The Video Game Theory Reader

Edited by **Mark J. P. Wolf and Bernard Perron**

ROUTLEDGE
NEW YORK AND LONDON

Published in 2003 by
Routledge
29 West 35th Street
New York, NY 10001
www.routledge-ny.com

Published in Great Britain by
Routledge
11 New Fetter Lane
London EC4P 4EE
www.routledge.co.uk

Routledge is an imprint of the Taylor & Francis Group.

10   9   8   7   6   5

Library of Congress Cataloging-in-Publication Data

The video game theory reader / edited by Mark J. P. Wolf and Bernard Perron.
    p.   cm.
  Includes bibliographical references and index.
  ISBN 0-415-96578-0 (hardback : alk. paper)—ISBN 0-415-96579-9 (pbk.: alk. paper)
  1. Video games.   I. Wolf, Mark J. P.   II. Perron, Bernard.

GV1469.3.V57   2003
794.8–dc21   2003001764

The Video Game Theory Reader

Contents

Foreword

WARREN ROBINETT

Video game history was made in 1978 when the ideas behind the all-text game Adventure *by Will Crowther and Don Woods inspired Warren Robinett to write a graphical adventure program for the Atari 2600, which he also entitled* Adventure. *In several online polls, Robinett's* Adventure *has been voted the best cartridge for the 2600, despite the fact that it was among the earliest cartridges to appear. The game also has an important place in video game history as it contained a number of firsts, including the first Easter Egg (hidden feature) to appear in a game; first screen credit; first significant off-screen events; and the first use of multiple screens that cut from one to the next, with conservation of screen direction used to continue the action, making* Adventure *the first to take advantage of cinematic conventions to orient the player in the game's diegetic world. The game contained the first use of identically-shaped characters whose behavior differed; the three dragons were different colors, each had different duties, and moved at different speeds.* Adventure's *Bat was the first computer-controlled character to have more than one behavioral state (agitated and not agitated). And, finally,* Adventure *was the first game to feature graphical, portable objects on-screen (as opposed to being located in an inventory) that a player-character could pick up, use, and drop, and that could be carried by a computer-controlled character as well (the Bat). In this regard, Robinett is among the foremost innovators of the video game during the era when the medium was coming into its own, and one whose work shows an active concern for the theoretical aspects of the medium.*

It is hard to say what ranks lower on the artistic food chain than video games. Comic books? TV sit-coms? X-rated films? These ratlike vermin at the bottom scurry to avoid the thunderous footfalls of the towering behemoths of the art world. Everyone knows that:

- Violinists, conductors, and composers are real artists.
- Novelists, poets, and playwrights are real artists.
- Painters, photographers, and filmmakers are real artists.

But video-game designers? Is that even art?

The established art forms have their prestigious awards (Grammies, Pulitzer Prizes, Academy Awards). They have academic departments devoted to their study (music departments, English departments, art departments). They have Godlike practitioners of the past to idolize (Beethoven, Shakespeare, Picasso), and, as archangels, the living masters (McCartney, Vonnegut, Spielberg). And for these living masters, has climbing to the top of the Food-Chain of Art benefited their wallets or their sex lives? The true answer to this may perhaps strain the imagination of all but the horniest of nerd-programmers, hacking at 2:00 A.M. on his 3-D monster.

But wait! Despair not, horny nerds! Sometimes ratlike vermin can triumph over towering dinosaurs. Things do change. New art forms do come into existence—not often—but, if you think back, there was a time when there were no novelists or poets or playwrights. Before the invention of writing, there was only storytelling and oral ballads. The written stories were a new art form spawned by a new technology (writing). Perhaps the oral balladeers scoffed at the time. But from our perspective in a literate culture, there is skill, technique, and yes, an art, to piling word on word to make a novel or a poem. Likewise, from a perspective slowly emerging, there is not only skill and technique but also an art to piling bit on bit to make a video game.

There is a natural progression in the emergence of a new art form. Often there is an enabling technology that must first be invented and made to work. In the case of cinema, for example, this was the motion-picture camera, projector, and film. Then come the first works exploring the new medium. The pioneers are often clueless, from the point of view of later practitioners, about what you can do with the medium, and a great deal of experimentation occurs, with a few successes, and with some bizarre and interesting relics that soon disappear. If the public likes what they see, they continue to buy, and the medium has a chance to develop. The ideas that work give rise to genres, and all too quickly, the youthful efflorescence is over ("Alas, that Spring should vanish with the Rose!/That Youth's sweet-scented Manuscript should close!") and the genres harden. Critics arise when there are enough works that the public needs help sorting out the good from the bad. And trying to analyze what separates the good from the bad naturally leads to a theory, or theories, about the medium. Throughout the progression outlined here, in a healthy and developing medium, there is a continuous competition among the practitioners making new works. The critics and theorists cannot get started without a body of works to winnow and analyze, and their work is meaningless without a stream of new works being created, presumably being informed (somewhat) by their efforts. The wolf keeps the caribou strong. The players, the designers, the critics, and the theorists are natural members of a healthy ecosystem.

This homespun theory of art-form emergence is based on what I have observed in the field of video games. (For a homespun art theory, there are no doubt theorists waiting, vulturelike, to claw out its eyes and pick its bones. But hey, vultures, I was there and you weren't.) The enabling technology (computers and computer graphics) became cheap enough to reach consumers in the 1970s. A great many video games were created in the first ten years, and genres came to be recognized (shooters, racing games, sports sims, side-scrollers, etc.). Critics were born when the game magazines began rating various games (C+, A−, etc.). As far as I know, this book is the first to focus exclusively on the theory of video games. There is a set of questions that fall to the theorists to address, but before trotting out the Big Questions, let's return briefly to the early days of the medium.

The ideas that we, the early video game designers, had about what video games were, or could be, were based on the games that had been created up to that time. Ivan Sutherland, who pioneered computer graphics in the 1960s, did not make games, but he made an interactive visual simulation (*Sketchpad*) demonstrating compelling possibilities—for example, a bridge truss whose beams could be pulled with an input device, with a structural simulation running continuously to calculate restoring forces. *Spacewar!*, done by MIT students on expensive research computers, was a game in which a pair of spaceships (represented by small 2-D icons on the screen) shot missiles at each other, while orbiting a central star. Al Alcorn created the first commercial video game "hit"—*PONG*, an abstraction of Ping-Pong, with a square "ball" bouncing back and forth between the rectangular "paddles" controlled by two players. In the early 1970s, the dominant form of video game was the "coin-op" (coin-operated) game, which was placed in bars and pinball-machine arcades, and paid for by a stream of quarters from the pockets of the players.

When home video game consoles, which could be purchased by individual consumers, became the dominant form in the late 1970s, a rapid change occurred in video games. This change was driven purely by economics. Coin-op games existed in order to suck quarters out of the pockets of players; the games had to exciting, yes, but they could not be long. Typical coin-op games lasted two or three minutes. But for a consumer who had already paid $200 for his Atari 2600 video-game console and $25 for a game cartridge, games that took an hour or more to complete were not only permissible, but good. The phrase was "hours of play-value." Most of the current video game genres originated either in the coin-op era or the early console era. Shooters and racing games were feasible as exciting fast-action coin-op games, but the games that took more time, such as adventure games, were first done on home video game consoles.

My vantage point was as a twenty-six-year-old programmer working for Atari, the company that first popularized commercial video games, at the time when video game consoles first reached the consumer. At that time, Atari gave its young designers almost complete design freedom. Just as I was finishing my first video game on the Atari 2600 console, I got a chance, at a Stanford research lab, to play the original text adventure game, which was called *Adventure*. (Thank you, Don Woods and Willie Crowther.) I decided that this idea—a journey through a network of rooms, with objects you could move from place to place, and obstacles and monsters to get past—could work as a video game.

Woods and Crowther's wonderful game used no graphics at all—it was entirely text. Text described where you were: **You are in a debris room filled with stuff washed in from the surface. A low wide passage with cobbles becomes plugged with mud and debris here, but an awkward canyon leads upward and west. A note on the wall says "MAGIC WORD XYZZY."** Text described objects you could carry: **A three-foot black rod with a rusty star on an end lies nearby.** And text commands were typed by the player to move around and do things: **GO WEST** or **TAKE ROD** or **SAY XYZZY**.

In spite of various practical and political obstacles that I faced—severe memory limits, my boss telling me it was impossible, the Atari marketing department telling me to change it into a game about Superman—the idea did work as a video game. *Adventure* for the Atari 2600 console was the first action-adventure game. (It ended up with the same name as Woods and Crowther's public-domain game.) It was also a commercial success, selling one million copies. Both versions of *Adventure* helped to define the genre for later adventure games, such as *Legend of Zelda* and the *Ultima* series.

I had to solve various problems in designing *Adventure*:

- How do you represent an adventure game "room" graphically? *Use the entire screen to depict a maplike view of the current room.*
- How do you represent movable objects graphically? *Use hardware sprites to show them as little icons.*
- How do you represent your "self" and where you are in the game world? *Use another little icon.*
- How do you move within a room? *Use the joystick to move your self icon.*
- How do you move from room to room? *Drive yourself off the edge of the screen into an "adjacent" room.*

- How do you constrain where you can go? *Interpret the graphics depicting each room as walls and passages. Walls constrain where you can go.*
- How do you show the "inventory" of objects you have picked up? *You don't: the player can only carry one object at a time. Show the object beside you as you carry it.*
- How do you pick up an object? *Drive yourself into it. Touching it picks it up.*
- How do you drop an object? *Use the joystick button. (The Atari 2600 joystick had only one button.)*
- What kind of obstacles can be created? *Maze walls, locked doors, dragons that eat you.*
- How do you get past these obstacles? *Create tool-objects: a bridge to cross walls, keys to open doors, a sword to kill dragons.*
- How do you make autonomous creatures? *Associate a subroutine executed each frame with a graphical object. Control their motions (toward or away from other objects in the game) by giving them "desires" and "fears."*
- What's the goal of the game? *It's a quest: you must find and retrieve the Holy Grail.*
- How do you fit all this into 4096 bytes of ROM and 128 bytes of RAM? *A good data structure, and efficient coding.*
- How do you get public credit for your cool game when Atari's policy is anonymity of the game designers? *Create a secret room that's really hard to get to, and hide your signature in it. Don't tell anyone until they've manufactured a few hundred thousand cartridges and shipped them all over the world. (This was the first Easter Egg.)*

My website ⟨http://www.WarrenRobinett.com/adventure⟩ has more information on the design of *Adventure*.

These design problems and solutions for *Adventure* illustrate that the evolution of the video game medium has a *history*. At the time that I write this (2002), the inventors of most of the genres are still alive, each with quirky design histories of their own. They probably still have their design notes somewhere, in a bookshelf or an attic. Back when video games were a nonartform, nobody seemed to care about the design history of early video games. But now, hey . . . maybe someone should interview these people while they are still alive. If you accept the idea that a new artform is emerging, then interviewing the genre-creators is equivalent, for a classicist, to interviewing Homer; for an English professor, to interviewing Shakespeare. (I pause to dodge the rotten tomatoes thrown by classicists and Shakespearean scholars.) The yellowed design notes in the attic are the equivalent of the literary manuscript. There may be other artifacts, as well. For example, I wrote a book on the design of *Adventure* in 1983, but my publisher went out of business just as I finished it, so I have a twenty-year-old manuscript that was never published on my bookshelf. If you believe this stuff has value, realize that there are people, artifacts, and relics accessible now, but that after some period of time—it's hard to say exact how long—they will have vanished into the bit-bucket of time.

This is a book about video game theory, and I think a reasonable person might well wonder why a theory is needed for video games. I'll give my answer here. In the video game ecosystem I described earlier, the ecological niches were player, designer, critic, and theorist. The roles of designers and players seem obvious—designers design games and players play them—but what are the jobs of the critics and theorists? I believe that the critic's job is to ask, "Which are the good games?" and the theorist's job is to ask, "Why?" From those basic questions, many new ones spring up:

- What makes a good game? What are the desirable qualities? Fun? Realistic? Playable? Winnable? Responsive?
- What are the elements of video games? By "elements" I mean such things as the game world, objects, autonomous creatures ("AI"s), other human players, goals, obstacles, weapons, tools, user-interfaces, controllers, and sounds. For comparison, some elements from which novels are built are: plot, character, description, and dialogue; and for poems: alliteration, meter, and rhyme. Some elements from which music is built are melody, harmony, rhythm, repetition, tempo, dynamics, and phrasing. Can we identify the essential and fundamental elements of video games?
- What are the genres of video games? People seem to naturally want to group works into classes according to their similarities. What are those classes? These would be analogous to the genres we find in music (classical, rock, jazz, country) and among novels (detective novels, romance novels, historical novels).
- What are the principal forms of video games? (For comparison, some literary forms are: novels, poems, plays, and essays.) What are the powerful techniques? (Some literary techniques are suspense, humor, irony, metaphor, metonomy, and exaggeration.) If you compare turn-based games (such as online card games), branching-video games (such as the classic *Dragon's Lair*), and real-time simulations (such as *Doom*), these exemplify very different types of gaming experiences. What terms should we use to talk about these differences?

Of course, these are only my ideas about the questions that theorists ought to ask. The variety in this book illustrates that video-game theorists—now enjoying their own youthful efflorescence—currently get to write their own job descriptions.

For my part, I will now follow my own advice, and try to analyze *why* my own game *Adventure* succeeded.

My main breakthrough, I think, was figuring out how to adapt the adventure game idea from its birth medium (with the player reading text descriptions and typing text commands) to the video game medium (with color, motion, animation, sounds, and joystick controllers). There were three powerful ideas in *Adventure* that were, at the time, different from how most video games were done.

1. A large game world (in this case, the network of rooms) that was bigger than a single screen, and that could be explored by the player.
2. Objects that the player could pick up and move around, which functioned as tools to do things in the game world, and that interacted with one another.
3. Creatures that moved around on their own within the game world, initiating actions. ("AI"s, in modern terminology).

Putting these elements together in a video game produced what we now call an action-adventure game. This has shown itself, over the last few decades, to be a very fertile genre. At the time that *Adventure* was designed, game designers were very experimental and were trying to figure out what you could do that was cool with this new medium of interactive computer graphics. I think you could now say that I discovered one of the "sweet spots" in the medium.

Of course, to make a finished and playable game, the details were important—what the objects and creatures did, and what they looked like, how the game world was laid out, and how the controls worked. Here is a distillation of my meditations on why *Adventure* worked so well.

Story
- Simple, understandable story, theme, and goal. The story (quest for the Holy Grail) was consistent with the fantasy theme (Dungeons and Dragons) and the goal of the game (find and retrieve the Grail). The Atari marketing department confused this a bit by renaming the Holy Grail to be the Enchanted Chalice, but it still worked.
- Nice-looking box that conveyed the theme. Good manual.

Controls
- The controls for moving yourself were intuitive. I used the joystick for what it is best at—moving an icon in 2-D on the screen.

- Square cursor (self-icon) and walls. Most games that followed *Adventure* have used an animated character as the user's avatar. An advantage to the square cursor is that it is easy to see when the cursor will run into a wall, and where the paths are. The visual feedback (jiggling cursor) when running into a wall was valuable. You also could slide along a wall when the joystick was attempting a diagonal movement. Because you spent most of your time in the game moving through mazes, it was important to have this interaction smooth, intuitive, and glitch-free.
- The user interface for grabbing and dropping objects was very easy to learn and remember. There was something simple and satisfying about grabbing objects and carrying them around. The "picking-up" and "putting-down" sound effects used three-note ascending and descending arpeggios to convey "up" and "down," which people seemed to readily understand.
- Allowing only one object to be carried at a time was a good decision. It simplified the user-interface. It meant the game could stay always in real time (never going to an inventory screen). It created strategic choices. (Should you carry the weapon or the treasure?)

Technical Enablers
- Efficient, pointer-based data structures for the room-list and object-list.
- Treating all objects in a unified manner, including the square cursor (the player's self), tool-objects, and creatures. All these objects used the same routines for movement, room-to-room motion, and collision detection.
- The chase/flee priority list data structure, which allowed me to efficiently specify complex behaviors for the creatures in the game.
- The space-efficiency and time-efficiency of these data structures, together with the uniform treatment of all object types, is the main reason I could fit such a relatively complex game into the game cartridge's small (4K) ROM memory.

Game World
- The game world was a good size: thirty rooms, divided into eight regions. It was small enough that you could explore and become familiar with all of it.
- Disjoint regions. The game world was partitioned into disjoint regions when the castle doors were locked. Also, two of the mazes consisted of two disjoint parts, requiring use of the bridge to get into the other part of the maze.

- Mazes. The multiscreen, nonplanar mazes were interesting.
- Object permanence—objects and creatures were never created or destroyed. Each one was always somewhere in the game world. The game simulation proceeded independently of whether you could see an object or creature, so that you sometimes saw the effects of things that happened offscreen, such as the Bat picking up a new object. This gave the game world a very believable feeling.
- No randomness during game-play. Algorithmically generated complex behavior is more interesting and understandable than just generating a new monster every so often based on a random number generator.
- Objects as tools to get past obstacles. This meant that with a simple user interface (that let you move yourself and pick up one object at a time), you could do a lot of things. Each new tool-object in the game gave you a new capability (sword, key, magnet, bridge, dot) without complicating the user interface.
- Problem solving. If a needed object (say the Black Key) was behind an obstacle (say the Green Dragon), this spawned a subgoal. Get the sword to get past the dragon; then use the key to get into the castle.
- Object-object interaction was easy to understand. These interactions were triggered by overlap of object shapes (which were called "collisions"). For example, the dragon was killed by having the sword touched to it. This is like in the real world: when two objects touch each other, they affect one another.
- Creatures (objects that moved around on their own, initiating actions). The creatures in the game were similar to animals in real life—they moved around, they did things, they had "motivations" that could be inferred from their behavior. Each creature was implemented by a subroutine that controlled what it did, which was executed twenty times per second. I came up with a data structure to represent a creature's goals—a prioritized list of objects and whether to go toward or away from that object (thus representing the creature's "desires" and "fears"). The subroutine went down its priority list until it found an object on the list in the same room with it. Then it went toward the object, or away from it. (I called this chasing and fleeing.) In other words, it responded only to its highest priority object in the same room with it. Each creature had its own priority list, and so each creature had different behaviors. There were four creatures altogether—three dragons and one bat. Since each of the three dragons had slightly different priority lists, they had different behaviors. This was a pretty good scheme, because it

modeled limited perception (creatures couldn't "see" across room boundaries), and it allowed a creature to "change its mind" when a new object came into the room.

- Surprises. Bat steals your sword. Bat carries dragon. (This always got a laugh the first time someone saw it.)

Display

- Using animation of the dragon graphics tied to its state in the game (Chasing, Biting, Swallowed-You, and Dead) worked extremely well.
- Animation of the bat flapping its wings was effective.
- Tying short sound effects to game events was effective.
- The sound effects were good, given the Atari 2600 sound hardware. The sounds evolved over time, which was made them more interesting than the sound effects of most contemporaneous Atari 2600 games.
- The color-cycling through the entire color palette for the Enchanted Chalice worked very well to show that it was important and magical.
- (Flaw) The dragons looked like ducks.
- (Flaw) The objects flickered when there were more than two of them in the same room. There wasn't much I could do about this, given the 2600 hardware, but it was still ugly. However, the flickering did provide a clue to the existence of the Gray Dot, which in turn provided a clue to the existence of the secret room.

Playability

- Chase/bite cycle. The dragon would chase the square cursor that represented your self. If the dragon touched you, it emitted a roar, displayed the Biting graphics, and paused for a fraction of a second. If it was still touching you after the brief pause, then it ate you (moving the square that represented you into the dragon's stomach). If you had managed to recoil away from it, then it resumed chasing you. Thus, the interaction could go like this: Bite-Recoil-Bite-Recoil-Bite-Recoil-Escape. Or Bite-Recoil-Bite-Recoil-Swallowed. I felt that this was a more interesting and less frustrating interaction than having it kill you the first time you touched it.
- Bat and dragons could go through walls, but you had to follow the maze paths. This created a good balance in the game since the player is actually smarter than the simple AI routines of the bat and dragons.
- Reincarnating when you were eaten by the dragon. Simple and understandable. Leaving all the objects where they were was a good

decision. This meant getting killed did not cause you to start over completely. But it did penalize you. Bringing all dead dragons back to life when the player reincarnated was analogous to being vulnerable in the game of bridge. The closer you got to winning, the more you had to lose.

- I chose not to have a timer in the game to emphasize exploration and problem solving, which I felt would not be enhanced by arbitrary time limits.
- You can win the game. In many video games of the period (for example, *Space Invaders*), you just kept playing until you finally got killed. In such games, you could not win.
- Progressive difficulty levels. Level 1 was designed for beginners, and Levels 2 and 3 were harder. Flipping the difficulty switches made the dragons significantly more challenging.
- Variety. Random object placement at the start of Level 3 (analogous to shuffling the cards before a hand of bridge) gave the game much more variety. The bat, which moved objects around, kept the game from being *too* predictable. It had enough variety to not be a pure puzzle, which can be solved the same way every time.

Secret Room

- I created the secret room in order to hide my signature in the game. Even though each game cartridge for the Atari 2600 console was created by a single person, Atari was keeping us game designers anonymous, which I found irritating. Also, I was kind of proud of the game. It was hard to figure out at the conceptual level, and hard to implement, too. And I had to fight through my boss at Atari telling me that it was impossible and not to work on it (which I ignored). Then when I had it half-implemented, the marketing department saw it and liked it (allowing me to continue working on it), but they then told me to keep the rooms and objects, but change it into a game about Superman, because Atari's parent corporation, Warner Communications, also owned the first Superman movie, which was coming out a few months later. But I stubbornly kept to the Dungeons-and-Dragons theme (while my co-worker John Dunn took over a copy of the half-finished code and did the Superman game). I finished *Adventure*. No royalty, no bonus, no pat on the back, not even a pizza. Atari really didn't treat its game designers very well during that period. All in all, I was pretty satisfied with the little surprise I left hidden in the final game code I handed over to be manufactured. Then I quit.

- Getting into the secret room was pretty hard. You had to first discover the Gray Dot hidden in an inaccessible part of one of the mazes, and then by trial and error, somehow figure out that the Gray Dot would get you through a certain wall into the secret room.
- Once into the secret room, well, hey, why hold back at that point? My name filled the screen like a throbbing, multicolored movie marquee.
- Also, it was a bit of an experiment. I wasn't sure any player would discover the secret room. It was pretty obscure. But it turned out that some kids mapped all the mazes, and therefore found the little chamber that contained the Gray Dot. Then they went crazy trying to figure out what it was for, refusing to let their parents turn off the video game or the TV for weeks . . . the Gray Dot was one pixel in size, the smallest possible object. It was my attempt at irony, I guess. Small and insignificant-looking, yet important. (Pay no attention to that little man behind the curtain.) At least a few kids did discover how to get into the secret room on their own, without any clues other than those in the game. And then the rumor mill started churning.
- Having a really hard-to-find secret place in the game, that was so secret it was hidden even from Atari was kind of cool. It fueled a good rumor buzz. My model in creating the secret room had been the secret messages supposedly hidden in Beatles records in the late 1960s—if you played certain Beatles songs backward, you could supposedly hear the words "I buried Paul"—and then people went crazy, playing every Beatles song backward, hunting for secret messages.
- For the players, the secret room was the meta-level, the way to truly beat the game and get to the real conclusion. For me, it was the meta-game I was playing with Atari management. They had the power to keep my name off the box, but I had the power to put it on the screen.

Many things about video games and the culture that surrounds them have changed enormously since *Adventure* was released twenty-three years ago. Yet some other things have not changed at all.

Back at Atari in the late 1970s, each game cartridge for the Atari 2600 console was created by one person. You had the idea, wrote the program, created the graphics, did the sound effects, chased down bugs, tested the game on kids, revised it until you were satisfied, and wrote a draft of the game manual. This made sense at that time, because with only 4K of ROM memory available to hold the game program, it only took a few months of programming to fill up the ROM. And not only was the memory extremely limited, but the processing power was also very limited (the Atari 2600's processor was a 1.2 MHz, 8-bit processor). To top it off, the display, although flexible, was also extremely limited, providing only two decent hardware sprites for displaying moving objects on the screen. It was the designer/programmer's job to make the tradeoffs and come up with an interesting game, given these resources. A finished game cost Atari four to six months salary for one programmer, which amounted to less than $10,000.

Nowadays, game consoles have thousands of times the memory capacity of the Atari 2600, and the processors are also thousands of times faster. Games are normally made by teams of several dozen people, with the work done by several types of specialists: designers, producers, writers, programmers, artists, sound-effects specialists, and musicians. Budgets of more than a million dollars for a game are common. The game world is usually 3-D in current games, not the 2-D of yesteryear.

However, our perceptual and motor systems have not changed. Thirty frames per second still produces the illusion of smooth motion. Human visual acuity is still one sixtieth of a degree. Reaction time is still around 150 milliseconds.

And little boys haven't changed. (Not even the ones who are now thirty or forty.) They still like to blow up bad guys, fight scary monsters, and drive noisy, powerful vehicles.

Many billions of dollars and billions of hours are now spent each year on video games. We've tried quite a few things by now. Will another factor of 10, or 100, or 1,000 in memory, or computing power, or textured polygons enable amazing new game experiences that are not yet possible? It's hard to say.

It's a good time to think and debate about what interactivity is, what it means, and what it could be. It's a good time for video game theorists to analyze, to make us think, to question old dogmas, to formulate new principles, and to ask the questions the rest of us didn't even know enough to ask.

Chapel Hill, North Carolina
December 2002

Acknowledgments

A book like this could only be possible in an academic environment where video games are finally being recognized as a serious area of study, and so we would like to first thank our audience, those readers and scholars who have an interest in developing video game theory as a field of study. A big, hearty thanks goes especially to all our contributors, who graciously joined this endeavor: Mia Consalvo, Chris Crawford, Patrick Crogan, Miroslaw Filiciak, Markku Eskelinen, Gonzalo Frasca, Torben Grodal, Walter Holland, Henry Jenkins (whom we would also like to thank for his comments on a draft of the introduction), Martti Lahti, Alison McMahan, Bob Rehak, Warren Robinett, Kurt Squire, and Ragnhild Tronstad. Thanks also go to others whose help and support we are grateful for, including Matt Byrnie and Routledge for asking for this anthology and supporting it along the way, Konrad Lischka, Mattias Persson, Mathew Weise, and the members of the Society for Cinema Studies who attended our panels on video games in 2000 and 2001, and gave their comments and support.

Mark would specially like to thank: my parents, of course, who let me play video games as a kid long before I knew I was actually doing useful research; my wife Diane Wolf and son Michael Wolf who were patient with the time taken to work on this book; and I of course must thank my coeditor Bernard who gladly joined me in the making of this anthology, and with whom I enjoyed collaborating. And, as always, thanks be to God.

Bernard would specially like to thank: Shantal Robert and Léa Elisabeth Perron to have accompanied me in this other "autumnal tour"; my parents, as always; Sébastien Babeux for his appreciated help and also Carl Therrien for our discussions about play, games, interactive cinema, and video games; Clayton George Bailey for his English grammatical advice; Diane and Michael Wolf for their warm welcome on my visit to Milwaukee for the writing of the Introduction; and, finally, last but not least, Mark, with whom it was so agreeable to collaborate.

Introduction

MARK J. P. WOLF
BERNARD PERRON

> It has been my conviction that most members of the computer pro-
> gramming community are also game players. Computerized game
> playing may be found to some degree at almost every computer
> installation. This is primarily because most computer profession-
> als agree that information gained while programming computers to
> play games is directly transferable to other areas of scientific and
> business programming.
>
> Donald D. Spencer,
> *Preface to Game Playing With Computers* (1968)

After forty years since it appeared, the video game has recently become the
hottest and most volatile field of study within new media theory. At last
the idea of video game theory is gaining acceptance in academia, even as
pockets of resistance still remain. A few years ago this reader could not
have come into being, not only for lack of an audience, but because of the
scarcity of scholars willing to take the video game seriously as a cultural
object worthy of attention.[1] In past years, video games, when they were
mentioned at all, usually appeared only as one example among many of new
media technologies (and often a marginal one at that). But as the medium
continues to mature it has in many ways become a centerpoint among digital
media and its importance is finally being recognized.[2]

The video game is now considered as everything from the ergodic (work) to the ludic (play); as narrative, simulation, performance, remediation, and art; a potential tool for education or an object of study for behavioral psychology; as a playground for social interaction; and, of course, as a toy and a medium of entertainment. Likewise, the emerging field of video game theory is itself a convergence of a wide variety of approaches including film and television theory, semiotics, performance theory, game studies, literary theory, computer science, theories of hypertext, cybertext, interactivity, identity, postmodernism, ludology, media theory, narratology, aesthetics and art theory, psychology, theories of simulacra, and others. The collection of essays in this anthology is testimony to this diversity, and underscores how the study of video games has become a nexus of contemporary theoretical thought.

And yet—the terrain is only beginning to be explored and mapped, the first walkthroughs are just being written. The medium itself is a moving target, changing and morphing even as we try to theorize and define it.[3] But its trajectory can be traced through the writings of the past three decades that set the groundwork for video game theory.

A Brief History of the Study of Video Games

A number of histories have already given accounts of what is commonly considered to be the first real video game (*Spacewar!* [1962]), the first commercial video game (*Computer Space* [1971]), the first home game system (The Magnavox Odyssey [1972]), and the first hit game (*PONG* [1972]), but little has been written about how the study of them arose. Although the term "video games" first appears as a subject heading in the March 1973–February 1974 *Reader's Guide to Periodicals*, articles on games appeared as early as 1970 under the headings "Electronic Games" and "Computer Graphics."[4] Even today, when games are written about they are variously referred to as "video games" (or even "videogames"), "computer games," or "electronic games." (Occasionally two terms appear together; for example, the "VCS" of the Atari VCS 2600 stood for "Video Computer System.") While the term "electronic games" is so broad as to include any games that have an electronic component (such as Milton Bradley's *Simon* [1978] or Parker Bros.'s *Merlin* [1978], neither of which has any visuals apart from blinking lights), the terms "video games" and "computer games" are more specific to the subject matter at hand; they are the terms most often used in popular and scholarly discourse. Because of its more exclusive and accurate nature, we have decided to use "video games" throughout this book.[5]

The earliest writings on video games were typically written by and directed at computer enthusiasts and hobbyists, with articles appearing in such venues as *Popular Mechanics, Popular Science, Popular Electronics,* and

Radio-Electronics, as well as general magazines such as *Newsweek* and *Time.* Many of these articles featured "how to" perspectives for building simple electronic games at home, such as electronic coin toss or tic-tac-toe programs, and there were even two books addressed to the computer programming community, Donald D. Spencer's *Game Playing With Computers* and A. G. Bell's *Games Playing With Computers* in Great Britain.[6] Like Spencer, Bell even makes a prediction as to the future of the video game medium:

> Apart from the educational aspects and training of programmers there are commercial benefits. Manufacturers have realised that they are more likely to improve their sales if their new machines can win at chess than if they can invert nonsensical matrices. The lay purchaser is more likely to prefer a chess program (which he believes he understands) as a measure of the power and speed of a machine. Indeed, as consoles become more and more common, then eventually computers will become as available as the television set. If so, it is very likely that future generations will use them in their leisure time to interact with game playing programs. The commercial profits of such entertainment could well exceed that of any "useful" activity.
>
> Unfortunately, at the moment, most people who wish to play games with computers do not have the eminence of a Turing et al. Rather than convince the "reader," they have to convince the firm that such work is useful. A word of advice: do not say you wish to "play games." Much better is a wish to study "dynamic technique of search and evaluation in a multi-dimensional problem space incorporating information retrieval and realised in a Chomsky Type 2 language."[7]

As the latter half of the quote demonstrates, the attitude considering video games as useless toys was already present even while the video game was still in a purely experimental stage.

After the appearance of commercial video games in the arcade and the home, game reviews began appearing, as well as articles examining the market for video games. By the late 1970s, the majority of articles focused on commercial video games and all the new systems appearing, with fewer mentions of the amateur home-built variety. As the arcade game industry grew, several trade journals for coin-op arcade owners appeared: *Play Meter* in 1974, *RePlay* in 1975, and *Star Tech Journal* in 1979. Some of the first books on video games were published in the late 1970s; Creative Strategies' *Consumer Microelectronics: Electronic Video Games* (1976), Len Buckwalter's *Video Games* (1977), and Consumer Guide's *The Complete Book of Video Games* (1977). For the electronics hobbyist, there was Robert L. Goodman's *How to Repair Video Games* (1978), David L. Heiseman's *How to Design and Build Your Own Custom TV Games* (1978), Walter H. Buchsbaum and Robert Mauro's *Electronic Games: Design, Programming, and Troubleshooting,* and others.[8]

The late 1970s and the early 1980s saw a growing market for home computers, fueled by electronics enthusiasts as well as video game players interested in home game systems. Both audiences were met with a variety of publications. Between 1981 and 1983, game companies including Activision, Atari, Coleco, Imagic, Mattel, and Magnavox produced magazines in-house covering their own products, along with over a dozen other independent magazines covering the video game craze.[9] In 1982 alone, the peak year for video game publications, over forty books appeared, the vast majority of which were collector's guides and strategy guides, such as Craig Kubey's *The Winner's Book of Video Games*, Michael Blanchet's *How to Beat the Video Games*, or the 670-page *Ken Uston's Guide to Buying and Beating Home Video Games*. Video game history, however, did not fare nearly as well. The first history of the medium, George Sullivan's *Screen Play: The Story of Video Games* (1983) was a short ninety-three-page book published for a juvenile audience, and the first history of video games written for adults, Leonard Herman's *Phoenix: The Fall and Rise of Home Video Games* (1984) was initially self-published when no commercial publisher could be found.

Prior to 1982, the only theory to be found was in the practice of video game designers who innovated changes and developed the medium with each advance in game design they made. Programmers such as Warren Robinett, author of the groundbreaking game *Adventure* (1979)[10] for the Atari 2600, were self-conscious about their methods even if they only articulated them in programming code rather than in print. But in 1982 Chris Crawford wrote *The Art of Computer Game Design*, the first book devoted to theorizing about video games, which would later be published by McGraw-Hill/Osborne Media in 1984. Crawford's book asked what games were and why people played them, and proceeded to suggest design precepts, describing methods and techniques, all the while defending the video game as an art form; "The central premise of this book is that computer games constitute a new and as yet poorly developed art form that holds great promise for both designers and players."[11] The end of the book even looked ahead to the development of the medium:

> To conclude: I see a future in which computer games are a major recreational activity. I see a mass market of computer games not too different from what we now have, complete with blockbuster games, spin-off games, remake games, and tired complaints that computer games constitute a vast wasteland. . . . I also see a much more exciting literature of computer games, reaching into almost all spheres of human fantasy.[12]

Video games were also given serious consideration in Geoffrey R. Loftus and Elizabeth F. Loftus's *Mind at Play: The Psychology of Video Games*

(1983), which looked at the psychological motivations of game players, how games relate to the cognitive system of the mind (attention, perception, short-term and long-term memory, and expectancy), motor performance, and problem-solving skills. The Loftus's book, along with Patricia Marks Greenfield's *Mind and Media: The Effects of Television, Computers and Video Games* (1984) began the tradition of the video game as object of psychological study and a tool to be used in laboratory experiments. This tradition still continues today, including work such as Anderson and Dill's 2000 study linking video games with aggressive thoughts and behaviors.[13]

After the video game industry crash of 1984, the video game industry rebounded with a new generation of technological advances, beginning with the release of the Nintendo Entertainment System (NES) in 1985. Elsewhere, interest in so-called interactive multimedia, such as the newly developed CD-ROM technology, was growing in academia, with video games receiving at least tangential mention as a form of "new media" (despite the fact that the medium was almost a quarter century old). Interest in the video game as a cultural artifact was also on the rise, resulting in *Hot Circuits: A Video Arcade*, a retrospective exhibition of video games presented by the American Museum of the Moving Image from June of 1989 to May of 1990. Museum director and founder Rochelle Slovin recalled how the exhibition was seen by some as questionable or even controversial:

> Reaction from peers and Trustees was, in the beginning, mixed. Within and without the Museum, the idea was met with raised eyebrows. Our institution, after all, was founded in 1981 as the first museum in the United States devoted to the art, history, technique, and technology of motion pictures and television.[14]

An essential part of the exhibition was an essay by Charles Bernstein, which also situated the video game as a cultural object worthy of attention, indirectly becoming a kind of apologetics for video game study.[15] Although such an apology might have been needed in 1989, the video game soon gained greater respectability and academic interest as its representational power and status as cultural object grew throughout the 1990s.

In 1991, Marsha Kinder's *Playing With Power: Movies, Television, and Video Games from Muppet Babies to Teenage Mutant Ninja Turtles* treated video games on a par with other media and looked at connections between them and transmedia franchise crossovers. Instead of being treated as a special case or a marginal form of "new media," the video game was regarded as a cultural object that fit into a larger social and economic context. Kinder's book demonstrated that it was no longer possible to talk about transmedia franchises without including video games. And some video games had even become the basis of franchises. Since the mid-1970s, stories and characters had typically originated in film and television and made their way into video games, not the other way around. This began to change in the 1980s when *Pac-Man* became an animated TV series and the movie *The Last Starfighter* was based on an Atari game that was never finished or released due, in part, to the 1984 industry crash.[16] By 1993,*Super Mario Bros.* was adapted into a big-budget feature film, and soon after other Movies such as *Street Fighter* (1994), *Double Dragon* (1994), and *Mortal Kombat: The Movie* (1995) found their way to the silver screen. Video games were now a source of material for film and TV, and became important to any discussion of them.[17]

Another reason for growing interest in games was the introduction of CD-ROM-based games in 1992. The increased storage capacity allowed for more detailed graphics and even full-motion video clips to be used in home games,[18] and the representational power of the medium grew. Despite the popularity and success of the CD-ROM, it took a while before the technology itself became the subject of study. Throughout the late 1980s and the 1990s, articles and books on CD-ROM technology tended to focus either on "interactive multimedia" or on technical aspects of the medium rather than on its place in culture. It was not until 1999 that a book-length scholarly work appeared on the topic, the anthology *On a Silver Platter: CD-ROMs and the Promises of a New Technology*. According to the editor, Greg M. Smith, the book was "intended to announce a kind of "coming of age" of CD-ROMs as a commercially, socially, and aesthetically significant medium worthy of close critical attention by media scholars."[19] Moreover, Smith underlined an important fact: while studying new media texts and the contexts of their reception, academics have been neglecting the multimedia form that was between the avant garde (i.e., hypertexts for instance) and the online (i.e., chatrooms or MUDs), that is, video games. As Smith noted, "Michael Joyce's hypertext *Afternoon, a story* has received more scholarly attention than the blockbuster CD-ROM *Doom*, although only a fraction of new media users have heard of Joyce's innovative text."[20]

Doom was released[21] in 1993, the same year as another landmark game, *Myst*, the game perhaps most responsible for the popularity of the CD-ROM. Both games became instant classics. They would come to represent the ends of a spectrum of gaming experience: *Myst* was a slow, contemplative game set amidst lush, painterly graphics, while *Doom* was a fast-paced shoot-'em-up set in claustrophobic tunnels and hallways where monsters lurked around every corner. In either case, the CD-ROM allowed games to grow to hundreds of megabytes in size while making their production cheaper than cartridges. The increased size and complexity of the games and their diegetic worlds also meant that game criticism would become more of a challenge as its object of study enlarged. More time and more game skills would be needed to see enough of a game to write authoritatively on it, and to write something more in-depth than merely a game review.

Two other debuts made 1993 an important year for video game studies: the first school for video game programming, and the World Wide Web. With the spread of graphical browsers, the Web quickly became one of the best research tools for video game study, beginning with websites of collectors, hardcore gamers, reviewers and publishers, and expanding to journalistic, research, and academic sites. Game communities grew and produced large-scale repositories of game information compiled from hundreds of contributors. For example, "The Killer List of Videogames," at <www.klov.com>, is a searchable database of over four thousand arcade video games including technical information, screenshots, cabinet art, and even Rotatable models of game cabinets created with QuickTime VR. Another site, <www.gamedex.com>, features a database for home video games. At the same time, game collectors were able to enlarge their collections and share them on-line along with the fruits of their research (for example, David Winter's website <www.pong-story.com>, which is one of the best sources of information on *PONG* and its imitators). As anyone who has surfed the Internet knows, websites vary greatly in their quality, but many of the best video game sites are as rigorous as any academic paper due to the scrutiny of hundreds of gamers, the use of e-mail as a way of providing feedback, and the ease and speed of web page updating.

Around the same time home computers were getting graphical web browsers, the DigiPen Applied Computer Graphics School began offering a two-year curriculum in video game programming, the first of its kind. DigiPen had begun as a computer animation and simulation company in 1988, and began training employees, until a 1991 discussion with Nintendo of America initiated the idea for a school for video game programming. According to the DigiPen website:

> With advisory support from Nintendo of America, DigiPen's engineers developed a two-year program with a unique curriculum in video game programming. In 1993, DigiPen Applied Computer Graphics School opened in Vancouver, BC, Canada, offering programs in computer/video game programming as well as continuing the training in 3D Computer Animation. Prior to DigiPen's course offering in video game programming, this type of training was unheard of in North America. The inaugural class graduated in 1996, nineteen graduates gathered about thirty job offers from various game development companies, such as Nintendo, Iguana, Sierra Online, Konami, Electronic Arts, Bandai Entertainment, and Sony of America.
>
> To fulfill the growing number of positions available in the digital entertainment industry, DigiPen decided to offer a unique degree program—a Baccalaureate of Science in Real-Time Interactive Simulation. As many of DigiPen's students came from the US, DigiPen decided to apply to the Washington State Higher Education Coordinating Board for the authorization to grant such a degree. The authorization was received in 1996. Digipen Institute of Technology

was opened in Redmond, WA in January 1998, offering both Baccalaureate and Associate degree programs in Real-Time Interactive Simulation. In September 1999, DigiPen added an Associate degree program in 3D Computer Animation to the programs available.[22]

Not only was the video game now considered a suitable object of study, it was declared an art in France. In their 1993 book *Qui a peur des jeux vidéo?*, Alain and Frédéric Le Diberder declared that, after the six classical arts and the three newer ones (cinema, the comic strip [*bande dessinée*] and television), video games were the tenth art, a provocative proclamation for the time echoed in the tone of the introduction. The Le Diberder brothers wrote about the epidemic of home game systems in the 1970s and all the myths about the danger of video games that followed in the 1980s.[23] It is interesting to note that the Le Diberders's book was revised and rereleased under a new title in 1998, with a revealing change of title; in a few years, the study of video games went from being presented as an object of anxiety, *Qui a peur des jeux vidéo?* [Who's Afraid of Video Games?], to being characterized as a distinct and worthwhile whole, *L'Univers des jeux vidéo* [The Universe of Video Games].[24]

For the Le Diberders, the video game industry was the new Hollywood. The relationship between video games and cinema has long been understood in France, and is even more remarkable today. Cradle of the French New Wave, the notion of *mise en scène*, and the "*politique des auteurs*," the famous and vastly influential journal *Cahiers du Cinéma* welcomed video games with open arms in mid-1990s. The journal's first leading article devoted to the video game medium was written by Alain Le Diberder in 1996 and designated video games a "new frontier of cinema."[25] This rank was later confirmed in a special issue of April 2000 about "The Frontiers of Cinema." Video games were examined along with digital cinema, cinema on the Internet, television, video clips, and experimental films. And in September 2002, *Cahiers du Cinéma* dedicated an entire special issue to video games. Revealing their bias in favor of narrative games with an affinity to cinema, they gave importance to the medium in an editorial addressed to both film and game buffs:

> Henceforth, the video game no longer needs to imitate the cinema to exist because it proposes hypotheses that cinema has never been able to formulate, as well as emotions of another nature. If video games have looked to the cinema in the past (their designers are also moviegoers), today they allow us to look at the cinema differently, to question it in its modes of functioning and its theoretical principles. Video games are not only a social phenomena, they are the essential crossroads of a redefinition of our relation to the narrative world in images, prolonging what Godard had formulated ("A film: between the active and the passive, between the actor and the spectator"), without knowing that the video game was going to seize this question, to reply to this demand, while leaving the cinema without reply.[26]

Just as the generation of young directors in the French New Wave had grown up with cinema and had an intimate knowledge of the medium, the children who grew up with video games in the 1970s started coming of age in the 1990s, bringing with them a relationship between the image and the viewer (player) very different than that of the generation before them. This generation entered graduate school during the 1990s, and is now moving into the ranks of university faculty, where their video game playing experiences are being articulated in theoretical terms.

On a wider scale, the 1990s also saw a growing nostalgia for the 1970s and early 1980s, and interest in classic video games that turned them into collectibles. Primitive and strangely archaic compared to their contemporary descendents, classic games were remediated through emulators and ported to newer systems on CD-ROM, and new versions of old games like *Pac-Man* and *Frogger* appeared with three-dimensional graphics. Websites for collectors listed old games and home systems, and groups such as the Video Arcade Preservation Society (VAPS) were born. In 1996, Keith Feinstein's traveling exhibition Videotopia (<www.videotopia.com>) began bringing dozens of classic arcade games to museum audiences, introducing classic games to a whole generation of players younger than the games.

In the last few years, a number of books have joined in looking back to the video game's first golden age, including a few with academic or journalistic leanings. Nostalgic about the old arcade era, J. C. Herz focused her attention specifically on video games in *Joystick Nation: How Videogames Ate Our Quarters, Won Our Hearts, and Rewired Our Minds* (1997). Unfolding the rise and evolution of video games, she suggested that they were perfect training for life in fin de siècle America. She also showed how the medium has shaped the minds of a whole generation, stating that if *Citizen Kane* had taken place in the twenty-first century, Kane would have sighed "Mario" instead of "Rosebud."

Another book appeared in 1997 that contained serious academic writing on video games. Espen Aarseth's *Cybertext: Perspectives on Ergodic Literature* looked at the much wider field of all texts that require nontrivial user input to function, of which video games are only a part. Aarseth's emphasis was on the cybernetic nature of the text (that is, the feedback loop between the user and the text), and he viewed the text as a network:

> The cybertext reader *is* a player, a gambler; the cybertext *is* a game-world or world-game; it *is* possible to explore, get lost, and discover secret paths in these texts, not metaphorically, but through the topological structures of the textual machinery. This is not a difference between games and literature but rather between games and narratives. To claim that there is no difference between games and narratives is to ignore essential qualities of both categories. And yet as this study tries to show, the difference is not clear-cut, and there is significant overlap between the two.[27]

Aarseth is also the founder of the Digital Arts and Culture series of conferences and the online journal *Game Studies* <www.gamestudies.org>.[28]

Another theoretical account came in 1998 from the debates about gender and games, *From Barbie to Mortal Kombat: Gender and Computer Games,* edited by Justine Cassell and Henry Jenkins. As they wrote: "Too often, the study of computer games has meant the study of *boys* playing computer games. In fact, too often the very design of computer games for children has meant computer games for boys" [the proof being, as Jenkins mentions in further reflections, Nintendo's *Game Boy*].[29] Cassell and Jenkins also discussed the "girls' game" movement which "document[ed] one moment in that process of translating feminist theory into practice." Cultural theorists, developmental psychologists, academic technologists, computer game industry representatives, and female game players studied the state of the market and the difference between the genders, and gave their thoughts as to whether it was necessary to design video games for girls or to have a broader view in order to create games for both girls and boys. And just as *From Barbie to Mortal Kombat: Gender and Computer Games* took an interest in entrepreneurial feminism, revealing the vision and goals of girl-specific companies, Brenda Laurel's *Utopian Entrepreneur* (2001) explored the demise of her company Purple Moon, which was dedicated to designing and producing software for girls, and the battles she faced while trying to keep her company true to its mission.[30]

Academia was not the only area where more serious study of video games was taking place. While most journalistic writing approached video games from a sociological and popular cultural perspective, Poole's *Trigger Happy: The Inner Life of Videogames* (2000) took a different one. For him, the inner life of video games was bound up with the inner life of the player whose response was *aesthetic*. Comparing them with other media, especially with cinema, Poole wished to present the *charm* of video games and their unique properties. With many references to games, he described the psychological and physical involvement of the player. He examined the ways worlds were built, stories were told, and Western or Japanese characters were turned into idols. But, even more important, Poole had some theoretical propensity. *Trigger Happy* was riddled with quick references to philosophers and numerous thinkers such as Adorno, Benjamin, Plato, Huizinga, Peirce, and Wittgenstein. Steven Poole arguably pushed the journalistic accounts of video games into a more theoretically oriented direction.

By the end of the twentieth century, the video game had gained recognition (if not respect) in academia and had acquired the status of nostalgia and a historical, cultural object. In 1997, *Film Quarterly* featured its first essay on video games and the Society of Cinema Studies (now the Society for Cinema and Media Studies) had its first paper on video games at its annual conference, with its first entire panel on video games appearing in 2000. No longer just a tangent or offshoot of new media theory, serious academic writing on the video game was finally beginning to carve out its own niche in the theoretical landscape.

Video Game Theory Comes of Age

At the turn of the millennium, video game theory, as a field of study, included a handful of books, several academic programs,[31] the first online academic journal (*Game Studies*), and over half a dozen annual conferences. As interest grows and the amount of academic work on video games multiplies, different trends in research and theorizing are already evident, especially in North America and Europe. Just as early film theory had its bifurcations (for example, Eisensteinian montage vs. the Bazinian long take), video game theory is already diverging into a variety of approaches, including narratology, cognitive studies, theories of representation, and ludology (the study of play). Examples of all of these can be found in this volume.

Many writings on video games, especially earlier ones, attempt to connect video games to other media, seeing elements shared between them, and much of the marketing and cross-franchising of video games does this as well. And there are, of course, many formal properties, organizational strategies, and elements of other media that are found in some video games but which are not in any way essential to the medium. For example, conservation of screen direction, sound perspective (or even sound itself), and narrative are found in some video games but certainly not all of them.[32] At the same, however, the video game is unlike any media to come before it, being the first to combine real-time game play with a navigable, onscreen diegetic space; the first to feature avatars and player-controlled surrogates that could influence onscreen events; and the first to require hand-eye coordination skills (except for pinball, which was much more limited and not as complicated). Massively multiplayer online role-playing games (MMORPGs) are the first persistent (twenty-four hours a day, seven days a week) worlds, and the first instance of individualized mediated experiences within a mass audience (each player's experience is unique despite the large number of simultaneous participants). And, apart from computer programming out of which it grew, the video game was the first truly algorithmic medium.

Even as the video game is clearly a unique medium and worthy of attention and forms of theory that can address it specifically, narrative elements and conventions taken from other media are still present to a great degree in many games, and a spectrum of positions exist combining ideas and terminology from various movements, even as the terms and definitions are not always agreed upon (for example, a number of scholars find the notion of "interactivity" problematic, suggesting that the term is misleading[33]).

Academic debates on the nature of video games have begun heating up, and one finds discussions of them at conferences devoted to the study of media, like the newly renamed Society of Cinema and Media Studies (formerly the Society for Cinema Studies), and at conferences aimed more specifically at digital media or concentrating solely on video games. Such conferences can be found throughout the world. The Digital Art and Culture conferences have had an international emphasis from the start, taking place in 1998 and 2000 at the University of Bergen (Norway), 1999 at Georgia Institute of Technology (Atlanta, Georgia, United States), 2001 at Brown University (Providence, Rhode Island, United States), and 2003 at RMIT University (Melbourne, Australia). The online journal *Game Studies* is likewise international in its makeup, with its eleven founding members coming from seven different countries, and the two Danish members, Jesper Juul and Lisbeth Klastrup, also organized the first academic conference on video games, *Computer Games and Digital Textualities,* held at the IT-University of Copenhagen in March 2001.[34]

Other conferences on video games have been appearing in recent years: the International Games Culture Conferences, the International Game Developers' Association (IGDA) Conferences, the Challenge of Computer Games Conference (Lodz, Poland, August 25–27, 2002), Conference on Computational Semiotics for Games and New Media (COSIGN) conferences, the Game On conferences, Computers and Games 2002 (Edmonton, Canada, July 25–27, 2002), and others. More books are appearing, in Europe as well as the United States. Regarding the state of books on video games in Germany, Konrad Lischka, author of *Spielplatz Computer,* writes:

> Within the last two years Germany has experienced a boom of literature on computer games—at least if you compare the amount of published books with what came before. Before the turn of the millennium, an interesting book about computer games appeared only once a decade. In the eighties it the was semiotically-inspired *Pac-Man & Co.* (1984) by the film critics Georg Seesslen and Christian Rost, and in the nineties there was the essay collection *Schöne Neue Welten?* [*Beautiful New Worlds?*] (1995) edited by Florian Rötzer. But since 2000 almost ten books of that kind appeared in Germany.
>
> There are three reasons for this. At present, the generation that grew up in the eighties indulges itself in its collective memory. Books like *Generation Golf* or the revival of German Punk arose from this development. Old video and computer games are part of this nostalgia wave. The coffee table book *Electronic Plastic* provides the pictures (of old hand-held games and table-top games) and the book *Wir waren Space Invaders* [*We Were Space Invaders*] by Mathias Mertens and Tobias O. Meissner provides the text. They define the culture of their youth through games.

The second reason for the high output of titles is the discussion about the effects of computer games. After the Columbine shootings of Littleton, Colorado, a tighter control of games by the authorities was discussed in Germany, and realized after the gun rampage of Erfurt. One book on this topic addressed to the broad public but remarkably differentiated is Hartmut Gieselmann's *Der Virtuelle Krieg* [*The Virtual War: Between Appearance and Reality in the Computer Game*] (2002).

The third reason for the variety of books is a growing interest in computer games as cultural phenomena. The first impressive works of human scientists about games have been published (for example, Claus Pias's *Computer Spiel Welten* [*Computer Game Worlds*] (2002). That this new perspective on games is also growing among museums and within the German game industry is shown by two exhibitions and catalogs (Förderverein für Jugend- und Sozialarbeit, Verband der Unterhaltungssoftware Deutschland, 2002; Museum für Sepulkralkultur, 2002).[35]

While there is growing cross-fertilization of ideas and academic debate between scholars of Europe and the Americas, there is much less so between Western countries and Japan. Part of the reason is the availability of writings translated into English, as well as the emphasis on game design and production as opposed to academic study of video games. According to Matthew Weise, a game researcher on MIT's Games-to-Teach Project team:

> As for existing writing available in English, I can only point to interviews with and lectures by Japanese video game designers. Shigeru Miyomoto, creator of Mario and Zelda, has spoken a number of times at game shows and conferences worldwide, and he is probably the closest thing to a Japanese video game designer (that I'm aware of) who frames his ideas in way that sound like what to a westerner would sound like "theory." Hideo Kojima, creator of *Metal Gear*, has spoken (mostly in interviews) in a similar fashion.[36]

In any event, the increasing number of books, periodicals, and conferences on video games suggests that an international network of video game researchers is forming, and that video game theory as an academic field is coming into existence. As it does, the question remains as to when (and perhaps if) agree-upon theoretical foundations and a common vocabulary will arise among the international research community. While it is certainly beyond the scope of this introduction to attempt to address such a question in full, we might examine a few possible starting points.

Basic Elements of Video Game Theory

As a multidisciplinary field of research, video game theory, by nature, must be a synthesis of a wide range of approaches, but at the same time focus on the unique aspects of video games. As Espen Aarseth wrote at the end of his editorial in the first issue of *Game Studies:*

> Of course, games should also be studied within existing fields and departments,
> such as Media Studies, Sociology, and English, to name a few. But games are too
> important to be left to these fields. (And they did have thirty years in which they
> did nothing!) Like architecture, which contains but cannot be reduced to art
> history, games studies should contain media studies, aesthetics, sociology etc.
> But it should exist as an independent academic structure, because it cannot be
> reduced to any of the above.[37]

Indeed. Nor can the video game be seen only as a remediation of film,
television, computers, or even games. The irreducibility of the video game
is precisely why it has been hard to define formally and why there is heated
discussion not only around what it *should be,* but also around what exactly it
is. While a spectrum of definitions are already in use by academics, gamers,
retailers, and designers, we can begin by trying to find essential elements
that are generally agreed upon as constituting a "video game."

Probably everyone would agree that *PONG* (1972) is a video game. As
video games go, it is hard to imagine a commercially feasible game that is
simpler than *PONG.* Therefore, *PONG* can be seen as fulfilling the criteria for a video game in the most minimal way possible. What does *PONG*
consist of? Competing players had to return the bouncing ball as in table
tennis; players were restricted to vertical movement; game play took place
on a video monitor; and a score was kept that determined who won and who
lost. While detailed discussions of how the term "video game" can be defined
exist elsewhere,[38] we can, from these basic features, begin to demarcate what
we mean when we say something is a video game. Of the first half of the term,
"video" would seem to require that game action appear in some visual form
on a screen (although "video" originally referred to the cathode ray tubes
[CRTs], which were used in arcade games and home video games, handheld
games with pixel-based displays also are now commonly referred to as video
games). The second half of the term, "game," is less easily defined. Attempts
to define it generally refer to the definition given by Johan Huizinga in his famous *Homo Ludens: A Study of the Play-Element in Culture* ([1938] 1950) or
to works ranging from Roger Caillois' *Man, Play, and Games* ([1958] 1961) to
Elliott M. Avedon and Brian Sutton-Smith's *The Study of Games* (1971), and
to recent works specific to video games by Gonzalo Frasca, for instance.[39]

Of all the various approaches that have been taken in defining the video
game, a few elements seem to appear persistently, under various names and
descriptions. These elements are at the heart of what makes the video game
a unique medium, and need to be addressed in any discussion of them.
The most fundamental of these elements are: an *algorithm, player activity,
interface,* and *graphics.*

The simplest of the four to define is *graphics,* which refers to some kind of changing and changeable visual display on a screen, involving some kind of pixel-based imaging. Graphics seem to be required, after all, if a game is to be a "video" game (but, as noted earlier, they are not necessarily a criterion for a "computer" game or an "electronic" game, although the majority of them do have graphics[40]). Although not explicitly mentioned in many definitions of "video game," there is almost always an implicit assumption that some form of graphics will be present. One also would expect the video game's graphics to differ from imagery in print or on film in that they are on an electronic screen of some kind (a CRT, an LED or LCD screen, for example) and have some moving component under player control.

Graphics should not be confused with the next element, the *interface,* since an interface may or may not contain graphics just as not all graphics represent an interface. The interface occurs at the boundary between the player and the video game itself, and can include such things as the screen, speakers (and microphones), input devices (such as a keyboard, mouse, joystick, trak-ball, paddles, steering wheels, light guns, etc.), as well as onscreen graphical elements such as buttons, sliders, scroll bars, cursors, and so forth, which invite player activity and allow it to occur. The interface, then, is really a junction point between input and output, hardware and software, and the player and the material game itself, and the portal through which player activity occurs.

Player activity is arguably the heart of the video game experience, and perhaps the most important thing from a design perspective. It is the element of the video game that is most written about, and every theory of video games thus far seems to agree with the idea that without player activity, there would be no game. The nature of player activity is also necessarily *ergodic* (to use Espen Aarseth's term) or nontrivial and extranoematic, that is, the action has some physical aspect to it and is not strictly an activity occurring purely on the mental plane. Player activity is input by means of the user interface, and is limited and usually quantized by it as well. We could further divide player activity into two separate areas, diegetic activity (what the player's avatar does as a result of player activity) and extradiegetic activity (what the player is physically doing to achieve a certain result). The two should not be conflated, as the translation from one to the other can differ greatly. For example, some shooting games could move a gunsight about with a joystick and use a button to fire, while another could use a controller shaped like a handgun for the same input; the onscreen action could be the same, while the means of input vary. Likewise, the joystick is used to input a wide variety of onscreen actions, including steering, rotating a point of view, or choosing from a menu.

Finally, at the heart of every video game program is an *algorithm,* the program containing the set of procedures controlling the game's graphics and sound, the input and output engaging the players, and the behavior of the computer-controlled players within the game. Dividing up its tasks, we could say that the algorithm is responsible for the *representation, responses, rules,* and *randomness* that make up a game. *Representation* is the rendering of the game's graphics, sounds, and gameplay (and the simulation of its diegetic world, if it has one), and the unification of them that make for a persistent and coherent player experience. *Responses* include the actions and reactions made by the algorithm in response to the changing situations and data within the game. This includes control of game events and non-player characters, as well as the on-screen action of the player's avatar, the action of which is determined by the player's input. *Rules* are the limitations imposed upon and determining the game's activities and representations, which regulate responses and gameplay. Even the most abstract video games or open-ended ones have some kind of rules, even if they are merely limitations on what the player can do within the context of the game. Finally, most games have some element of *randomness* (or "unpredictability," perhaps, since true randomness is computationally impossible). Randomness keeps the game from being exactly the same every time it is played, keeping players guessing and the game interesting, through the variation of events and the times and order in which they occur. Strictly speaking, randomness is not a necessary element; puzzle games and games which rely heavily on narrative and are generally played only once may contain little or no randomness (like *Myst* [1993], *Gadget* [1993], or *Star Trek: Borg* [1996], for example). But most games have some degree of randomness, to keep the game from boring predictability (most computer chess games, for example, will not use the same opening every time).

These four basic elements, the *algorithm, player activity, interface,* and *graphics,* are often referred to in discussions of video games, though the terminology used varies. For example, in *Hamlet on the Holodeck: The Future of Narrative in Cyberspace* (1997), after describing her experience of playing the laserdisc arcade movie game *Mad Dog McCree* (1990), Janet Murray pointed out four essential properties of digital environments:

> Digital environments are procedural, participatory, spatial, and encyclopedic. The first two properties make up most of what we mean by the vaguely used word *interactive*; the remaining two properties help to make digital creations seem as explorable and extensive as the actual world, making up much of what we mean when we say that cyberspace is *immersive*.[41]

What Murray calls procedural[42] and participatory can be mapped onto what Lev Manovich, in *The Language of New Media* (2001), identifies as algorithmic, whereas Murray's spatial and encyclopedic aspects coincide with Manovich's idea of navigable space and the database:

> Of course, not all media objects are explicitly databases. Computer games, for instance, are experienced by their players as narratives. In games, the player is given a well-defined task-winning the match, being first in a race, reaching the last level, or attaining the highest score. It is this task that makes the player experience the game as a narrative. Everything that happens to her in a game, all the characters and objects she encounters, either take her closer to achieving the goal or further away from it. Thus, in contrast to a CD-ROM and Web database, which always appear arbitrary because the user knows additional material could have been added without modifying the logic, in a game, from the user's point of view, all the elements are motivated (i.e., their presence is justified).... While computer games do not follow a database logic, they appear to be ruled by another logic—that of the algorithm. They demand that a player execute an algorithm in order to win.[43]

In both cases, the use of a spatial metaphor is indirectly reliant upon the presence of graphics, though neither acknowledges this overtly. The similarities between some of Murray's and Manovich's ideas and their differences in terminology is a good example of the diversity of approaches and lack of a common terminology that can be found in the writings converging in the area we could call video game theory. As video game theory begins to demarcate its territory and conceptual overlaps become apparent, the field may finally begin to coalesce and define itself. In the thirteen essays that follow, one can already see shared ideas, themes, and concepts despite the different disciplines out of which they arise.

Essays from Around the World

Featuring the work of sixteen scholars from eight countries,[44] this anthology is a sampling of the wide range of approaches being brought to the study of video games, and suggests a potential for interdisciplinary dialogue. The first essay, "Theory by Design" by Walter Holland, Henry Jenkins, and Kurt Squire, explores how the gap between theory and practice might be bridged in the context of emerging media technology. "What happens when theorists become game designers?" they ask, and "How does the design task force them to reconsider their theoretical assumptions?" The essay describes the work of MIT's Games-to-Teach Project, which examines the challenges and potential of edutainment with the goal of developing conceptual prototypes for games outside of a commercial context. Design is also the topic of the next essay, Mark J. P. Wolf's "Abstraction in the Video Game," which looks at graphical abstraction in games. Ever since the early days, when technological limitations severely restricted graphical detail, game design has pushed toward more representational imagery, and has ignored the possibilities offered by abstraction. Wolf's essay looks at how abstraction was used and how it related to game design, suggesting that much potential for the use of abstraction remains untapped. As the video game moves beyond the relatively narrow stylistic palette conformed to by most commercial games, its potential as art, educational tool, and training simulation will perhaps be better realized.

One of the main concerns of video game design is the relationship the game has to the player, including such things as the interface, the avatar, and the way the player is positioned by the game. Alison McMahan's essay, "Immersion, Engagement, and Presence: A Method For Analyzing 3-D Video Games," examines ideas behind the terminology surrounding the notion of "presence" and how it has been defined, and then constructs a model for analyzing the degree of presence enabled by a particular video game using aesthetic criteria. Closely tied to the notion of "presence" is that of "identity," which Miroslaw Filiciak examines in "Hyperidentities: Postmodern Identity Patterns and Massively Multiplayer Online Role-Playing Games." Filiciak suggests that the use of online personae is analogous to the postmodern condition of multiple or split identities and networked selves, taking his examples from the worlds of role-playing games in which hundreds of thousands of players have avatars embodying their online identities.

Expanding in a different direction regarding identity and the avatar, Bob Rehak's "Playing at Being: Psychoanalysis and the Avatar" traces the evolution of avatars from the earliest games to current first-person shooting games, revealing a symptomatic concern with the onscreen body's capabilities and vulnerabilities, as well as its relationship to player corporeality. His essay shows how suturing effects of point-of-view in the first-person shooting games constitute a powerful interpellative system in which players take on avatarial perspectives as their own, using film theory and psychoanalytic concepts to explore this aspect of avatarial operations. Cognitive psychology also can be applied to the study of video games, and in "Stories for Eye, Ear, and Muscles: Video Games, Media, and Embodied Experiences," Torben Grodal argues that computer games and other types of interactive virtual reality are simulations of basic modes of real-life experiences. He suggests that the tools of cognitive psychology are more successful at describing video games than those used in a semiotic approach, since most game activity consists of seeing, hearing, and doing in simulations of real-world interaction.

Taking up the theme of embodied experience, Martti Lahti's essay "As We Become Machines: Corporealized Pleasures in Video Games" explores how video games construct a new relationship between corporeal experience and subjectivity, and the role of the technology and the interface in the process. The way that video games allow the player to try out (at least in a virtual sense) different bodies, races, genders, and sexualities is also discussed in Mia Consalvo's essay "Hot Dates and Fairy-Tale Romances: Studying Sexuality in Video Games," which looks at the construction of sexuality and the way it is represented in a game's characters, narratives, visuals, and situations, and the presumed worldviews they imply, and the impact on the game's storyline and players' performances.

In "Video Games and Configurative Performances," Markku Eskelinen and Ragnhild Tronstad look at video games as remediated games and see a continuum between video games and ergodic art. They compare the performative aspects of video games with that of theater, performance art, and Allen Kaprow's notion of the Happening, and examine the distribution of information and modalities of action in video games, including such things as motivation, exposition, and orientation. Moving from performance to simulation, Gonzalo Frasca's essay, "Simulation versus Narrative: Introduction to Ludology," also contests the necessity of narrative in video games, arguing for an approach that views games as simulations instead of representational narratives. He compares the characteristics of video games with those of traditional media, and demonstrates a variety of ways that an author can use a video game as a vehicle for the expression of an ideology, through the rules that regulate gameplay and the game's possible outcomes, suggesting that the video game is ripe for use as a rhetorical tool for art, philosophy, and education. Also writing from the standpoint of ludology, Bernard Perron's essay "From Gamers to Players and Gameplayers: The Example of Interactive Movies" examines the bipolarity of the range of games from "paidia" to "ludus." Basing his argument on the ludic attitudes at play during movie games and interactive movies, he attempts to lay out a common terminology that would articulate the distinction between players and gamers more accurately, and applies his ideas to the genre of "interactive movies," which attempts to combine storytelling and interactivity. "Interactive Storytelling" is the subject and title of Chris Crawford's essay, which begins by surveying early attempts to combine interactivity and storytelling and the resulting models. Following his survey, he proposes his own model for an interactive storytelling engine, and describes its functioning.

Narrative is also one of the main concerns of the last essay in the anthology. Patrick Crogan's paper, "Gametime: History, Narrative, and Temporality in *Combat Flight Simulator 2*," traces the connections between war-related computer games and recent Hollywood war films, exploring key aspects of the transformation of mainstream visual culture under the impact of computer-based digital imaging. With a particular focus on the game Microsoft *Combat Flight Simulator 2: WW II Pacific Theater* (2000) and the movie *Pearl Harbor* (2001), his essay draws out some of the implications of this relation between war and imaging for the analysis of visual culture, and ways in which video games can act as training for action in the real world, as well as ways video games can remediate history.

Finally, to help situate the study of home video games historically, we include an Appendix listing home video game systems that have appeared over the last three decades. Whereas most video game study focuses on more recent games, due in large part to their more complex and detailed content as well as their availability, this list is a good reminder of the rich history the video game has, much of which has yet to be addressed by historians and theoreticians.

On to the Next Level: Future Directions of Study

As the field of video game studies grows, it may well find its way to the center of media studies, as games eclipse other forms of digital technology and art. As Henry Jenkins argues:

> Games represent a new lively art, one as appropriate for the digital age as those earlier media were for the machine age. They open up new aesthetic experiences and transform the computer screen into a realm of experimentation and innovation that is broadly accessible. And games have been embraced by a public that has otherwise been unimpressed by much of what passes for digital art. Much as the salon arts of the 1920s seemed sterile alongside the vitality and inventiveness of popular culture, contemporary efforts to create interactive narrative through modernist hypertext or avant-garde installation art seem lifeless and pretentious alongside the creativity and exploration, the sense of fun and wonder, that game designers bring to their craft.[45]

As both game designers and theorists explore the possibilities and potential that the video game has to offer, and historians begin to record where the video game has been and what it was, new strains of formal exploration may emerge, much as experimental cinema or electronic music led in directions away from mainstream industry productions, while at the same time exerting their influence on them and indicating future avenues for development.

Like an endlessly scrolling adventure game map, so much territory remains to be explored. The production of video games calls for an account of the video game's economical and political functions, and the ideologies that shape games as well as those for which the games are propaganda. The reception of games will have to be examined; how are they played, received, understood, and interpreted by the players. The international popularity of video games will require that they be viewed in a larger cultural and geographical landscape. And the cultural landscape is broad; with the integration of video games into operating systems, cell phones, PDAs, and practically every type of electronic screen technology available, video games have a ubiquity and availability unlike any other medium in history.

And the many uses of video games are also being explored. MIT's Games-to-Teach Project and George Kosmetzsky's I.C. Squared are both researching ways that video games can be used in education and training. The increasing availability of digital media-producing tools and programs means more individual production is possible, and perhaps even an avant garde of experimental game designing will be able to arise outside of mainstream commercial production. Already, younger scholars such as Jesper Juul (<www.soup.dk>) or game designers such as Eric Zimmerman (<www.gmlb.com>) are making games as well as developing their theoretical approaches. Just as simulations can embody theoretical ideas, perhaps games embodying theories will someday hold as vaunted a position in academia as the book and the film does today. Whatever the case, it is clear that the video game is an important part of popular culture and will likely remain so for some time to come, regardless of the future forms that it may take.

Notes

1. In a 2001 interview in *Joystick101.org,* Steven Poole, the author of *Trigger Happy: The Inner Life of Videogames,* gave evidence of the remaining resistance: "There has been a small current of dissent, however, with the common theme that my attempt to place videogames in a wider cultural context by relating them to film theory, semiotics and so on is just 'pretentious.' This is a criticism I don't really understand, and I don't think anyone will think it's pretentious in 50 years, when videogame criticism has attained the same status as film criticism has now. A minority of hardcore gamers have resisted the idea of their pet hobby being analysed and explained by someone who is in their eyes an 'outsider,' but I don't apologise for that." In Kurt Squire, "Interview with Steven Poole, Author of Trigger Happy," *Joystick 101.org* (January 24, 2001). Available online at <http://www.joystick101.org/?op=displaystory&sid=2001/1/16/174911/133>.

    The gaming community also can be hostile toward the theorizing of video games. The premiere issue of the first academic peer-reviewed online journal *Game Studies* provoked a harsh response from the gamers at *slashdot.org.* See <http://slashdot.org/articles/01/08/03/1147242.shtml>.

2. And protected. See Henry Jenkins, "Power to the Players: Why video games need the protection of the First Amendment," *Technology Review* (June 7, 2002). Available online at <http://www.technologyreview.com/articles/wo_jenkins060702.asp>.

3. The first chapter of Wolf's book *The Medium of the Video Game* deals with the definition of "video game," looking at the range popular uses of the term. See *The Medium of the Video Game,* ed. Mark J. P. Wolf (Austin: University of Texas Press, 2001).

4. The first three times the subject heading "Video Games" appeared in the *Reader's Guide,* it was merely followed by "See Electronic Games."

5. Although the two terms are often used interchangeably, a distinction between them could be made; "computer games" would not require any visuals, while "video games" would not require a microprocessor (or whatever one wanted to define as essential for being referred to as a "computer"). The board game *Stop Thief* (1979), for example, has a handheld computer that makes sounds that relate to game play on the board. Therefore the game could be considered a computer game, but not a video game. More of these kinds of games exist than games that involve video but not a computer, making "video games" the more exclusive term. "Video games" is also more accurate in regard to what kinds of games are meant when the term is used in common parlance.

    Another blurred boundary arises when one considers the place of text adventure games, which are made up solely of text. While the distinction between text adventures and graphical adventure games remains (and is a useful and logical distinction), text displayed on a monitor screen is arguably also a visual display and a form of computer graphics.

6. Donald D. Spencer, *Game Playing with Computers* (New York: Spartan Books, 1968); and A. G. Bell, *Games Playing With Computers* (London: George Allen & Unwin Ltd., 1972).

7. Bell, *Games Playing With Computers*, 10–11.

8. For a list of early books on video games, a good source is Lee K. Seitz's Classic Video Games Literature List. Available online at <http://fly.hiwaay.net/~lseitz/cvg/cvglit.shtml>.

9. A list of these magazines can be found at <http://www.digitpress.com/faq/vgmags.txt>.

10. Warren Robinett began work on *Adventure* in 1978, which, according to him, gives some validity to the copyright date of 1978 found on the Atari cartridge and manual for *Adventure*. But the actual code was finished and turned over to Atari in June of 1979, making 1979 the actual year of release. Going by the copyright date found in the game manual and cartridge, I mistakenly gave 1978 as the date of release in the initial print run of *The Medium of the Video Game*.

11. Chris Crawford, *The Art of Computer Game Design* (Electronic Version, 1984), 1. Available onilne at <http://www.vancouver.wsu.edu/fac/peabody/game-book/Coverpage.html>.

12. Crawford, *The Art of Computer Game Design*, 87.

13. Craig A. Anderson and Karen Dill, "Video Games and Aggressive Thoughts, Feelings, and Behavior in the Laboratory and in Life," *Journal of Personality and Social Psychology* 78, no 4 (April 2000): 772–790. Available online at <http://www.apa.org/journals/psp/psp784772.html>.

14. See Rochelle Slovin, "Hot Circuits: Reflections on the 1989 Video Game Exhibition of the American Museum of the Moving Image," in Wolf, *The Medium of the Video Game*, 137–154.

15. See Charles Bernstein, "Play it Again, Pac-Man," in Wolf, *The Medium of the Video Game*, 155–168.

16. For more on *The Last Starfighter* game that was almost made, see *The Last Starfighter* FAQ. Available online at <http://www.paulbunyan.net/users/wayland/arcade/laststar.html>.

17. About the symbiosis between the film and video game industries, see, for instance, Sue Adamo, "Hollywood is Game," *Film Comment* 19, no 1 (January/February, 1983): 40–41; Marc Graser, "New Playground for Studios," *Variety*, May 17, 1999, available online at <http://www.findarticles.com/cf_0/m1312/1_375/54701191/print.jhtml>; Marc Graser, "H'W'D Can't Crash Vidgames (motion pictures inspired by video games)," *Variety*, August 9, 1999, available online at <http://www.findarticles.com/cf_0/m1312/12_375/55578478/print.jhtml>; and Josh Spector, "Hollywood puts on its game face," *Hollywood Reporter*, daily electronic edition, June 1, 2001, 2.

18. Prior to the CD-ROM, only laserdisc games featured full-motion video clips, overlaying computer graphics over them or creating games entirely from them. Sega's *Astron Belt* introduced the technology in Japan in 1982 and later in America in 1983, the same year that Cinematronic's *Dragon's Lair*, the first successful laserdisc game, appeared. In 1984, Rick Dyer created a home laserdisc game system, the RDI Halcyon, that also used full-motion video. For a nice summary of the rise and fall of laserdisc games and information on individual games, see <http://www.atarihq.com/coinops/laser/>.

19. Greg M. Smith, "Introduction: A Few Words about Interactivity," in *On a Silver Platter. CD-ROMs and the Promises of a New Technology*, ed. Greg M. Smith (New York: New York University Press, 1999), 2.

20. Smith, "Introduction: A Few Words about Interactivity," 2. The anthology begins to make up for this oversight by studying *Phantasmagoria, Civilization II, Sim City 2000*, and *Sim Town*.

21. *Doom* was released as shareware in 1993 before it appeared commercially.

22. From the *Catalog for Academic Year 2001–2002*, Digipen Institute of Technology, Redmond, Washington, 6.

23. The Le Diberders underscored an important fact:

> The project of this book is born from the observation that analysis [of video games] did not precisely exist. The specialized press proliferates, but for the exclusive usage of an already convinced community. While the one who wants to document himself on the sailing board or on the manufacture of lampshades in leather has a suitable bibliography, the favorite leisure of several tens of millions of Westerners remains largely a *terra incognita* for parents wanting to understand.

In Alain and Frédéric Le Diberder, *Qui a peur des jeux vidéo?* (Paris: La Découverte/Essais, 1993), 8. Freely translated.

24.   Another French book about pedagogy was published with the same objective in 1994. Évelyne Esther Gabriel's *Que faire avec les jeux vidéo?* [What to Do with Video Games?] (Paris: Hachette, 1994) was wishing to rehabilitate the player and the spirit of play and to show that the teacher would gain something from the ludic to the pedagogic.

25.   Alain Le Diberder, "L'interactivité, une nouvelle frontière du cinéma," (Dossier: Numérique, Virtuel, Interactif. Demain le Cinéma) *Cahiers du Cinéma* 503 (June 1996): 122–126.

26.   Erwan Higuinen and Charles Tesson, "Éditorial: Cinéphiles et Ludophiles," (Jeux Vidéo) *Cahiers du Cinéma* Hors-Série (September 2002): 5. Freely translated.

27.   Espen Aarseth, *Cybertext: Perspectives on Ergodic Literature* (Baltimore and London: Johns Hopkins University Press, 1997), 4–5.

28.   Although the majority of the original eleven members of the *Game Studies* team were present at the first DAC conference, it was after the third conference in 2000 that the preparation for the launching of the first academic peer-reviewed online journal began. *Game Studies* was launched in July 2001 with a specific mission: "To explore the rich cultural genre of games; to give scholars a peer-reviewed forum for their ideas and theories; to provide an academic channel for the ongoing discussions on games and gaming" (<http://www.gamestudies.org/about.html>).

29.   Justine Cassell and Henry Jenkins, "Chess For Girls? Feminism and Computers Games," in *From Barbie to Mortal Kombat: Gender and Computer Games*, eds. Justine Cassell and Henry Jenkins (Cambridge, MA: MIT Press, 1998), 5.

30.   Thanks to Henry Jenkins for this reference.

31.   For a list of schools, see for instance <http://www.gamasutra.com/php-bin/companies.php3?cat=153138>.

32.   Conservation of screen direction, sound perspective, sound, and narrative are also not essential to film, yet one does not find film scholars vehemently arguing that film is not narrative and should not be considered as such. But claims like these are made in the narrative versus interactivity debates among video game theorists.

33.   For example, see the discussions of "interactivity" in Aarseth, *Cybertext: Perspectives on Ergodic Literature*; Mark J. P. Wolf, *Abstracting Reality: Art, Communication, and Cognition in the Digital Age* (Lanham, MA: University Press of America, 2000); and Lev Manovich, *The Language of New Media* (Cambridge, MA: MIT Press, 2001).

34.   Previous conferences, such as MIT's *Computer and Video Games Come of Age: A National Conference to Explore the State of an Emerging Entertainment Medium* held in February 2000, mixed industry professionals, software designers, and scholars of media and culture. As to the international makeup of the Game Studies crew, Markku Eskelinen has described the original eleven members as "3 Norwegians, 2 Danes, 2 Finns and one each from Uruguay, Spain, Germany and the U.S/Switzerland." E-mail correspondence with the editors.

35.   An annotated list of German publications on video games by Konrad Lischka is available from the editors, at <mark.wolf@cuw.edu> or <bernard.perron@umontreal.ca>.

36.   E-mail correspondence with the editors.

37.   Espen Aarseth, "Computer Games Studies, Year One," *Game Studies* 1, no 1 (July 2001). Available online at <http://www.gamestudies.org/0101/editorial.html>.

38.   For examples of detailed discussions of how the term "video game" can be defined, see the section "Defining the Video Game" in Chapter One of Wolf, *The Medium of the Video Game*, and "Towards a Definition of "Videogames," *Videotopia.com* (1998–99). Available online at <http://www.videotopia.com/errata1.htm>.

39.   See Frasca's website <http//:www.ludology.org>.

40.   See note 5.

41.   Janet H. Murray, *Hamlet on the Holodeck. The Future of Narrative in Cyberspace* (New York: The Free Press, 1997), 71.

42.   "Authorship in electronic media is procedural. Procedural authorship means writing the rules by which the texts appear as well as writing the texts themselves. It means writing the rules for the interactor's involvement, that is, the conditions under which things will happen in response to the participant's actions. It means establishing the properties of the objects and potential objects in the virtual world and the formulas for how they will relate to one another.

The procedural author creates not just a set of scenes but a world of narrative possibilities." Murray, *Hamlet on the Holodeck. The Future of Narrative in Cyberspace,* 152–153.

43.   Manovich, *The Language of New Media,* 221–222.
44.   Australia, Canada, Denmark, Finland, Norway, Poland, the United States, and Uruguay.
45.   Henry Jenkins, "Games, the New Lively Art," in *Handbook of Computer Game Studies,* eds. Jeffrey Goldstein and Joost Raessens (Cambridge, MA: MIT Press, forthcoming). Available online at <http://web.mit.edu/21fms/www/faculty/henry3/GamesNewLively.html>.

CHAPTER 1

Theory by Design

WALTER HOLLAND
HENRY JENKINS
KURT SQUIRE

Why game theory? What functions does theory serve during a moment when a medium is undergoing rapid transformation, when it is still defining its aesthetics, its functions, and its audiences? What forms will give theory maximum impact? Does theory serve a different function when a medium is new than when a medium is well established?

If one looks at the emergence of film theory, the most important early work did not come from distant academic observers but, rather, from direct participants. It came from trade press reporters like the *Moving Picture World*'s Epes Winthrop Sargent who documented cinema's evolving formal vocabulary and pushed the medium to achieve its full potential.[1] Sargent's readers were filmmakers, distributors, and exhibitors, who made a direct impact on the kinds of films produced. Early Soviet film theory came from expert practitioners, such as Eisenstein, Vertov, Kuleshov, or Pudovkin, who wanted to record and share discoveries made through their own production practice and, in the case of Kuleshov, to train future professionals.[2] It came from public intellectuals like Gilbert Seldes who wanted to spark a discussion about the aesthetic merits of contemporary popular culture and thus wrote for mass market magazines, not specialized academic journals.[3] Theoretical abstraction and distanced observation came much later, once cinema was more fully established as a medium and had achieved some cultural respectability. More specialized language emerged as cinema studies struggled for acceptance as a legitimate academic discipline. In the process, many now feel it sacrificed the potential for dialogue with media practitioners and consumers.

Game theory seems to be teetering on a threshold: many academics want to see game theory establish itself as a predominantly academic discipline, while others seek to broaden the conversation between game designers, consumers, journalists, and scholars. The opportunity exists for us to work together to produce new forms of knowledge about this emerging medium that will feed back into its ongoing development.

Writers such as Gill Branston and Thomas McLaughlin have made the case that academic theorizing is simply a subset of a much broader cultural practice, with many different sectors of society searching for meaningful generalizations or abstract maps to guide localized practices. Branston draws parallels between the productive labor of a car mechanic and the intellectual work of academic theorists: "Theory, always historically positioned, is inescapable in any considered practice. Our hypothetical car mechanic may find her work intolerable, and indeed replaceable, if it consists entirely of behaving like a competent machine. She will be using some sense of the whole engine to fix bolts successfully; she has to operate creatively with something close to theories—those buried traces of theories which we call assumptions or even, if more elaborated, definitions—of energy, combustion. Should she ever want to drive the car she will need maps."[4]

Theory thus governs practice and practice in turn contributes to our theoretical understanding. McLaughlin writes, "Practitioners of a given craft or skill develop a picture of their practice—a sense of how it is or ought to be practiced, of its values and its worldview—and many are quite articulate about this 'theory,' aware for example that there are competing theories, that not all practitioners work from the same premises. These practitioners' theories may contrast sharply with the theories of their practice constructed by academic theorists. . . . It would be possible to find the nurse's theory of disease, the musician's theory of audience, the computer designer's theory of interpretation, the athlete's theory of sport, the bookstore designer's theory of reading, the casting director's theory of character."[5] Or, one might add, a game designer or game player's theory of games. Theoretical terms are most often articulated by expert practitioners, McLaughlin argues, during moments of transition or disruption, when existing language prove inadequate to changing situations, common wisdom has not yet been established, competing models demand adjudication, contemporary developments demand new vocabularies, or the practice comes under fire from the outside and has to justify its own assumptions. We ascribe theoretical insights to avant-garde artists, for example, when they push their media in new directions or provide aesthetic rationales for their work. Yet, when a medium is sufficiently new, all works produced are in a sense avant garde—they are mapping still unfamiliar terrain, requiring a heightened consciousness about the medium itself.

McLaughlin's formulation would suggest, then, that as game designers develop their genre and formal vocabulary, expand their audience, introduce new production processes, or contend with governmental and policy challenges, this "vernacular theory" production will play a central role in their lives. Expert practitioners, such as Eric Zimmerman, Brenda Laurel, Doug Church, Will Wright, Peter Molyneux, and Warren Spector, among many others, have made significant contributions to our early understanding of this emerging medium. Professional conferences, such as the Game Developers Conference, have been at least as important academic conferences in formulating and debating game theory, if not more so. And the gamer community also has been actively and publicly involved in making sense of the medium, its audience, and its impact.

The MIT Comparative Media Studies Program has been actively involved in those public debates about games and game theory over the past several years. We hosted one of the first conferences to bring together academic theorists with game design professionals to talk about the current state and future development of the medium. We have conducted workshops at E3, GDC, and other major industry gatherings, demonstrating how a broader humanistic knowledge of media might enhance game design. Many of our faculty members have participated in a series of workshops with some of the top "creatives" at Electronic Arts, examining such core questions as genre, narrative, character, emotion, and community.[6] We also have been involved in public policy debates, testifying before governmental bodies, speaking to citizens, educators, parents, and reporters. We are motivated by a commitment to applied humanism—that is, the effort to mobilize theories, concepts, and frameworks from the humanities to respond pragmatically to real world developments during a period of media in transition.

The Games-to-Teach Project represents a new phase in our efforts to provoke discussion between game designers, players, policy makers, and scholars. A collaboration between the MIT Comparative Media Studies Program and Microsoft Research, the project seeks to encourage greater public awareness of the pedagogical potentials of games by developing a range of conceptual frameworks that show in practical terms how games might be deployed to teach math, science, and engineering at an advanced secondary or early undergraduate level. Much of the existing work in "edutainment" has focused on the primary grades. We feel games can also be used to communicate more complex content aimed at older players, who now constitute the core gamer market.[7] Our research has showed that incoming students at MIT are more apt to turn to games for their entertainment than film, television, or recreational reading; many respondents expressed enthusiasm for the idea of mastering classroom content through gaming.[8] Our group starts from the assumption that educational games need to be inserted into larger learning contexts, not operate in a vacuum. Games can no more turn kids into scientists and engineers than they can make kids psycho killers; our task is to identify what things games do well, and how educators can leverage existing game genres and technologies.

Science and engineering faculty have long utilized digital models, simulations, and visualizations as teaching aids. There is an all-or-nothing quality to visualizations and lecture-style materials, however. Rather than presenting an explanation for a phenomenon (or a canonical illustration of "how things work"), games present players microworlds; games offer players (students) a contexts for thinking through problems, making their own actions part of the solution, building on their intuitive sense of their role in the game world. A gamer, confronting a challenging level, finds personal satisfaction in success—and personal motivation as well, rehearsing alternative approaches, working through complex challenges (often well into the night!). Many parents wish that they could get their children to devote this determination to solving their problem sets—it is an open question, however, whether simply working toward a better grade is an effective educational challenge. Games confront players with limits of space, time, and resources, forcing them to stretch in order to respond to problems just on the outer limits of their current mastery. The best games can adjust to the skills of their players, allowing the same product to meet the needs of a novice and a more advanced student. Indeed, the concept of advancing in "levels" structures the learning process such that players can't advance without mastery—something that curriculum- and test-designers have struggled to build into their work.

And games can enable multiple learning styles: for example, arts students might better grasp basic physics and engineering principles in the context of an architectural design program. Many of us whose eyes glaze over when confronted with equations on a blackboard find we can learn science more thoroughly when it builds on our intuitive understandings and direct observations, yet many important aspects of the physical world cannot be directly experienced in the classroom. Students often complain that they see few real-world applications for what they learn in advanced math and science classes, yet they might draw more fully on such knowledge if it was the key to solving puzzles or overcoming obstacles in a game environment—if the knowledge were a tool rather than an end. It is both a motivational distinction and a matter of mindset (and what is the object of teaching if not literally to *change one's mind?*).

Games model not only principles but processes, particularly the dynamics of complex systems; students develop their own languages for illustrating those systems and grow incredibly adept at explaining them in their own terms. Researchers have found that peer-to-peer teaching reinforces mastery[9]; why, then, do we dismiss such information exchange in the context of gameplay (a website devoted to strategies for a particular game, or picking apart the rules of a simulation to ensure maximum efficiency) as somehow intellectually illegitimate? Such interactions are a critical part of the gaming context, and in the case of educational games, perhaps the most pedagogically important interactions.

Games also may enable teachers to observe their students' problem-solving strategies in action and to assess their performance in the context of authentic and emotionally compelling problems. Teachers may stage a particularly difficult level during a lecture, comparing notes on possible solutions. And the gaming world represents a rich model for sharable content, putting authoring tools into the hands of consumers and establishing infrastructures for them to exchange the new content they have developed. The question for educators, then, is not whether games could someday work to teach students; they already do so. The question is how to help these two worlds, that of gaming and that of education, to work together.

By design, our conceptual frameworks constitute thought experiments that seek to address core questions in game theory, pointing toward directions still largely unexplored by the mainstream industry. One could draw an analogy between these thought experiments and the early work of the Kuleshov group. For more than a year, Kuleshov taught his students at the VGIK school how to make movies without having any access to film stock; they conceptualized movies, blocked movies, imagined ways of dividing the action into shots, and even reedited existing movies, trying to develop a better understanding of how cinema operates. Kuleshov's experiments and insights have, however, guided decades of filmmakers as they sought to master the building blocks of film language. Similarly, our students are working through games on paper, examining existing games, brainstorming about future directions, and through this process, trying to address central issues surrounding games and education. As we developed these prototypes, we consulted with game designers, educational technologists, and the scientists and engineers most invested in the content areas, using them as a catalyst to get feedback and insight from practitioners.

We see these design documents as a form of game theory, one that starts with broad conceptual questions but addresses them through concrete examples. In the process of developing these frameworks, we have developed a much firmer grasp of the core challenges and opportunities that will shape the emergence of an educational games market. Operating within an academic space, removed from the immediate need to ship product, we were able to ask more fundamental questions about the medium and to imagine new directions games might take. This essay will discuss four of those frameworks—*Hephaestus, Supercharged!, Biohazard,* and *Environmental Detectives*—describing the conceptual and practical challenges we confronted and what we think these examples reveal about the potentials of educational gaming.

The "games" we are describing have not been built—so far—though the next phase of the Games-to-Teach Project involves the development of playable modules that can be tested in educational contexts and the development of a government, foundation, industry consortium that can fund the actual production and distribution of the games. This essay describes games that are in a very real sense theoretical—games that might exist, someday, but whose current value lies in the questions they pose and the directions they point for future development.[10]

Remediating Real World Play: *Hephaestus*

Hephaestus presented the challenge of translating the successful FIRST robotics competition to a digital space. FIRST[11] is a "non-profit, educational organization that was founded to inspire and excite young people about science and technology by bringing together professional mentors with high school students from around the country."[12] Started in 1989, FIRST was founded by Dean Kamen in the hopes that "the act of invention—that is, the work of scientists, engineers and technologists—[will be] as revered in the popular culture as music, athletics and entertainment are today." FIRST consists of two main competitions—the FIRST Robotics design competition and the Lego League, two competitions in which players design, construct, and operate robots in competitions. While *Hephaestus* incorporates elements of these other competitions, it is primarily based on the FIRST Robotics Competition.[13]

Every January, the FIRST Robotics Competition pits over 650 teams from nearly every state in the United States as well as representatives from Canada and Brazil. Each team is typically comprised of thirty-five students and an adult mentor (mostly engineers who volunteer to work on FIRST). Teams have six weeks to design and construct their robots from a basic kit of robot parts, and a list of optional parts that they might cast or purchase. They must develop a team of remote-control robots and work in alliance with another team to move balls from one zone in the playing field to another, scoring points by placing the balls in a goal (the playing field is depicted in Figure 1.1). One point is awarded for each ball that is in the goal at the end of the competition. Ten points are awarded for each ball that is in a goal inside the

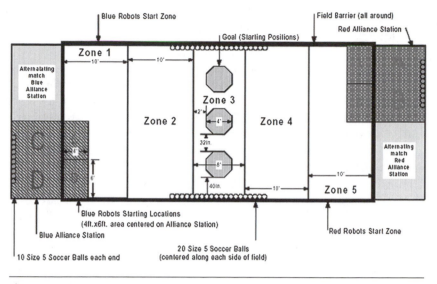

Figure 1.1. The Robot Playing Field.

alliances' territory. This rule encourages players to move the goals, which are initially placed in the center of the field, into their own territory.

The two-minute long matches are designed to foster both collaboration and competition. Each alliance scores points as a team, and alliances shift every match. Both the winners and the losers of the match receive Qualification Points that determine their place in the FIRST Robotics Competition Standards. Unlike most competitive events, where teams receive points for a win (or tie) or perhaps even by goals scored, the winning alliance earns triple the points of the losing alliance. So, if the blue alliance beats the red alliance by a score of 100 to 50, the red alliance, who lost, earns 50 points, and the winning blue alliance earns 150 points. This point structure is designed to minimize sabotage between alliances. Knocking out an opponents' robot or preventing him from scoring points ultimately lessens the winning alliances' score.

The FIRST Competition shares much in common with established game genres. Most obviously, FIRST is a competitive game, with elaborate game rules and structures. The game itself has two phases—a design phase, in which players are given fixed resources and limited time which constrain their design decisions, and a real-time action game, in which players deploy their robots to move balls, baskets, and robots across the floor. The robots' movements across the game floor, evading other robots, strategically positioning themselves near goals, and moving robots, baskets, and balls for their strategic advantage are elaborate contestations of space, which as we have argued in "Games as Contested Spaces," is also a hallmark of computer and video games.[14]

More than simply machines designed to score points, the robots quickly become personalized avatars for the players, who decorate and paint them, and in some cases, create movies and computer animations personifying them. In a live action film created by students in Hammond, Indiana, two robots prom dance in a high school parking lot. In another short, a computer-rendered robot flies through outer space. Emerging through hundreds of hours of work by dozens of people, each robot embodies not only functional design decisions and aesthetic considerations, but also, according to FIRST Competition cofounder Woodie Flowers, aspects of the players' collective identities.[15] This design and decoration are quite literally *performances of understanding* whereby the robots embody designers' understandings of robotics and aspects of their identities as designers; we wanted to leverage this identification process and preserve this pride in possession (and use) of knowledge in *Hephaestus*.

In designing *Hephaestus,* the Games-to-Teach team wrestled with how to leverage the engaging and educational aspects of the FIRST competition within a compelling computer game.[16] How could we balance single and multiplayer game dynamics? How could we create a rule set that fosters collaboration and competition, an online system that encouraged peer-to-peer teaching through the interaction between novices and experts? How could we integrate online and offline game play? And how could we support a variety of different player tastes? How does the computer-mediated nature of digital gaming change the robotic design process? How does the computer-mediated nature of gaming affect social interactions?

Hephaestus is a massively multiplayer game in which players design robots, down to the gear level, to colonize a fictitious planet located in the Alpha Centauri system. Heavily volcanic, the planet Hephaestus is currently too dangerous for human colonization. Lava serves as both a danger and reward to players. Players can perish by falling into a lava crevice but also can earn rewards by diverting lava into pools for thermal energy collection. Players also can set up collectors for wind and solar energy. If players gather enough resources, they can collaborate with other teammates to construct bridges, walls, and buildings. Although players begin the game with simple stock robots, they gradually earn enough resources for customization. Players might change gear ratios, buy treads with greater friction, or add extra battery holders. Consistent with basic engineering principles, players must make tradeoffs—for instance, between energy capacity, mass (which affects their fuel economy), and speed. The computer offers powerful methods for visualizing these tradeoffs in real time.

Massively multiplayer games are not only games but also social systems—living, breathing communities with their own ecologies, life cycles, and cultures. One way to characterize designed social systems is through the notion *of illuminative tensions.* In *Learning by Expanding,* Yuro Engestrom describes tensions as complementary and conflicting needs that reciprocally define one another and drive the dynamics of a social system.[17] Mapping these tensions can enable researchers to identify the core activities and predict sources of change within a social system. For example, in their studies of a community of preservice teachers (*Community of Teachers*), Sasha Barab and colleagues used design tensions to examine the practical and theoretical issues that "fuel change and innovation."[18]

In conceptualizing *Hephaestus,* the Games-to-Teach team identified several potential tensions: competition versus collaboration, robust simulation tools versus accessibility to new users, engrossing game dynamics versus appeal to broad audiences, and offline versus online activity. These tensions, which drive change and innovation in a system, are overlapping and often mutually reinforcing. FIRST cofounder Woodie Flowers describes the process of balancing FIRST as one of manipulating rules so that players are recognized for achievement and motivated to excel within a competitive framework, yet encouraged to collaborate and play fairly.[19] Players are motivated by a desire to excel and gain recognition within their school communities, among the FIRST competitors, and from their adult mentors. However, success demands collaboration with their teammates, their alliances, and their adult mentors. The competition values collaborative design, teamwork, mentorship, and constructive (as opposed to destructive) goals.

For the purposes of this essay, we will focus on one such tension in greater depth: online and offline practices. Our initial interviews with Flowers and students revealed that much of the appeal and educational value of FIRST came through interacting with physical materials—building drive trains, wiring circuits, and creating a physical robot that scoots across the floor.[20] For many participants, the thought of learning engineering without interacting with actual steel, rubber, circuitry, and plastics is inconceivable. The *Hephaestus* team, then, didn't want to displace the physical aspects of the FIRST competition, but rather identify ways that computer games could extend that experience in new directions. By remediating the FIRST competition as a massively multiplayer game on a fictitious planet, *Hephaestus* enables players to confront novel challenges that would be harder to model in real-world spaces, such as building robots to withstand immense amounts of heat, traverse in snow, or operate in high winds or on a planet with increased gravitational pull. *Hephaestus* players also face different design tradeoffs. Players might need to design a robot with sufficient energy to cross an entire planet, or to traverse under water; such requirements might make it impossible to include certain features. The parallels to management or survival training (or experimental design—the game offering a way of reflecting on its own genesis as *theory*) suggest something of the polyvalence of this approach. In later phases of the game, players also are given access to materials and parts not available in FIRST, such as titanium alloys or solar panels. We incorporated a structural engineering component into the game, in which players can pool their resources and purchase bridges, walls, or other structures.

We also wanted to explore the ways that online and offline robotics competitions might inform one another. Engineers use computer-based tools in designing and prototyping, and *Hephaestus* could be used as a prototyping tool for FIRST competitors. Digital simulation technologies make robotics engineering accessible to a broader audience of students, and *Hephaestus* could be used by students who are looking for a less intensive introduction to robotics engineering, may not have opportunities to join a FIRST team at their local school, or might want to explore robotics engineering during the off season. In order to support this fluid interplay between online and offline practices, we envision a separate robot design tool that enables prototyping and testing robot configuration, premade robots that novices could use, and a massively multiplayer game dynamic that encourages sustained participation. Finally, we hope that success in *Hephaestus* might motivate more players to build their own robots, and the *Hephaestus* robot design tools includes actual part numbers and links to facilitate purchasing actual robot parts or schematics.

Fostering Intuitive Knowing: *Supercharged!*

Hephaestus illustrates how digital gaming facilitates complex engineering practices within massively multiplayer worlds. A second unexplored application of gaming technologies is in using gaming environments as visualization tools. As Steven Poole highlights in *Trigger Happy*, game worlds are entirely fabricated spaces: everything that exists on the screen was placed there by a designer for some reason.[21] While recent press attention has focused on the increased realism of current gaming graphics, game fans themselves just as frequently admire the whimsical landscapes of Shigeru Miyamoto's Nintendo games, or the romantic, gothic, surrealistic, or cyberfuturistic environments in other contemporary games.[22] New improvements in game graphics may enable a much broader array of visual styles and game atmospheres—allowing players, for instance, to interact in landscapes designed to illustrate scientific phenomena. Imagine playing as a virus trying

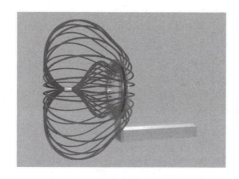

Figure 1.2. A visualization of Faraday's Law. Photo used courtesy of John Belcher.

to infect the human body, fighting off antigens and phagocytes (*Replicate*). Or, much like *SimEarth,* the game board might be expanded to an entire ecosystem or solar system (with the player "writing" the rules governing its behavior). In addition to changes in scale, gaming technologies can make invisible phenomena visible, as in *Supercharged!,* where players fly through and navigate around electric and magnetic fields demarked with field lines. Educators note that students have difficulty grasping core concepts of electromagnetism because they run counter to their own real world experiences, yet playing a game that requires mastery of those principles in order to win may give them an intuitive grasp of how they work that can be more fully developed in the classroom. *Supercharged!* builds on existing visualization and simulation techniques in science education to create a compelling gaming experience.

Supercharged!, is a 3-D action/racing game designed in conjunction with Professor John Belcher, a Physics professor at MIT who has been researching the use of digital visualization tools in supporting learning in electromagnetics (see Figure 1.2). The player is a student in a college physics class. The class begins with an old (and we later find out, evil) physics professor showing a crackly black-and-white educational film on electromagnetism through an old 1950 16mm film projector. The projector is struck by lightning and the students are mysteriously sucked inside, trapped in the depths of the projector's ancient circuitry. Drawing on themes from 1950s science fiction films, the game puts the player in control of a small metallic space pod which has adopted the properties of a charged particle. The player eventually learns to navigate by placing electromagnetic charges throughout the environment—an indirect kind of motor control, in which the player learns to describe her environment by changing it.

The gameplay consists of two phases: planning and playing. As the player encounters a new level, she is given a limited set of charges that she can place throughout the environment; she will move either toward or away from the charge, enabling her to shape the trajectory of her ship. In the "playable" portion of the game, the player switches her charge (either positive, negative, neutral, or dipole), and manages a limited amount of fuel that can be used to directly propel the ship. Each level contains a set of obstacles common to electromagnetism texts, including points of charge, planes of charge, magnetic planes, solid magnets, and electric currents. Each of these obstacles affects the player's movement, according to laws of electromagnetism. The goal of *Supercharged!* is to help learners build stronger intuitions for how charged particles interact with electric and magnetic fields and use the laws of electromagnetism to solve novel problems in a variety of contexts.

Notably, *Supercharged!* is not designed to completely teach the student all there is to know about Electromagnetism. We do not believe that *Supercharged!* will ever replace Physics teachers, textbooks, or other educational materials. Rather, *Supercharged!* can be used as an instructional tool or resource within a broader pedagogical framework. Teachers might begin a unit on Electromagnetism by having students play several levels before encountering textbook or lecture explanations. Other teachers might use levels as demonstrations or as homework problems. One can even imagine Physics teachers using levels for testing purposes. However, *Supercharged!* affords players few opportunities for interacting with the laws of Electromagnetism quantitatively; those kinds of understandings may be best taught by more traditional means.

As Alex Rigopulos, cofounder of Harmonix Music Systems (makers of the PlayStation 2 game *FreQuency*), commented in one of our design meetings, electromagnetism is an intriguing area to explore through games, because Maxwell's equations translate readily into game mechanics. Much as *Super Mario Brothers* game players learn that ice causes Mario to skid across the floor, and quickly learn to predict where the intrepid plumber will *stop* skidding, *Supercharged!* players can learn that a positively charged particle traveling through a magnetic field careens in a specific direction, and get a "feel" for the mechanics of it. As Ted Friedman suggests in "Civilization and Its Discontents: Simulation, Subjectivity, and Space," part of the joy of playing a game such as *Civilization* is learning to "think" like the computer; players intuit not only the rules of the game world, but the likely results of specific interactions.[23] Expert *Supercharged!* players might be able to predict the end location of a positive charge traveling at a given velocity through a magnetic field, just as experienced Civilization players might predict how a geographically isolated, resource-rich civilization will evolve. As Eric Zimmerman and Katie Salen argue, the process of gameplay can be thought of as observing a situation, making a decision, observing the results, and then continuing to make new decisions based on the outcomes of earlier decisions.[24] These stages closely mirror the "scientific method" of constantly revising hypotheses through experimentation.

On the surface, *Supercharged!* has much in common with E+M visualization tools, such as Belcher's animations,[25] as well as traditional simulation exercises where players can change parameters of a system and observe the results. However, embedding challenges within the tool requires users to actively monitor their performance, observing, hypothesizing, acting, and reflecting. In addition to being potentially more motivating for learners,[26] engaging in such critical thinking processes is generally thought to be the basis of meaningful learning.[27] As John Bransford and colleagues have shown, knowledge developed in the context of solving problems, is typically recalled better than knowledge learned by rote, and more readily mobilized for solving problems in novel contexts.[28]

Despite the pedagogical potential of *Supercharged!* many questions remain. Just how robust are the understandings developed playing *Supercharged!*? Will players use concepts learned through playing the game to solve novel problems that arise in other contexts? There's still a large gap between, on the one hand, observing patterns and interactions in digital environments, placing charges, and devising strategies for solving puzzles, and, on the other hand, using knowledge of electromagnetism to design circuitry, performing experiments, or solve engineering problems. We think it is only by explicitly coupling the game with a range of other pedagogical models, such as problem-based or inquiry-based learning, that this transfer across contexts is likely to occur. Regardless, these challenges, the limitations of *Supercharged!* for learning the quantitative aspects of electromagnetism, and the importance an instructor can play in providing explanations, demonstrations, and structuring learning experiences, remind us that a game is a tool or a resource in a learning environment, not a magic box that ensures mastery over the content.

Stories for Learning: *Biohazard*

The pitch for *Biohazard* is straightforward: the relentless pace and shotgun presentation of medical material of NBC's *ER,* and the eerily plausible apocalypse of Crichton's *Andromeda Strain* or the nonfiction novel *The Hot Zone,* in the interface style of the award-winning PC game *Deus Ex* (a first-person "sneaker"/role-playing game from Ion Storm, considered one of the best PC games of recent years). What makes the project interesting to us as educational researchers, however, are its goals: to teach AP-level biochemistry material, and to try to communicate the feeling of "doing science," all the while making the presentation of the material interesting for players who are *not* students, and thorough enough for classroom teaching. Whew!

The educational theorist/computer scientist/software designer Roger Schank (among others) argues that, since understanding is to be *performed* in certain contexts (bus drivers do not drive in classrooms, they sit in buses on roads; managers manage under particular office conditions, not in idealized training situations), information should be taught in similar contexts.[29] This "learning by doing" approach seems like common sense to those who've taught or learned by apprenticeship or on-the-job training, but the method is foreign to most in-school instruction (in which the retention of facts is tested very deliberately *out of context*, the rationale presumably being that the students should "know the material cold").

However, not all tasks are equally well suited to this instructional approach. Training bridge builders by having them build bridges seems sensible enough, and the task of bridge building scales straightforwardly from the road to the classroom (balsa wood offers a good analogical medium for experimentation); training doctors without pathogens or patients, by contrast, presents a problem of representation. The power of a learning-by-doing approach comes from its simultaneous stimulation of all the senses, a total acculturation of the learner *in the moment* that enables strong, extensible conditioning.[30] But an instructional video can only offer visual and aural cues (and the links between them); a textbook presents problems linearly, offers textual solutions (explanations, answers), and gives a particular spatial organization that doesn't reflect physical (lived) experience; lab work cuts students off from the breakneck pace of the ER, the limited materials of in-the-field engineering, the minute conversational cues that characterize office politics. For activities that can't simply be replicated in the classroom (firefighting, emergency medical care, race car driving, real estate sales, etc.), a richer training medium is needed to acclimate students to a broader portion of the sensory spectrum associated with those practices.

Moreover, narratives have the peculiar quality of making readers (players, viewers, *interactors*) care a great deal about the events they represent. Everyone has had the experience of being lost in a story; being lost in a textbook is an entirely different prospect. Indeed, the word "lost" is misleading, because readers or filmgoers who lose track of their physical surroundings are often hyperaware of what's going on in the story. The events are rendered with a vividness that leaves permanent memories, which can be evoked later with a turn of phrase or musical strain. That power of persuasion is used to full advantage in moral education (how many children *learned* to seek inner beauty from the story of the Ugly Duckling?), but the power of narrative contexts for teaching is underutilized in schools.

A walkthrough of the early moments of the game will make clearer the link between *Biohazard*'s educational goals and its method (and its qualities as entertainment). At startup, the player is presented with her world, seen over the avatar's shoulder (as in adventure games such as *Tomb Raider*). She is in a hospital; her character is in the garb of a doctor, and an onscreen character is talking animatedly about the player's new job, while motioning for her to follow. Players familiar with the mouse-and-keyboard interface of first-person games will instantly recognize the visual style: the keyboard is used to move the character and conjure up menus, while the mouse activates items presented in a *Deus Ex*-style series of inventory boxes, menus, and text streams. Moving through the hospital after the tour guide, the player is surrounded by the ebb and flow of medical technicians at work; one of the game's characters approaches to assign the player a task—in this case, something as simple as checking in with a lab down the hall. The character speaks hasty directions; the player's real task at this point is to get acclimated to the layout of the hospital, which—although it is a fictional setting—is a slightly simplified amalgam of actual hospital layouts.

But the heart of the game is its *dramatic* force; rather than a lecture, the player is compelled by a visceral or an *emotional* logic. Rather than regurgitating context-free facts, the player must take the next step and utilize knowledge in tense, contextually rich situations. A little girl endures uncontrollable coughing fits, her suffering audible as the player confirms the steps of a testing procedure in an online manual before clicking the mouse and *seeing herself perform the procedure*. Shots from the first-person perspective are intercut with schematics of the body, establishing shots of the entire operating hospital wing (the flow of foot traffic made visible and useful for later play), reaction shots of the little girl, her coughing a rhythmic counterpoint to the frenetic activity. . . . The representational conventions of film and television are known to nearly every American; they provide a shorthand for engaging our emotions in service of aesthetic experience. In the filmic or literary moment we are alert to subtle cues, hidden information, logics beyond the merely deductive; isn't this precisely what educators want for their students? Can't we remember AP Chemistry as vividly (and as fondly) as we remember *Casablanca*? To date, games have had more success at creating emotional reactions through visceral action than through compelling storytelling.[31] Elsewhere,[32] we have argued that game designers tell stories through the organization and manipulation of space. In *Biohazard,* we developed some of these ideas further, exploring how emotional intensity can be heightened through evocative spaces, embedded narratives, or emotionally reactive third parties.

Video game players are familiar with the concept of the in-game tutorial: the skills they need to play the game are taught in the context of some sort of in-game "training period." The opening of *Biohazard* works this way, starting with genre assumptions (about everything from TV medical dramas to the preferred interfaces for first-person video games) and the willingness of the player to go along with a story that begins *in medias res*. We (as "readers") accept the limits and assumptions of the narrative and tailor our expectations to them *as if* they were "real"; this iterative process of expectation-testing is itself a kind of learning, perhaps the most elemental kind (knowing what to expect from the world—whether expressed in language of physical causality or narrative logic). By matching the conditions of *Biohazard*'s virtual medical practice as closely as possible to those of the real world—accepting the limitations of a digital operating room, but simulating tempo, presenting real-world problems, demanding that students apply what they know to novel situations—we give students a sense of the *practice* for which they're being trained. Video games can suggest, then, a model of learning as a kind of "in-game tutorial" for *real life*.

While *Biohazard* may well be used to train doctors and emergency workers, we see its primary value in giving affective force and contextual relevance to AP science material. Rendering a six-hour emergency operation wouldn't work on a computer; telescoping into the body of a patient during a cutscene, to show internal state at a microscopic level, wouldn't work in real life. A video game can bridge between these two representations. *Biohazard* can present information *in situ*. Actual physicians have access to encyclopedic resources in which are organized centuries of medical knowledge; providing an even more efficient interface to such information, in "heads-up" fashion, is a soluble task for video games. Students who have difficulty finding text in the dictionary often blast through the information landscapes of video games without a second thought. Students are using textbook information "just in time"—that is, in practical situations—rather than constrained in the arbitrary conventions of the classroom exercise (forty-five minutes for a test, always think of calculus at 12:45 P.M.). They will form the mental maps that make the most sense for them, associating information with its practical uses and real world consequences. And since, within a game, a given piece of information might be needed at any given time (players know this well!), players will demand of themselves a high degree of information-retention and recall. We read stories because we want to; we learn to go along with their logic because, in order for the stories to make sense, we *have* to; compelling stories stick with us long after the screen has darkened. We have no choice in the matter.

At Play in the Fields: *Environmental Detectives* and Wireless-Enabled Simulation

We see the *Biohazard* proposal as the presentation of a complex problem and a real, implementable solution; there is no technology in the *Biohazard* précis that doesn't exist already. But one of the follies of the field of education is its conservative approach to new technologies; they tend to be met with initial enthusiasm, and on occasion find early adopters in schools, but new tools generally take a long time to reach their potential in schools (held back by a combination of very medium-based standards, unreliable performance, the need for technical education for teachers, and an ill-fittedness between the technologies' affordances and teachers' needs). Wireless computing is among the latest batch of panaceas to come out of Silicon Valley; in answer to the titular question of a CMS conference, "We wired the classroom—now what?", new technologies promise an elegant solution: *unwire it* (the phrase is borrowed from another MIT research initiative, the "Unwiring the World" initiative at the Media Lab). Network infrastructure will be gaseous; word processors will be handheld and voice-activated; the Web will be everywhere; computing will happen without computers.

But the revolution in the way we approach computers is all promise; right now we need solutions for bringing handheld, wireless networked technology into the classroom in ways that, to borrow a formulation from constructionist pioneer Seymour Papert, addresses issues for both the next decade and next Monday (when the kids arrive for class at 8 A.M.). Revolutions in education, ironically enough, can't just happen overnight.

Environmental Detectives is GTT's entry into a new, wide-open field— handheld (computer) games for education. The possibilities that the technology holds should be clear: instant access, anywhere, to web-based information and specifically tailored apps for education, along with lightning-fast communications in and out of the classroom (between students and teacher(s), and among students). But there are important questions to be answered: How does wireless technology offer richer *learning* experiences? How do they facilitate the *teaching* of material in and out of the classroom? If we afford this new distributed technology a central role in the teaching process, what changes should the classroom undergo to enrich and enable the exchanges that constitute the act of *education*? And perhaps the most immediate questions: when is the technology going to work consistently, seamlessly, and logically? And what do we do in the meantime? The broader work of theorizing about the unwired classroom (and more broadly, the learning environment afield) can't be divorced from the practical matter of making it work in the first place.

Consider a relatively minor sample problem: *Detectives* relies on GPS hardware, connected to a PocketPC via the serial port; the software is written in Microsoft's young object-oriented language, C# (a descendent of C++, a cousin of Java in appearance); there is no official, documented method for interfacing with the serial port on a PocketPC in C#.[33] We realized this days before the software framework was to be demoed to our collaborators in the MIT Environmental Engineering department—well *after* we had pitched the simulation. In sheer man hours, the knowledge was pricey, though *in theory* there was nothing to the job of writing it. In developing a framework for educators to design scenarios (described later in this essay), such straight-forward development snags translate into major usability considerations for end-users.

Environmental Detectives[34] is set to be beta-tested with MIT freshmen in Fall 2002; they will essentially take the part of environmental consul-tants, working in teams to determine the extent of contamination from a possible source of pollutant on MIT's campus, the affected locations, and possible plans for remediation (treatment of the contaminated area) if nec-essary. Their handheld devices—PocketPCs equipped with GPS radios and 802.11b network cards—will allow them to simulate in-the-field data collec-tion (testing for contaminant concentration based on GPS location data), site interviews and desktop research (the wireless networking cards offer access to miniwebs of data for the sake of conciseness and focus, from EPA documents to executive summaries of resident interviews), and plan formu-lation and analysis. An important consideration for us is that the PocketPCs are not simply digital notebooks; they offer the unique ability to maintain a consistent underlying simulation. The distinction is a vital one: a traditional view of wireless computing allows us to bring our work (or play) wherever we go (reading email on the subway, playing *Quake* at the doctor's office), but we see wireless technology as a tool for switching around the relation between place and activity—in effect, bringing "wherever" into our work (or play).

From a practical standpoint, making the machine more aware of its sur-roundings makes the act of stepping outside more palatable to teachers for whom *outdoors = field trip,* with concomitant harm to student attention spans. Moreover, an activity that maps physical space and curricular space onto one another—in which physical location is another data structure for the software—lends continuity to the experience; the idea that setting should work in service of stories is old hat to authors of fiction, but that lesson has yet to be taken to heart by educational designers. But it's easy to make this pronouncement in a book chapter or corporate pitch; it must be tested by teachers, with students, on finicky hardware, or it remains an empty promise.

Conclusion: How and Why Game Theory?

As our four case studies illustrate, educational software design is neither a solved problem nor a single problem to be solved. But our conceptual designs respond to individual theoretical and practical concerns. Taken as a group, they also offer a methodology for "doing theory" in a way that can be of use to both the academic world and those "in the trenches" (a description that fits teachers and students equally well). Each design addresses different needs within the educational community; each reveals limitations in the ways that gaming and education are currently understood, and identifies opportunities for productively transforming that relationship. In this way, we see game design and learning as linked theoretical activities: the imaginative process of conceiving and testing frameworks for understanding, with the motivating need to communicate those frameworks to listeners with various knowledge bases.

The current phase of the Games-to-Teach Project involves implementing versions of some of the designs (*Supercharged!, Environmental Detectives*) in-house and testing them with groups of students. This is a necessary, arguably the most important, phase in the process of theory construction; we can ask the question, "What can we *possibly* make?" and follow a project through to its conclusion, asking the final questions, "What did the *players* think?" and "What did they learn?" The current media technologies, which are lower in cost, easier to use, and more accessible than traditional media production tools, enable a material component to brainstorming, blurring the lines between theorists and practitioners. Janet Murray has argued that the next generation of storytellers—the cyberbards—will be both artists and programmers; the same should also be said of critics and educators; blurring the lines between thinking about and making media should open up new opportunities for conversations across those various sectors. The language of critical theory can benefit from grounding in the experience of gameplay and game design; games themselves can be made immeasurably richer through the development of new models of interaction and representation (beyond the straightforwardly competitive and rigidly mimetic).

This is not to say, of course, that GTT offers a magic bullet for the problems of contemporary education, educational software, or game theory. Our team consists of students and faculty from across disciplines and areas of expertise, in the sciences, humanities, and outside the academy; a lingua franca does not develop overnight. And, throughout our first year, we encountered the typical problems associated with projects of this scale (the tradeoff between lowest-common-denominator design and the complexity of new concepts; the competing research interests of more than a half-dozen graduate students; the need to work toward a common goal with common deadlines). Moreover, maintaining a balance between the academic rigor of an MIT graduate program and our sponsors' desire for deliverables on a certain date meant that the role of the students underwent continuous redefinition. But we see these as productive challenges, not mere stumbling blocks; the very nature of our program is an object for further study and development. We all learned from each other as we collaborated on meeting the challenge of putting theory into practice and meeting our ideal of applied humanism. Students not only mastered an existing body of theoretical literature but also found ways to expand it, bringing it to bear on the practical challenges of creating games which would meet real world contexts. In the end, we argue that it is in the best interests of students, theorists of games and gaming, and designers to endeavor to bring not only Hamlet but Habermas and high school to the Holodeck.

Acknowledgments

This research was supported by an iCampus Grant from Microsoft Research. Comparative Media Studies Department, Massachusetts Institute of Technology, Cambridge. Correspondence should be addressed to Kurt Squire, Comparative Media Studies Department, 14N-211, Cambridge MA 02139.

The authors would like to thank members of the Games-to-Teach team for their intellectual contributions to this essay, including Randy Hinrichs, Alex Chisholm, Robin Hauck, Heather Miller, Zachary Nataf, Alice O'Driscoll, Sangita Shresthova, Jill Soley, Elliot Targum, Philip Tan Boon Yew, Katie Todd, and Tom Wilson.

Notes

1. For a discussion of Sargent's role, see David Bordwell, Janet Staiger, and Kristen Thompson, *Classical Hollywood Cinema* (New York: Columbia University, 1985).
2. On the context that generated Soviet film theory, see David Bordwell, *The Cinema of Eisenstein* (Cambridge, MA: Harvard University Press, 1994).
3. On the relevance of Gilbert Seldes to game theory, see Henry Jenkins, "Games, the New Lively Art," in *Handbook of Computer Game Studies*, eds. Jeffrey Goldstein and Joost Raessens (Cambridge, MA: MIT Press, forthcoming).
4. Gill Branston, "Why Theory?" in *Reinventing Film Studies,* eds. Christine Gledhill and Linda Williams (London: Arnold, 2000): 30.
5. Thomas McLaughlin, *Street Smarts and Critical Theory: Listening to the Vernacular* (Madison: University of Wisconsin Press, 1996), 22.
6. The word "creative" in this context warrants comment. It is a term used in the games industry—and in the entertainment industry more generally—to refer to those involved in the process of creating cultural products. They often maintain a strict separation in perspective and orientation from the front office personnel, who make the practical or business decisions. In any creative industry, there is a potential tension between those who control the purse strings and those who make the creative decisions and this tension gets embodied not only in academic theories of authorship and mode of production but the language used by expert practitioners.
7. Part of what has given "edutainment" a bad name is that it has been done cheaply, often by educators who had limited awareness of the current state of game design and technology or by developers who knew little about current thinking about pedagogy. We have tried through the Games-to-Teach Project to bring those two groups together, to develop games that reflect both the current state of game design and the current thinking about the best ways to teach.
8. This data was collected through a web-based survey of all MIT students in the fall of 2001 and is reported in Kurt Squire, Henry Jenkins, and Games-to-Teach Team, *Games-to-Teach Project Six Month Report* (Cambridge, MA: MIT Press, 2001).

9.   See, for example, Timothy Koschmann, ed., *CSCL: Theory and Practice of an Emerging Paradigm* (Mahwah, NJ: Lawrence Erlbaum, 1996).
10. All of the game design documents and supporting materials have been published on the web and can be found at <http://cms.mit.edu/games/education/>. Take a look and send us your feedback.
11. See <http://www.usfirst.org>.
12. For Inspiration and Recognition of Science and Technology (FIRST). FIRST website. <http://www.first.org>. July 20, 2002.
13. For the sake of convenience, we say, "*Hephaestus* incorporates the following..." rather than "*Hephaestus* would include the following" or "The design for *Hephaestus* proposes...." These games possess features in the same way that they exist: *in theory.*
14. Henry Jenkins and Kurt Squire, "The Art of Contested Spaces," in *Game On: The History and Culture of Videogames*, ed. Lucien King (New York: Universe, 2002), 64–75.
15. Woodie Flowers. Personal Interview. August 30, 2001.
16. Our use of the term "remediation" here owes much to Jay David Bolter and Richard Grusin, *Remediation: Understanding New Media* (Cambridge, MA: MIT Press, 1999).
17. Y. Engestrom, *Learning By Expanding: An Activity-Theoretical Approach to Developmental Research* (Helsinki: Orienta-Konsultit Oy., 1987).
18. Barab and colleagues "present these tensions in both an experience-near (local to the CoT experience) and experience-far (has possible connections to other projects) manner with the goal that the reader might take in these experiences, apply these experiences to new cases as situational constraints permit and, hopefully, develop a more refined gaze toward new phenomena." Using tensions, Barab et al. hope to characterize the core elements of practical and theoretical interest in a manner that can be of use to designers of other social systems. Sasha Barab, Michael Barnett, and Kurt Squire, "Developing an Empirical Account of a Community of Practice: Characterizing the Essential Tensions," *Journal of the Learning Sciences* 11, no 4 (2002) : 489–542.
19. Woodie Flowers. Personal Interview. August 30, 2001.
20. In preparing to create *Hephaestus,* the Games-to-Teach team interviewed several MIT students who completed robotics engineering, and attended the annual FIRST competition kickoff held at Dean Kamen's home in Manchester, NH on January 4, 2002.
21. Steven Poole, *Trigger Happy* (London: Arcade, 2000).
22. See, for example, *Newsweek,* March 6, 2000.
23. Ted Friedman, "*Civilization* and Its Discontents: Simulation, Subjectivity, and Space," in *On a Silver Platter: CD-ROMs and the Promises of a New Technology,* ed. Greg Smith (New York University Press, 1999): 132–150.
24. Eric Zimmerman and Katie Salen, *Game + Design.* (Cambridge, MA: MIT Press, in press).
25. This can be found at: <http://web.mit.edu/jbelcher/www/anim.html>.
26. See Tom Malone, "Toward a theory of intrinsically motivating instruction." *Cognitive Science* 4 (1981): 333–369.
27. John D. Bransford, A. L. Brown, and Rodney R. Cocking, *How People Learn: Brain, Mind, Experience, and School* (Washington, DC: National Academy of the Sciences, 1999).
28. John D. Bransford and Daniel Schwartz, "Rethinking transfer: A simple proposal with multiple implications." *Review of Research in Education* 24: 61–101. Edited by A. Iran-Nejad and P. D. Pearson (Washington, DC: American Educational Research Association, 1999).
29. R. Schank, A. Fano, B. Bell, and M. Jona, "The Design of Goal-Based Scenarios," *Journal of the Learning Sciences* 3: no 4 (1993): 305–345.
30. Like "dogma," "conditioning" is a word used all too often as a pejorative, robbing it of its illustrative power for instructional design. Knowledge is most useful as *second nature,* it is dangerous for teachers to remain ignorant of the conditions of their environment, the condition of their students... Hans Vaihinger, in his *Philosophy of As-If* (1911/trans. 1924), provides a useful view of dogma as part of a continuum of assuredness, along with fictions and hypotheses (each with its own usefulness). A powerful extension of Vaihinger's ideas is found in Wolfgang Iser's *The Fictive and the Imaginary* (1993); Iser treats reading as a process of acculturation, in which we *learn* (in collaboration with the text) new ways of comprehending fictional worlds of meaning, as if they were "real."

31. Gamers will frequently cite games such as *Planetfall* or *Grim Fandango* as exceptions to this pattern.
32. See Henry Jenkins, "Games as Narrative Architecture," in *First Person*, eds. Pat Harrington and Noah Frup-Waldrop (Cambridge, MA: MIT Press, 2002.)
33. To be sure, there are a couple of user-written libraries for doing this; we had the devil's own time tracking them down. The wireless development community is young and dispersed enough to make finding publicly available code a nonnegligible project.
34. At the time of this writing, the game is still in development, and the particulars are subject to change.

CHAPTER 2

Abstraction in the Video Game

MARK J. P. WOLF

Most writing on video games considers either narrative concerns or game-play and what is usually referred to as "interactivity." Instead of focusing on the "game" aspects of the video game, this essay looks at the video game as "video," or rather, as a medium of visual imagery. The video game began with perhaps the harshest restrictions encountered by any nascent visual medium in regard to graphic representation. So limited were the graphics capabilities of the early games, that the medium was forced to remain relatively abstract for over a decade. Gradually as technology improved, designers strove for move representational graphics in game imagery, and today they still continue to pursue ever more detailed representations approximating the physical world. At the same time, video games have come to rely on conventions from film and television, allowing the depiction and navigation of their diegetic worlds to seem more intuitive and familiar to players. Yet by limiting themselves to conventions established in other media, game designers have neglected the realm of possibilities which abstraction has to offer. This great, untapped potential will only be mined by a deliberate move back into abstract design that takes into consideration the unique properties of the video game medium.

In order to get a better sense of how abstraction has been used in video games, we might first examine some of the ways in which the video game can be seen as an extension of abstract art, and the different types of abstraction that can be present within a video game.

Abstraction, Time, and Interaction

To *abstract* something is to simplify it, reducing it to a few essentials and basic forms instead of trying to reproduce it. *Representation,* which seeks to create resemblances and reproduce something, is the polar opposite of abstraction (and is sometimes conflated with *realism*). Most artwork falls in the spectrum between the two extremes, since even very representational artwork usually falls short of fully reproducing its subject. Abstraction has appeared throughout art history, from the earliest cave paintings, to mosaics, tilework, geometric patterns and ornamentation, to the works of Cézanne and the Impressionists, Cubists, and Surrealists, whose work inspired the Abstract Expressionist movement in New York during the 1940s and 1950s. Finally, as abstract art moved more and more into the conceptual realm, it began to raise questions as to what exactly constituted a work of art.

During the second phase of Abstract Expressionism, an approach to abstract art developed known as "action painting," of which Jackson Pollock is perhaps the best-known practitioner. For the action painters, the process of creating the art, including the elements of time and performance, became important. In his 1952 essay, "The American Action Painters," art critic Harold Rosenberg wrote,

> At a certain moment the canvas began to appear to one American painter after another as an arena in which to act, rather than a space in which to reproduce, redesign, analyze, or "express" an object, actual or imagined. What was to go on the canvas was not a picture, but an event.[1]

Rosenberg's description of the direction in which abstract art was developing, one that was time-based, interactive, and event-based, seems to anticipate the video game, which would appear on mainframe computers a decade after the essay.

Besides action painting, the idea that a work of art could be an event was found in areas of conceptual art and performance art of the late 1950s and 1960s, such as Allen Kaprow's Happenings, the Fluxus festival, Jordan Belson's Vortex Concerts, and the Japanese group Gutai Bijutsu Kyokai. Although many of these events centered around the performance of the artist, some began to incorporate the audience into the event, for example, John Cage's piece for piano, 4:33, which contained no notes at all and consisted solely of the ambiance of the auditorium, including sounds made by the audience. Audience participation varied from mere attendance as a spectator at art events to active engagement with interactive artwork such as Nam June Paik's closed-circuit video installations in which a live video image of the viewer appeared, or Myron Krueger's *VIDEOPLACE* (1970), which featured wall-projected video imagery that combined the user's live image with interactive computer graphics produced in real time. In some cases, the point or experience embodied in the artwork could only be understood through active interaction rather than passive spectatorship.

The video game, appearing when it did, took advantage of the interest in interactive art and the intersection of art and electronic technology, and it is perhaps no coincidence that many early game programmers were counterculturally engaged.[2] Because of the limitations of early video game technology, graphics were stark and minimalist for the most part, and rather abstract as a result, which happened to coincide with certain minimalist tendencies of the time. Interactivity was, of course, what the made the games interesting; like certain video installation pieces, one could affect the image onscreen in real time and watch it change.

When it left private mainframe computers, however, the video game met the public in the arcade and later in the home, not in the art museum. Video games also differed from interactive art because of their status as games, which meant that there was usually some motive or goal toward which the player's interaction was directed, whereas in art, the experience itself was the goal. The addition of a goal or challenge to the experience connected the video game to such things as pinball and other arcade games, table-top games, and board games, all of which would influence the shape the video game would take both aesthetically and commercially. But the video game, as an audio-visual medium, stood apart from other games, for its gameplay lacked the solidity of game pieces or the physicality of pinball action and the Newtonian collisions of pool balls. The video game took place within an image, whose interactivity required a new way of reading and understanding abstract imagery.

Reading the Abstract Image in the Video Game

Just as the understanding of cinematic conventions seems second nature to us today, the playing of video games has likewise come to feel natural and automatic. It is easy to forget that the video game interface, with its hand-eye coordination linked to onscreen action, was not always as intuitive as it now seems. The first arcade video game, Nolan Bushnell's *Computer Space* (1971), failed commercially, because players found its controls difficult to understand and use, and it was not until Bushnell's second effort, *PONG* (1972), which had a single control and simplified graphics, that the video game as a commercial entity finally found success.

In this sense, the video game required abstract imagery to be read in a new way. Since the substance of video games is simultaneously both *imagery* and *events,* their elements can be abstract in both *appearance* and *behavior.* Among the first tasks a player encounters while learning to play a game is the identifying of the different elements seen onscreen and understanding how they function and behave. Elements occurring in video games can be divided into four general categories: those indicating the player's presence in the game (the player-character); those indicating the computer's presence in the game (computer-controlled characters); objects that can be manipulated or used by game characters; and the background environment that generally serves as the setting and is not manipulated or altered by any of the characters during the game.

Among these elements, the most important is arguably the player-character. Player-characters, which represent the player's influence and effect on the game's diegetic world, can be either surrogate-based or implied. *Implied* player-characters are not visible onscreen. In these games, player interaction is indicated through onscreen events that occur as a result of the player's actions, including changes in the game's point of view (particularly in first-person games in which the point of view is controlled by the player), by changes in informational graphics that indicate what the player is doing (like the crosshairs in *Missile Command* [1980] and the radar in *Battlezone* [1980]), or by the direct manipulation of onscreen objects (such as is found in *Tetris* [1989] or *Video Chess* [1979]). In any of these games, the player-character is constructed outside of the screen, both *visually* (sometimes through perspective, the way a photograph constructs a point of view and implies a spectator) and *interactively* through the game interface and the coordinated onscreen action under the player's control.

Surrogate-based player-characters appear as onscreen graphics representing the player's character (see Figure 2.1). Since the 1980s, most onscreen player-surrogates are character-based (such as Pac-Man, Mario Mario, Lara Croft, Sonic the Hedgehog, and so on), but this has not always been the case. In the earliest video games, the player-surrogate was function-based; instead of an anthropomorphic character, the player was represented onscreen by a graphic of a tool or vehicle that the player controlled. Function-based players surrogates included spaceships, (as in numerous outer space games), tanks or planes (as in *Combat* [1977] and *Air-Sea Battle* [1977]), cars (in racing and driving games), or even a "paddle" (as in *PONG* [1972] or *Breakout* [1976]). One advantage of function-based player-surrogates was that they often represented rigid objects for which a minimum of animation was needed. When they moved, spaceships, cars, tanks, and paddles traveled in straight lines or turned in place, whereas characters with moving arms and legs required more animation and computing power. Atari's *Football* (1976), for example, used a series of "X"s and "O"s to represent the players, similar to football diagrams, instead of human figures.

As graphics improved, games began moving towards human figures as character-based player-surrogates, beginning with simple blocky forms such as those found in Midway's *Gun Fight* (1975), Project Support Engineering's

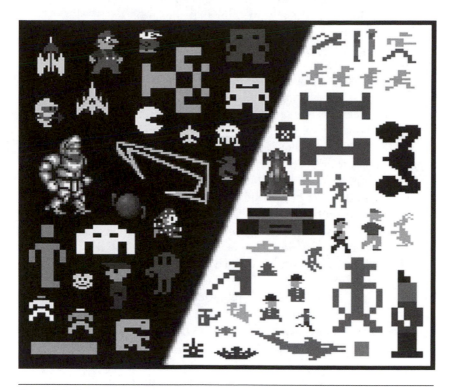

Figure 2.1. Examples of player-characters (avatars) in early video games. Characters are designed to appear on either dark or light backgrounds. Note the five different styles of race car icons.

Knights in Armor (1976), Atari's *Outlaw* (1976), *Homerun* (1978), and *Basketball* (1978), and Meadows's *Gypsy Juggler* (1978). Animals appeared as player-surrogates beginning with *Frogs* (1978). The player-surrogates in these games, however, were still functional in that they were differentiated only by color, and given no names or individual traits that made them different from each other. Only later in games such as *Pac-Man* (1980) and *Donkey Kong* (1981), and games adapted from other media such as Atari's *Raiders of the Lost Ark* (1982) and *E.T.: The Extraterrestrial* (1982), did the player-surrogates have names and identities of their own apart from the player. From the early 1980s on, however, character-based player-surrogates were by far the most common form of player-character in video games, no doubt due in part to the stronger identification they could engender. Simple avatars are similar to cartoons, of which Scott McCloud writes, "The cartoon is a vacuum into which our identity and awareness are pulled, an empty shell that we inhabit which enables us to travel to another realm. We don't just observe the cartoon, we become it!"[3] Abstraction, then can become an aid to identification, rather than something that alienates.

Player-surrogates, whether they are function-based or character-based, can be abstract to varying degrees. In some cases, they are visually abstract but perform recognizable functions. Pac-Man, for example, is only a yellow circle with a wedge-shaped gap. As the gap faces forward as Pac-Man moves, and opens and closes erasing the yellow dots, it functions as a mouth, making Pac-Man appear less abstract and more like an eating head. Some player-surrogates, however, are completely nonrepresentational, like the square in *Adventure* (1978), the yellow C-shaped surrogate in *Tempest* (1981), or the "spark" surrogate in *Qix* (1981). The player controls each of these onscreen, but no attempt at visual resemblance with something outside the game is made, and so the player-surrogates in these three games cannot really be said to be based either on characters or functions without imposing an interpretation onto the abstract forms.

Although an understanding of the player-character and how it operates is central to interfacing with and the playing of a video game, the other three categories mentioned above, computer-controlled characters, objects that can be manipulated, and the unalterable background environment, also can be abstract to varying degrees. Knowing the role and function of each game element, where they begin and end, and how they affect the player-character is crucial to learning the game. As these elements grow more abstract, however, so can the game's objectives, as both the interface and gameplay grow less intuitive. Thus, another reason for making game elements representational are the default assumptions and diegetic structures that accompany them and make both the interface and gameplay more transparent and intuitive.

Games with representational graphics often rely on conventions from other audiovisual media, and increasingly, on conventions established in earlier video games, giving them a built-in familiarity that allows players to begin playing without having to learn the interface. Still, early games were abstract enough, even when they were representational, that an explanation of play had to be included, either as a demo running in between games, instructions printed on the game cabinet, or in an instruction manual in the case of home games. Such explanations were especially important for games with unusual goals or gameplay, or deliberately abstract games, like *Qix* (1981) and *Q*bert* (1983). Often the titles of games, such as *PONG*, *Asteroids*, *Tank*, *Football*, and so on, helped players to interpret what the graphics were meant to represent. Home games, purchased instead of played in an arcade, could afford to have more complex gameplay and even feature glossaries defining the games' low-resolution iconography. For example, *Raiders of the Lost Ark* (1982) for the Atari 2600 had over a dozen objects the player could use, which were represented in two different sets of graphic icons, one for the playfield and one for the inventory strip at the bottom of the screen (both sets were depicted and defined in the game's instruction manual).

The simplicity of the early games helped players to read and understand the images and action onscreen during a game. Later games built on earlier conventions, adding graphical complexity, spatial navigation, and a greater mixture of diegetic and nondiegetic graphics on the same screen, as players grew more sophisticated. Likewise, early games helped players grow accustomed to the hand-eye coordination and input devices used to control the action. *PONG* and games like it familiarized players with the paddle controller, while other games used firing buttons, joysticks, and trak-balls, all of which now seem elementary compared to controllers commonly in use today, like the multibutton two-handed controller used in the Sony PlayStation, Microsoft Xbox, or the 12-button controller for the Nintendo 64. As the medium grew and conventions began accumulating, video games grew from a novelty into an industry and popular pastime.

The Golden Age of Abstraction in the Video Game

The Golden Age of the video game is generally considered to be the period from the rise of the video game in the early 1970s to 1984, the year of the great video game industry crash, which was brought on by a market glutted with game systems and their pale imitators. In many ways this period was also the Golden Age of abstraction in the video game, due in large part to the technological limitations of the time.

Just as early film audiences thrilled to see anything move in the one-shot actualities of the 1890s, early video games, with their abstract and often minimalist graphics, had no competition and generally found success (a plethora of *PONG* imitations, based on the AY-3-8500 chip, testify to the high demand for home games). As games proliferated and the initial novelty of controlling objects onscreen wore thin, competition among systems increased, especially with the industry changeover from hard-wired consoles to those that used interchangeable cartridges. The number of games available for a given system was one consideration for system buyers, along with graphical complexity. Game graphics were, and to a large extent still are, the main criteria by which advancing video game technology is benchmarked by the buying public; thus representational graphics act as a means of visually benchmarking the computer's graphics against the visual experience of unmediated reality, while abstract graphics are unable to serve such a purpose.

Even the earliest games claimed to represent something, from space battles to ping-pong games. Market pressure for more representational and "realistic" graphics in games is certainly one of the forces that shaped the look of games and pushed the technology forward. Another was the game programmers themselves. According to Atari 2600 programmer Rob Fulop, whose games include *Demons to Diamonds, Cosmic Ark,* and *Missile Command,* as well as the 2600-ported versions of *Space Invaders* (1978) and *Night Driver* (1980), game complexity naturally evolved as programmers attempted to outdo one another. Certain types of material were chosen because they were easier to do; for example, outer space games required only a black background (usually with stars) and a few spaceships and laser bullets.[4]

Working against the desire for representation were the technological restrictions embodied in the programming of the games. Even today, video games' appearance and behavior are still subject to limitations regarding the number of polygons used, rendering speeds, moving objects and collision detection, and screen resolutions. Some of the limitations Atari programmers were confronted with can be found in the "Stella Programmer's Guide" of 1979 by Steve Wright ("Stella" was the in-house name for the 2600 at Atari). For example, the Atari 2600 had only 128 bytes of RAM (and no disk storage), and a graphics clock that ran at roughly 1.2 MHz.[5] Early cartridges for the Atari 2600 contained as little as 2 or 4 kilobytes of ROM. The television image produced for the games had only 192 lines vertically and 160 color clocks, or pixels, across.[6]

Because the microprocessor was so slow, most games used only half of the 192 lines available, and roughly half of the horizontal resolution as well. As the Guide describes it:

> The actual TV picture is drawn one line at a time by having the microprocessor enter the data for that line into the Television Interface Adaptor (TIA) chip, which then converts the data into video signals. The TIA can only have data in it that pertains to the line being currently drawn, so the microprocessor must be "one step ahead" of the electron beam on each line. Since one microprocessor machine cycle occurs every 3 clock counts, the programmer has only 76 machine cycles per line (228/3 = 76) to construct the actual picture (actually less because the microprocessor must be ahead of the raster). To allow more time for the software, it is customary (but not required) to update the TIA every two scan lines.[7]

In addition to the low resolution, the graphics making up the playing field (or playfield) laid over the solid-color background were drawn only on the left side of the screen and then duplicated on the right half of the screen, either as a repetition or a mirror image of the left side, accounting for much of the horizontal symmetry found in the early Atari games. This limitation is particularly noticeable in games with more complex graphics, for example, the mazes and castles of *Adventure* (1978), the city screens in *Superman* (1979), and the forest and buildings in *E.T.: The Extraterrestrial* (1982) (see Figure 2.2).

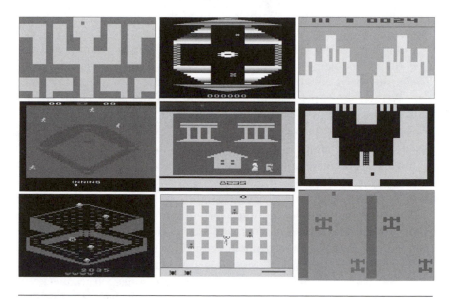

Figure 2.2. Because of the way the Atari 2600 was programmed, the right side of the background had to either be a duplication of the left side or a mirror image of it, resulting in symmetrical screens, a graphical limitation that had to be worked into the games.

Motion was also subject to restraints. Because of the way in which the raster scan occurs, horizontal and vertical movement had to be programmed in different ways. As the positioning of objects on the horizontal axis was limited by the machine cycle and writing of registers, horizontal motion had to be further fine-tuned through a separate register that would fill in the resultant gaps in movement.[8] In the end, horizontal motion was more difficult to achieve than vertical motion, resulting in a bias toward having action occur on the vertical axis.[9]

The playfield consisted of blocks of a single foreground color placed over a solid color background, and on top of the playfield were the "moveable objects graphics," which were limited to five objects: two players, two missiles (one for each player), and a ball. The players were the characters controlled by either the human game player or the computer, while the missiles and ball were objects used or fired by the players. Each player graphic was eight bits (pixels) wide, while the missiles and balls were only one bit wide, although the single bit could appear as 1, 2, 4, or 8 clock counts of horizontal line time (a full line being 160 clock counts). Player graphics also could be stretched horizontally, and up to three copies of the player could appear horizontally, though they would have the same attributes (color, width, movement, and missile action). An example of this appears in games 19–20 and 25–27 of *Combat* (1977) in which two or three identical planes always fly in horizontal formation, rotate together, and fire simultaneously.

Color, luminance, and sound were also limited. A programmer had sixteen colors (including transparency) to choose from, and eight levels of luminosity (brightness), but only four of each could be used at any given time. As there were only four color-lum (color and luminosity) registers, the objects were grouped so that the first player and its missile were the same color, the second player and its missile were the same color, the ball and playfield were the same color, and the background was a separate color. For sound effects, there was a "noise-tone generator" that created sixteen types of sound, which could be produced at sixteen different pitches and sixteen levels of volume (including silence).

These programming restrictions, and others, account for much of the style, graphics, and gameplay of the early Atari games. But more memory and programming tricks helped game developers overcome some limitations; for example, only four color-lum registers were available, meaning that a game character could only be one color. Some games, like *Superman* (1979) and *E.T.: The Extraterrestrial* (1982) got around this by changing the color-luminosity values on a line-by-line basis (see Figure 2.3), which allowed characters to be multiple colors, although any given horizontal line of pixels had to be the same color; a stylistic limitation due to the way the monitor scans the image onto the screen. Graphic complexity, then, was often a sign of programming prowess and graphics evolved as programmers tried to outdo each other.[10]

Advances in software and hardware allowed graphics to become more detailed and representational, but there was still some interest in the creation of purely abstract graphics. In 1978, Atari released the Atari Video Music C-240, which connected a stereo system to a television screen, translating an audio signal into abstract video graphics. The idea of machines to produce abstract graphics determined by sounds, or "visual music," can be traced back to the Ocular Harpsichord built by the Jesuit Father Louis Bertrand Castel in 1730, and extends through optical toys like the chromatrope slide for magic lanterns in the 1800s, to the early 1900s and the projected-light electrical "color organs" of A. Wallace Rimington, a British painter, and Italian futurists Arnaldo Ginna and Bruno Corra. The 1920s and 1930s saw the invention of several color organs, Thomas Wilfred's Clavilux, Mary Hallock Greenewalt's Sarabet, and Charles Dockum's MobilColor projectors, which in some ways were the forerunners of the video synthesizers that appeared in the 1960s and 1970s.[11]

Video synthesizers used analog electronics to generate a real-time video image from an audio signal, resulting in abstract graphics that were displayed

Figure 2.3. Another limitation of the Atari 2600 involved the color-luminance register. Onscreen characters have only one color-luminance register assigned to them, limiting the character to a single color. But if the register is changed for every scan line (see the fourteen scan lines in the image in the black box), a character made up of multiple colors can be displayed, although there will still be only one color on any given horizontal line of the character. The top row of characters and the helicopter on the lower left are from *Superman* (1979), and the three characters in the second row are from *E.T.: The Extraterrestrial* (1982).

on a television screen. While most video synthesizers were experimental units used by artists and were not available to the public, the Atari Video Music was simpler, mass-produced, and marketed to the owners of the Atari 2600. The Atari Video Music was not a game itself but its successor, the Atari Jaguar Virtual Light Machine (VLM) was built into the Atari Jaguar console.

The audience for abstraction and experimental graphics, however, was not as large as the audience for games and increasingly detailed representational graphics, and market pressure for increased realism moved game design away from abstraction as video game graphics improved in the mid-to-late 1980s.

The Decline of Abstraction

As graphics improved and became more representational, abstraction became more of an artistic choice instead of merely a technical default. The simple, iconic graphics of the early games looked more and more archaic as newer, more advanced consoles like the Nintendo Entertainment System (NES) and the Sega Master System (SMS) appeared, as well as the Coleco ADAM, Texas Instruments 99/4a, and Commodore 64, which were home computers that also could play video games. Atari produced several home computers itself, as well as the 5200 and 7800 console systems, making their own 2600 seem primitive by comparison. The "realism" of the games was the simplest and quickest way that consumers could compare systems, and the complexity of graphic detail and gameplay became the main areas in which home games would compete for players.

Home video games were not as technologically advanced as arcade games, and while arcade games cost a quarter to play, cartridges for home systems could cost $20 to $30 each (in addition to the cost of the console itself). The home game had one advantage, however, in that it was bought by stores based mainly on the packaging, allowing games to be advertised as representational despite their highly abstract graphics (see Figure 2.4). Although the earliest boxes featured only text, later boxes for Atari 2600 games, and even the cartridges themselves, featured collages of detailed representational artwork depicting scenes of fast action, while the actual screenshots of the games

Figure 2.4. Box claims versus actual game screens.

themselves were relegated to the backs of the boxes if they even appeared at all. The games, then, were sold based on their supposed connections to the narrative contexts shown on the games' boxes, or through their connections to known franchises such as movies, television, comic books, or even arcade video games. The boxes and advertising were eager to help players imagine that there was more to the games than there actually was, and actively worked to counter and deny the degree of abstraction that was still present in the games. Inside the box, game instruction manuals also attempted to add exciting narrative contexts to the games, no matter how far-fetched they were. Several games that were more abstract in their design, like *Centipede* (1982) and *Yars' Revenge* (1981), even came packaged with small comic books that set up the narrative that was supposedly continued in the game.

Arcade games, on the other hand, always remained several steps ahead of home games technologically and in their representational ability, although simplicity and fast action had to remain priorities if they were to keep a steady stream of quarters rolling in. Apart from the graphics featured on their cabinets, arcade games were sold less through packaging and advertising than through actual gameplay; one decided to play either by watching the game in demo mode between games or by watching the game being played by someone else. Elaborate narrative contexts, then, are often less important in the selling of an arcade game than are fast action, interesting graphics, and good sound effects. With these elements a few abstract games survived and even flourished, such as *Pac-Man* (1980), *Tempest* (1981), *Qix* (1981), *Q*bert* (1982), *Quantum* (1982), *Marble Madness* (1984), and *Tetris* (1988). A number of these games even inspired sequels (*Qix II: Tournament* [1981], *Super Qix* [1987], *Twin Qix* [1995], *Q*bert's Qubes* [1983], *Tetris Plus* [1990], *Hatris* [1990], *Tetris Plus 2* [1997], and *Marble Madness 2: Marble Man* [1991], and over half a dozen *Pac-Man* sequels[12]), a phenomenon more typical of games with narrative content.

Despite a few successes, however, game design leaned increasingly toward representational games and fewer abstract ones were produced. While technological improvements allowed games to become more representational, they cannot, in and of themselves, explain why pure abstraction was so overwhelmingly rejected. One reason may be found in the work of the art theorist Wilhelm Worringer, whose 1908 treatise, *Abstraction and Empathy*, remains a classic. Worringer suggested that there are two fundamental aesthetic impulses that are mutually exclusive, the desire for abstraction and the desire for empathy. He writes:

> In the forms of the work of art we enjoy ourselves. Aesthetic enjoyment is objectified self-enjoyment. The value of a line, of a form consists for us in the value of the life that it holds for us. It holds its beauty only through our own vital feeling, which, in some mysterious manner, we project into it.[13]

Thus, the urge toward representation is due to a desire for empathy, even though, as noted above and in Scott McCloud's work, abstraction can help to increase identification, the game's diegetic world is easier to enter into if it resembles the real world. But what happens when the real world is seen as an uncomfortable or threatening place? Of the opposing urge to the pole of abstraction, Worringer writes:

> Whereas the precondition for the urge to empathy is a happy pantheistic relationship of confidence between man and the phenomena of the external world, the urge to abstraction is the outcome of a greater inner unrest inspired in man by phenomena of the outside world; in a religious respect it corresponds to a strongly transcendental tinge to all notions.[14]

The need for empathy does seem to explain the great popularity of representational art among the general public compared to that of abstract art, which seems to be more of an acquired taste. In most media, abstract works are relegated to a marginalized genre, created and seen by only a few. Abstraction comes closest to reaching a broad audience in music, but even there the majority of albums produced include the human voice as an empathic anchor and link to human emotional experience. Worringer sees the need for empathy as a kind of understanding of, or being able to relate to, the object or scene being depicted:

> ... the process of empathy represents a self-affirmation, an affirmation of the general will to activity that is in us. 'We always have a need for self-activation. Indeed this is the basic need of our nature.' In empathising with this will to activity into another object, however, we *are* in the other object. We are delivered from our individual being as long as we are absorbed into an external object, an external form, with our inner urge to experience.[15]

The player-character surrogate in the video game is, in a very concrete sense, the external object into which the player is absorbed, which receives the player's will to activity. This may help explain why the majority of player-character surrogates in video games are character-based. Even in abstract games one can find them; *Pac-Man* and *Q*bert* and their sequels are character-based, although both are still very abstract and personify their characters through cabinet art, the cut scenes in *Pac-Man,* and embedded names that suggest personhood ("Man" and "bert"). As in many character-based games, a simple chase narrative is also present, making the games less abstract in function, if not in appearance. The fact that Pac-Man flees, eats with a moving mouth, and even "dies" further personifies what would otherwise be merely a yellow circle with a wedge missing. (In some sense, the condition of a player learning to control an onscreen surrogate and developing hand-eye coordination is similar to the "mirror stage," in which an infant learns to recognize and control his reflection in the mirror.)

During the 1980s, the video game also became more integrated with other forms of media, both commercially and aesthetically, and many of its conventions had codified. Although the iconic graphics of video games still retained a degree of abstraction, purely abstract games had become a minor genre, which, apart from *Tetris,* had relatively few hit games in the latter half of the 1980s. But during the early 1990s, as the technological advances of computer graphics began to spread from the laboratory and university to film, television, and video games, new possibilities and uses for abstraction developed.

New Possibilities for Abstraction

Besides purely abstract games, there have always been games that are abstract in that they are representations of abstract things, for example, games that are adaptations of board games, card games, table-top games, and pinball games. Versions of pencil-and-paper games (like Tic-tac-toe and Hangman) are not based on physical objects, yet each is a representation of something found outside of the video game, making them ontologically similar to the two-dimensional objects depicted in Jasper Johns's paintings of flags, targets, maps, letters, and numerals. Abstraction, then, can appear as an element within representational game graphics, or even as part of the subject matter, for example, the patterns and designs appearing as surface textures found on three-dimensional objects and settings in video games.

Although attempts at three-dimensional graphics can be found in earlier games like *Night Driver* (1976), it was not until the 1980s that games with real 3-D computation appeared, including the wireframe landscape of the vector arcade game *Battlezone* (1980), and the abstract but three-dimensional world of *I, Robot* (1983), the first 3-D game to feature filled-polygon graphics (as opposed to wireframe graphics). Computing and rendering speeds continued to increase, and the next advances in game graphics would include 3-D lighting and shadow effects and eventually texture mapping.

The idea behind texture mapping, which places a two-dimensional texture, pattern, or image onto a surface in a 3-D computer-generated object, first appeared in 1974 in the doctoral dissertation of Ed Catmull at the University of Utah.[16] As hardware and software grew more sophisticated, texture mapping spread from university computers to film during the late 1980s, most notably in Pixar's award-winning short films *Luxo Jr.* (1986), *Red's Dream* (1987), *Tin Toy* (1988), and *Knickknack* (1989), which vividly illustrate the advances taking place. With the release of Intel's 64-bit Pentium chip in 1993, home computers and game consoles were ready to incorporate texture mapping into video games. Two hit games also appeared in 1993 that incorporated texture mapping and changed the standards of computer games; *Doom* and *Myst*.

Doom featured texture-mapping in a 3-D environment rendered in real time during game play, while *Myst* had prerendered high-resolution images with finer textures and subtler lighting effects. Both games signaled the beginning of a new era in video game graphics, and *Myst*'s sequel, *Riven* (1997), used larger and more detailed texture maps to achieve its photorealism. Although the objects the textures are mapped onto are representational, the texture maps display patterns of rust, cracks, grain, splatter, corrosion, and wear, which are often the very subject matter explored in works of abstract art. Ironically, it is through the application of these abstract texture maps that video game imagery achieves heightened realism and greater representational ability.

Even as representational games strive for greater photorealism, the abstract game has not vanished entirely. In January of 2002, Sega's game *Rez* was released for the Sony PlayStation 2. Graphically, the game is a nostalgic throwback to the days before texture mapping, and its luminous solid-colored polygonal figures with glowing vertices and vectors are at times reminiscent of the film *Tron* (1982) (see Figure 2.5). It also features "Wave Master club beats and a laser light show,"[17] which, along with its psychedelically-inspired graphics, also link it to the video synthesizer tradition. Despite its dazzling graphics, *Rez* is still given a clichéd save-the-world frame story that involves going into the cyberworld "inside" a computer, as in *Tron*. It features several different designs of player-characters through which the player advances, a number of which are anthropomorphic, as are some of the "bosses" or enemy characters in the game. Gameplay itself is relatively simple, and the only controls are a targeting cursor and a fire button. The narrative context, anthropomorphic figures, and simple play may indicate Sega's reluctance to think too far outside the box of video game conventions, but the game does reveal possibilities for video game design even if it does not embrace them entirely.

Although abstract video games may not be learned as intuitively as representational games, abstraction need not imply simplicity. With the sophistication of today's hardware and software, a vast amount of potential in the area of abstract gaming remains untapped. Complexity may even help bring about a rebirth of the abstract game. A study published in *Empirical Studies of the Arts* by Tsion Avital and Gerald C. Cupchik regarding the perceiving of hierarchical structures in abstract paintings found that "affective ratings were tied to interesting complexity, but not to disorder," and that "hierarchically complex artworks facilitate both affective orienting and an exploratory search for meaning."[18] Discussing experiments in which

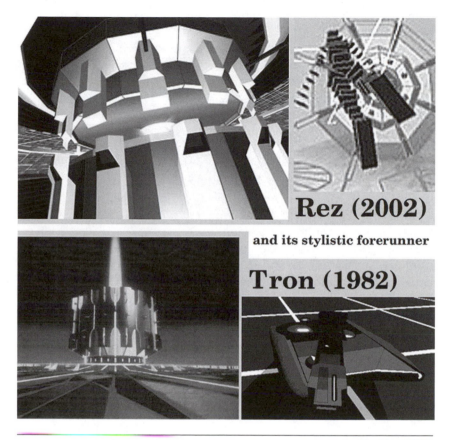

Figure 2.5. The PlayStation 2 game *Rez* (2002) and its stylistic forerunner, the film *Tron* (1982). *Rez* features an avatar (in the upper-right-hand corner) which has the same black-paneled, red-verticed look of *Tron*'s Recognizers, as well as a large cylindrical object (in the upper-left-hand corner) reminiscent of *Tron*'s MCP.

the subjects viewed a series of paintings in sequence, the authors write, "serial presentation attracts the viewer's attention and stimulates affective response because it raises expectations and curiosity regarding the emergent structures."[19] The time and motion present in a video game, coupled with complex graphics, could add to the stimulation of attention and curiosity, and play with expectations in a variety of ways. Games could even be designed such that the rules by which they are played, and the ways actions and consequences are connected, could be varied from game to game, requiring a player to learn them anew every time. A variety of non-Euclidean spaces could be used, making navigation less intuitive. In any event, abstraction represents perhaps the greatest area of potential for the developing video game medium.

Finally, it should be noted that even the most representational games available, or perhaps even imaginable, will always be to some degree an abstraction of the things or situations they are trying to represent or simulate. Will Wright, the designer of the line of "Sim" games from *SimCity* (1989) to *The Sims* (2000), believes abstraction to be a key design element, in the same way that Japanese rock gardens are an abstraction of nature.[20] The player's mind is forced to complete or imagine game details, which engages and involves them more in the game. At the same time, the simplified versions of situations found in video games allow players to feel a sense of order and understanding that may be more difficult to find in their own real lives, an idea that echoes Worringer's notion that uncertain times bring about a resurgence in the urge to abstraction.

Abstraction's role in the video game medium has changed over the years, from perceptual abstraction to conceptual abstraction, but it appears to be both a necessary and inevitable part of the video game-playing experience. Rather than try to avoid or sublimate abstraction, game design can usefully incorporate abstraction, resulting in new gaming experiences and game conventions. Just as computer simulations and mathematical visualization have taken graphic design in directions other than photorealistic representation, abstraction can expand and explore the great potential that the video game medium has to offer.

Notes

1. Quoted in Marilyn Stokstad, *Art History*. Revised Edition. New York: Harry N. Abrams, Inc., 1999, 1114.
2. Many were "hippie programmers," according to Rob Fulop, a programmer who worked at Atari during the 1970s. (Rob Fulop, phone conversation with the author, March 5, 2002.) Atari programmer Bob Polaro also described the Atari workplace environment in a similar manner. See Backiel, Al. "Dinner with Bob Polaro : An interview by Al Backiel." Available online at <http://www.digitpress.com/archives/arc00054.htm>.
3. Scott McCloud, *Understanding Comics* (New York: Harper Collins, 1993), 36.
4. According to Rob Fulop, phone conversation with the author, March 5, 2002.
5. According to Warren Robinett, "the 6502's clock speed was the color clock divided by 3, which was roughly 1.2 MHz." (Warren Robinett, e-mail to author.) The "color clock" refers to the color sub-carrier signal, the frequency of which is 3.58 MHz.
6. The entire image produced was slightly larger, but portions of it were not visible onscreen:

   The actual TV picture is drawn line by line from the top down 60 times a second, and actually consists of only a portion of the entire "frame". . . . A typical frame will consist of 3 vertical sync (VSYNC) lines, 37 vertical blank (VBLANK) lines, 192 picture lines, and 30 overscan lines. Atari's research has shown that this pattern will work on all types of TV sets. Each scan line starts with 68 clock counts of horizontal blank (not seen on the TV screen) followed by 160 clock counts to fully scan one line of TV picture. When the electron beam reaches the end of a scan line, it returns to the left side of the screen, waits for the 68 horizontal blank clock counts, and proceeds to draw the next line below.

From the "Television Protocol" section at the beginning of Steve Wright, *Stella Programmer's Guide* (December 3, 1979). Reconstructed online in 1993 by Charles Sinnett. Available online at <http://www.classic-games.com/atari2600/stella.html>.

7. Wright, *Stella Programmer's Guide.*
8. An object would be positioned, and then motion could be added to its relative position:

> Since there are 3 color clocks per machine cycle, and it can take up to 5 machine cycles to write the register, the programmer is confined to positioning the objects at 15 color clock intervals across the screen. This coarse positioning is fine tuned by the Horizontal Motion....
>
> Horizontal Motion allows the programmer to move any of the 5 graphic objects relative to their current horizontal position. Each object has a 4 bit horizontal motion register...that can be loaded with a value in the range of $+7$ to -8.... This motion is not executed until the HMOVE register is written to, at which time all motion registers move their respective objects. Objects can be moved repeatedly simply by executing HMOVE. Any object that is not to move must have a 0 in its motion register. With the horizontal positioning command confined to positioning objects at 15 color clock intervals, the motion registers fill in the gaps by moving objects $+7$ to -8 color clocks. Objects cannot be placed at any color clock position across the screen....
>
> There are timing constraints for the HMOVE command. The HMOVE command must immediately follow a WSYNC (Wait for SYNC) to insure the HMOVE operation occurs during horizontal blanking. This is to allow sufficient time for the motion registers to do their thing before the electron beam starts drawing the next scan line. Also, for mysterious internal hardware considerations, the motion registers should not be modified for at least 24 machine cycles after an HMOVE command. (From sections 7.0 and 8.0 of Wright, *Stella Programmer's Guide*)

9. According to Rob Fulop, phone conversation with the author, March 5, 2002.
10. Rob Fulop, phone conversation with the author, March 5, 2002.
11. The history of color organs is described in William Moritz, "The Dream of Color Music, And Machines That Made It Possible," *Animation World Magazine* 2, no 1 (April 1997). Available online at <http://www.awn.com/mag/issue2.1/articles/moritz2.1.html>.
12. For example, *Ms. Pac-Man* (1981), *Ms. Pac-Man Plus* (1981), *Baby Pac-Man* (1982), *Pac-Man Plus* (1982), *Jr. Pac-Man* (1983), *Pac & Pal* (1983), *Pac-Land* (1984), *Pac-Mania* (1987), and *Hyper Pac-Man* (1994).
13. Wilhelm Worringer, *Abstraction and Empathy: A Contribution to the Psychology of Style*, trans. Michael Bullock (Chicago: Elephant Paperbacks, Ivan R. Dee, Inc., [1908] 1997), 14.
14. Worringer, *Abstraction and Empathy: A Contribution to the Psychology of Style*, 15.
15. Worringer, *Abstraction and Empathy: A Contribution to the Psychology of Style*, 24.
16. Ed Catmull, *A Subdivision Algorithm for Computer Display of Curved Surfaces* (Ph.D. thesis, University of Utah, 1974).
17. According to the game's official website, at <http://www.sega.com/games/post_gamegame.jhtml?PRODID=843>. Thanks to Keith Feinstein for alerting me about *Rez*.
18. Tsion Avital and Gerard C. Cupchik, "Perceiving Hierarchical Structures in Nonrepresentational Paintings," *Empirical Studies of the Arts* 16, no. 1 (1998): 59–70.
19. Avital and Cupchik, "Perceiving Hierarchical Structures in Nonrepresentational Paintings."
20. Wagner James Au, "Dispatches from the Future of Gaming : Page 3: Will Wright Speaks...To Arnold Schwarzenegger?" *Gameslice.com* (2001). Available online at <http://www.gameslice.com/features/gdc/index3.shtml>.

CHAPTER 3

Immersion, Engagement, and Presence

A Method for Analyzing 3-D Video Games

ALISON McMAHAN

...Video games allow the viewers to engage actively in the scenarios pre-sented.... [Adolescents] are temporarily transported from life's problems by their playing, they experience a sense of personal involvement in the action when they work the controls, and they perceive the video games as not only a source of companionship, but possibly as a substitute for it.[1]

Hotshot digital cinematography doesn't make a digital story immersive. What makes it immersive is a world where no territory is off-limits, anything you see is fair game, and all your actions have consequences.[2]

A recent shift in computer game design involves a move away from 2-D level design in games like *Prince of Persia* (1992), or from isometric design in games like *Warcraft,* to 3-D design and a first-person point of view. This shift increases the sense of immersion by replicating the aesthetic approaches of first-person shooter games in other types of games, such as adventure games, role-playing games, and even strategy games, which previously used 2-D levels or isometric views. The shift in design is indicative of an overall trend to make desktop video games feel more like virtual reality. My approach here is to reexamine our concept of immersion in video games and suggest that immersion has become an excessively vague, all-inclusive concept. It is necessary to break down the concept of immersion into its more specific meanings and develop a more specific terminology. In this essay, I take the concept of "presence," as it is used in technical literature on virtual reality for scientific applications, as the basis for developing of a set of aesthetic criteria for analyzing 3-D video game design.

Immersion

As we can see in the quotations at the beginning of this essay, *immersion* means the player is caught up in the world of the game's story (the diegetic level), but it also refers to the player's love of the game and the strategy that goes into it (the nondiegetic level). It seems clear that if we are talking about immersion in video games at the diegetic level and immersion at the nondiegetic level, then we are talking about two different things, with possibly conflicting sets of aesthetic conventions. No specific terminology has yet been proposed to clarify those issues. In addition, humanities scholars have started to pick up, from scientific literature on virtual reality, the term *presence,* defined loosely as "the feeling of being there." The terms *immersion* and *presence* are seen together more and more often, although both have been so loosely defined as to be interchangeable—which they often are.

The first step is to define each term carefully. The most accepted definition of *immersion* is Janet Murray's:

> A stirring narrative in any medium can be experienced as a virtual reality because our brains are programmed to tune into stories with an intensity that can obliterate the world around us.... The experience of being transported to an elaborately simulated place is pleasurable in itself, regardless of the fantasy content. We refer to this experience as immersion. *Immersion* is a metaphorical term derived from the physical experience of being submerged in water. We seek the same feeling from a psychologically immersive experience that we do from a plunge in the ocean or swimming pool: the sensation of being surrounded by a completely other reality, as different as water is from air, that takes over all of our attention, our whole perceptual apparatus... in a participatory medium, immersion implies learning to swim, to do the things that the new environment makes possible... the enjoyment of immersion as a participatory activity.[3]

Most scholars and scientists seem to agree that total photo- and audio-realism is not necessary for a virtual reality environment to produce in the viewer a sense of immersion, a sense that the world they are in is real and complete, although this awareness has not stopped VR producers from aiming for photo- and audio-realism. Also taken for granted is that the more surrounding the VR exhibition technology is (the bigger the screen, the better the surround-sound) the more immersive it will be. However, it is quite possible to become very immersed in a desktop VR, for immersion is not totally dependent on the physical dimensions of the technology. Three conditions create a sense of immersion in a virtual reality or 3-D computer game: (1) the user's expectations of the game or environment must match the environment's conventions fairly closely; (2) the user's actions must have a non-trivial impact on the environment; and (3) the conventions of the world must be consistent, even if they don't match those of "meatspace."[4] Narrative and narrative genres are often used as a way of defining the conventions of a world and to help the user align their expectations with the logic of the world. It is no accident that role-playing and adventure games, the video game genres that have the most in common with more linear time-based narrative forms such as the cinema, were among the first to go 3-D.

Engagement

However, narrative is not a key component of most video games. Instead, many users appreciate games at a nondiegetic level—at the level of gaining points, devising a winning (or at least a spectacular) strategy, and showing off their prowess to other players during the game and afterward, during replay. To be so engaged with a game that a player reaches a level of near-obsessiveness is sometimes referred to as *deep play.* The term originated with Jeremy Bentham, in his *The Theory of Legislation* (1931). Bentham was referring to a state of mind in which users would enter into games almost irrationally, even though the stakes were so high it was pointless for them to engage in them at all. The example given was: a man whose fortune is a thousand pounds; if he wagers five hundred of it on an even bet, the marginal utility of the pound he stands to win is clearly less than the marginal disutility of the one he stands to lose. "Having come together in search of pleasure [both participants] have entered into a relationship which will bring the participants, considered collectively, net pain rather than net pleasures."[5]

The anthropologist Clifford Geertz extended the meaning of the term to the kind of substantial emotional investment humans make in violent rituals such as Balinese cock fighting. Geertz found the deepest investment of human meaning in matches where the odds are more or less even and the stakes "irrationally" high. His "deep play" requires a parity of force.

According to Diane Carr, the term *deep play,* as used in gaming magazines, refers to "a player accessing/accumulating layers of meaning that have strategic value . . . like 'deep play' in a Dungeons and Dragons [board game] context would mean knowing all the monsters and the different schools of magic, for example, whereas 'shallow' play would mean more 'up and running hack and slash' style of play."[6] The term *deep play,* when referring to video games, then, is a measure of a player's level of engagement.

Presence

The shift to 3-D design in games has already led to the adoption of the term *presence,* usually applied to virtual reality environments (VREs), to be used when discussing certain types of video games. However, the term *presence* is often used synonymously with *immersion,* which simply adds to the confusion. By specifically applying the criteria for presence developed for virtual reality design to 3-D video games we can develop a set of design criteria that will enable us to judge a game's degree of immersiveness, engagement, and the degree of presence possible. The development of such a tool takes on a certain urgency in a legal environment in which games are routinely labeled as addictive, as inductive of hallucinatory trances, and blamed as the source for crimes such as the Columbine shootings.

The Trend Toward 3-D Design

As Mark J. P. Wolf has pointed out, most 3-D games represent their navigable space using the conventions of Classical Hollywood Cinema, at least to a degree. The difference, of course, is that these spaces are navigable; first-person shooters and virtual reality games, for example, "provide players with an unbroken exploration of space, allowing them to pan, tilt, track, and dolly through the space, which is usually presented in a first-person perspective view and is navigable in real time."[7]

Game historians generally agree that *Battlezone,* a 1980 Atari arcade game described as a "hyperrealistic tank combat simulator"[8] was probably the first game depicted from a first-person perspective[9] as seen through a periscope that simulated the interior of a tank. *Battlezone* was drawn in vector graphics, that is, straight lines that connect any two points on the screen. Games like *Lunar Lander* (1979) and *Battlezone* pioneered the vector look. The mountains and other landscape elements were depicted in luminous green polygonal shapes but were realistic enough for the Army to ask Atari to design a training simulator for them (it's not clear if this simulator was ever built).[10]

"Wireframe" is the term used for objects that are outlined, but without the planes filled in.[11] Wireframe is still an acceptable way of depicting virtual reality, and is used in films such as *The Thirteenth Floor* (1998). The first game to use polygon-based 3-D graphics was *I, Robot,* designed by Dave Theurer, and released in 1983.[12]

In 1982, isometric (i.e., "constant measurements") perspective was introduced in a Sega game called *Zaxxon.* The term isometric comes from the architectural practice of isometric drawings, "in which all horizontal lines are drawn at an angle of thirty degrees to the horizontal plane of projection."[13] The result is no vanishing points and equal emphasis given to all three planes. As Poole writes: "In video game terms, this means that an illusion of solidity is created while preserving an external viewpoint. You could see three sides of an object rather than just one; and now, crucially, the game screen was not just a neutral arena; it had become an environment."[14]

Isometric perspective had its heyday and is now still used for games like *SimCity, Civilization,* and *Command and Conquer,* all games in which the player controls numerous units (people, tanks, factories, etc.) within a vast playing area and with an omniscient overview.

But the foreshortening of scientific perspective had certain advantages: it implied a subjective, individual viewpoint, and it promised a degree of immersiveness that the God's-eye-view of isometric perspective could never deliver.[15] Scientific perspective made a comeback with the first truly "immersive" 3-D game, *Wolfenstein 3-D* (1992).[16] *Wolfenstein* put the player into rooms, separated by doors, with walls receding realistically into the distance and populated with bots that took the form of Nazi soldiers for the player to destroy. There was no texture on the walls or ceilings so only the walls moved with forward movement, and the bots looked 2-D as they were drawn with bit-mapped sprites whose pixels enlarged as they got closer. *Wolfenstein* made another innovation, which was adopted by the genre, which was to include a representation of hands (the player's hands) clutching a gun at the bottom of the screen. The gun is not used for aiming, but it does make the player feel more like they are incorporated into the space. These conventions were continued and developed in other first-person shooters, such as *Doom* (1993), *Hexen* (1994), *Quake* (1996), and *Unreal* (1998). Technical literature on presence in VR often make reference to the conventions of first-person shooters as the standards for a sense of presence and a transparent interface, especially *Doom, Quake,* and *Unreal.* For example, Randy Pausch et al. say that *Doom* "... get[s] users to the point where the interface becomes transparent and the user focuses on task performance."[17] In another example, Michael Lewis and Jeffrey Jacobson assert that: "The most sophisticated rendering pipelines are now found not on specialized scientific machines but on PC video cards costing less than $500. The most sophisticated, responsive interactive simulations are now found in the engines built to power games."[18] And finally, John Laird, comparing the possibilities for artificial intelligence research in robotics and first-person shooters, prefers the latter: "Simulated virtual environments make it possible to bypass many of these problems, while preserving the need for intelligent real-time decision-making and interaction ... computer games provide us with a source of cheap, reliable, and flexible technology for developing our own virtual environments for research."[19]

As we can see from the above quotations, first-person shooter games and game editors are used in virtual reality research because they promise a high degree of immersiveness, engagement, and presence in an affordable, manageable format. But when researchers ascribe a high degree of presence to first-person shooter games, what exactly are they referring to?

Origins of the Term *Presence*

Steuer gives a useful outline of the provenance of the term *presence:*

> Presence is closely related to the phenomenon of *distal attribution or external-ization,* which refer to the referencing of our perceptions to an external space beyond the limits of the sensory organs themselves. In unmediated percep-tion, presence is taken for granted-what could one experience other than one's immediate physical surroundings? However, when perception is mediated by a communication technology, one is forced to perceive *two* separate environ-ments simultaneously: the physical environment in which one is actually present, and the environment presented via the medium. . . . Telepresence is the extent to which one feels present in the mediated environment, rather than in the immediate physical environment. . . . Telepresence is defined as the experience of presence in an environment by means of a communication medium. . . . In other words, "presence" refers to the natural perception of an environment, and "telepresence" refers to the mediated perception of an environment. This envi-ronment can be either a temporally or spatially distant "real" environment (for instance, a distant space viewed through a video camera), or an animated but non-existent *virtual world* synthesized by a computer (for instance, the animated "world" created in a video game).[20]

Steuer's definition, which dates from 1992, is useful because it shows us how the current usage of the term *presence*—which Marie-Laure Ryan has defined as "we experience what is made of information as being material"—is derived from *telepresence,* which, as Steuer wrote in 1993, originally meant a successful experience of presence in a teleoperation environment, such as scientists on Earth using devices to work on satellites in space, which gave them the feeling of being astronauts. As Ryan noted, the word *presence* is currently used to indicate a successful feeling "being there" in a synthetic en-vironment, while *telepresence* has been reserved for teleoperation situations such as surgery, research in space, and so on.[21] I will explore further changes in the meaning of the the the word *telepresence* later in this essay. For more detail on what is meant by presence, Ryan refers to the work of Sheridan,[22] but a more detailed and more referenced series of studies are those by Lombard and Ditton.[23]

Matthew Lombard and Theresa Ditton define presence as "the artifi-cial sense that a user has in a virtual environment that the environment is unmediated."[24] They surveyed the literature on presence and found that other researchers had conceptualized presence as the result of a combina-tion of one or all of six different factors. Their summary indicated that an increased sense of presence can result from a combination of all or some of the following factors: quality of social interaction, realism in the environ-ment (graphics, sound, etc.), from the effect of "transportation," from the degree of immersiveness generated by the interface, from the user's ability to accomplish significant actions within the environment and the social impact of what occurs in the environment, and from users responding to the computer itself as an intelligent, social agent. Lombard and Ditton's elements of presence are reminiscent of Michael Heim's initial definition and categorization, in his essay, "The Essence of VR."[25] Heim defines VR as "an event or entity that is real in effect but not in fact. . . . The public knows VR as a synthetic technology combining 3-D video, audio and other sensory components to achieve a sense of immersion in an interactive, computer-generated environment." According to Heim, there are seven elements of VR: Simulation, Interaction, Artificiality, Immersion, Telepresence, Full-Body Immersion, and Networked Communications.[26] For scientists, especially cognitive scientists and therapists using VR as a treatment tool, Lombard and Ditton's definitions make up the standard, and I shall follow that approach here.

Lombard and Ditton agree that each of these six dimensions of presence are very different from each other but, rather than focus on the differences, they focus on what each dimension has in common: "the perceptual illusion of nonmediation." Clearly, some of these elements work against others; for example, the learning curve required to act effectively can conflict with the sense of immersiveness.[27] It is worthwhile to look at each of these aspects of presence in turn.

Quality of Social Interaction

The first element of presence is the quality of the social interaction available within the VRE, that is, if it was perceived as "sociable, warm, sensitive, personal or intimate when it is used to interact with other people."[28] Lombard and Ditton surveyed studies which measured how different communication media could "(a) overcome the various communication constraints of time, location, permanence, distribution, and distance, (b) transmit the social, symbolic, and nonverbal cues of human communication; and (c) convey equivocal information." Key concerns were how intimacy and immediacy were achieved in the medium in question, especially how language choices helped reach those goals.[29]

Durlach and Slater[30] assert that the sense of being with someone, or the sense of togetherness, contributes to a heightened sense of presence; this definition includes the ability for all the participants in the VRE to interact with the space as well as with each other.

The goal of their research is to improve virtual systems such as telecommunications by increasing the sense of presence by adding the sense of "togetherness." They assume that the criteria for establishing a common environment are essentially the same as the criteria for defining a common environment in the real world, and the same problems will appear: for example, the different backgrounds, viewpoints, and sensitivities of the participants can complicate social interaction.

The key to a sense of presence derived from social interaction is that alterations of the environment caused by the actions of one participant are clearly perceived by the other participants, and interactions with the environment in which the environmental changes are not only perceived by many or all of the participants but also are the result of collaborative work on the environment by the participants (an example given is moving heavy furniture together).

In writings about 3-D environments (as well as in text-based MUDs and 2-D MUDs), discussions of social realism often focus on the use of avatars (textual or graphic representations of users that include a character designed to fit into the fictional environment in question, complete with a set of personality traits, skills, and health status) and the methods players have for communicating with each other. How the avatars are designed is a key concern here; in particular, how each participant relates to his or her avatar. How is the sense of presence in the common environment and the sense of togetherness influenced by the choice of viewpoints?

Participants can choose an egocentric viewpoint, see the environment through the eyes of the avatar, and see one's own avatar in the same manner as one sees one's own body in the real world. Alternatively, participants can assume an exocentric viewpoint and view one's own avatar in much the same manner as one views the avatar of the other participants. A goal of Durlach and Slater's research is to discover in what ways such choices influence the sense of presence in the common environment and the sense of togetherness.

Alluquère Roseanne Stone[31] describes presence as the result of the unique persona within the physical body being transported to a mediated world, rather than the transformation of persona or instances of multiple persona within the same physical body. Stone is distinguishing presence from what the users aim for in MUD and MOO environments which Jay Bolter and Richard Grusin have described as "... the freedom to be oneself is the freedom to become someone (or something) else."[32] MUDs and MOOs offer users a variety of subject positions to choose from, from creating multiple avatars, to networking with others to jointly make up the psyche of a single avatar, to riding invisibly on the back of someone else's avatar, to encountering an AI form who has an agentless subject position.[33]

The effectiveness of avatars as a way of facilitating social interaction has not received much in the way of academic attention. How players relate to their own avatars in a single-player environment, however, and—of course— how well an avatar works for a player in a multiplayer environment depends on how the player engages with the avatar to begin with. Some avatars have inspired enough devotion to achieve an independent cult status. For example, the figure of Lara Croft from the *Tomb Raider* series was one of the humanoid avatars[34] who achieved stardom (twenty-six million copies sold[35] between 1996 and 2001 and her own Hollywood films). Lara appeals to players across genders, ages, and social classes and has generated a fairly large body of criticism.[36]

The quality of a game's social interaction also depends on its networks. Many games are designed as stand-alone, but playing the stand-alone game is often seen as a prelude to playing the networked version. These can range from six to eight person games, such as those possible with *Warcraft III* and similar games, to massive multiplayer online role-playing games such as *Lineage, EverQuest, Ultima Online, Asheron's Call,* and *The Sims Online.*[37]

Realism

A sense of realism is also an important factor, that is, how accurately does the virtual environment represent objects, events and people. Realism is subdivided into social realism (the extent to which the social interactions in the VRE matched interactions in the real world), and perceptual realism (how closely do the objects, environments, and events depicted match those that actually exist).

"Social realism is the extent to which a media portrayal is plausible or 'true to life' in that it reflects events that do or could occur in the nonmediated world."[38] Perceptual realism is what is usually vaguely meant by "realism" or "photorealism"—how well the environment looks and sounds like the real world. An animated cartoon, for example, could have a low degree of perceptual realism but a high degree of social realism. Social realism is achieved by designing the world to match the real one, with streets and stores and homes and parks, as well as organizing rituals and ceremonies that enable players to identify their social place in the world. In most MUDs, for example, ceremonies such as "beheadings," funerals, and MUD weddings are common practices.

Clive Fencott[39] believes that as presence is based on perception, it is the content of the virtual environment, and how that content is designed, that is most important; in close agreement are Prothero et al.[40] who believe that presence is enhanced by how the user perceives the space, specifically, an increased sense of presence results from a wide field of view and a sense of foreground and background, which enables the user to orient themselves in space and understand the orientation of virtual objects in the same space. Clive Fencott's research focuses on the perceptual realism necessary to generate a feeling of presence in a virtual environment, or VRE. According to Fencott, "presence is a mental state, it is therefore a direct result of perception rather than sensation. In other words, the mental constructions that people build from stimuli are more important than the stimuli themselves." The aim of Fencott's research is to discover how content affects perception. To aid him in this goal he has come up with the model of *Perceptual Opportunities:* "The art of V[R]E design is surely to provide users with carefully structured opportunities to allow them to explore, strategise, and generally feel some sense of control over what they are doing." Perceptual opportunities include Sureties, Shocks, and Surprises.

"Sureties" are mundane details that are attractive because they are highly predictable. Examples of sureties include: Architectural details such as lamp-posts, street furniture, and marks to indicate distance; indicators to tell us where to go such as railings, paths, doorways; and background sound that reassures us (cars in distance, etc.).

Shocks are poor design elements that jar the user out of the sense of "reality" of the VRE, such as the "end of the world" shock—the user can see where the environment ends; "film set shock"—buildings are incomplete; polygon leaks—seeing through cracks; and latency and motion sickness caused by poor design or overlong use of the hardware.

Surprises are nonpredictable details that arise logically out of the VRE design. There are three types of Surprises: attractors, connectors, and re-tainers.

Attactors tempt the user to go or do something. These include mystery objects the user may want to examine, such as moving objects that attract attention (such as animation), objects needed for tasks in the VRE, objects that cause fear, alien objects that indicate the end of a level, sensation objects that attract attention through the nonvisual sense, awesome objects that impress by their size, and dynamically figured objects that relocate in space and time.

Connectors are configurations of perceptual opportunities that help the visitor figure out how to use/explore the VRE, such as axes or direction signs, choice points that should indicate outcome of both choices, and deflectors such as a closed door.

Retainers are the interesting things that make users linger and enjoy the VRE such as hot spots, learning areas, puzzles, gadgets, and so on.

Perceptual Maps are designs that show how sureties, surprises, and shocks work together.

Telepresence, Teleoperation, Teleportation

Lombard and Ditton, in their 1997 article, referred to this as "transporta-tion." (When they wrote the abstract for their study in 2000, they re-ferred to this category as "teleportation" or "telepresence," using the words interchangeably).[41] Lombard and Ditton have identified three types of transportation: (1) "You are there," in which the user is transported to another place, the oldest version of presence; (2) "It is here," in which another place and the objects within it are transported to the user—the example given is of how television "brings the objects and people from another place to the media user's environment"[42]; and (3) "We are together," in which two or more communicators are transported to a common space, such as in immersive video conferencing.

For the the purposes of humanities scholarship, however, especially when it comes to the analysis of 3-D games, it seems better to abandon the first meaning of "transportation" as this is too similar to the conventional definition of the word *presence* itself. By the same token, it seems better to retain the term "telepresence" for the second meaning Lombard and Ditton ascribed to *transportation,* that is, "telepresence systems use video signals and computer graphics to place the user at a remote or inaccessible location."[43] *Telepresence* can also cover the "we are there together" meaning, as this is only different from "You are there" in that it covers more users, whereas *teleoperation* will keep its meaning of people controlling tools, such as surgical instruments, and performing manipulations such as surgery on a patient that is made present to them through the use of virtual reality, covering Lombard and Ditton's second meaning.

Finally, a third term needs to be added to cover something that does not, as yet, happen in real life but is quite frequent in games: *teleportation.* In *Diablo,* for example, players can open portals that will transport them from the dungeons below to the village above and vice versa. Other games, such as *Titanic,* have maps as interfaces; the player can click on where they want to go on a map and they are instantly there.

Perceptual and Psychological Immersion

Presence is also the result of perceptual and psychological immersion. The first is accomplished by blocking as many of the senses as possible to the outside world and making it possible for the user to perceive only the artificial world, by the use of goggles, headphones, gloves, and so on. The second results from the user's mental absorption in the world. Theorists such as Schuemie et al.[44] have followed Lombard and Ditton in assuming that the ability to interact with the mediated environment is the most important factor in the sense of presence, and that this explains why immersive virtual reality environments have been shown to be effective in the treatment of fear of heights, fear of flying, arachnophobia, claustrophobia, and agoraphobia, and the fear of being in places from which escape might be difficult or embarrassing.

A well-known example of a VRE with a very high level of immersiveness is *Osmose,* by Char Davies. Davies believes that full body immersion in a virtual environment can lead to shifts in mental awareness. She also felt that the technology associated with the Cartesian types of virtual reality inherited from the Western-scientific-industrial complex is not neutral. Davies set out to deliberately circumvent these conventions. "*Osmose*... shuns conventional hand-based modes of user interaction which tend to reduce the body to that of disembodied eye and probing hand in favour of an embodying interface which tracks breath and shifting balance, grounding the immersive experience in that participant's own body."[45] The metaphor for *Osmose* is scuba diving: the environments are slightly blurred and without horizon lines, much like the ocean; users move from space to space by breathing or adjusting their balance. Some users have strong emotional reactions to Davies's environments, suggesting that the high degree of immersion, with an interface that involves the kinesthetic sense as well as hearing and sight, results in a high degree of presence.

The Use of a Social Actor in the Medium

The use of a synthetic social actor also can lead to a heightened sense of presence. Users respond to virtual guides and virtual pets in much the same way they respond to the direct address of newscasters on TV.

Synthetic social actors can be of different types. For example, an interaction with a social actor can be preprogrammed. In the text-based MUD *Angalon,* users can battle with a scarecrow, a battle that plays like a cut-scene in a graphic game: the user's actions instigate the struggle, but once started it plays out according to the MUD's programming. More interactive encounters are possible, for example, in the same MUD users also can adopt one of the kittens that are nested in a barn, and the kitten will make its presence felt by perching on the user's shoulder or climbing up their leg. In spite of the clearly programmed nature of these synthetic social actors, users tend to respond to them realistically. An excellent example is "The Thing" in *The Thing Growing,* a virtual animated character in a CAVE (Computer Automated Virtual Environment) designed by Josephine Anstey and Dave Pape. *The Thing Growing* takes advantage of everything that VR in CAVEs has to offer to create a situation in which the user takes a leading role and develops an emotional relationship with the Thing. First the user follows the sound of the Thing's voice and lets it out of its box; then the Thing insists on a sort of couple relationship, expressed mainly through dancing (with the Thing and the user alternating in leading). No matter how cooperative the user is, however, the Thing is never emotionally satisfied and even takes revenge by locking the user in a space where they can no longer interact. The user gets a chance for revenge, however, only to discover that such intimacy between virtual character and human user is "forbidden" and other police-things are on their way to judge and sentence the Thing and the user.[46]

Intelligent Environment

Finally, a sense of presence can result from users responding to the computer itself as an intelligent, social agent. Humans tend to do this, even though they consciously understand that such responses to computers are illogical. Responses, such as treating a computer with politeness and ascribing it with gender stereotypes are aimed at the computer itself, and not to the programmer. Therefore, when the virtual medium itself follows basic social cues, the user will feel a higher sense of presence. This includes most artificial intelligence (AI) programming, such as natural language programming, which is designed to make the machine seem more human.

I am currently conducting an experiment in how the sense of presence is altered if a 3-D CAVE environment responds to the user's subconscious cues as well as conscious ones. The name of the project is *The Memesis Project.* It is an experiment in interactive narrative designed to test certain theories of presence and immersion in the environment and transparency or immediacy in the interface. In this version of *Memesis,* the environment is designed to resemble a haunted house that collects information about the user's phobias and deep-seated psychological fears in order to provide an ultimate, more thrilling "haunted house" experience. If the first, single-user version is successful, future versions of *Memesis* are planned to carry the interactive narrative and engagement research even further.[47] The principle goal is to see how much and in what way a more intelligent environment can affect the user's sense of presence.

As we can see from the above, *immersion* and the nondiegetic level of involvement with a game that I have labeled *engagement* are both aspects of what researchers in virtual reality have labeled *presence.* As we have seen, many elements, some overlapping, some fairly incompatible with each other, go into making up a sense of presence. In summing up their six conceptualizations of presence, Lombard and Ditton emphasize that: "Because it is a perceptual illusion, presence is a property of a person. However it results from an interaction among formal and content characteristics of a medium and characteristics of a media user, and therefore it can and does vary across individuals and across time for the same individual."[48] Individual scientists working in virtual reality have focused on particular elements that make up a feeling of presence. We can now take advantage of their findings to devise a method for the aesthetic and cultural analysis of 3-D video games. This investigation can take two forms: a quantitative, analytical one or a qualitative, aesthetic one. My goal in this article is the articulation of a theoretical tool for the qualitative, aesthetic analysis of 3-D video games. The important thing to remember is that the various elements of presence should be seen as a continuum that each game will embody differently. Once we analyze how different elements of presence are weighted in each game, we can ask ourselves what purpose that serves in this particular game. As an example of application of this method, I have conducted my own analysis of of *Myst: Exile* (2001).

Myst III: Exile: The Case Study

Exile is the third in the series of groundbreaking video games released by Cyan, beginning with the original *Myst* in 1993, which was a breakthrough in 3-D rendering in its day and became a bestseller across all game categories and stayed on the bestseller list for 104 weeks. The original *Myst* was composed on Apple computers, and consisted of still images linked together in HyperCard. The images were of stunning beauty, a tradition kept up in the sequels. In the original, the Miller brothers, the game's creators, focused on realistic images, especially textures. There were puzzles to be solved involving fanciful but mechanical (and therefore easily understandable) machines. There were some short video clips in which the user was addressed by a limited number of characters, but these were rare. The user was addressed as someone known to Atrus, who could help repair the tragic effect of the actions of Atrus's sons. The sequel, *Riven,* (1997) continued the conventions of *Myst,* although it was a much larger game, this time composed on SGI machines using SoftImage. *Riven* added journeys in a variety of mechanical contrivances, to great effect, and there were more characters. Although not produced by the Miller Brothers, *Exile* builds on and continues the convention of both games. Images for *Exile* were modeled in Discreet's 3ds max on Mac computers.

Like its predecessors, the game is not designed for multiplayer play, so social interaction is limited to conversing with the artificial characters. As in the earlier games, the game characters, depicted through video footage, speak to the player but the player has no way of speaking back.

The game begins with the player finding him or herself in a sheltered garden, overlooking a dry landscape. After a moment the player realizes that he or she is being addressed by Catherine, Atrus's wife, who is holding a baby. Catherine directs the player to go into Atrus's office, as Atrus is expecting them.

This first scene sets up most of the elements relating to presence for the entire game. The user has no avatar, other than the most basic cursors (pointer for setting a direction, open hand for grasping an object, zoom in/zoom out, and the lighting bolt for indicating a site where fast transitions to another part of the game environment is possible). The player has a first-person perspective at human eye-level (following the cinematic convention, this eye-level is set roughly at the level of a six-foot-tall human) throughout the game. Players cannot see their own reflection in glass or water, or even see their own feet when they look down, but they can take rides in elevators and zeppelins and other related contraptions, can turn the pages of books, peer closely at objects, and "pick up" certain items as well as manipulate mechanical contraptions. As a result of these measures, the game has an extremely high degree of social realism, as the majority of the elements in this fantastical world conform quite closely to how things would be in our world. The carefully designed, beautifully elaborated 3-D graphics and a soundtrack consisting of well-timed ambient sounds as well as sound effects give the game a high degree of perceptual realism.

Beyond the introductory scene, however, the player does not see another character for very long stretches of game time. The player's journey through the *Exile* environment takes the form of pursuit of a character called Saavedro, who has stolen the book of a new age Atrus had just composed, called Releeshan. Occasionally the player gets a glimpse of Saavedro, and sometimes Saavedro has left recorded video messages that help the player advance through the game. But, apart from that, the world of *Myst III: Exile* is as lonely and empty as its predecessors were. This makes the environment feel less like the real world and more like a dreamscape, part of the designer's goal. Nevertheless, although the characters (when they appear) look very realistic, the fact that their appearances are rare and do not allow the user to talk back, lowers the sense of presence that would be provided by more synthetic characters.

The game does have a sense of environmental intelligence built into the puzzles. The puzzles must be solved in an exact way, but they are built into the environment very creatively. Players familiar with the prequels will have a sense of how to solve the puzzles, as they are a reflection of Atrus's way of thinking and philosophy. So the player has a relationship with Atrus in a removed sense, and the game is partly a treasure hunt that can be solved by how well the player understands Atrus's mind. In *Exile,* the Atrus layer in the environment is there, as Atrus designed and built the environment and puzzles, but a new layer has been added on top, Saavedro's, who has altered and reset all the puzzles to make life difficult for anyone who might come looking for him (he assumes in fact that it is Atrus who is looking for him and addresses the player as Atrus in the middle of the game; only later does he realize his mistake). So the player finds themself inserted into a long game of cat-and-mouse that is really taking place between Atrus and Saavedro, with the player assumed to be on Atrus's side (there is no option to play from any other perspective). The way to lose the game is by not understanding Saavedro and being taken advantage of by him. Though subtle, this intersubjective triangulation between Atrus, Saavedro, and the player gives the game environment a feeling of presence that it would otherwise lack, based on the intelligence of the environment.

Teleportation is used in this game through the linking books, as in the original *Myst*. The designers have included many references to other forms of virtual reality, such as three telescopes that need to be carefully lined up, to holograms, to portals (the linking books) that transport the player to other parts of the game. Ironically, these mediations add to the feeling that the world itself is nonmediated.

Because the game is a desktop computer game, the degree of perceptual immersion is limited. The player is always aware of the relatively small screen and the need to use the mouse. Using the mouse properly can be a challenge on certain puzzles. This low degree of perceptual immersion is amply made up for, however, by a very high degree of psychological immersion. Once the player adapts to the game's conventions it is possible, if one is so inclined, to lose oneself in the beauty and peacefulness of the environment. There is not much need to strategize as the realistic environment also uses sureties, shocks, and surprises to guide the player from one place to another and from one puzzle to another. If the player does not resist the logic of railings and closed doors (trying to jump down the elevator shaft, for example, or off a cliff, does not accomplish anything) then it is perfectly clear where to go and how to get there. There is no time limit to solving the puzzles and therefore no sense of hurry. This contributes greatly to the overall sense of psychological immersion.

For a sense of how the perceptual realism works in *Myst III: Exile,* let's take a closer look at the first age, J'nanin: The Lesson Age. J'nanin is full of sureties that guide and show the player where to go: catwalks, stone steps, stepping stones, sandy paths, curving metal stairways, and ladders. Only by following these paths can the player move through the game (and of course, link to different Ages through books, a *Myst* convention that would be familiar to players from other games with similar devices, such as the portals in *Diablo*). So "Sureties," as Fencott has defined them, are one of the principle elements that add to the presence in this world. Shocks, the signs that we are playing a game, are rare. If a player insists on trying to jump into a pool of water, off a cliff, or down an elevator shaft, nothing will happen, and they will hear a whispery warning sound, the closest thing this game has to a shock. Of course the game is very large and requires switching

CDs regularly, but once started on a CD the player can play for a long time without other interruptions.

What makes the *Myst* franchise special are its surprises. Attractors abound: players want to read the diaries scattered throughout the world (and know that the information in them functions as a retainer, as a device for helping them solve the puzzles). They want to play with the numerous gadgets like lamps, gears, and levers, and, best of all, go for wild rides in rail cars or blimps. They know that in order to do this they need to solve the puzzles. Attractors that appear early in the game, such as the Venus flytrap and the scale that balances wooden and crystal balls, serve as connectors to other parts of the game, because the player will encounter puzzles later that can be solved with the information garnered from the scale or the flytrap. This type of surprise is typical to adventure games and therefore feels very intuitive to players with a minimum of experience.

To sum up, *Myst III: Exile,* like its predecessors, offers players the opportunity to explore a particular kind of world—the typical adventure game experience. *Exile* provides a more meditative experience, the result of the way the game's design emphasizes perceptual realism and minimizes social interaction. All of this is in keeping with the game's genre and theme. Other games emphasize different elements of presence. For example, *Diablo II* has an isometric view; the player can choose from a number of avatars; the game is populated by numerous nonplayer characters and can be played alone or in multiplayer versions. Compared to *Exile,* however, the world is not all that visually immersive, and each new dungeon does not look all that different from the next. *Diablo* emphasizes social interaction. Social realism is low, which means that there is a lot of information the player must learn about weapons and monsters in order to succeed. However, once this is accomplished, psychological immersion can be very high, as battling the various monsters and other players requires the player's constant attention and strategic calculation. The monsters are not very complex social actors, unlike *Exile*'s Saavedro, who has a long history and a complex set of motivations. But the *Diablo* player does not have time to really think about such issues, anyway.

In short, Lombard and Ditton's conceptualization of presence enables critics and analysts to conduct an aesthetic analysis of various types of games, which can contribute to a fuller overall analysis as well as to a badly needed elaboration of game genres, which have experienced some rapid changes recently. An elaborated concept of presence also can help those working in virtual reality, those working in games, and those working in interactive instruction design develop a common vocabulary and therefore learn from each other. It also provides players with a terminology to discuss the games that they like, so they can ask for more.

84 · Alison McMahan

Notes

1. Eugen Provenzo, *Video Kids: Making Sense of Nintendo* (Cambridge, MA: Harvard University Press, 1991), 64–65.
2. J. C. Herz, *Joystick Nation: How Video Games Ate Our Quarters, Won Our Hearts and Rewired Our Minds* (Boston, New York, Toronto, London: Little, Brown, and Company, 1997), 155.
3. Janet Murray, *Hamlet on the Holodeck: The Future of Narrative in Cyberspace* (Cambridge, MA: The MIT Press, 1997), 98–99.
4. Two representative discussions of the nature of immersiveness can be found in Thomas B. Sheridan, "Interaction, Imagination and Immersion: Some Research Needs," in *Proceedings of the ACM Symposium on Virtual Reality Software and Technology*. Seoul, Korea, (2000), 5, and in George Robertson, Mary Czerwinski, and Maarten van Dantzich, "Immersion in Desktop Virtual Reality," in *Proceedings of the 10th Annual ACM symposium on User Interface Software and Technology*. Banff, Canada (1997), 11.
5. Clifford Geertz, "Deep Play: Notes on the Balinese Cockfight," in *The Interpretation of Cultures* (New York: Basic Books [1972] 1973), 432.
6. Personal communication.
7. Mark J. P. Wolf, *The Medium of the Video Game* (Austin: University of Texas Press, 2001), 66.
8. Van Burnham, *Supercade: A Visual History of the Videogame Age 1971–1984* (Cambridge, MA: The MIT Press, 2001), 216.
9. See Steven Poole, *Trigger Happy: Video games and the Entertainment Revolution* (New York: Arcade Publishing, 2000), 112, and Wolf, *The Medium of the Video Game.*
10. Van Burnham, *Supercade.*
11. Poole, *Trigger Happy,* 211.
12. Van Burnham, *Supercade,* 382.
13. Poole, *Trigger Happy,* 121.
14. Poole, *Trigger Happy,* 121.
15. Poole, *Trigger Happy,* 122–23.
16. Atari's vector arcade game, *Star Wars* (1983), had an immersive first person perspective, like *Battlezone,* with guns at the edge of the screen and the ability to steer through the space. This article focuses primarily on 3-D games with polygonal graphics, but we are not done learning from older vector games.
17. Randy Pausch, Jon Snoddy, Robert Taylor, Scott Watson, and Eric Haseltine, "Disney's Aladdin: first steps toward storytelling in virtual reality," in *Proceedings of the 23rd annual conference on Computer Graphics and interactive Techniques* (1996), 95.
18. Michael Lewis and Jeffrey Jacobson, "Game Engines in Scientific Research" (Special Issue: Game Engines in Scientific Research), *Communications of the ACM* 45, No. 1 (January 2002): 27.
19. John E. Laird, "Research in Human-Level AI Using Computer Games," *Communications of the ACM* 45, No. 1 (January 2002): 32.
20. Jonathan Steuer, "Defining Virtual Reality: Dimensions Determining Telepresence," *Journal of Communication, 42,* No. 4 (Autumn, 1992): 73–93. Available online at <http://www.cyborganic.com/People/jonathan/Academia/Papers/Web/defining-vr.html>.
21. Marie-Laure Ryan, *Narrative as Virtual Reality: Immersion and Interactivity in Literature and Electronic Media* (Baltimore, MD: The Johns Hopkins University Press, 2001), 67–68.
22. For example, see Thomas B. Sheridan, "Interaction, Imagination and Immersion: Some Research Needs," in *Proceedings of the ACM Symposium on Virtual Reality Software and Technology,* Seoul, Korea, 2000.
23. See especially M. Lombard et al., "Measuring presence: a literature-based approach to the development of a standardized paper-and-pencil instrument." Project abstract submitted for presentation at *Presence 2000: The Third International Workshop on Presence.* Available online at <http://nimbus.temple.edu/~mlombard/P2000.htm>.
24. Jay David Bolter and Richard Grusin use *immediacy* to define a similar concept, in their book *Remediation* (Cambridge, MA: The MIT Press, [1999] 2000):

    > *Immediacy* (or *transparent immediacy*): A style of visual representation whose goal is to make the viewer forget the presence of the medium (canvas, photographic film, cinema, and so on) and believe that he is in the presence of the object of

representation. One of the two strategies of remediation; its opposite is *hyperme-diacy*, "A style of visual representation whose goal is to remind the viewer of the medium. One of the two strategies of remediation." (272–73).

25. Originally published in Michael Heim, *The Metaphysics of Virtual Reality* (New York: Oxford University Press, 1993).

26. By simulation, Heim means the trend in certain kinds of VR applications that try to approach photo-realism, using graphics or photographs, and also use surround-sound with an aim toward "realism." Heim points out that we think of any interaction mediated by a machine as a virtual one (including phone calls with people we never meet). By *Artificiality*, Heim means what other scholars such as Cubitt mean by *Simulation*; in other words, an environment with possibilities for action (a world) that is a human construct. This construct can be mental, like the mental-maps of Australian Aborigines, or constructed, like a 3-D VR. For Heim,*Immersion* refers to VR technology's goal to "cut off visual and audio sensations from the surrounding world and replaces them with computer-generated sensations." *Full-Body Immersion*, which Heim also called "Projection VR," following Myron Krueger, is defined as "Interactive Environments where the user moves without encumbering gear" (such as a Head Mount Display) Projection VR requires more suspension of disbelief on the part of the user. Heim makes the distinction between VR and *telepresence:* virtual reality shades into telepresence when you bring human effectiveness into a distant location—for example, using robotics. For *Networked Communications*, Heim followed the definition of Jason Lanier: a virtual world is a shared construct, a RB2 (Reality Built for Two) Communication with others in an environment is essential; online networked communities strongly embodies this element of VR. Heim incorporates all seven elements into a new definition of VR: "An artificial simulation can offer users an interactive experience of telepresence on a network that allows users to feel immersed in a communications environment."

27. See, for example, M. Ryan, "Cyberspace, Virtuality and the Text," in *Cyberspace Textuality, Computer Technology and Literary Theory,* ed. Marie-Laure Ryan (Bloomington and Indianapolis: Indiana University Press, 1999), 78–107.

28. Matthew Lombard and Theresa Ditton, "At the Heart of It All: The Concept of Presence," *JCMC* 3, No. 2 (September, 1997): 4.

29. Lombard and Ditton, "At the Heart of It All: The Concept of Presence," 4.

30. Nat Durlach and Mel Slater, "Presence in Shared Virtual Environments and Virtual Togetherness," Research Laboratory of Electronics (Cambridge, MA: The MIT Press, 2000).

31. Alluquère Roseanne Stone, *The War of Desire and Technology at the Close of the Mechanical Age* (Cambridge, MA: The MIT Press, 1996), 83–92.

32. Bolter and Grusin, *Remediation*, 247.

33. Alison McMahan, "Spectator, Avatar, Golem, Bot: Interface and Subject Position in Interactive Fiction" (paper given at the Society for Cinema Studies Conference, Chicago, 2000). See also "The Effect of Multiform Narrative on Subjectivity," *Screen* 40, no 2 (Summer 1999): 146–157.

34. Pac-Man, of course, also achieved a high degree of recognisability and tie-in merchandising and spinoff TV show, hit song, and numerous sequel games.

35. Ad copy on back of *Lara Croft: Lethal and Loaded,* 50 min. West Long Branch, NJ: White Star Video, 2001, DVD.

36. See especially Diane Carr's article in *ScreenPlay: Cinema/videogames/interfaces,* eds. Geoff King and Tanya Krzywinska (London: Wallflower Press, 2002); and my chapter on avatars and bots in Alison McMahan, *Branching Characters, Branching Plots: A Critical Approach to Interactive Fiction* (forthcoming).

37. For a more detailed cultural analysis of networked communications and MUDs, see my essay "Verbal-Visual-Virtual: A MUDdy History," in *Gramma: Journal of Theory and Criticism* 7 (1999): 73–90.

38. Lombard and Ditton, "At the Heart of it All: The Concept of Presence," 5.

39. Clive Fencott, "Presence and the content of Virtual Environments," (1999). Available online at <http://web.onyxnet.co.uk/Fencott-onyxnet.co.uk/pres99/pres99.htm>.

40. J. D. Prothero, D. E. Parker, T. A. Furness III, and M. J. Wells, "Foreground/background manipulations affect presence" (paper presented at HFES '95). Available online at <http://www.hitl.washington.edu>.

41. Matthew Lombard et al., "Measuring Presence."
42. Lombard and Ditton, "At the Heart of it All: The Concept of Presence," 6.
43. Bolter and Grusin, *Remediation,* 214.
44. M. J. Schuemie, C. A. P. G. van der Mast, M. Krijn, and P. M. G. Emmelkamp, "Exploratory Design and Evaluation of a User Interface for Virtual Reality Exposure Therapy," in *Medicine Meets Virtual Reality,* ed. J. D. Westwood, H. M. Hoffman, R. A. Robb, D. Stredney, 468–474. IOS Press, 2002. Available online at <http://graphics.tudelft.nl/~vrphobia/mmvr2002.pdf>.
45. From the Immersence website at <http://www.immersence.com/publications/ephpaper-B.htm>.
46. Josephine Anstey and Dave Pape, "Animation in the Cave," *Animation World Magazine* (April 1, 1998). Available online at <http://mag.awn.com/index.php3?ltype=search&sval=Animation+in+the+Cave&article_no=532>.
47. Alison McMahan, "Sentient VR: The Memesis Project (Report of a Work in Progress)." In *Proceedings of the 6th World Multiconference on Systemics, Cybernetics and Informatics,* ed. Ngib Callaos, Marin Bica and Maria Sanchez. International Institute of Informatics and Systematics, Vol. XII (2002): 467-472. Available online at <http://faculty.vassar.edu/almcmahan/memesis/home/index.html>.
48. Lombard and Ditton, "At the Heart of it All: The Concept of Presence," 10.

CHAPTER 4

Hyperidentities

Postmodern Identity Patterns in Massively Multiplayer Online Role-Playing Games

MIROSLAW FILICIAK

Our era is defined by computer-based technologies. Computers subtly model our way of thinking about the world.[1] Through computers, new cultural phenomena and abstract ideas are presented to the public in a simple and accessible way. For example, Sherry Turkle claims that "computers embody postmodern theory and bring it down to earth."[2] I would like to show here the common dealings of video games—especially MMORPGs—in the context of general transformations of our culture occurring along with the expansion of electronic media. By MMORPGs (Massively Multiplayer On-line Role-Playing Games), I mean any computer network-mediated games in which at least one thousand players are role-playing simultaneously in a graphical environment. Every player uses one or more avatars, which are described by various statistics. Changing the statistics influences the interaction with game's environment. MMORPGs—despite their large-scale nature, and perhaps because of it—are in the forefront of some of the cultural trends now materializing. Naturally, it is impossible to determine whether the popularity of these games is just the effect of their compatibility with such processes. However, MMORPGs have much in common with the rules governing the lives of people—often unaware of such relations—now living in the industrial countries.

In my opinion, MMORPGs are the most fascinating phenomena to appear in recent years in the field of interactive entertainment. They are the first mass games (their popularity considerably surpasses the more difficult to use and more elitist MUDs) using the Internet on such a large scale. MMORPGs also are revolutionary within the video game medium, in which it is increasingly difficult to get real novelties. Also, they are the best argument against current views that perceive video games as a medium that alienates people. MMORPGs do not alienate; on the contrary, the games make sense only when people are joined through it (albeit by cooperation or competition). The games require interpersonal interaction and, as experience shows, MMORPGs are in principle one more medium in which to communicate. While they may seem "bizarre" in comparison to telephone or e-mail, their growing popularity clearly shows that people to whom communication with others comes more and more difficult in the real world, communicate eagerly in a virtual world. Paradoxically, it is easier for some people to talk through the computer than through face-to-face contacts. Last but not least, the argument for the special position of MMORPGs is that they constitute a sort of experimental arena in which we can watch mechanisms that, along with the development of sophisticated communication technologies, will increasingly be found in our daily lives. Hundreds of thousands players are finding themselves in situations described by postmodernism theorists, even though the vast majority of them have never heard of Baudrillard. The larger part of the phenomena as analyzed below refers not only to MMORPGs but also to other forms of communication on the Internet; however, in my judgment, only MMORPGs realize the postulates of postmodern identity in the most complete way.

MMORPGs are the first interactive mass medium to unite entertainment and communication in one phenomenon. MMORPGs include features typical of electronic entertainment (such as interactivity, plot, possibility of exploring virtual lands) as well as features that are specific for World Wide Web. One of these features is free communication on both person-to-person and many-to-many level.[3] We are living in a culture of simulation, in which the role of new technologies is continuously growing. This is the reason why *identity*—cogitation on how to define our "self" under the new conditions—is a key notion for the analysis of the present-day human condition. Intensive comprehension of identity has been evolving since the modernist era (the idea of the "self" as a construction is now around two hundred years old); however, today such transformations have reached their zenith. Digital media, video games included, enable us—for the first time in history on such a scale—to manipulate our "selves" and to multiply them indefinitely.

Networked "Self"

Today, nearly all media are undergoing convergence, becoming concentrated around the computer technologies. As "computer technologies," I mean here any platforms that serve digital formats and exchange information with each other. It is this opportunity to exchange information that seems to be the key one—the surrounding media make one stream, and it is not a single information source that is important anymore, but media in general as such. For the same reason, a strict separation of knowledge obtained by direct experience from what we know through the media becomes impossible—even the information coming from our closest friends more and more often reaches us through technological instruments. Many noticeable variations in modern human life were brought about by the Internet, which altered not only aspects of human communication but of entertainment as well. Today, the possibility for users to be interconnected through the Internet is a feature of a vast majority of games and there are many indications that in future net-games will become one of the mainstays of electronic entertainment. These games are becoming more and more popular—the Sony PlayStation's success made the game console a common part of a modern household, just like furniture. Also, unstable political situations in the world since the events of September 11 make more and more people concerned about their safety, resulting in more of them staying at home, creating a kind of cocooning effect. The fear of leaving home and the avoidance of direct contacts with other people both stimulate development of Internet and the MMORPGs found there.

The players participating in MMORPGs often are called users, not players, because of the lack of defined time and spatial confines and impossibility to actually end MMORPGs, which in principal do not meet many classic game definitions. Every MMORPG user begins by creating his or her own character. Depending on game universe, the user can freely—of course within the confines of some "realities"—select sex, appearance, profession, and physical features for his or her character. For example, in *EverQuest,* one of today's most popular MMORPGs, the action takes place in a land called Norrath, a rather typical fantastic setting. Creating an avatar—the user's representative in the virtual universe—begins with the choosing of a breed. While playing I couldn't decide between human and elf so I chose a half-elf, a breed that reduces the number of possible occupations from fourteen to five. I chose a ranger, therefore I received adequate modifiers for rangers. Then I divided my initial pool of ability points between Strength, Stamina, Agility, Dexterity, Wisdom, Intelligence, and Charisma. By the end, I'd created a character who is not very intelligent and charismatic, but (for a newbie) a quite able-bodied ranger. Then I have to choose a name. If a user can't think of a name matching the game's universe, an automatic name generator can be used. I used it, and the computer gave me the name Taeryen. I chose a face for my avatar, and the last thing to do was to pick a deity and my avatar—and my half-elf (but he could also be a halfling rogue or ogre shaman) called Taeryen—found himself in Norrath. The avatar develops while acting in the game's universe, he or she gets money and equipment, scores experience points, acquires new skills as well as makes virtual acquaintances, and successive possibilities become available to the user. For example, in the beginning, Taeryen is able to kill only small bats. After a few hours of training, he is able to fight with orcs, skeletons, or pixies. The avatar's development applies not only to fighting but also to any other ability.

It is easy to notice that the MMORPG user situation is an idealized image of the situation of the postmodern human creature, in which a user can freely shape his own "self." On the Internet this freedom reaches a heretofore-unprecedented extent, since we have full control over our own image—other people see us in the way we want to be seen. A huge role is played here by the ability to choose appearance, which has become an obsession in the postindustrial societies. There is no doubt that physical attractiveness is of great importance in our interpersonal relations—more than one Internet friendship was killed by photo exchanges, and research has shown that taller and more beautiful people earn more money and are more pleased with their own life.[4] On the Internet our appearance is—at least at present, when video image transmission in real time is not generally available—a matter of choice. In case of MMORPGs, there is no need for strict diets, exhausting exercise programs, or cosmetic surgeries—a dozen or so mouse clicks is enough to adapt one's "self" to expectations. Thus, we have an opportunity to painlessly manipulate our identity, to create situations that we could never experience in the real world because of social, sex-, or race-related restrictions. What Elizabeth Reid writes about avatars in MUDs applies to MMORPGs as well: avatars "are much more than a few bytes of computer data—they are cyborgs, a manifestation of the self beyond the realms of the physical, existing in a space where identity is self-defined rather than pre-ordained."[5] The majority of users create avatars bearing their resemblance to simplify identification. An extreme example can be placing one's own photo in some networked games. Nevertheless, users take advantage of a game's possibilities to improve their representations, making them smarter, prettier, and stronger. It is also significant that people talking about their activities in the game world use the pronoun "I," each identifying his or her "self" with the avatar created for the game purposes. Hava Bechar-Israeli arrived at similar conclusions in the research conducted on IRC channels.[6] He studied pseudonyms chosen by the chat room users, and found that as many as 45 percent of the users chose nicknames related to them somehow,

8 percent used names from the real world, and 6 percent used names of people known from pop culture. It follows, then, that the presentation of one's own person on the Internet resembles to some extent the user's real-life identity. I am convinced that we are dealing here with the mechanism of transference as described by John Suler in his work *Identity Management in Cyberspace.* This mechanism consists in transferring concealed emotions— often unconsciously—to the fictitious character. There are enough niches in the Internet to deconstruct one's identity, giving it a transparent form through the placing of various identities in a number of environments. There are separate places for sexual fantasies, various hobbyists, and so on. Their MMORPG equivalents can be different avatars corresponding with the particular fantasies of each. However, maintaining only one, long-term avatar seems to be an optimal variant, because of the advantages that follow from its development, which also leads to a deepening of the player's investment in and identification with the avatar. It clearly shows that the residents of virtual lands treat their net-life much more seriously than it would seem to people from the outside.

Of course, the possibility of modeling the characters we play in the virtual world is not only a mechanism supporting identification. There is also one important fact—that the user plays an active role in modulating the transmissions that reach him, and has control over them. Of course to some extent, what he watches on the screen depends on his actions and the choices he makes. Obviously, it is easier to identify ourselves with something that is partly created by us than with pictures imposed on us by somebody else. The possibility of transmission modulation (through influencing the game appearance in real time) enhances the game comfort to a large extent; it allows the user to adapt the game to his or her own preferences.

The process of secondary identification taking place in cinema theaters depends paradoxically on distance while in the case of games we encounter something more than just intimacy. Identification is replaced by *introjection*—the subject is projected inward into an "other." We do not need a complete imitation to confuse the "other" with the "self."[7] The subject (player) and the "other" (the onscreen avatar) do not stand at the opposite sides of the mirror anymore—they become one. While using an electronic medium in which subject and object, and what is real and imagined, are not clearly separated, the player loses his identity, projecting himself inward, becoming the "other," and identifies with the character in the game. During the game, the player's identity ends in disintegration, and the merger of user's and character's consciousness ensues. Another extremely important element exerting an influence on deepening the user-avatar identification is the development of the character's set of features, present today in most role-playing games (RPGs) and of course in MMORPGs. The ability to change an avatar's characteristics and its possibilities to act in the game universe also appears in games of other kinds, from sport games to strategy games, in which the player has an opportunity to upgrade the character's skills or buy new equipment. Nevertheless, it is in MMORPGs that the possibilities are most abundant, and avatars operate in an entirely virtual society, in which the emotional relationship between the player and the character directed by him is the closest. "The process of developing avatar capital seems to invoke exactly the same risk and reward structures in the brain that are invoked by personal development in real life," writes Edward Castronova in his innovative economical analysis of the virtual universe of *EverQuest*.[8] The virtual identity thus becomes one of the many "selves" included in the user's identity, perhaps the one in which the user realizes himself in the most complete way because of the lack of limitations existing in the real world; which is all the more reason that networked games, because of interaction with other people, become a part of someone's inner life.

Role-playing is one the social life's basic elements, and is used in our everyday functioning. Networked games can imitate such an ideal place; within them, people usually do not think in terms of deceptions. While visiting various chat rooms many Internauts assume (or would like to assume) they are talking with "real" people (i.e., people acting as they would in everyday life and not giving false personal data). In case of MMORPGs, total convergence between an avatar and its user is impossible. For example, when I chat with someone in Norrath, no one thinks that I'm really a half-elf. At the moment of writing this essay, *The Sims Online* has just been released. This game will be the first MMORPG whose universe won't be a fantasy or sci-fi land, but a contemporary Western-style environment. Nevertheless, I don't think that such a game will change the notion of convergence dramatically. Thus, virtual environments will still be the domain of liquid identity. The freedom of playing is restricted only by the realities of the game we choose. It is much more difficult to catch involuntary messages, which in everyday life consists partly of what is transmitted nonverbally. In any case, we also have greater comfort with regard to communication, as our voice is replaced by text on the screen and our interlocutor sees only those things that we allow him or her to see. The objectivizing role of the body disappears. I do not think that isolating the body from the mind has any justification, but in cyberspace this Cartesian dualism is being weakened in some ways and strengthened in others, and I intentionally do not examine this issue here. On the Internet people perceive us as our avatar, and such a perception is highly appropriate because when I play I am more my own avatar than the person sitting by the console/computer. To specify which of these identities is more true or more false is probably impossible. In any case, it would appear that our virtual "self" is closer to our images of ourselves than the one we present, which is governed by requirements and expectations of "real" life. The fact that one's identity is often the product of society ceases to limit us here, because there are not many transgressive whims which could not come true on the Internet. For example, in reality I can't shoot my boss when he or she puts me off, but in games I can. Finally, human beings get a tool, thanks to which they are sufficiently flexible to cope with new existence conditions.

From Identity to Hyperidentity

The notion of identity is one of the most important questions in any study dealing with the human creature; in Western culture, "self" is the measure of reality. The problems of our "self" become more pronounced now that the conventionally understood human identity has undergone erosion. By conventionally understood human identity, I mean the identity based on the constancy of physical and mental traits that allow us to differentiate our self from others. In society, this applies to identification with particular social groups. Changes in the surrounding world have given us tremendous freedom in shaping our "self"—unlike our ancestors, who had little opportunity to break out from their social caste or to change their residence. Before the Industrial Revolution, social roles were predefined, and thus an individual had solid and stable frames in which to exist within the community. In the age of mass media, however, a static concept of identity can no longer be preserved. In Western countries, standards of living have changed dramatically. These changes had their start during modernism, and they are related to big urban agglomerations arising. People living in big cities each day have far more interpersonal contact than their small-town ancestors had during one week or even one month. Therefore, compared to past years, the number of social roles we play has considerably multiplied.

William James, considered one of the fathers of modern psychology, noted that we match our "selves" to social relations, and in specific situations we present a different "version" of ourselves. He claimed that he was a completely different person in the stable, while breaking in his horse or talking with horse-boys, than on the psychological congress. As human beings are social creatures, they are thus able to determine their own identity only in reference to others (comparison or identification with the group). Sigmund Freud, Carl Jung, and Jacques Lacan all argue that ego existence is an illusion. Jung writes about a *persona*, the mask being an integral part of our personality and shaped according to the need to match it with cultural requirements. The concept was developed by Jung's student, Jolande Jacobi, in her book *Masks of the Soul* (1976). According to Jacobi, masking is forced by the growing complexity of social relations; it is simply the effect of adaptation to the environment's expectations. Roger Caillois researched the role of the mask in primeval communities. He also investigated masks in modern societies (for example, uniforms). In his book *Man, Play, and Games* (1961), he wrote that the use of masks is so tempting to human beings that their roles cannot be simply reduced to children's amusement and aberrant behavior.[9] Therefore, these masks come back as avatars.

Normal human relations require appearances to be kept up. The psychologist Ronald D. Laing, whose book *Self and Others* (1961) attempts to negate the dualism between what is inside us and the world outside, presents an extreme attitude here. He writes that man cannot be anybody other than what is required by his environment. The mask and the identity do not oppose each other any more; they are merged. It is impossible to distinguish between what is "original" in us and what is caused by other people's expectations. What is interesting is that Laing arrived at these conclusions long before more recent postmodern thinkers did.

Postmodernity is, according to Zygmunt Bauman, the leading sociologist of postmodernism, a certain developmental stage of individuals and social relations. The postmodern lifestyle is featured by lack of cohesion; it is fragmented. The postmodern man's personality is not quite definite, its final form is never reached, and it can be manipulated. We receive no implied form of our "self," but, instead, we construct it incessantly.[10] The effect becomes stronger as the constant elements in our life grow fewer and fewer; we can repeatedly change our profession, our residence, everything is transient and temporary today. In Europe, 14.5 million workers have chosen to work from home, mostly as freelancers or the employees of blue-chip companies. In Great Britain alone, there are seven million, and the consultancy *Datamonitor* estimates that by 2005 it will be 8.3 million.[11]

The role of institutions in making an individual's life cohesive has been reduced, and for many, the role of family also has weakened. Therefore, the social frames within which the individual's experience resides have changed. These changes were encouraged by mass media such as television, movies, and especially by the Internet and the World Wide Web. The media's ability to loosen social frames is relatively new, and even by the standards of Western civilization (which has always been individualistic), quite a new period is beginning. It is more and more difficult to talk about the continuum of experience even within two successive generations; thus, flexibility and a knack of matching ourselves with the changes are now among the most important features of the modern human being.

The postmodern context, with its tendency for fragmenting the self, favors a lack of strictly defined identity. Today, the individual is encouraged to create his or her persona according to standards presented by mass media. It is a source of new opportunities, though powerful stresses result as well. We are creating our "self" not as a linear process of construction and striving toward some original target—each identity we create is a temporary formation. Erosion of our individual "self" in macro scale is reflected in the fall of collected identities, like a nation. Of course, it must be added that the functioning of such mechanisms does not mean they permeate all of society. On the contrary, they are true only for a part (how big a part, remains to be discussed) of postindustrial Western societies. However, I am convinced that very soon such a model will become dominant in more and more of the Western world.

For postmodern people, background and residence are less and less important, as they are liquid. As mentioned above, we are today less likely to identify ourselves with dominant institutions,[12] including our place of employment, which assigns us a position in the manufacturing process. In postindustrial societies, the trend is just the opposite: minimizing the role of work in human life, constructing ourselves through our occupation ceases to be popular (especially now that we have a liquidity of roles), we are more willing to identify ourselves with our hobbies or pleasures. Work is not the essence of life anymore, it is not a value in itself—it is, rather, a necessity enabling us to get resources for other activities. Thus, as workers, we ceased to be institutions, while the changing employment system (working at home to specific orders, rejecting the "9 to 5" model) may allow those taking the new conditions in stride to reach a level of individualism and independence which was not possible earlier.

It must be noted that the pressures influencing identity are augmented by mass media along with the lifestyle promoted by consumerism, multiplying our "self" as an effect not only of complex social relations (in which people did participate earlier, though with less intensity) but also—and maybe even mainly—of shaping ourselves through consumption and constructing our own image. We construct this image by surrounding ourselves with the objects, which, beside their utility, are used to define and emphasize our image. It can even be said that the image offered is the one of the most important values of the product. At the same time, we ourselves become like the products, which by means of their image, engage in competition; for an attractive partner, for a well-paid job, for a social respect. Jean-Luc Godard said: "When you have no identity, look for image." Today, image and identity are interchangeable notions. In his conversation with Philippe Petit,[13] Jean Baudrillard calls identity the "label of existence." Peter Wagner, in his turn, notes that what we have today is a superabundance of material products, cultural orientations, and consumer practices. The multitude of opportunities to shape our identity/image that is now available is unprecedented in the history of mankind. Therefore, the individual is required to control his life actively in an incessantly varying social context.[14]

The postmodern identity is a self-aware identity. We understand the mechanisms running and ruling today's world; we know that complex social relations require maximum flexibility. Therefore, we relinquish the attempts to maintain a single constant "self." What would be condemned in the old paradigm (inconstancy which is associated to insincerity, hypocrisy or even mental illness) gets an affirmative dimension in the postmodern world. We do not have to talk about the individual as a monolithic self anymore. A new, more useful model replaces the nonfunctional one, efficiency being a new religion, and a dynamic "self" being undoubtedly better realized under the new conditions. As in a game, which is, after all, one of the metaphors used by postmodernists. Everybody is a player, and we are doing everything to match our "self" to the conditions and thus to play better. The game is for pleasure and what gives the greatest pleasure is a complete control over the "self" evading the bans and commands.

Manuel Castells, author of *The Power of Identity* (1997), notes that in a network society (as he calls the information society) our identity is defined by our relation to the net instead of the family, the clan, the tribe or nation. This is reflected in the notion of "Real Virtuality" that Castells proposes; the media are merging into one big medium, which supplies the net-society with the information for experience. Besides Castells, other postmodernists (Baudrillard first of all) emphasize that we live in a world of simulation where the boundary between the real and the fictional has disappeared; we have entered into hyperreality, which is more real than reality itself. Because nothing in our surroundings is real, we cannot be deluded to keep a constant, invariable, and only one true "self." Because, as I already said, the majority of institutions with which we heretofore identified ourselves have now been dramatically weakened, we define ourselves through varying values as well; it is more and more difficult to find something we can identify ourselves with permanently. Thus, wealthy and educated people construct and develop their personal identity, using any means available, redefining their social position and maintaining their mental balance under the new conditions. By contrast, the masses, who have less opportunity to take advantage of the transformative potential of techonology, look for collective and communal identities to replace the weakened official institutions.[15]

Today, people are no longer assigned to territories. With the development of transportation and communication, the process of deterritorialization intensifies, and this can also be applied to the notion of one's identity, which can be changed just like territories. Stuart Hall claims that "the subject assumes different identities at different times, identities which are not unified around a coherent 'self'. Within us are contradictory identities, pulling in different directions, so that our identifications are continually being shifted about. If we feel that we have a unified identity from birth to death, it is only because we construct a comforting story or 'narrative of the self' about ourselves."[16] Therefore, identity can be described as a rhizome. The rhizome model stands in opposition to the model of "the tree," which symbolizes hierarchical structures, extreme stratification, and linear thinking.[17] The rhisome is a labyrinth, a centerless universe that rejects any form of hierarchy and centralization while tending toward anarchy. It is the perfect metaphor to describe the user of electronic media; we cannot talk anymore about a single identity that produces temporary identities subordinate to itself. Thus, in the era of electronic media we should rather talk about hyperidentity, which is related to identity as a hypertext to a text. It is, rather, more a process than a finished formation, a complex structure that we update incessantly by choosing from the multitude of solutions. Any moment, we actively create ourselves. One's "self" arises just to be revoked a moment later and replaced by another "self"—equally as real (and at the same time apparent) as the previous one. A list of thinkers proclaiming the death of identity in conventional formulation should not omit Michel Foucault, who stressed that there is no inside "self," no essence making me who I am—it is only one of the possible ways of thinking, a discursive construct. Hence, a "self" is only a temporary construction. This is similar to the situation of the MMORPG user who is given simple tools for creating his or her own avatar— the representation of user's identity. The user creates one avatar and by its mediation she or he contacts other users, but at any moment the user can exchange one avatar for another. Parallels that occur between the modeling of one's identity in everyday life and in games are one of the user's pleasures, especially because the RPG elements created for "playing" with identity have been present in all kinds of games, not only in online games. Even in sports games that are competition oriented and contain no elements of social life simulation, the possibilities of creating and developing one's character are available.

Changes in the identity model are also perceived by the postmodernism critics, such as Anthony Giddens, whose view is that we are living in a period of late modernism and a posttraditional era. Our social lives are less determined by the social forces that shaped the lives of former generations. Nowadays people are free to create their own history. Giddens describes that as the "narrative of the self." He believes our everyday activities consist in strengthening and reproducing a set of expectations (theory of structuration).[18] He perceives the growing effects of posttraditional nature; tradition is withering, thus, the individual's activities—which did not attract much attention earlier, being somehow determined—become an important subject to be considered. As we have no longer social roles attributed to us at the moment of our birth, we work them out ourselves. "Self" ceased to be static; we are free to choose out of the complete list of "lifestyles" continually presented to us by the media. Naturally, all options are available only to the richest.

In summary, as the social psychologist Kenneth Gergen writes in *The Saturated Self,* ego is some sort of a hollow tube through which, under different circumstances, different parts of our personality—each time a single one—find their expression.[19] We are existing in the state of continuous construction and reconstruction, and any attempts to provide for cohesion are only a defect of human mind; some sort of side effect of having memory (such an approach is by no means new; an example can be found in Zen Buddhism or in the works of eighteenth-century European philosophers such as Thomas Reid or David Hume) or a work of language. However, this does not have to mean an incoherence of the subject. Liquid identity is not in conflict with the constancy of the object that integrates the individual's activities. In the conventional terms of reasoning, postmodern identity can be considered schizophrenic;[20] however, it should not be looked on as pathology (from such a viewpoint, the millions of Internauts would be believed to be mentally sick). Certainly, our "self" is now more liquid than ever and this situation is often regarded as a virtue. As I mentioned before, if people play games eagerly to be able to shift their identities, they must be deriving pleasure from that.

I would like to raise one more question, which might be a vital one for all those criticizing hyperreality and hyperidentity. Construction of a new paradigm that obliterates the boundary between the inner and outer is essential to creating the kinds of thinking needed for the new conditions of our existence. In the foreseeable future, when simulations will be closer to perfection (the growing popularity and technical advancement of video game consoles leave no doubt as to the tremendous demand for them), differentiation between artificial and real or between outside and inside will be blurred. Such a troubled differentiation will not apply to all areas of life, but it will affect the field of human interaction, which is increasingly computer-mediated. Already today, our knowledge of the world comes to a huge extent from the media; thus, they shape our life experience. We could refer here to the concept of "complete reality of mental life" as proposed by Jung—he believes that when somebody dreamt about being on the Moon and is convinced that he was there, then in a sense he was actually there.[21] Something similar happens with video games—although any actions performed on the screen are excluded from real life and are in one way outside it, they induce some emotions in the subject and thus constitute a part of the subject's life experience. Although the user exists in a MMORPG not only as a character in the game but also outside of the character, it is the avatar that stands in the middle of the course of events. The avatar is also the subject of chats one has with other users. Janet H. Murray writes about the active creation of belief—we desire the experience of immersion, so we use our intelligence to reinforce rather than to question the reality of the experience.[22]

The Need for an Audience: Making the Screen a Fetish

Pleasure taken in playing video games is extremely complex. Escapism, getting away from everyday life worries, and deriving satisfaction in doing things that we could never do in the real world are popular subjects of academic discussions surrounding video games. In MMORPGs, making a name for oneself is relatively easier than it is in the real world (though as the number of players grows each player's chances become smaller and slowly become equal to the chances we have in the "analog" world). With regard to killing a dragon with the help of the team of colleagues or friends, it is not worth mentioning at all; there is no chance of finding a dragon on the street or even when taking a drive out of town. Pleasure derived from accomplishing imaginative quests is rather obvious, but it often eclipses other important aspects of games. What I mean here is the monotonous performing of an action that can result in better indexes of the player's character. Not only in networked games but also in entertainment programs of other kinds, the users simply *work;* the game is not always easy and pleasant. Producing impressive statistics through burdensome training (which often consists in nothing but the boring clicking of the same mouse button or the carrying of out simple commands) has little in common with an idealized exploration of what happens to us in our everyday life. As one can see, the efforts put into the development of a game character do not necessarily need to be the opposite of what happens to us in everyday life. Even worse, it often happens in games that we encounter things we would not want to do every day, and yet we do them. While playing *Shenmue,* I spent a dozen or so hours on working as a forklift operator. In reality I wouldn't like to do such a monotonous thing as carrying crates. Within online games there are even more examples of repetitive and boring actions. While playing *EverQuest,* I spent long hours running around the forest and looking for some creature or artifact. It would be boring in a real life, but in the context of the game it was fun. Many games contain those dull actions that make gaming similar to living. Yet we eagerly do those boring things while playing. Why?

Contemporary people have a fascination with electronic media, something we cannot define, something that escapes our rationalizations. Referring to the notion of control does not discuss the subject utterly and comprehensively. We make the screen a fetish; we desire it, not only do we want to watch the screen but also to "be seen" on it. One could say that game activity is ineffective, as all our efforts are being transferred to an unreal world. But we also could take the opposite view: since our actions are visible on a television or computer screen, it is there where we actually act, especially because our actions on the screen are highly visible to others. It may be the effect of incessant associating with mass media; we are not only voyeurs, but we want to appear on the screen as well. Since our "window on the world" was replaced by "Windows," we ourselves want to appear on the screen. The Internet allows us to fulfill this need. To be visible means to be real. When we make ourselves visible on the screen, our "self" becomes more real. The child becomes aware of its own identity and body while it enters the mirror phase—when it sees itself. Today, the mirror is replaced with the screen. Interestingly, research shows that the statements found in the newsgroups are being constructed like those in interviews. Milena Collot and Nancy Belmore analyzed messages from the newsgroups with the help of the same method that Douglas Biber used for examining letters, academics works, and mass-media speeches.[23] Even when a message is addressed to only one person, we are aware that there are more potential observers. We feel as if we were in front of a camera; the Internet is, in a sense, like a television on which everybody can star. On the one hand, appearance on the screen is easily available. For example, when one plays MMORPGs, he or she is visible on the screens as an avatar, and everybody can buy a webcam and appear on the screen. On the other hand, by analogy with earlier, more elitist media (which are more difficult to appear in), being on the screen ennobles. All the time we have feeling (more or less true) that others are watching us. The existence of audience is an absolute necessity, we simply cannot—or choose not to—exist without it.

Against Alienation

The picture of contemporary identity that is presented by postmodern theory and networked games seems to be negative; according to it, we deal with a completely perfect eradication of most frames traditionally normalizing our life. The possibility to negotiate our "self" minimizes the control that social institutions wield over human beings. It does not need to mean chaos, but on the contrary, it can mean liberation. I would also like to stress that treating new media as the crowning achievement of escapist tendencies ubiquitous in the pop culture may be wrong. Perhaps the converse is true; avatars are not an escape from our "self," they are, rather, a longed-for chance of expressing ourselves beyond physical limitations, they are a postmodern dream being materialized. On reflection, it becomes obvious that computers are a modern technology that help people build up close relations. Thus, is it a hindrance that the close relations they build are in virtual space, in media-instrumented electronic communication? The contemporary theory of communication removes all doubts—we use media not only for the playing of video games but also during many of our life activities. We cannot, or rather choose not to, live without television, telephones, and e-mail anymore. . . . That is why the dissemination of new ways of thinking which make the real and the virtual worlds equal, is only a matter of time. As shown by the above text, video games, and especially networked games, are one of the most accurate metaphors of contemporary life. Games are the medium that most perfectly describe our existence and express the way the human "self" functions in the contemporary world. It is on the screen that we can present our hyper-identity in the most imposing way. Thanks to computer networks, we have the possibility to freely form our "self" as well as the network-instrumented process of communication with other people. We watch them on the screen, but they see us there as well; thus do we make the television-era fantasies come true. The combination of all these features was impossible for earlier media, and only such a combination can fully express the complexity of processes ruling the life of postindustrial societies. The identity we use in MMORPGs is another incarnation of contemporary man, the one incarnation that dominates the others. What is this superiority? Having a free hand when creating our own images is a commonly-accepted convention in Internet, but not in the offline world; or, rather, not yet, because the future belongs to interactive media and hyperidentity. From the player's point of view, the question "Are we still in the game?" at the end of the David Cronenberg's movie *eXistenZ* is not so disturbing anymore. It seems to be a rhetorical question.

Notes

1. Jay David Bolter, *Turing's Man: Western Culture in the Computer Age* (Chapel Hill: University of North Carolina Press, 1984).
2. Sherry Turkle, *Life on the Screen: Identity in the Age of the Internet* (New York: Touchstone, 1997), 18.
3. Howard Rheingold, *The Virtual Community* (1993). Electronic version available online at <http://www.rheingold.com/vc/book/intro.html>.
4. See: "Tall men and slim women earn more," *BBC News*, 24 November, 2000. Available online at <http://news.bbc.co.uk/2/hi/uk_news/1038531.stm>; and "Shorter Men Earn Less Money in Careers," *Cosmiverse.com* (April 19, 2002). Available online at <http://www.cosmiverse.com/news/science/science04190206.html>.
5. Elizabeth Reid, "Text-based Virtual Realities: Identity and the Cyborg Body," in *Cultural Formations in Text-Based Virtual Realities* (Ph.D. Thesis, University of Melbourne, 1994): 75–95. Available online at <http://www.rochester.edu/College/FS/Publications/ReidIdentity.html>.
6. Haya Bechar-Israeli, "From <Bonehead> to <cLoNehEAd>: Nicknames, play and identity on Internet relay chat," (Play and Performance in Computer Mediated-Communicaton) *Journal of Computer-Mediated Communication* 2, no 1 (1995). Available online at <http://www.ascusc.org/jcmc/vol1/issue2/bechar.html>.
7. Margaret Morse, "What Do Cyborgs Eat? Oral Logic in an Information Society," in *Culture on the Brink: Ideologies of Technology*, ed. Gretchen Bender and Timothy Duckrey (Seattle: Bay Press, 1994).

8.   Edward Castronova, "Virtual Worlds: A First-Hand Account of Market and Society on the Cyberian Frontier," *CESifo Working Paper Series* (December 2001): 16. Available online at <http://papers.ssrn.com/sol3/papers.cfm?abstract_id=294828>.

9.   Roger Caillois, *Gry i ludzie,* trans. Anna Tatarkiewicz and Maria Zurowska (Warszawa: Volumen, 1997), 113.

10.   Zygmunt Bauman, *Dwa szkice o moralnosci ponowoczesnej* (Warszawa: Instytut Kultury, 1994).

11.   Valerie Hannah, "Switching on Teleworking," *The Electronic Herald,* April 10, 2002. Available online at <http://www.theherald.co.uk/business/archive/10-4-19102-0-9-52.html>.

12.   "Kofi Annan in the fall of 2000 commissioned a global survey of citizens' opinions in the world, which showed that two thirds of citizens in the world did not consider themselves represented by their governments. And this was also true for the advanced democracies, the United States and others, with the only exception being the Scandinavian democracies." Harry Kreisler, "Identity and Change in the Network Society: Conversation with Manuel Castells," *Conversation with History* (Institute of International Studies, UC Berkeley, May 9, 2001). Available online at <http://globetrotter.berkeley.edu/people/Castells/castells-con5.html>.

13.   Jean Baudrillard, *Le Paroxyste indifférent* (Paris: Grasset, 1997).

14.   Peter Wagner, *A Sociology of Modernity. Liberty and Discipline* (London: Routlege, 1996), 165.

15.   Manuel Castells, "Materials for an Exploratory Theory of the Network Society," *British Journal of Sociology* 51, no 1 (January/March 2000) : 5-24. Available online at <http://sociology.berkeley.edu/public_sociology/castells.pdf>.

16.   Chris Barker, *Cultural Studies: Theories and Practice* (London: Sage, 2000), 170.

17.   Gilles Deleuze and Félix Guattari, *Mille plateaux* (Paris: Éditions de Minuit, 1980).

18.   David Gauntlett, "Anthony Giddens: The theory of structuration," extract of *Media, Gender and Identity: An Introduction* (London and New York: Routledge, 2002). Available online at <http://www.theory.org.uk/giddens2.htm>.

19.   Quoted in Turkle, *Life on the Screen,* 257.

20.   As I've already mentioned, according to the modern paradigm, the distortion of identity's stability is considered to be mental illness. In postmodern theory the polymorphous identity is regarded as the most advisable.

21.   Tomasz Grzegorek, "Tozsamosc a poczucie tozsamosci. Proba uporzadkowania problematyki," in *Tozsamosc czlowieka,* ed. Anna Galdowa (Krakow: Wydawnictwo Uniwersytetu Jagiellonskiego, 2000), 61.

22.   Janet H. Murray, *Hamlet on the Holodeck* (Cambridge, MA: MIT Press, 2000), 110.

23.   Milena Collot and Nancy Belmore, "Electronic Language: A New Variety of English," in *Computer-mediated communication: linguistic, social and cross-cultural perspectives,* ed. Susan C. Herring (Amsterdam: John Benjamins Publishing Company, 1996), 13–28.

CHAPTER 5

Playing at Being
Psychoanalysis and the Avatar

BOB REHAK

Christian Metz, writing of the psychodynamic effects at work in cinema reception, observes that film is like the "primordial mirror"—the original instance in which subjects are constituted through identification with their own image—in every way but one. Although on the cinema screen "everything may come to be projected, there is one thing and one thing only that is never reflected in it: the spectator's own body."[1] Because processes of identification are clearly involved in film viewing, and yet the cinema screen fails to "offer the spectator its *own* body with which to identify as an object,"[2] Metz is forced to distinguish between primary (ongoing) and secondary (intermittent) identifications with, respectively, the camera that records a given scene and the human actors that appear within the field of vision.

But the application of psychoanalytic theory to technological mediations of identity is surely both simplified—in one obvious sense—and complicated in unexpected ways when it comes to figures that appear on screen in place of, indeed as direct *extensions* of, the spectator: sites of continuous identification within a diegesis.[3] The video game avatar, presented as a human player's double, merges spectatorship and participation in ways that fundamentally transform both activities. Yet film theory, particularly the psychoanalytic turn popularized by the journal *Screen* in the 1970s, offers one productive way to understand the processes of subjectivization from which video games derive their considerable hold on our eyes, thumbs, and wallets.

The recourse to film theory also seems logical given the accelerating convergence between video games and certain movie genres—science fiction, action, and horror—notably in the registers of thematics (similar storylines and dramatic exigencies), aesthetics (lighting, camera angles, and conventions of mise-en-scène, as well as the use of narrative space and nondiegetic music), and visual traces of the cinematic apparatus itself (the simulation of lens flares and motion blur, for example). Video games *remediate* cinema; that is, they demonstrate the propensity of emerging media forms to pattern themselves on the characteristic behaviors and tendencies of their predecessors.[4] That video games are starting to resemble movies more than they do "real life" suggests that games, as a cultural form, are produced and consumed in phenomenological accord with preexisting technologies of representation. At the same time, video games plainly rework the formulas of cinema—and spectatorship—in ways that demand addressing.

The traditional first-person shooter (FPS) organizes its user interface around a software-simulated "camera" that, in the game's representational system, serves double duty as a body situated within the diegesis. The avatar's navigation of "contested spaces"[5] and its often violent interactions with other avatars (either human- or computer-controlled) generate the narrative-strategic pleasures of the video game experience. But the crucial relationship in many games—both contemporary standards like the *Quake* series (1996–1999) and its ancestors from the 1960s and 1970s such as *Spacewar!, Space Invaders,* and *Battlezone*—is not between avatar and environment or even between protagonist and antagonist, but between the human player and the image of him- or herself encountered onscreen.

Often collapsed in discussions of virtual reality (VR) to a transparent, one-to-one correspondence, players actually exist with their avatars in an unstable dialectic whose essential heterogeneity should not be elided. Players experience games through the exclusive intermediary of another—the avatar—the "eyes," "ears," and "body" of which are components of a complex technological and psychological apparatus. Just as one does not unproblematically equate a glove with the hand inside it, we should not presume the subjectivity produced by video games or other implementations of VR to transparently correspond to, and thus substitute for, the player's own (although it is precisely this presumption that appears necessary to secure and maintain a sense of immersion in "cyberspace"). To blur the distinction between players and their game-generated subjectivities is to bypass pressing questions of ideological mystification and positioning inherent to interactive technologies of the imaginary.[6]

Jacques Lacan's account of the mirror stage constitutes an entry point to this investigation of the ways in which video games "reflect" players back to themselves. Whereas first-person shooters remain the clearest example of the suturing effects of interactive technologies, it is helpful to consider how avatars first came into being as a defining component of such technologies, long before the advent of hardware and software required for the simulation of embodiment in three-dimensional spaces. This abbreviated history therefore touches on key moments of avatarial "evolution" (in games such as *Spacewar!, Space Invaders, Pac-Man, Battlezone, Myst,* and *Quake*) in order to build a case that models of identification and discursive address derived from film theory sharpen our understanding of video games as powerful interpellative systems with profound implications for subjects—and subjectivity—in densely mediated societies.

As described by Lacan[7] and elaborated by Samuel Weber,[8] the mirror stage occurs in human infants between the ages of six and eighteen months, when they first encounter and respond to their own reflection as an aspect of themselves. Unlike other animals, which rapidly lose interest in mirrored surfaces, the human infant seems engrossed, and commences a kind of gleeful experimentation:

> A series of gestures . . . in which he experiences in play the relation between the movements assumed in the image and the reflected environment, and between this virtual complex and the reality it reduplicates—the child's own body, and the persons or things, around him.[9]

Lacan stresses two important aspects of this "jubilant assumption" of the image. First, it precipitates the "I" or ego within a symbolic matrix, producing for the child a perception of itself as observing individual and sign in a differential series of signs. Second, it is a *taking-place* (in that phrase's full meaning) in which the infant, at that point mostly helpless and unable to control its body, responds to the attraction of unity, wholeness, and power promised by the reflected form. For Lacan, this move is at heart a mistake or misrecognition, permanently dividing one from oneself as sign and referent are divided:

> The important point is that this form situates the agency of the ego, before its social determination, in a fictional direction, which will always remain irreducible for the individual alone, or rather, which will only rejoin the coming-into-being (*le devenir*) of the subject asymptotically, whatever the success of the dialectical syntheses by which he must resolve as *I* his discordance with his own reality.[10]

The ego formed through identification with a reflection or representation of itself is thus forever split, rendered incomplete by the very distinction that enables self-recognition. The subject that comes into being stands in sharp contrast to the Renaissance category of the unitary self: a stable, autonomous individual, capable of accessing all truth through reason and possessing "a human essence that remains untouched by historical or cultural circumstances."[11] Indeed, the split subject goes through life alienated from itself and its needs, endlessly seeking in external resources the "lost object" (*objet petit a*) from which it was initially severed—an object that "derives its value from its identification with some missing component of the subject's self, whether that loss is seen as primordial, as the result of a bodily organization, or as the consequence of some other division."[12]

In his reading of Lacan, Weber emphasizes the fundamentally *aggressive* nature of the child's assumption of the image: "The ego comes to be by taking the place of the imaginary other."[13] The roles of *self* and *other* take on a paradoxical or mutually contradictory quality; each contests its counterpart's privileged wholeness even as it depends on the counterpart to confirm those qualities. The reflected image must be recognizably related to the physical body in order to maintain the image's fascination—a requirement that may necessitate willful misrecognition. "The ego is thus initially constituted through the child's identification with an image whose otherness is precisely overlooked in the observation of similarity."[14] Yet in order for the image to function as a projective ideal, it must ultimately resist or thwart that similarity: "Despite the effort to ignore it . . . such alterity can never be entirely effaced, since it is what permits the identification to take place."[15]

The formation of identity through dialectical synthesis, then, conceives subjectivity as a tense, oscillatory motion toward and away from the other: a process in which first originating consciousness and then idealized reflection are alternately embraced and rejected. Furthermore, this "fictional" aspect of the ego is not just an originary instance—the installation of an "I" remaining stable thereafter—but a gesture of maintenance, opening notes of a discordant melody that will play throughout the subject's life.

> The *stade du miroir* is thereby defined not primarily as a genetic moment, but rather as a *phase* and as a turning-point or trope, destined to be repeated incessantly, in accordance with a schema whose moments are inadequacy, anticipation, and defensive armoring, and whose result is an identity that is not so much *alienated* as *alienating*, caught up in "the inexhaustible squaring of its own vicious circle of ego-confirmations."[16]

The video game avatar would seem to meet the criteria of Lacan's *objet petit a*. Appearing on screen in place of the player, the avatar does double duty as self and other, symbol and index. As *self*, its behavior is tied to the player's through an interface (keyboard, mouse, joystick): its literal motion, as well as its figurative triumphs and defeats, result from the player's actions. At the same time, avatars are unequivocally *other*. Both limited and freed by difference from the player, they can accomplish more than the player alone; they are supernatural ambassadors of agency.

But most significant (and often overlooked thanks to the event's ubiquity), avatars differ from us through their ability to *live, die, and live again.* Their bodies dissolve in radioactive slime or explode into a mist of blood and bone fragments, only to reappear, unscathed, at the click of a mouse. In terms of extradiegetic frame—the apparatus of software, operating system, and computer hardware—avatars are "killed" and "resurrected" with the flick of a power switch or the selection of a QUIT command on the File menu.[17] Rapid-fire representations of violence and death in video games, and the formal mechanisms by which avatars can be paused, erased, or restarted, are necessary moments in a cycle of symbolic rebirth: a staging, *within* technology, of the player's own "vicious circle of ego-confirmation."

In a specifically agential sense, avatars reduplicate and render in visible form their players' actions—they complete an arc of desire. This relationship is evident from the outset of video games in the linkage of players with avatars of spaceships, tanks, even ping-pong paddles. The emergence in recent games of simulated first-person perspectives, graphically sophisticated bodies, and camera movement suggesting corporeal presence underscores an obsessive concern with the avatar's function as acting stand-in for the player.

But the long history of video games also makes clear that there is no perfectly "reflective" avatar, that is, one that resembles the player visually and (in the fashion of a real mirror) seems to gaze back on him or her.[18] If the avatar is a reflection, its correspondence to embodied reality consists of a mapping not of *appearance* but of *control.* Somewhat in the manner of a customer in an appliance store, who, catching sight of himself on a wall of monitors, waves his arms—"a series of gestures . . . in which he experiences in play the relation between the movements assumed in the image and the reflected environment"[19]—players pleasurably experiment with the surprising, often counterintuitive articulation between their manipulation of the interface and the avatar's obedient responses. If anything, such pleasures seem amplified by the uncanny difference between reality and reflection: an alterity enabling players both to embrace the avatar as an ideal and to reject it as an inferior other.

The avatar is not simply a means of access to desired outcomes, but an end in itself—a desired and resented lost object, existing in endless cycles of renunciation and reclamation. Willingly inverting self-other distinctions, players invest an acted-on object with the characteristics of an acting subject. That status is then rescinded in moments of avatarial rupture to prove the object's fundamental alterity and confirm, through contrast, the player's (fictive) ego unity. The contradictions opened up by this figure enhance, not detract, from gameplay, which consists—at least in part—of a toying with unstable categories of identity, presence, and subjectivity.

Contradictions in self-image opened by the avatar must be reconciled as part of the game's process. This reconciliation—the collapse of belief structures necessary to the assumption of an idealized other—takes the symptomatic form of the avatar's destruction: its fragmentation by shotgun blast or consumption by zombie. Graphic portrayals of dismemberment and death, the wounded bodies notoriously common to video games, are a mandatory punctuation to the out-of-body experience. The animated *grand guignol* shores up players' wholeness, working out in technological form our aggressive response to our reflected images, our constitutive others.[20]

Refining Our Reflections: An Avatarial History

If the release in 1992 of the first-person shooter *Wolfenstein 3D*—a game that popularized the genre's signature over-the-gun viewpoint—marked the moment at which avatarial operations matured into a formal system, the roots of avatarial fascination extend back more than forty years, to early experiments in recreational computer programming. Before we turn to an examination of the suturing and misrecognition that subtend interactive technologies of the imaginary, it may be helpful to consider how the onscreen "other" has developed over time, for avatars are shaped as much by players' psychological needs as by advances in computer hardware and software. Our search for and rejection of digital ego ideals—a search that, like desire itself, is without end—has worked in combination with technological, economic, and aesthetic factors to refine avatarial look and behavior, embroidering a diversity of game "surfaces" atop a fundamental relationship of reflection and rejection.

This very diversity renders any taxonomy of the avatar provisional at best. Therefore, my intent in delving into history is neither to recapitulate video games' development in detailed sequence, nor to represent every genre. The games discussed later in this essay mark significant junctures in avatarial operations: the first appearance, in *Spacewar!*, of avatars in the form of player-controlled icons; the shift during the dominant years of the arcade from avatars coded as mechanical to avatars coded as organic; and the ultimate emergence, with the FPS and its relatives, of realistic human(oid) avatars whose troubled relationship to players' bodies becomes the game's primary concern—and primary source of pleasure. Crucial to this evolution is the avatar's gradual but relentless acquisition of "liveliness." In appearance, movement, and character, avatars have ever more clearly come to mimic their players, developing personality, individuality, and an ability to act within the (virtual) world—as must any infant on its way to maturity.

It is also important to note the increasing *subjectivization* of video games: a move from the God's-eye perspective utilized in early games to perspectival rendering that simulates three-dimensionality, first as static scenery, then as fluidly navigable space. Avatarial operations flow from two elements that interdepend in various ways. First is the foregrounding of an onscreen body, visible in whole or in part. Second is the conceit of an offscreen but assumed body constituted through the gaze of a mobile, player-controlled camera. Differing articulations between camera-body and avatar-body lead to different, though related, modes of play and subject effects. In every case, the intent—to produce a sense of diegetic embodiment—announces itself from the dawn of video game history.

> In May 1962, at the annual MIT Open House, the hackers fed the paper tape with twenty-seven pages worth of PDP-1 assembly language code into the machine, set up an extra display screen—actually a giant oscilloscope—and ran *Spacewar!* all day to a public that drifted in and could not believe what they saw. The sight of it—a science-fiction game written by students and controlled by a computer— was so much on the verge of fantasy that no one dared predict that an entire genre of entertainment would be spawned from it.[21]

Retold with little variation across many different folk histories of the computer, the creation of *Spacewar!* has come to be viewed with a reverence befitting the Book of Genesis. Indeed, the first video game was seminal in several respects. As a "hack" of unprecedented popularity—a program whose original code, written by Steve Russell, J. M. Graetz, and others, was distributed to and modified by students and faculty at the Massachusetts Institute of Technology—*Spacewar!* exemplifies the steps by which avatarial operations—and the narrative-strategic context on which they depend—first came into being and continue to operate today. Russell, along with Alan Kotok, AI theorist Marvin Minsky, and other programmers, had developed numerous display hacks: elegant or visually impressive graphics routines. Russell, however, envisioned a more active role and rewards for the user. Building on his love of the pulp space operas published by E. E. "Doc" Smith,[22] he wanted *Spacewar!* to absorb the user in an *experiential* simulation. Russell "let his imagination construct the thrill of roaring across space in a white rocket ship . . . and wondered if that same excitement could be captured while sitting behind the console of the PDP-1."[23] Russell produced what amounted to the first avatar: an onscreen blip subject to user control, accelerating and changing direction based on toggle-switch settings. Eventually these points of light would evolve into icons of rocket ships, which, set against a starry background, engaged in warfare. Suggestive of a human ensconced within a mechanical shell, the rocket-ship imagery of the first avatars harkened to the external reality of the player seated at the terminal, hands on the controls.

Spacewar! established a set of elements vital to avatarial operations in most video games that followed:

1. Player identification with an onscreen avatar.
2. Player control of avatar through a physical interface.
3. Player-avatar's engagement with narrative-strategic constraints organizing the onscreen diegesis in terms of its (simulated) physical laws and semiotic content—the "meaning" of the game's sounds and imagery—that constitute rules or conditions of possibility governing play.
4. Imposition of extradiegetic constraints further shaping play (for example, timer, music, scorekeeping and other elements perceptible to the player but presumably not by the entity represented by the avatar; an instance of this in the relatively austere *Spacewar!* would be the software function that ended a game when one player "died").
5. Frequent breakdown and reestablishment of avatarial identification through destruction of avatar, starting or ending of individual games and tournaments, and ultimately the act of leaving or returning to the physical apparatus of the computer.

This final trait, at once the most common and least discussed dynamic of gameplay, is central to the *repetition* from which video games, perhaps more than any other medium, take their structure. Systematic rupture of the agential and identificatory linkage between players and avatars is a defining characteristic, suggesting that the mirror-image's *loss* is as vital as its acquisition. As I will discuss later in this essay, repetition is central to another aspect of psychoanalytic theory: the game of *fort/da* in which an object that "stands in" for a lost and desired other is repeatedly tossed away, retrieved, and tossed again. Sigmund Freud[24] observed that his grandson, disconsolate at being left alone by his mother, used *fort/da* to substitute an arbitrary object—a spool—for his absent caregiver, and to bring that caregiver under (symbolic) control. But this mastery, as Silverman points out, is ambiguous:

> The game through which he masters the trauma of her departures, however, proves the vehicle through which that trauma returns, now in a guise which will prove much more significant for his future history. The child puts himself in an active relation to his mother's disappearances by throwing away and then recovering the toy which is her symbolic representative, while uttering the words "*fort*" ("gone") and "*da*" ("there"). In so doing, he employs language for the first time as a differential system, and so stages the trauma of his own disappearance. His ostensible mastery is consequently based upon a radical self-loss, and upon his subordination to the order of discourse.[25]

Repetition aside, the other elements listed above characterize (with minor modifications) our engagement with computer operating systems as standardized in the WIMP (Windows-Icon-Menu-Pointer) interface developed at Xerox PARC and adopted by Apple Macintosh and Microsoft Windows. As real-time processes, video games demand continuous involvement. Players' hands are always at the joystick, mouse, or keyboard, performing actions immediately reflected in the onscreen behavior of avatarial forms. This behavior in turn creates new exigencies to which players respond. Video games from their birth depended on a particularly *reactive* programming paradigm, one that updated screen content moment to moment in response to user input.

This mode of activity, where "what happens on a computer matches the frame of reference in which human beings are actually working,"[26] inaugurated a different way of thinking the human-computer agential circuit, and influenced future development of both hardware (toward processing power for improved graphic responsiveness) and software (toward icon-based operating systems and applications organized by visual and spatial metaphor). *Spacewar!* was the first of many games that

> repurposed the mainframe and the mini[computer] as well as the desktop computer, with an implicit suggestion that gaming, or at least an immediately responsive, graphical interface, is what computing should really be about. . . . There was a vast difference between this graphic behavior and the operations of a traditional computer, which manipulated symbols and presented its results only in rows of alphanumeric characters on the screen or on perforated printer paper. The game suggested new formal and cultural purposes for digital technology.[27]

Through gaming, then, the concepts of *avatar* and *interface* became linked; part of what users seek from computers is continual response to their own actions—a *reflection* of personal agency made available onscreen for reclamation as surplus pleasure. Russell and the other *Spacewar!* programmers were among the first to bind human agency to discrete graphical bodies on the computer screen. Furthermore, the situation of those bodies within a systematic context limited, and thus helped define, their activity and purpose.[28] As an early avatarial mirror, *Spacewar!* shared with its descendants—video games as well as nonrecreational applications such as word processors and web browsers—an apparatus that directed user agency and subjectivity, creating a spectatorial/participatory relationship with onscreen traces of self.

Although rendered in text, Will Crowther and Don Wood's *Adventure* (1972–1977) marks an important movement toward the immersive mechanisms of later video games. Its themes of puzzle-solving, treasure-hunting, and interaction with fictional characters within a rule-bound otherworldly environment—as well as its branching structure of decision nodes navigated by the player—set the model for contemporary games such as *Myst* (1993) and *Half-Life* (1998). *Adventure*'s interface invited players to imagine themselves as the observing/participating "I" in an unfolding narrative and brought to gameplay a sensation of first-person experience. Produced through textual collaboration between player and program, *Adventure*'s hybrid player-avatar epitomized the simultaneous splitting/suturing at the heart of video games.

Adventure powerfully conveyed a sense of depth generated by players' exploration of fictive territory—a territory populated by creatures and objects that could be interacted with and manipulated systematically. *Adventure*'s diegesis was described in textual passages, to which the player responded with typed commands.[29]

> Computer: YOU ARE STANDING AT THE END OF A ROAD BEFORE A SMALL BRICK BUILDING. AROUND YOU IS A FOREST. A SMALL STREAM FLOWS OUT OF THE BUILDING AND DOWN A GULLY.
> Player (typing): GO SOUTH.
> Computer: YOU ARE IN A VALLEY IN THE FOREST BESIDE A STREAM TUMBLING ALONG A ROCKY BED.[30]

The sense of embodiment produced by *Adventure*'s exchanges prompts the question of who and where the player "is" within the diegesis. While screen output was usually phrased in second person ("YOU ARE IN A MAZE OF TWISTY PASSAGES, ALL ALIKE"), the grammar of the interface required imperative interjections from the player (GO EAST, EXAMINE CARPET, and so on), commands presumably addressed to an implied intermediary body: a textual avatar. In one sense, this differs only slightly from the procedure that vision-based games use to map players' positions. For example, a subroutine might generate the sign-of-the-player at a particular set of screen coordinates ("YOU ARE OUTSIDE A HOUSE"); the player then nudges the joystick ("GO EAST"); a subroutine reads the signal from the input device and redraws the sign-of-the-player an inch to the left ("YOU ARE INSIDE A HOUSE").

This breakdown reveals a shared workload between player and computer: a halved (or doubled) agency undercutting the apparent unity that encourages imaginary investment in avatarial bodies and perspectives. As I will argue later, the discursive gaps opened in *Adventure*'s interface—and, by extension, any interface—seem to beckon us as unique individuals. Imagining ourselves as the addressee of the computer screen's discourse, the "I" misrecognizing itself in the computer's "YOU," is part of video games' lure, as programmer Roberta Williams discovered in her first encounter with *Adventure* more than a decade after the game appeared:

> From the moment [she] tentatively poked GO EAST she was totally and irrevocably hooked. . . . She would be up until four in the morning, trying to figure out how to get around the damn snake to get to the giant clams. And then she

would sit up in bed thinking, *What didn't I do? What else could I have done? Why couldn't I open that stupid clam? What's in it?*[31]

In his analysis of the sim (simulation) game genre, Ted Friedman locates within the human-machine collaboration a cybernetic circuit "in which the line demarcating the end of the player's consciousness and the beginning of the computer's world blurs."[32] This blurring constitutes an effacement of self, in that agency is simultaneously diluted by being transferred to a mechanical other, and amplified in resulting onscreen behavior. Construction of an office building, slaying of a monster, casting a magic spell: these achievements are only experientially possible (for the meager price of a mouse click) within the game diegesis. Friedman labels this "strange sense of self-dissolution"[33] both a denial of one's own material existence and a seductive generator of new perspectives: effectively a cyborg consciousness that identifies with the computer.[34]

The 1970s saw the rise of arcades as popular entertainment venues in the United States and Japan. During a decade that began with the placement of the first dedicated cabinet or arcade machines in bars and pinball parlors and the subsequent founding of Atari by Nolan Bushnell in 1972, video games and the social contexts in which they were played underwent rapid change, with corresponding alterations of both diegetic and avatarial content. *PONG* (a hit when released in 1972) sold players brief sessions of head-to-head combat for a quarter a turn. Because of limitations of integrated-circuit technology—the first game to use a dedicated microprocessor, Midway's *Gun Fight*, didn't appear until 1975—single-player games were rare; technology and aesthetic trends had yet to reach the point where a "machine enemy" could take on individuals.

One exception was *Breakout*, an Atari product designed for solo play. *Breakout* was essentially *PONG* turned on its side; a paddle at the bottom of the screen deflected a bouncing ball into rows of bricks hovering above. Like *PONG*, *Breakout* offered little in the way of embodiment; yet its rudimentary interface held a certain fascination, as David Sudnow attests:

> The *Breakout* hand doesn't move a paddle freely among all facets of bodily space and surroundings. It encircles the knob, to be sure, but all actions transmit back and forth between the mere surface of things. I look down and watch my fingers quickly adjusting the control, the shot made to happen with superrapid, flexible-looking motion. But it's as if the fullness of things, and of myself, has been strangely halved. I could even say that I wasn't so much interfaced on screen as I was "interpictured" there.[35]

The lack of a computer-controlled other changed in 1978, when Midway unveiled its version of Taito's *Space Invaders*. Refashioning the bricks of *Breakout* into rows of insectoid or skull-like aliens ("invaders" of a formerly safe recreational "space"), the game imbued computer-controlled avatars with militaristic malevolence. Players steered a gun platform—an armed version of *PONG*'s paddle—from side to side, firing up at the descending aliens. It is difficult to say whether the gun's blunt utility as a representation of self, the leering faces of the invaders, or some combination of both, were responsible for the game's hold on the public imagination, but something certainly spoke to audiences; only a year after its introduction, there were 350,000 *Space Invaders* cabinets worldwide, 55,000 in the United States alone.[36] In addition, the game's popularity spurred sales of Atari's VCS 2600, a console system designed to be hooked to a television, bringing *Space Invaders* into the home—a second invasion, this time of domestic, and to that point uncomputerized, space.

The game's aliens, with their oversized heads, small legs, and disproportionately large faces, were, for the player, plainly "not-I," but in another sense they were the player-avatar inverted—in the spatial coordinates of the screen as well as the flipped ethical map of their destructive agency. *Space Invaders*' introduction of nonhuman others restructured screen identity, disarticulating avatarial forms from material bodies and shifting the mode of consumption from two-player dyads to solitary space. Although the aliens always began the game moving in collective lockstep, each was potentially capable of surviving as an individual to the end, racing across the screen and dropping bombs. This implacable purposefulness modeled for players an ideally tireless, ever accelerating style of play—which the computer, of course, always finally won. At the same time, there was pleasure in defeat by *Space Invaders* and similar games structured around ever-faster enemies: surrender to the inevitable as opposing forces finally reached overwhelming intensity. *Missile Command* (1980), an Atari game in which players defended cities against nuclear assault, was capable of prompting euphoria as the mushroom clouds bloomed.[37]

> You knew that you were gonna die, that you were within seconds of everything going black. . . . You're dying. You're dead. And then you get to watch all the pretty explosions. And after the fireworks display, you get to press the restart button, and you're alive again, until the next collision with your own mortality. You're not just playing with colored light. You're playing with the concept of death.[38]

This aspect of gameplay—the simulated experience of death and resurrection—is a key function of the avatar, one that would become more explicit as avatarial forms metamorphosed from the crosshairs, spaceships, and missile bases of the late 1970s to the "living" bodies of the early 1980s.

The commercial space of the arcade—whose darkened interiors were raucous with robotic sounds and strobe-lit by video explosions—was like a large-scale, physical analog of video games themselves. Indeed, many games that appeared between 1978 and 1984 shared thematic elements that could be taken as ironic commentary on the arcade environment: *Asteroids, Defender, Centipede, Missile Command, Galaxian, Star Castle, Tempest, Qix*, and *Zaxxon* all featured claustrophobic diegeses filled with deadly obstacles in constant motion. Player-avatars had to maneuver safely through this maze of shifting spatial relationships, a task not unlike that faced by individuals in a crowded arcade.

The threat in most of these games was impersonal, often automated assault. In *Asteroids*, the danger was posed by a colliding field of rocks, though flying saucers intermittently appeared to fire upon the player. *Centipede*'s eponymous peril was a segmented insect that, vivisected by the player's weapon, would merely continue its attack on separate fronts. Against such tireless synthetic threats, a player was only as good as his or her gun; indeed, collapsed by avatarial synecdoche, a player-avatar *was* the gun.

This began to change with the arrival of Namco's *Pac-Man* (1980), which dispensed with mechanistic signs of gun and spaceship, embodying players instead as a round yellow "voracious dot."[39] The avatar's organic status was marked by its color as well as by its only feature, a gaping mouth whose obvious function was as consumptive orifice. Rather than spitting dots, Pac-Man—the game's title designated the avatarial protagonist rather than the villain to be defeated—endlessly absorbed them, a reversal in thematic focus from anal expulsion to oral incorporation.

> Before this epoch-making game, the player controlled spaceships, gun turrets, or other mechanical devices. Suddenly, though, the player of *Pac-Man* controlled a *being:* an animated, eating thing. The game's designer, Toru Iwatani, says that he got the idea for Pac-Man's form after eating a slice of pizza, and seeing the shape that was left.[40]

The Pac-Man avatar semiotically collapsed *subject* (a thing that eats) with *object* (a thing that is eaten) to constitute a closed circuit of desire. Equally important, the body acquired its signification through a missing part ("the shape that was left"); Pac-Man was recognizable *as* Pac-Man because of what was excluded from its form. This pie-slice absence also structured Pac-Man's agency within the game, its ceaseless voracity. Like the player for whom it stood in, Pac-Man was never at rest within its infinite progression of mazes, consuming dots—his own *objets a*, frail reflections, perhaps, of an eternally missing slice.

Atari's *Battlezone* (1980), while not the first video game to shift camera position from an elevated, omniscient viewpoint to a gaze located at eye level—sports and racing games had experimented with this throughout the 1970s—did originate first-person perspective. *Battlezone* situated the player behind the controls of a tank capable of movement, allowing players to change their perspective at will by driving through an environment rendered in green vector wireframes. The game thus created a dual sense of enclosure: immersing players not only in an artificial world (a desert patrolled by enemy tanks and hunter-killer satellites), but in an artificial vehicle capable of free navigation.

Battlezone's graphic conceit would be repeatedly copied, adapted, and refined by its descendants, culminating in the FPS. By locating players at the still center of a world that seems to pirouette around them, subjective-viewpoint displays blend enclosure and embodiment, implying the existence of a body—logically and physiologically associated with the presence of eyes and ears at a specific set of coordinates—as it simultaneously feeds players sensory imagery of created environments. The shift *Battlezone* signaled is like the introduction of perspective in post-Renaissance painting, which gave

> landscapes their formal focus in the human figures in them. The paired tech-niques involve the creation of a dreamscape, and the provision of figures for identification that call the viewer to enter fictive space, changing with their movements, inviting their co-authorship. They are fundamentally navigable.[41]

An *Adventure*-like meander over deserted islands in multiple "ages," *Myst* (1993) substituted ray-traced scenes of near-photographic quality for the descriptive textual passages of its predecessor. Yet, *Myst* emulated *Adventure* in fundamental ways, including a puzzle format, absence of explicit instruc-tions, and an emphasis on spatial exploration over linear plot development. In addition to the still frames that parceled out the island topography, *Myst* used ambient sound effects to deepen the player's sense of immersion: wind whistling through trees, waves washing up on shore, and mechanical objects that whirred and clicked. The game also made use of nondiegetic music, the equivalent of a movie soundtrack, to build suspense or indicate proximity to clues.[42]

Just as *Myst* formally combined old and new media—"three-dimensional, static graphics with text, digital video, and sound to refashion illusionistic painting, film, and, somewhat surprisingly, the book as well"[43]—its diegesis involved the superimposition of two sets of events. The first, an Oedipal struggle[44] between a father and two sons, was over before the game even began: buried in the past, this conflict drove the second, contemporary sequence of the player's point-and-click search for clues, the successful assembly of which rendered the fragmented back story comprehensible, solving the mystery. The subject position offered to players was that of pri-vate detective in a "whodunit,"[45] ironically gesturing toward the subjective point-of-view (POV) experiments of *film noir* that presented the detective as scientist/voyeur.[46]

Most striking to many was the eerie sense of stillness and solitude produced by *Myst*'s interface, which lacked visible avatarial forms. Players moved through the diegesis as though watching a slide show, clicking at the borders of each image to choose where they would go next. The only mark of this control onscreen was a cursor in the shape of a pointing hand. Omitting representations of the body in favor of a single, stylized point of control, *Myst*'s interface epitomized the "tourist mouse" aesthetic[47] in which access to the computer's imaginary takes the form of a restless search for "an impossibly pristine discovery"[48]—the pursuit of an object to fill an essential lack.

> The cursor as perpetual tourist meanders through a landscape which is always foreign, in which it seeks perpetually a home that it will recognize less by identification than by an impossible welcome which its denizens will give it. . . . The impossibility of this quest derives from the tourist's fate: always to be seeking to arrive, not "here," but "there."[49]

For some, *Myst*'s appeal was less in its puzzles than in its ability to transport players to a detailed environment; the game was "a grand exercise in virtual tourism."[50] At the same time, technological limitations made both an onscreen body and fluid navigation unfeasible; other subjective-viewpoint games of the period, like *Wolfenstein 3D* (1992), could not approach the rich level of detail offered by *Myst*. The avatarial point of presence consisted of *Myst*'s relatively inflexible camera, an apparatus that produced a corresponding sense of ghostliness for the player. Able to observe with relative freedom and work small-scale effects on the environment—opening books, turning knobs, pressing buttons—players were nonetheless barred from the (illusory) corporeality afforded by avatars in later games. The result was a diegesis in which the player could not die and was at risk of little more than frustration.

Id Software, responsible for the archetypal "shoot-'em-up"s *Wolfenstein 3D* and *Doom*, refined the FPS formula further with the launch of the *Quake* series in 1996. Incorporating both a single-player mode and multiplayer or deathmatch scenarios, *Quake* emphasized the avatar's physical boundaries and tolerances, subjecting it to near-continuous assault from environmental forces. The multiple diegeses of *Quake*—a game now in its third official iteration, not including expansion packages or countless player-created levels—have successively stripped away the trappings of narrative, leaving only a plot based on the protection and loss of bodily integrity. *Quake III: Arena* (1999) was geared solely around deathmatch battles, with an option for solo players to train against bots: artificially intelligent avatars.

The *Quake* avatar, represented on screen by a gun-holding hand, could be customized through the use of "skins" to have different appearances in the virtual environment of networked play. Players cloaked themselves as men, women, cyborgs, demons, and cartoon characters, and other guises, suggesting that, in the contemporary FPS, visibility is the first order of interaction. Avatars both *see* and are *seen*; as seer, players

> are called on to conduct an ongoing surveillance. They are assigned explicitly or implicitly the role of security guards, whose simple task is to shoot anything that appears threatening. Because the ultimate threat is that the enemy will destroy the equilibrium of the system and eventually halt the game by destroying the player himself, the player must constantly scan the visual field and direct his fire appropriately.[51]

An inverse logic, of course, applies to the body as *seen*—the avatarial extension that enables players' presence within the game also places them at the focus of the other's destructive surveillance. Constituted through a routinized, ceaseless hunt with violence an inevitable endpoint, the player-avatar bears authority's gaze even as he or she is disciplined by it.

Yet, in *Quake* and its ilk, the avatar's visual attributes were overshadowed by its somatic character, a "material" vulnerability conveyed through multiple codes of representation. Players heard their own avatars' footfalls and breathing. Collision detection bounced avatars off walls and forced them into crouching or crawling positions to enter tight spaces. Forces of gravity prevented avatars from jumping too high, and made falls from a sufficient distance lethal. Impact wounds were signaled by a shaking of the camera coupled with the sound effect of a groan or gasp, and a corresponding loss of health points (replenished by running over "medkits," white crates iconically labeled with a red cross). As avatarial damage mounted, players watched their own blood spray; "death" was signified by a toppling of the avatarial camera, which lay motionless—but still feeding visual and auditory information to the screen—until reborn with a mouse click.

As this brief survey shows, video games have evolved toward ever more complex simulations of corporeal immersion, subsuming economic, social, and technological determinants under an overarching goal: to confront players with detailed and lifelike "doubles." As the avatar took on character, history, and presence within increasingly detailed story worlds, the coded representation of sensory immersion epitomized by the FPS brought video games into dialogue with the dominant representational system of Hollywood filmmaking. In multiple ways—from the simulation of first-person perspective to the illusory wholeness that editing conventions offer the spectator—video games and movies invite comparison.

The Speaking Mirror: Video Games and Cinema

If the pleasures of the video game stem as much from avatarial "reflection" as from narrative and strategic engagement with its diegesis, then spectatorship is clearly central to the form. As we play we also watch ourselves play; video games are by turns, and even simultaneously, participatory and spectatorial. Thus it is more accurate, or at least more inclusive, to speak of the *avatarial relation*: a "structure of seeing" in which the subject, acting on its desire to see itself as other, pursues its reflection in the imaginary like a cat chasing its tail.

The study of cinema has been informed in multiple ways by psychoanalytic insight into the role played by vision—looking as well as being looked at—in the inscription of sexual difference and power.[52] In addition, much attention has been given to the ways in which the material apparatus of camera/projector and stylistic devices of editing and narrative operate, with varying degrees of effectiveness, to produce a coherent space of reception for the viewing subject.[53] In order to analyze related effects on subjectivity in video games, I touch on two aspects of film theory. First, the use of subjective POV to create a newly participatory role for the spectator; and second, the concept of interpellation and its function, within discourse, in constructing apparently unified subject positions.

In any application to one medium of theory developed for another, care must be taken to distinguish the codes organizing each. The FPS borrows certain aspects of cinematic storytelling, most explicitly the tracking POV shot, but makes little use, at least while players are controlling the avatar, of editing or montage in a traditional sense.[54] Rarely, for example, do conventional video games rely extensively on shot-reverse-shot constructions, which counterpose two images—a viewed object, person, or scene and a corresponding image of a viewing subject—to create for spectators the illusion of a contiguous space which they inhabit as an invisible presence. Crucial to the account of suture advanced by Jean-Pierre Oudart and Daniel Dayan,[55] the subject position created through shot-reverse-shot is replaced in the FPS by a camera simulated through software rendering of three-dimensional spaces. Individual control over this camera's behavior—its ability to tilt, pan, track, even climb ladders and descend staircases at the behest of the player—literalizes the conceit of an embodied diegetic participant that cinema, because of its material technologies, can only imply. The FPS's direct (visual) address, updated in real time, presents one ongoing and unbroken half of the shot-reverse-shot construction, enabling a snug fit between the player and his or her game-produced subjectivity.

As an example of film's failure to convincingly assert the embodiment that avatars routinely generate, it is instructive to consider Robert Montgomery's *film noir* experiment *Lady in the Lake* (1947), which exemplifies the costs of truly subjective narration. *Lady in the Lake* takes as its narrative and formal task the construction of a seamless subjective and embodied POV. As private eye Philip Marlowe, actor-director Robert Montgomery makes only desultory appearances on screen, directly addressing the audience to introduce the story and provide updates on its progress, or appearing as a reflection in the many mirrors sprinkled throughout the film's locations. The majority of his role, however, is "performed" by a camera whose diegetically situated look we are meant to adopt as at once Marlowe's and our own.

What follows is an experience that audiences and critics found more exasperating than engrossing. Some rejected the story as "an insipid anecdote that would not have required any innovation to be developed adequately,"[56] but most criticized the subjective camera itself as an awkward gimmick, the technological limitations of which nullified its ability to substitute for a novelistic "I."

> There is therefore a misinterpretation here which fails to understand that it is not at the place of the subject that the camera operates, but at the place of the Other. . . . We cannot identify with someone whose face is always hidden from us. And if we cannot identify ourselves, we cannot share the anxieties of the character. In a thriller this can become rather annoying.[57]

Underlying many reactions of the time, however, is an acknowledgment that subjective narration through the simulation of first-person presence is a desirable goal, even a workable one if the technique were appropriately modified—by taking into account, for example, that the human eye discards extraneous detail when looking at an image, or that our attentiveness to scenic elements is determined as much by affective interest as by optical properties. This suggests an implicit endorsement of narrative immersion and embodiment as a pleasurable frontier for the spectator; indeed, some critical rhetoric prefigures the current hyperbole surrounding video games and other interactive technologies of the imaginary:

> The subjective camera can explore subtleties of experience hitherto unimaginable as film content. As the new technique can clearly express almost any facet of everyday human experience, its development should presage a new type of psychological film in which the camera will reveal the human mind, not superficially, but honestly in terms of image and sound . . . permitting the audience to see a human being both as others see him and as he sees himself.[58]

Hyperbolic dreams of "psychological film" aside, Montgomery's failed attempt to subjectivize cinema bears examining, for it points the way toward a broader agenda of particularized embodiment realized more than forty years later in the FPS. While *Lady in the Lake*'s first-person camera amounted to little more than tiresome artifice, its later mobilization in video games attests to the technique's effectiveness when transferred to a medium offering greater interactivity.

According to Lacan, the ego produced through identification with an image attains its entry into language and meaning at the price of determination/domination by the governing symbolic order. Social theorists, notably Louis Althusser,[59] have linked this alienation and the psychic mis-recognition on which it is based to ideological forces that reproduce them-selves through naturalization in discourse and self-image. For Althusser, subjectivity is shaped, even generated, by social institutions and processes, acting through systems of signification that supply individuals with their identifications.

In the 1970s, cinema came under investigation as one of the social tech-nologies included in Althusser's account of the ideological state apparatus (ISA). This critique studied cinema as a signifying system that produces specific ideological effects by positioning its spectators as the understood subjects of screen discourse. The constructed quality of this discourse, in turn, is made invisible through the same effects—for example, shot-reverse-shot constructions, discussed above, are central to the suture by which spec-tators are "stitched into" the signifying chain through edits that articulate a plenitude of observed space to an observing character. This onscreen figure, presented as author/owner of the gaze, serves also as identificatory site for the spectator willing

> to become absent to itself by permitting a fictional character to "stand in" for it, or by allowing a particular point of view to define what it sees. The operation of suture is successful at the moment that the viewing subject says, "Yes, that's me," or "That's what I see."[60]

Suture's coercive effects consist precisely in "persuading the viewer to ac-cept certain cinematic images as an accurate reflection of his or her sub-jectivity . . . it does this *transparently* (i.e. it conceals the apparatuses of enunciation)."[61]

While the frustrations of extended first-person POV in cinema have been noted, fewer pitfalls occur in video games that operate according to a similar code of signification. The game apparatus—a software engine that renders three-dimensional spaces from an embodied perspective, directed in real time by players through a physical interface—achieves what the cinematic apparatus cannot: a sense of literal presence, and a newly participatory role, for the viewer. Yet the question of ideological positioning is as pertinent to this new medium as it is to cinema. More so, in fact, because of video games' amplified effect on subjectivity and corresponding elision of authorship. The film spectator's role as an implied observer of narrative events—an "absent one" flickering ghostlike through the diegesis, positioned anew from shot to shot—is concretized in the video game imaginary through the figure of the avatar, a "present one" standing in for the player, who chooses the path of the camera-body with apparent freedom. The disavowal necessary to gameplay is like the "Yes, that's what I see" of successful cinematic suture, but goes further: it is "Yes, that's what I *do*."

Interfaces, then, are ideological. They work to remove themselves from awareness, seeking transparency—or at least unobtrusiveness—as they channel agency into new forms. Whatever the aesthetic by which a given interface has been designed, the computer's interactive address produces an additional, *anesthetic* effect, threatening mystification for the user. More-over, interfaces are discursive, in that their signifying elements are orga-nized around a continuous hailing of the human beings who use them—a beckoning spatial representation marked by the cursor, the startup beep, the avatarial gun. This is the uncanny power of what we might call *speaking tech-nologies:* the perception, produced even through mundane interaction, that we are the subject of their address, that we have been recognized. Joseph Weizenbaum's ELIZA (1966), written to simulate psychotherapeutic dis-course by parroting back typed input in interrogative form, also provoked enthusiastic responses from its users:

> Weizenbaum thought that ELIZA's easily identifiable limitations would discour-age people from wanting to engage with it. But he was wrong. Even people who knew and understood that ELIZA could not know or understand wanted to confide in the program. Some even wanted to be alone with it.[62]

Recognition-by-interface situates the user within a software-driven signi-fying chain, a discourse full of gaps that invite participation. To sit at a computer and handle mouse and keyboard is to be physically positioned; to misrecognize oneself as the addressee of the screen's discourse is to be interpellated as a subject. Under this model, the FPS becomes an extreme form of subject positioning, a scenario of continuous suture.

But the model described above runs a risk in postulating a completely deterministic system, the smooth functioning of which precludes any space of negotiation. This does not square with most people's experience of com-puters in general or video games in particular. Interactions with computers are complicated by the interruptions of everyday life, hardware and soft-ware failure, and an affective user response ranging from joyful transport to seething rage. In addition, the discourse of the screen is itself a collage of different hails that compete for recognition and attention: multitasking op-erating systems "window" applications so that users move jarringly among word-processing documents, games of Solitaire, and the World Wide Web. In this sense, the computer screen is more closely related to television than to movies.[63]

Subjective-viewpoint video games, however, *do* resemble cinematic ad-dress, in the specialized ways described above. Where, then, is the space of resistance in the video game? The answer is in the relationship between player and avatar—a relationship that, because of the intersubjective mech-anisms on which it is predicated, is an always-already "contested space." In addition to games' preferred meanings, players derive pleasure from avatar-ial instability. On the most basic level, avatars enable players to think through questions of agency and existence, exploring in fantasy form aspects of their own materiality.

If the mirror stage initiates a lifelong split between self-as-observer and self-as-observed, and the video game exploits this structure, then, in one sense, we already exist in an avatarial relation to ourselves. Our experience of the world itself is based on equal parts participation and spectatorship; we are certainly here, acting, but we do so in a constant tension between the illusory unity of self that our observing consciousness delivers to us, and the fragmented multiplicity of a self riddled with unbridgeable gaps. Egos are founded on the assumption of wholeness, a wholeness misperceived in the form of a symbolic other. The other that functions retroactively to bestow authenticity on the self could be described as a living avatar.

Movement back and forth across the border separating self from other might therefore be considered a kind of liminal play: an attempt to isolate and capture (fleetingly) the oscillatory motion of consciousness by which we are sutured into this reality. As argued above, video games seem to enact the *fort/da* game. If our unity is itself a misrecognition, then the video game, for all its chaotic cartoonishness, may constitute a small square of contemplative space: a laboratory, quiet and orderly by comparison with the complexity of the real world, in which we toy with subjectivity, play with being.

As small-scale implementations of VR and other interactive technologies of the imaginary, video games seem to offer the potential for profound redef-initions of body, mind, and spirit. In theory, avatars need not be hampered by any semblance of physicality—not even a unitary, ground-level perspec-tive. They need not pretend to tire as they struggle uphill, need never "die." Yet, the avatar's structuring metaphor, source of its believability and, per-haps, its fascination for users, is the very vulnerability that attends embodied existence. We create avatars to leave our bodies behind, yet take the body with us in the form of codes and assumptions about what does and does not constitute a legitimate interface with reality—virtual or otherwise.

Why should experiential simulations be limited in this way? Why should any tics of corporeality, any perverse obsessions or "slips of the tongue," interrupt the carefully engineered flow of virtual fantasy? The answer, I have argued, can be found in the origin of subjectivity itself—in the moment of mistaken recognition that ties self-consciousness to an idealized represen-tation of self and launches a lifelong struggle for guarantees of authenticity. If, as Lacan argues, we win our experience of wholeness through the estab-lishment early in life of a permanent divide, then our extension through technological networks becomes both possible yet restrictively conditional. If we already understand our bodies to be in some sense "escapable," then the magical projections of telephone line, movie screen, and computer-generated battlefield flower before us as spaces into which we can nimbly step—then step back as suddenly, without suffering any consequences save, perhaps, the memories left by a vivid dream.

But if our extension through various media is predicated on the body as root metaphor, then the body becomes an inescapable aspect of fantasized experience. Images of self demand recognition through identification. Yet, once established, this identification must be demolished, so that players can remember where and who they "really" are—and the cycle can begin again.

That the total control promised by the avatar has not been fully exploited is a positive sign: an indication that engagement with interactive technologies of the imaginary will be limited in ways specific to embodied human existence and discursively determined subjectivity. It suggests further that the ideological potential of immersive interfaces is doomed to operate in contention, forever breaking its own flow by violating the seamless suture between its technologically produced perspective and our own. The ambivalence that marks our experience of ourselves will continue to manifest itself in the rules, images, and interactions produced through technologies of the imaginary. The worlds we create—and the avatarial bodies through which we experience them—seem destined to mirror not only our wholeness, but our lack of it.

Notes

1. Christian Metz, *The Imaginary Signifier: Psychoanalysis and the Cinema*, trans. Celia Britton, Annwyl Williams, Ben Brewster, and Alfred Guzzetti (Bloomington: Indiana University Press, 1982), 45.
2. Elizabeth Cowie, *Representing the Woman: Cinema and Psychoanalysis* (Minneapolis: University of Minnesota Press, 1997), 99.
3. *Diegesis,* from the Greek term for "recounted story," is conventionally employed in film theory to refer to the "total world of the story action" (David Bordwell and Kristin Thompson, *Film Art*, 6th ed., New York: McGraw-Hill, 2001, 61). I use it here to designate the narrative-strategic space of any given video game—a virtual environment determined by unique rules, limits, goals, and "history," and additionally designed for the staging and display of agency and identity.
4. In introducing the concept of remediation, Bolter and Grusin emphasize the hybrid, dialectical nature of media appropriation:

   > The new medium can remediate by trying to absorb the older medium entirely, so that the discontinuities between the two are minimized. The very act of remediation, however, ensures that the older medium cannot be entirely effaced; the new medium remains dependent on the older one in acknowledged or unacknowledged ways (Jay David Bolter and Richard Grusin, *Remediation: Understanding New Media* [Cambridge, MA: MIT Press, 2000], 47).

5. Arguing that video games are as much about architectural, sculptural, and other "spatial" properties as they are about narrative or cinematic pleasures, Jenkins and Squire remind us that

If games tell stories, they do so by organizing spatial features. If games stage combat, then players learn to scan their environments for competitive advantages. Game designers create immersive worlds and relationships among objects that enable dynamic experiences (Henry Jenkins and Kurt Squire, "The Art of Contested Spaces," in *Game On: The History and Culture of Video Games,* ed. Lucien King [New York: Universe, 2002], 65).

6. Here and throughout, I use the term "imaginary" in the Lacanian sense, to denote the realm of subjective experiences formed and maintained through identification, dualism, and equality. In Kaja Silverman's words, the imaginary order

    precedes the symbolic order, which introduces the subject to language and Oedipal triangulation, but continues to coexist with it afterward. The two registers complement each other, the symbolic establishing the differences which are such an essential part of cultural existence, and the imaginary making it possible to discover correspondences and homologies (Kaja Silverman, *The Subject of Semiotics* [New York: Oxford University Press, 1983], 157).

7. Jacques Lacan, "The Mirror Stage as Formative of the Function of the I as Revealed in Psychoanalytic Experience," in *Écrits,* trans. Alan Sheridan (New York: W.W. Norton, 1977), 1–7.
8. Samuel Weber, *Return to Freud: Jacques Lacan's Dislocation of Psychoanalysis,* trans. Michael Levine New York, NY. Cambridge University Press, 1991).
9. Lacan, "The Mirror Stage," 1.
10. Lacan, "The Mirror Stage," 2.
11. Silverman, *The Subject of Semiotics,* 126.
12. Discussing the ways in which external entities—the mother's breast, the feces, the gaze of another—take on erotic significance for the developing child, Silverman observes that "[t]here will be many such objects in the life of the subject. Lacan refers to them as '*objets petit a,*' which is an abbreviation for the more complete formula '*objets petit autre.*' This rubric designates objects which are not clearly distinguished from the self and which are not fully grasped as other (*autre*)." Silverman, *The Subject of Semiotics,* 156.
13. Weber, *Return to Freud,* 14.
14. Weber, *Return to Freud,* 14.
15. Weber, *Return to Freud,* 14.
16. Weber, *Return to Freud,* 14.
17. Another version of this occurs when loading a saved game, which, in effect, obliterates the current avatar in order to substitute an earlier version.
18. One way to consider such "reflective relationships" in third-person games such as the *Tomb Raider* series (1996-present), in which a "chase camera" follows the avatar but rarely reveals its face, is by analogy to a two-mirror system. Positioning a hand mirror so that its reflection is visible in a larger mirror, I can, for example, glimpse the back of my own head: the image is still recognizable as me, yet I do not return my own gaze.
19. Lacan, "The Mirror Stage," 1.
20. In her analysis of historical trauma and the death drive, Silverman identifies the subject's repetitive (symbolic) staging of its own destruction as a particularly *male* syndrome; one that, furthermore, even the father of psychoanalysis could not bring himself to confront:

    Masculinity is particularly vulnerable to the unbinding effects of the death drive because of its ideological alignment with mastery. The normative male ego is necessarily fortified against any knowledge of the void upon which it rests, and—as its insistence upon an unimpaired bodily "envelope" would suggest—fiercely protective of its coherence. Yet the repetition through which psychic mastery is established exists in such an intimate relation with the repetition through which it is jeopardized that Freud shows himself unable to distinguish clearly between them. . . . Disintegration constantly haunts the subject's attempts to effect a psychic synthesis." (Kaja Silverman, *Male Subjectivity at the Margins* [New York: Routledge, 1992], 61.)

21. Steven Levy, *Hackers: Heroes of the Computer Revolution* (New York: Anchor, 1984), 52.
22. Levy, *Hackers*, 46.
23. Levy, *Hackers*, 47.
24. Sigmund Freud, *Beyond the Pleasure Principle* (New York: Bantam Books, 1959).
25. Silverman, *Male Subjectivity at the Margins*, 61–62.
26. Levy, *Hackers*, 61.
27. Bolter and Grusin, *Remediation*, 90.
28. The *Spacewar!* diegesis—derived from the preexisting media form of printed science fiction—also foreshadowed the metaphoric borrowings of WIMP operating systems, which take their shape from preexisting material technologies of desktops, folders, trash cans, and so on.
29. Levy equates this line-by-line exploration of a fantasy world with programming itself, suggesting that the original players were able to achieve partial metaphorical contiguity between their actual lives and their experiences as avatarial presences within the domain of *Adventure*. A similar parallel might be drawn between *Spacewar!*'s battling vessels and its hacker combatants, whose social and professional lives were characterized by highly competitive struggles to demonstrate flamboyant programming abilities.
30. Quoted in Levy, *Hackers*, 132.
31. Quoted in Levy, *Hackers*, 295.
32. Ted Friedman, "*Civilization* and Its Discontents: Simulation, Subjectivity, and Space," in *On a Silver Platter: CD-ROMS and the Promises of a New Technology*, ed. Greg M. Smith (New York: New York University Press, 1999), 137.
33. Friedman, "*Civilization* and Its Discontents," 136.
34. Friedman, "*Civilization* and Its Discontents," 138.
35. David Sudnow, *Pilgrim In The Microworld* (New York: Warner, 1983), 66.
36. Scott Cohen, *Zap: The Rise and Fall of Atari* (New York: McGraw, 1984), 78.
37. *Missile Command* had its start in a Rand Corporation simulation of ICBM air-defense management, the goal of which was to determine how quickly human controllers would be overwhelmed (J. C. Herz, *Joystick Nation: How Video Games Ate Our Quarters, Won Our Hearts, and Rewired Our Minds* [Boston: Little, Brown, 1997], 216).
38. J. C. Herz, *Joystick Nation: How Video Games Ate Our Quarters, Won Our Hearts, and Rewired Our Minds*, 64.
39. Marsha Kinder, *Playing with Power in Movies, Television, and Video Games: From Muppet Babies to Teenage Mutant Ninja Turtles* (Berkeley: University of California Press, 1991), 106.
40. Steven Poole, *Trigger Happy: Videogames and the Entertainment Revolution* (New York: Arcade, 2000), 148.
41. Sean Cubitt, *Digital Aesthetics* (London: Sage, 1998), 75.
42. Janet H. Murray, *Hamlet on the Holodeck: The Future of Narrative in Cyberspace* (Cambridge, MA: MIT Press, 1997), 53.
43. Bolter and Grusin, *Remediation*, 94.
44. Kinder notes in video games a tendency toward Oedipal narratives "in which male heroes have traditionally grown into manhood and replaced father figures, and on myths . . . in which little guys beat giants" (Kinder, *Playing With Power*, 105); she sees this as a uses-and-gratifications strategy whereby "the games can help boys deal with their rebellious anger against patriarchal authority" (Kinder, *Playing With Power*, 104).
45. Herz, *Joystick Nation*, 150.
46. "*Myst* is an interactive detective film in which the player is cast in the role of detective. It is also a film 'shot' entirely in the first person, in itself a remediation of the Hollywood style . . . like many of the other role-playing games, *Myst* is in effect claiming that it can succeed where *film noir* failed: that it can constitute the player as an active participant in the visual scene" (Bolter and Grusin, *Remediation*, 97).
47. Cubitt, *Digital Aesthetics*, 85.
48. Cubitt, *Digital Aesthetics*, 90.
49. Cubitt, *Digital Aesthetics*, 90.
50. Herz, *Joystick Nation*, 151.
51. Bolter and Grusin, *Remediation*, 93.
52. The touchstone in this body of work remains Laura Mulvey's "Visual Pleasure and Narrative Cinema" (*Visual and Other Pleasures* [Bloomington: Indiana University Press, 1989],

14–26), which first articulated the connection between cinematic representation and the phallocentric imaginary.

53. See, for example, Jean-Louis Baudry, "Ideological Effects of the Basic Cinematic Apparatus," 531–542, and Jean-Luc Comolli and Jean Narboni, "Cinema/Ideology/Criticism," 22–30, both in *Movies and Methods,* Vol. 2, ed. Bill Nichols (Berkeley: University of California Press, 1985).

54. By contrast, video games often insert "cut-scenes" intended for viewing, not playing. At these moments, the game cues players (typically by shifting to a "letterboxed" mode with black bars at screen top and bottom) to remove their hands from the controls and simply watch information that advances the game's narrative. During cut-scenes, conventional codes of cinema reassert themselves; viewing competencies developed through movies (and, arguably, television and graphic novels) guide players in the proper interpretation of "unembodied" visual grammar such as shot-reverse-shot, dissolves, zooms, fade-ins and fade-outs, and so on.

55. Daniel Dayan, "The Tutor-Code of Classical Cinema," in *Movies and Methods,* Vol. 1, ed. Bill Nichols [Berkeley: University of California Press, 1976], 438–450. See also David Bordwell, *Narration in the Fiction Film* (Madison: University of Wisconsin Press, 1985), 110.

56. Julio L. Moreno, "Subjective Cinema: And the Problem of Film in the First Person," *Quarterly of Film, Radio, and Television* 7 (1953): 349

57. Pascal Bonitzer, "Partial Vision: Film and the Labyrinth." Trans. Fabrice Ziolkowski. *Wide Angle* 4, No. 4 (1981): 58.

58. Joseph P. Brinton III, "Subjective Camera or Subjective Audience?" *Hollywood Quarterly* 2 (1947): 365.

59. Louis Althusser, "Ideology and Ideological State Apparatuses (Notes toward an Investigation)," in *Mapping Ideology,* ed. Slavoj Žižek (London: Verso, 1994), 100–140.

60. Silverman, *The Subject of Semiotics,* 205.

61. Silverman, *The Subject of Semiotics,* 215.

62. Sherry Turkle, *Life on the Screen: Identity in the Age of the Internet* (New York: Simon and Schuster, 1995), 105.

63. Computers share with television a technological base—the CRT display—as well as domestic and professional spaces of consumption that stand in sharp contrast to the collective, uninterrupted viewing environment of theater-based cinema.

CHAPTER 6

Stories for Eye, Ear, and Muscles
Video Games, Media, and Embodied Experiences

TORBEN GRODAL

Video Games, Media, Stories, and the Embodied Brain

A common way of describing representational structures is by way of media. Central problems such as "narrative" or "point of view" are explained by referring to those media forms in which we ordinarily find manifestations of such structures. Some researchers, for example, define narratives by referring to literary works, others, like Brenda Laurel,[1] describe video games and other computer applications by reference to theatre and theatrical structures. Such descriptions have some advantages, but also problematic consequences, because phenomena such as "story" or "narrative" are then only defined in relation to their media realizations, not by their relation to unmediated real-life experiences and those mental structures that support such experiences. This raises special problems for describing mediated activities such as virtual reality and video games because these activities are in several dimensions simulations of real-life activities. Media representations are better described as different realizations of basic real-life experiences. As early as 1916, the Harvard psychologist Hugo Münsterberg[2] showed how the film experience might be described as a cued simulation of central mental and bodily functions. Such an approach provides many advantages for describing video games, because, as I will argue in detail in the following, video games and other types of interactive virtual reality are simulations of basic modes of real-life experiences. This also means that cognitive psychology provides many advantages as a tool for describing video games compared with a semiotic approach; even if games may be provided with some symbolic signs, most of the game activity consist in seeing, hearing and doing in a simulation of a real-world interaction.

Before proceeding further, let me provide a definition of "story":[3] a story is a sequence of events focused by one (a few) living being(s); the events are based on simulations of experiences in which there is a constant interaction of perceptions, emotions, cognitions and actions. An example: Harry sees the dragon coming, he is upset, thinks that he needs to grasp his sword, he does that, and he kills the dragon. The experience of stories is based on central embodied mental mechanisms. The primary story-regulating brain structures are probably located in amygdala-hippocampus, the left peri-Sylvian region, the frontal cortices and their subcortical connections,[4] but these structures rely on many other cognitive and emotional mechanisms.[5] Our experience of stories exist as representation of exterior worlds and they may be described as such, but at the same time they are body-brain-internal processes that need to follow the innate specification of that platform.

The story-mechanisms in the brain provide the superior framework for our experience of events by integrating perceptions, emotions, cognitions and actions. When going to the supermarket, for instance, a micro story in our mind tells us that we have left home because we desired to buy vegetables, that we are now at the entrance of the mall and tells us our ideas of how to find the grocery store. The micro story thus orients us in space, describes our desires and projects and thus guides our motor actions. Damage to some brain structures important for "narrative" may lead to confusion: where am I and why, where shall I go, and so on. The story includes a quest and its motivation. The story also can be a medium-sized one: I met Linda, we had some lovely days in San Diego, she disappeared, but I want to find her again. The story can furthermore be a macro story of my life up till now, including how the past set up some agendas for my future.[6] In such stories there are actors and settings, actions and happenings, but not because such elements exists in mediated representations, like novels dramas or video games, but because such things are important for my experience of, navigation in, and interaction with the world. Stories are based on innate mental functions that match the ecological niche of humans, they are not just social constructions or media constructions. Even if the basic story structure (agency, setting, actions, etc.) is based on functions shaped in our embodied brain by evolution, we may of course fill in real as well as invented material in our stories, and learning mediated stories may enhance our ability to structure nonmediated events.

Human motivations exist in a nested hierarchy. There are high-order goals, like those folktale motives of being married or becoming a king, or high-order existential goals such as survival, as in horror fiction. High-order goals may presuppose lower goals, like courting or fighting dragons; the last may presuppose getting a good weapon, a magic sword, or laser gun. Such goals presuppose that you sleep and eat. At a basic level, you may have simple muscular activations and very basic perceptions. The representation may focus on high-order goals and motivations, because such goals are emotionally very activating, and may to a varying extent recruit nested activities. Some scholars may think that such high-order "dramatic" events are essential to a definition of stories. However, realism or modern high art narratives may focus on low-level events, like kitchen sink realism, stream-of-consciousness, and Sarraute's *tropisms*. Video games may have some high-order motivations, but for a series of reasons games will often also have a strong focus on the execution of low-level (sub)goals like simple navigation and handling processes. An intro to the game may provide the superior motivation, say, to crush an evil empire, and this will provide motivation for the lower-order processes.

My characterization of "story" accords with state-of-the-art psychological descriptions and has the advantage in comparison to those definitions that define narrative as "cognitive-logical" patterns in that it makes explicit how many story events that are described as "logical" consist of emotional-motivational reaction patterns. In *Moving Pictures*,[7] I have shown how film experience may be described by a flow model: the fundamental narrative flow is based on the way in which incoming perceptual (story) information relevant for some vital protagonist concern cues emotional activation linked to the protagonist's preferences. The emotional activation of body and brain informs the problem-solving activity of the protagonist and motivates motor actions that are relevant for the concerns and preferences. The basic story experience consists of a continuous interaction between perceptions (I see a monster approaching), emotions (I feel fear, because I know or feel that monsters are dangerous), cognitions (I think that I better shoot the monster), and an action (the actual motor act of shooting that changes the motivational emotion fear into relaxation). The flow model also explains a series of experiential consequences that may be caused by blocking the canonical flow in different ways and at different stages of the perceptual-emotional-cognitive-enactional processing. Narrative forms based on autonomic reactions, like sorrow or laughter, are based on blocking the motor outlet. Associative forms are made conscious by a block of the flow in an earlier stage of the processing; and experiences based on "pure" perception, such as perception of abstract forms, only activate the first stage of the flow.

Narrative models, such as those of the French structuralists that dominate narrative theory, do not concern themselves with the brain implementation of narratives and cannot account for the intimate relation between perception, emotion, and action in narrative structures.

The story experience need not have any verbal representation, as the ability to "hold" the story in consciousness (including ideas of future possibilities) that is important for prolonged action patterns can take place on a nonverbal perception-emotion-motor-level. Thus, the neurologist Antonio Damasio describes core consciousness as a wordless storytelling:

> Movies are the closest external representation of the prevailing storytelling that goes on in our minds. What goes on within each shot, the different framing of a subject that the movement of the camera can accomplish, what goes on in the transition of shots achieved by editing, and what goes on in the narrative constructed by a particular juxtaposition of shot is comparable in some respects to what goes on in the mind, thanks to the machinery in charge of making visual and auditory images, and to devices such as the many levels of attention and working memory.[8]

This mental film is of course not a silent one, it is only lacking that possible "constant voice-over" of doubling the experiences with a phonological stream of words, that is, an inner monologue. As a verbal "voice-over," an inner monologue may strongly enhance our cognitive analysis of our experience and make it easier to manipulate the experience, for example, to compare it with other experiences or to imagine possible consequences. But the "inner monologue" may also mask part of the salience of the perceptual-motor experience.[9]

Damasio could have pointed out that in several respects video games of the 3-D kind typical, for instance, for first-person shoot-'em-up games or some types of virtual reality are even closer to our core consciousness, because not only are we able to see and feel, we are even able to act upon what we see in light of our concerns, our (inter)active motor capabilities allows us to so shoot at what frightens us or approach what activates our curiosity. Thus, video games and some types of virtual reality are the supreme media for the full simulation of our basic first-person "story" experience because they allow "the full experiential flow" by linking perceptions, cognitions, and emotions with first-person actions. Motor cortex and muscles focus the audiovisual attention, and provide "muscular" reality and immersion to the perceptions. Even visually crude video games such as *Pac-Man* (1980) might provide a strong immersion because of their activation of basic visuo-motor links.

An embodied brain-approach to story experience allows us to characterize the way in which verbal storytelling is a media-specific variant of the story experience. Many language-based story-descriptions have derailed descriptions of video games (and films) because they ignore the fact that semantic meaning is based on concrete perceptions and motor patterns, not on some abstract "semantics," kept in place by verbal signifiers. Humans have probably only acquired language within the last one hundred thousand to two hundred thousand years, whereas the basic story mechanisms may have existed for several million years. Some researchers have even argued that the use of language only took place sixty to seventy thousand years ago.[10] Language has certainly been important for communicating such story experiences and has been a superior tool for the retrieval of and the complex manipulation of the basic experiences.[11] But a purely linguistic model may seriously impede descriptions of those media like video games that rely on a series of nonverbal skills.

Stories are not the only way that we may experience the world. We may perform analytical reasoning similar to that in an essay, we may have thematic-categorical principles of organization or principles based on a network of lyrical associations.[12] Novels, films, or video games may be full of nonnarrative material, like philosophical reflections, descriptions unrelated to the narrative core, or lyrical segments.

Video Games in the Perspective of Media History

The basic story format is the one called the "canonical story,"[13] that is, a story with one (or a few) focusing characters that unfolds itself in a linear, progressive time, from beginning through middle to end, as Aristotle noticed. A canonical representation does not only accord with the way in which we experience unmediated reality as a series of events in a progressing time, it is also the one that is easiest to remember and represent.[14] People will tend to reproduce a story in a canonical fashion even if they have heard it "uncanonically," that is, heard it with temporal rearrangements. Thus, our innate mental machinery seems to take the canonical story format as its baseline. It is important to point out that the basic story experience must be described as taking place in the present, the experiencer is situated in a "now" that is anchored in the memory of a past that causes and informs the cognitions, emotions, and actions directed toward the future. Furthermore, the nucleus of the story experience is the first-person experience, because third-person perspectives are—from an evolutionary point of view—expansions of a first-person point of view[15] even down to the level of motor activation. We infer how other people experience things by extrapolation from our own experiences, using for instance the so-called mirror neurons.[16] In the following, I will show why media representations of experiences have lead many theoreticians into making misleading descriptions of stories. Theoreticians have focused on story mediation and left out those aspects of stories that the French structuralists called *l'enoncé*, the story as such, in order to define "story" as a discursive phenomenon (*l'énonciation*). They have further tended to define stories as being based on a "retelling" or "representation," not as an experience that takes place in a progressing present.

The first media representation of the brain's story experiences took place when language was invented. This has lead to several changes and additions to narratives. Linguistic representations stabilize the experiences and make them easier to recall and to manipulate. Furthermore, a central purpose of language is to provide stories with an intersubjective form and this refocuses the story experience from a mainly first-person to a mainly third-person perspective (that of the listener), although a basic story experience also includes perceiving others from a third-person perspective. Verbal representations enhance the already-existing possibility of providing a third-person perspective to stories, because even if the story is one of one's own experience, language enhances the possibility of reliving past experiences out of their direct perceptual context. Even a first-person "autobiographical" narrative is made by the storyteller from a distanced position to the previous on-line experiences. The distance is also possibly a temporal one, because retelling enhances the ability to mentally represent past experiences as past by means of linguistic tense markers.

The stable, intersubjective representation by language provides a symbolic filter (in the Peircian sense of symbolic) between the perceptions, emotions, and actions, and their communicative existence. Language enhances the possibility of describing fictitious events, because even if a central function of imagining a "story" is linked to those mechanisms that make it possible to imagine different possible future actions, language has removed all constraints on the veracity of stories by removing on-line indexicality. Vision (before paintings, film, and television) represented what existed and thus had strong indexical links, but in language (or even in paintings) it is just as easy to lie or fantasize as to "tell the facts."[17] This has lead many into making a link between "story" and "fiction," although story structures do not have a fixed reality status, they may have all kinds of truth values.

Oral narratives were and are predominantly canonical, because, due to memory constraints and cognitive constraints, radical changes in the temporal order raised and raise difficulties.[18] Thus, even for oral stories, the distinction between story and discourse is of limited value, because one of the main practical uses of the story-discourse distinction has been as a tool for describing texts with a scrambled temporal order and to compare several versions of the "same" story. But if there is no scrambled temporal order and no other versions, the degree of story compression and focus on important events seems to be the only use that one can make of the story/discourse distinction. Oral narratives enhance that aspect of stories that many find to be an important story-defining feature, namely, that a story mainly represents very salient events (love, fight, death, etc.) and leaves out trivial events. But to define "story" by a compression that focuses on high-order experiences, and thus to define story as the opposite of representations of trivial events, is problematic.

Prelinguistic "mental" narratives probably made a strong selection among those aspects that existed prominently in the ongoing "story": some aspects of the experience were probably more important than others in a nonverbalized story-experience. Thus, to compress and focus the story on salient events is an aspect of how the mind works by making priorities for access to a limited working memory space. Joseph Anderson has provided a description of how superior structures are important for the comprehension of detail.[19] Compression may thus be described as a "proto-discursive" phenomenon, because it is not really possible to distinguish between a story as "it really happened" and the presentation. But what is compressed in a given story depends on its purpose: if the purpose is also practical, it may focus on certain details and leave out a detailed description of the superior motivation. Thus, video games often focus on the "how" questions of a story.

The verbal form of narratives until the beginning of the twentieth century has led theoreticians, for instance Marie-Laure Ryan,[20] into thinking that the story phenomenon is centrally a verbal phenomenon, because they conflate the story experience with the verbal retelling. In principle, Ryan follows Jakobson's very prudent semiotic definition of stories as something that can be manifested in many forms and that is not defined in relation to one medium,[21] and her general description of narrative avoids a series of "linguistic" traps. Nevertheless, the verbal form seems to be the central one for her. She thus thinks that video games "embody a virtualised, or potential dramatic narrativity," because games provide some experiences that might be retold by means of language, although these virtual stories may ever be told, that is, provided a verbal form. But this conception is paradoxical, because by these criteria we would never experience any "stories" unless they got a linguistic form; even films would only become stories when we made a verbal resumé of a film.

The way in which verbal representations enhance the possibilities for taking a third-person perspective on stories also greatly enhances the experience of stories that rely on certain third-person emotions, like empathy. The most fundamental emotions like love, hate, jealousy, curiosity, sorrow, and fear rely on a first-person perspective for a full experience of these emotions.[22] But emotions also may be simulated in a third-person perspective in which these emotions are modulated by empathy, like pitying the tragic hero or admiring the superhuman hero. First-person emotions are dynamic action-motivating emotions, whereas third-person emotions like pity or admiration may motivate action, but also more static dispositions. Some theoreticians think that empathic emotions are more valuable than first-person emotions (especially those connected with active coping) and more typical of stories. Thus, Marie-Laure Ryan[23] uses such an emotional valorization as an argument against video game stories and possible VR stories because such stories are better at presenting first-person emotions than, for instance, novels that excel in evoking empathic involvement. It is, however, problematic to make empathic emotions a criterion for whether something is centrally a story or not. In an evolutionary perspective, first-person emotions like the urge for exploring, fighting (based on sympathetic reactions), or emotions linked to sex, food, and laughter (linked to parasympathetic reactions) are more fundamentally linked to stories than empathic emotions. But Ryan is right in her criticism of Janet Murray's claim[24] of the unimportance of media for the story experience, and in pointing out that video games better support some emotions than others. The centrality of motor control in video games makes emotions supported by sympathetic reactions based on coping more probable than emotions supported by parasympathetic reactions based on acceptance and relaxation,[25] and first-person emotions more probable than third-person emotions. A game that presupposed an active striving for causing the death of a nice game character would be perverse and not even attractive for players with suicidal tendencies. But those emotions that are centrally afforded in video games are sufficient for providing holodeck-like experiences as described by Murray.[26]

The invention of dramatic representations provided yet another expansion of the story experience. The dramatic form (re)infuses online perceptual qualities to story-representations. The actors are physically present and some dramatic representations rely on sets and props. The representation is perceived in a third-person perspective (the distanced position in the theatre seat as well as the phenomenological "outside" views on actors), although spectators might mentally identify with some of the protagonists. The physical constraints on dramatic performances made some stories more suitable for dramatic presentation than other stories. Verbal narratives have no cost in providing representations of movement through vast spaces, of handling complicated props and performing complicated actions, or to represent a quick temporal progression. Drama is much more confined to some limited spaces, and to representations of a few contiguous temporal scenes. But it is well suited to represent personal interaction based on strongly emotion-evoking events, from courting to tragic death. Theater has prompted a series of ancillary techniques, from the art of making sets to the art of structuring events and characters. Nevertheless, it is difficult to understand why Brenda Laurel[27] uses the theater as a special metaphor for computers. Those

Aristotelian elements that she uses as reasons for describing the computer as theater, namely action, character, thought, language, melody, and spectacle are a list of human capabilities that are neither exhaustive nor exclusive to theater. The reference to theater only provides a starting point for breaking down computer features into some functions that also could be derived from other domains.

Dramatic representations are mostly done in the present tense, and thus challenge the belief that the core element of stories in general is their pastness (that is evident in the experiential basis of story comprehension). There are good emotional reasons that make a present tense experience the core story mode. The activation of the central action-motivating or curiosity motivating emotions demands that a given point in the story is simulated with an open, undecided future. If the hero with certainty is going to fall in the pit there is no reason to feel fear or to simulate active coping in order to avoid the danger, but just to feel a distanced pity. If we are totally certain that the hero will get the heroine there is not much suspense. Even if folktales are told in the past tense, the listener will take that past point in time as the focus of "presentness" and construct an open future. The problem with some types of strongly narrative video games is that it is difficult to simulate such stories in a dynamic real time and this will deprive the player of a strong sense of experiencing the story in the present tense.

The dominant present tense of drama may be somewhat blurred by the fact that some dramas, for instance, the most famous Greek tragedies, are based on stories that are well-known on beforehand, so that the viewer may know what happens and only asks how it happens. Tragedies and melodramas are however a variant of stories because they rely on passive emotions and/or third-person emotions. For such stories, pastness, decidedness, and fatality is important in order to block a present-tense experience that would make the passive acceptance of the inevitable and painful more difficult,[28] that is, make the transformation from first-person to third-person emotions more difficult. Comedies do not ordinarily need nor presuppose such a pastness.

The invention of written story representations surpassed some of the memory constraints of oral stories. The written medium affords complex narratives, including discursive rearrangements. The written form may emphasize the pastness of the experience, and at the same time it enhances the experience of the "fixity" of the story, because beginning, middle and end of the story exists physically in a fixed form. That does not exclude that stories are read in a simulated present and that the reader may tend to experience a given narrative future as "undecided," just that the medium emphasizes the fixity of the story (and often the third-person perspective). In the twentieth century, film and television became the prime vehicles for basic storytelling, whereas high-art literature increasingly emphasized the discursive dimensions by a series of complex narrative strategies (or by filling in nonnarrative material such as philosophical reflections).

The invention of film created a new medium for the simulation of basic story experiences. Like theater, film makes it possible to present events in a direct perceptual form. In some respects the screen does not have the same intense physical "presence" of space and characters as theatre. But in other respects film affords a story-presentation that is free of some of the constraints of theater. Films make it possible to move freely through time and space. Films make it possible to cue and simulate an experience that is close to a first-person perception (either directly by subjective shots, POV-shots) or from positions close to the persons, contrary to the fixed and distant perspective in the theater.[29] The focusing and framing of persons, objects and events simulate and cue the working of our attention. The representation can furthermore represent various aspects of reality with photographic verisimilitude. As an audiovisual media, the dominant temporal dimension is the present tense; we directly witness the events. To present them "in the past tense" is possible but is not the norm, as it is in written stories. The medium more easily affords story development that focuses on a "now" with an undecided future that has to be constructed by the actions of the hero. Furthermore, there are also strong emotional reasons for a present tense presentation because this supports experiences based on emotions linked to active coping (hate, fear, love, desire), although the medium is also excellent for presenting passive emotions.[30]

The dominant mode of representation is a canonical one, because film viewing often works under strong time constraints that strain the viewer's cognitive capacities.[31] In mainstream cinema, mental capacity constraints impede narrative complexity. This does not mean that films—like written narratives—often use more complex forms of representation. They may use explicit narrators and discursive rearrangements, but in mainstream cinema such devices mostly serve special functions (explicit narrators are thus most typical for creating passive effects), and discursive rearrangements mostly serve to provide subjective dimensions (e.g., flashbacks to childhood experiences).

Video Games, Story Experience, and Game Playing

The computer is the newest medium for story simulation. By providing an "interactive" motor dimension to story experience the computer adds a powerful new dimension to the possibility of simulating first-person experiences. The motor link is still primitive compared to our capabilities to physically interact with a real-life environment (speech is in this respect also a motor act). However, eye and ear will not only be linked to an activation of the premotor cortex (as in previous media) but also to a full motor cortex and muscle activation. Like cinema, the video game screen predominantly simulates perceptions of spaces and objects that are present to the senses, but they can be influenced by actions. In several respects, then, video games are, as mentioned, the medium that is closest to the basic embodied story experience.

The interactive capability also raises a series of new problems that were absent in the earlier media, but are similar to those raised by interacting with real-life phenomena on a first-person basis. The reader/viewer of "traditional" mediated stories needs only to activate some general cognitive skills, including the ability to have some expectations. The story will proceed even without such expectations. The computer story, in contrast, is only developed by the player's active participation, and the player needs to possess a series of specific skills to "develop" the story, from concrete motor skills and routines to a series of planning skills. Therefore, the new activations also increase the capacity problems, and the increased demand on working memory space also increases immersion.

In earlier media, story progression is controlled by the author/director. To follow protagonists through space only demands rather vague mental models (for instance, to imagine that a character somehow gets from his apartment in Berkeley to Golden Gate Bridge), not detailed cognitive maps and hand-eye coordination. Watching John Wayne shooting an opponent only demands crude models for actions, not precise motor programs for grasping the gun and aiming precisely. But in video games such activities often demand rather detailed cognitive maps and motor skills, and playing therefore often requires extensive training of necessary skills. One of the reasons why video games are called *games* is precisely because the repetitive training of coping skills is an important element in many of those activities covered by the term "games."

However, the term "game" is very loosely-defined, and Wittgenstein used the term as a prime example of a category based on "family resemblance" and Lakoff used "family resemblance" to describe categorizations based on prototypes.[32] There are no necessary and sufficient conditions for belonging to or not belonging to the category "games," only a loose network of interconnected resemblances. Several video game researchers have used Roger Caillois's[33] categorization of games as a tool for characterizing video games in contrast to narratives. Caillois divides games into four types, *agôn* (competition), *alea* (chance), *mimicry* (simulation), and *ilinx* (vertigo). But a comparison between video games and Callois's categories creates more problems than it solves. Mimicry may be used when playing, but is also central in film and theatre. Ilinx is a central element in many action films.

Agôn is central in many action films, alea is prominent in lotteries, and so on, but neither typical of fiction nor of video games, although of course most events in this world may possess an element of chance.

It is more rewarding to take the point of departure for describing games in a more general definition of "play" and then describe games and fictions as special forms of play. The ability to play is a very general innate feature that characterizes all mammals.[34] To play means to perform an activity for pleasure, not out of a necessity, although the survival value of playing may be to train important skills, from motor skills to imagination and hypothesis-formation. Cats may play "fighting" or "hunting" and even if their playing may enhance their skills for real-life fighting or hunting, the play situation is not carried out with full real-life intentions, their claws are withdrawn. Humans may play cops and robbers, perform an act, play soccer or Monopoly, but it is only play as long as it is not carried out with real-life intentions, where the players kill each other or risk their fortunes. Thus, a central element in the concept of "play" is linked to what kind of reality status is manifested in a given play activity.

In some fictions (for instance, realist fictions) the fictive "playfulness" of the activity is only a general prescript that prevents the viewer (or actor) from confusing the fiction with reality, but they are in several respects consumed as if they were real. Other fictions are overtly playful. The fictions may be fantasy stories that activate the spectators' or readers' joy by seeing a series of laws of reality violated. But they may also be fictions that cue the spectators into seeing the events as playful, as it is often the case in comedies. Thus, when *The Cosby Show* is called a show and not just a film or comedy, the name clearly indicates that these are some "artist performances" that the characters do in order to please the audience, enhanced by the laugh track. Thus, the more the "fourth wall" of the "theater" is negated, the more the actors are not only communicating to other people in the diegetic world, but also to the spectators, the more we will think that the activity is "a performance," a "game." Such comic shows will never produce any final results, because in the next sit-com, all the activities will start again, just as we know that Laurel and Hardy will never develop, but repeat the same stupidities.

A central element in those playful activities that we call games is therefore their repetitiveness, because somehow repetitive (reversible) activities are felt as less serious, less "real" than activities like tragic stories that represent irreversible processes. A sophisticated viewer of, say, a tragic western might however see that film as a "game" and thus as something more formal (less real) that could be repeated in another western. Thus we might define games as a special kind of playfulness that is characterized by a virtual or actual element of repetitiveness, linked to a conscious feeling that the activity consists of exploring some pattern-bound, rule-bound possibilities (narrative schemas, comic schemas, etc.). The repetitiveness may diminish the felt seriousness. Although some activities may afford playfulness better than other, playfulness depends on subjective attitudes and skills as well as on object affordances. Just as we may either enjoy a western as a "serious" simulation of reality, but also as a "game" with some patterns, so we may also play a video game in a serious-realist mode, but also in a "playful mode." The ease with which we can start a new game certainly supports playfulness, but there is a tradeoff between depth of involvement and degree of playfulness.[35] The lack of depth of involvement may, however, be an advantage if the purpose is to try out roles that conflict with our normal set of identity-defining roles, and the playfulness may then function as an excuse (e.g., for playing monsters, killer-drivers, angels, or devils).

Mediated fictions are mostly enjoyed from a "perceptual" third-person perspective that eventually is simulated mentally from a first-person perspective, whereas many types of playing are enjoyed from a first-person perspective even in its motor dimensions, although many people also watch soccer games, and so on. Fictions are about the concerns of anthropomorphic beings, whereas some kinds of playing, like solitaire, lack an anthropomorphic dimension. And furthermore, most kinds of playing when experienced from a first-person perspective are repetitive in nature, although competition may change playing into distinct events. Thus, big professional soccer games may be experienced in a mode similar to a drama, and more so from the perspective of the spectators than the players. The question of repetitiveness versus unique events is based on subjective, experiential evaluations: players of all kinds of games or consumers of stories may experience a game or a story on the superior level of pattern repetition or focus on the unique variations of a genre or a game-world (or, in structuralist terminology, a system-based vs. a manifestation-based experience).

Stories and games are prototypical categories (or, in Wittgenstein's terminology, categories based on family resemblance). They bleed into each other and cannot sharply be delimited from yet other categorizations. Thus, the central prototype of stories are similar to those games that, like action, shoot-'em-up, and adventure video games, are based on intelligent agencies that act in space-time, whereas other games—like *Tetris*—have weaker links to stories.

Linearity, Non-linearity, and Interactivity as Agency

I noted that, contrary to the reader/viewer of mediated stories (and texts), the player of video games (and related phenomena such as hypertexts) needs to actively develop the story. This development is often described by means of some "hyped" terms like "interactivity" and "nonlinearity," especially when those terms are used in a semiotic context. My definition of "interactivity" in relation to computer application is simple: Interactivity means that the user/player is able to change the visual appearance of a computer screen (and/or sounds from speakers) by some motor action via an interface. The more this motor interaction takes place in a world that simulates being an agent in a world that simulates aspects of a possible real world the greater experience of interactivity. This definition is in accordance with our everyday experience of interaction (in contrast to mental processing). To describe an active reader or viewer of texts as interactive is confusing in relation to ordinary language. The definition furthermore focuses on the experience of the user/player (performing motor acts) and thus avoids those metaphysical speculations of whether the user/player is "really" in control or not. The media theoreticians Bordewijk and Kaam have tried to make an objectivist typology of different types of communication.[36] Traditional one-way media like television are "transmissions." Information that is produced by a "center" and distribution is controlled by the user (like a database or video games) are characterized as "consultation." The true interactive forms are telephone, e-mail, and chat groups, and so on, because only those media formats enable the user to produce and distribute information. But such a description clearly violates normal language. We do not "consult" *Doom* in order to find out what information the producers of that game have provided, we play the game in order to get an experience that is a simulation of the way in which we might act in a hypothetical world. Our primary model is the way in which we experience interaction in a real world.

In a real world as well as in simulated worlds our influence is limited by the general design of that world: we follow roads, tunnels or career tracks, and obey rules, but within a given framework we may alter some elements, take different roads, build houses, and so on. The only necessary condition for experiencing "agency" and interactivity is that our actions make a difference. Ryan (2001) provides a distinction between four kinds of interactivity, made up of two pairs internal/external (roughly equivalent to first-person/third-person) and exploratory/ontological. The last pair distinguishes between those games in which the player moves around the database but is unable to alter the plot and the virtual world, and those games in which the player can influence that world and consequently influence the possible stories. When exemplified, however, it becomes obvious that this distinction is difficult to maintain, because there is no clear distinction between exploring and altering. The reason for this is that the key element in agency and thus in the feeling of interactivity is the ability to change the player's experience. In real life, I may feel agency by changing my experiences by going to Italy, and this might be described as "exploring" the "database Italy" and that does not change much in the world. The "database Italy" is pretty much the same after my visit, but nevertheless I experience agency by my power to change my mental states by my "navigation." But I also may experience agency by building a house or making a table. Is the first experience just exploratory whereas the last is ontological? When I wander around in a mystery, adventure or a shoot-'em-up game, I cannot change the fundamental layout of the game-world just as I cannot change Italy by my visit, but nevertheless I control my navigation, my ability to shoot monsters, and so on, and create many different stories. Thus, interactivity is not centrally about changing a world; on the contrary, it is about changing the mental states of the player, whether that takes place by changing some objects in the world or by changing one's point of view.

Ryan describes some adventure and mystery games as (internal) exploratory whereas other adventure games are characterized as (internal) ontological. However, the difference between *Myst* and *Quake* is not one between a game in which the story is "predetermined" and one in which the player creates the story. In *Quake,* the player also needs to do certain things that are inscribed in the game by the producer of the game, to shoot certain adversaries and find certain paths, for instance. The main difference is the salience of the experience of the player's game alter ego in different games. In contemporary shoot-'em-up games the player more often navigates in a real-time 3-D world, the player may "die" or "crash" his or her plane, or whatever, whereas a problem in a mystery game would be more "external," some headache caused by game problems but projected out in the game world. Thus, even if both worlds are equally free or controlled by some built-in functions and trajectories, the surface of some games are more inviting for experiencing first-person involvement (including the speed of events). The slow and totally player-determined time in *Myst* may lead players into feeling that the "game-resistance" to agency, for instance, troubles with finding out the mysteries, is caused by "narration." However, the "game-resistance" to agency caused by troubles with steering an airplane through a tunnel or keeping a car on a racetrack in real time may be experienced as a personal failure to cope. The distinction between "exploratory" and "ontological" is very much created by an implicit "hype" that thinks that the essence of interactivity consists of free, demiurgic powers for world-making, instead seeing interactivity as the creation of experiences that appears to flow from one's own actions.

A description of the game experience cannot only be "objective" but must take its point of departure in a psychological description. Brenda Laurel has pointed out[37] that the computer experience is a first-person activity and that it is most activating if the proper sensory modalities are stimulated. Vividness of the sensory and motor interface provides salience to the experience of agency irrespective of objective control. The "subjective" aspect of the experience of agency can be observed in the difference in experience between film sequences in film and the same or similar "film"-sequences in a video game, that is, sequences that temporarily block interaction. Because such sequences in a video game are experienced in a context of interaction, they are experienced as more "dead," less "vivid" than in a film context.

Our experience of our interactive capabilities are, however, not constant over time. When beginning a new behavior and/or learning a new environment, we may feel that we have many options that depend on our own choices. However, as we learn those behaviors and environments, we may increasingly get a clear "map" of our options, and we may even feel that we are just alienated robots that follow the commands of society or our own fixed compulsions. To play video games provides a similar variation in our experience of interactivity. When starting a new game we may follow different routes and have an experience of controlling many options. But when we gain mastery we may not only experience the game as a series of routes that we may follow but also create a total "map" of the game and realize that we have a set of limited options. In this stage, the game is more likely to be experienced as a "message" from the game producers because we get insight into their game design. Experienced players may get to that stage sooner and shift more often between experiencing the game as an interactive world and reasoning about the possible intentions laid down by the producers. But it spoils some of the fun to see fictions and games as communication, although it creates other connoisseur pleasures. You may ask yourself the question Will Hitchcock kill this woman? instead of simulating her destiny as a real-life event. Similarly, some pleasures of game playing are linked to the simulation of an experiential flow, although other pleasures consist in getting insight into the intentions of the creators. Our experience of basic mimesis is one of "naturalness," "it has to be so." However, our experience of "art" is based on our insight into the way in which a given creator realizes specific intentions that are only fully understandable as a choice selected among several possible options, and this demands expertise. The metaphors "game as an experiential route" versus "game as a map and as a system" sum up the two poles in the game experience (novice to master), and may perhaps also cover the way in which "texts" may be either experienced as mimesis or as art.

The term "nonlinearity" is closely related to the question of interactivity, because for many scholars within the humanities, the idea of total interactivity and supreme agency is linked to that term. The term is heavily loaded with associations provided by different strands of postmodernist-deconstructionist thinking, for example, those derived from Derrida.

According to their philosophy, linearity is a product of a Western, metaphysical logos-thinking (e.g., causality), enhanced by the linearity of alphabetical writing. These ideas are often linked to rather patronizing ideas that consist in implicitly claiming that non-Western people should be more illogical than Western people. The computer "hype" version of nonlinearity consists in claiming that the computer media possibly emancipates one from these metaphysical and ideological constraints.

However, linearity is not a product of Western metaphysics but based on very fundamental features of the world, of action, and of consciousness. An experiential flow is—unless totally unfocused—a linear process in time. At the same time, linearity is a mental representation of the essential features of the world; that it exists in time, and that time is experienced as linked to irreversible processes. Such processes are represented mentally by concepts like cause and effect. The sun begins to shine and then the snow melts. The arrow pierced the heart, and then the person or animal died. The man entered the tunnel, went through and came out on the other side of the mountain, and so on. Lakoff[38] has shown how such causal links are universally represented by source-path-goal-schemas. By playing a film backward, it becomes obvious that our whole conceptual machinery is based on such linear processes, based on concepts of causality that we share even with animals. The role of linearity and causality in science is only a sophisticated version of innate mental mechanisms that have been developed because of their survival value. Actions are causes that make a difference of effect, and therefore it would be difficult to make a story that was not based on some kind of linearity and causality, because the actions of the story would otherwise make no difference.

A given effect may have different causes: the street may be wet because of rain or because a city water wagon has passed. We may construct video games that consist of different paths that cross each other at some points. In one of the storylines we may arrive to a given space after having followed a path that simulated rain, in another storyline we may arrive to the same space by another path after having witnessed how a water wagon made the street wet. Thus by providing several linear trajectories to the same point we may create ambiguity (seen from a "system" point of view: one effect, several possible causes, as in the deliberations of possible motives and causes in crime fiction, including representations of alternative possible scenarios). It is, however, evident that because a given effect cannot have an unlimited amount of different causes, there can only be a limited amount of such causally motivated crossing paths.[39] A hypertext-like computer story in which all the scenes of the game story were connected by a complex web of links, would have to be a fairly primitive one, or one with insignificant effects. It would be impossible to figure out hundreds of different paths crossing in hundreds of different scene-nodes that provided significant processes and actions irrespective of what concrete trajectory was taken in the web of links. Thus such "a-linear" hypertext web structures afford association-like phenomena (similar to those of dictionary cross-reference links, lyrical associations, literary allusions, etc.) that get their significance by the accumulation of associations. But complex hypertext-like networks do not afford those narrative actions well that rely on causality, a certain time direction, and some irreversibility. Networks of (lyrical) associations versus linear (narrative) trajectories are linked to two different types of emotions, the unfocused emotions that I have called "saturated"[40] and those "tense" emotions like aggression that motivate action, and that need a "linear-causal" setting. Media cannot change our innate cognitive and emotional architecture, only invent products that may activate and enhance the innate specifications.

The reason for wanting multiple choices and multiple possible storylines is the desire to simulate the feeling of a (relative) freedom of choice that we may have in real life, or an utopian-romantic wish for a virtual world that liberates from the restrictions of the real world. Seen from this point of view the creation of several alternative routes simulates freedom. We may, for instance, follow one path to the princess on which we need to kill a dragon in order to proceed to the princess, whereas the other path to the princess has a trial that consists in solving riddles. But choices based on path bifurcation and path separation also imply some constraints on "significance," because if one path implied that the hero lost an eye, and the other one did not, they could not meet. If the choice is "only" created by combining several alternative paths leading to different goals they are collections of linear stories. They just make something explicit which is implicit in other story forms; namely that our story comprehension is based on the fact that the story is a series of "forks" (of alternatives, as pointed out by Bremond[41]). We may go left or right, the hero may win or lose the battle, and so on. Normally, the options in stories are only virtual, even in the second reading or viewing, whereas a computer story may be constructed in such a way that what was virtual in the first playing is chosen and actualized in the second playing.

Thus, we may conclude that stories are essentially linear in their realization: (1) all texts and experiences are linear as experiential processes, because even when "reading" a hypertext the experiential flow would always be linear as it would be revealed if we taped our hypertext activity, our netsurfing, or our consultation of an electronic dictionary with links between articles and terms; (2) the story as a sequence of significant events is linear because a significant story relies on causality, on irreversible processes, and of choice of a trajectory of action. Freedom is the transient feeling that precedes a choice. This insight may be blurred by the fact that a given story world may support different stories, different choices of paths (and in computer stories different player performances). However, we need to distinguish between story experience and story world affordance, because a given story world or game world may afford one or several story experiences.[42] The experience of the way in which a game/story world affords one or several story experiences is however not an a-linear experience, but an insight into the difference between an "experiential route" and a game world as a "map," that is, a system of multiple linear routes. Described in psychological and experiential terms we might say that our visual perception is a two- or three-dimensional field that is supported by a multidimensional a-temporal web of associations, but our actions are based on linearity and time.

The Aesthetics of Video Games

Several theoreticians have pointed out that at least at present most video games have a less complicated story than films or novels. Thus, Jesper Juul compares some films with their game versions[43] (e.g., *Star Wars* and *Tomb Raider*). He points out that the game versions are much simpler than the film versions and uses this as one of his arguments for thinking that video games are not a storytelling media. The problem with this argument is that it is normative. That some stories are rather simple in some dimensions is not a reason for depriving them of their status as stories. There is obviously a tradeoff between control and some dimensions of complexity. Films based on novels may often in some dimensions be simpler than the novels because the richness of the perceptual presentation and the pressure of experiential time are in conflict with other dimensions of complexity that may characterize the printed medium. Similarly, the complexity of the active control of story development in video games is in conflict with other dimensions of complexity. Playing video games demands a detailed richness and specificity in cognitive maps of spaces and opposing agents, of causal inferences that do not only have to be vague premonitions as in films or novels in which the author/director is in control, but precise ideas in order to work. The perceptions have to be fast and precise, the motor control coordinated with the perceptions, and thus the computer story demands the acquisition of a series of procedural schemas. From another point of view, therefore, video games are not imploded stories, but on the contrary the full, basic story that the retelling has to omit, including its perceptual and muscular realization. Video games are based on learning processes and rehearsals and are therefore stories *in the making,* sketches of different stories, different coping strategies. In our first-person experience of a series of events the actual physical manipulation may be intriguing: how to dress oneself, how to control a car, how to deal with a given piece of machinery. All those procedures may be vital elements in our first-person experience. However, such "procedural" experiences are often not very interesting for other people, they do not like to hear about all those "low level" procedures and learning processes, but only to get the bottom line, whereas video games communicate such procedural knowledge. In retelling, there is often a conflict between the teller who wants to provide all the salient details and the listener who wants the big picture. Video games activate a first-person perspective and furthermore often possess a time-frame of many days that allow for a story that is realized on a procedural micro level as well as on a macro level. Films provide a rich access to those perceptual experiences that ground the basic story experience, whereas video games provide the full agency-dimensions of story experience.

In several respects, video games provide an *aesthetic of repetition*, similar to that of everyday life. A film is mostly experienced as a unique sequence of events, and we do not learn the physical outlay of a given simulated world very well, we are carried from space to space. In everyday life, however, we repeat the same actions over and over in order to gain mastery. When we arrive to a new city or a new building we slowly learn how to move around, and if we want to learn to drive or bike, we exercise those skills until we have acquired the necessary procedural skills. The video game experience is very much similar to such an everyday experience of learning and controlling by repetitive rehearsal. We often tell our everyday experiences to others, but often learn that all those details that we find intriguing may be boring for other people.

The video game experience consists of different phases. The first time a game is played, it is experienced with a certain unfamiliarity; the world is new and salient and poses challenges and mystery. By playing the game numerous times, the game world will become increasingly familiar. The peak result of such a learning process may be a trancelike immersion in the virtual world, because of the strong neuronal links that are forged between perceptions, emotions, and actions. But the end result of the learning process is what the Russian Formalists called *automation,* and what psychologists might call *desentization by habituation.* The virtual world becomes predictable, it loses its visual and acoustic salience, and the player will probably stop playing the game at this stage. Thus, this aesthetics of repetition is based on the sequence: first *unfamiliarity and challenge,* then *mastery,* and finally *automation.* The experience is thus in some respects similar to the way in which we enjoy music—musical appreciation is also strongly based on repeating the listening process until it has reached a stage of automation.

The repetitive and interactive nature of video games leads to changes in the function of central devices in the emotional experience of "narratives," namely *curiosity, surprise,* and *suspense.* In a film, the curiosity that is cued by secrets of the narrative world is a passive one, and mainly linked to first-time viewing. The viewer will activate a passive curiosity that supports the viewer's attention. In a video game, however, curiosity takes the form of *explorative coping*. The game only develops if the player performs a series of explorative actions. This self-controlled exertion of active agency is a central fascination in one type of game segment. However, other segments, especially in shoot-'em-up games, are based on the experience of personal agency as being *dynamic coping* by interacting with other *dynamic agencies,* from monsters to gravity, in a simulated *real time.* Explorative coping and dynamic coping provides two distinct experiences of agency as control and agency as playful interaction with other dynamic agencies.

In films, surprising events are mainly emotionally activating in the first viewing. But in video games, what was surprising in the first playing of the game is transformed into a suspenselike coping anticipation in subsequent playings. When the player advances toward the space in which the "surprising" event previously has occurred, for example, the sudden appearance of a fierce antagonist, it will induce an increased arousal. The arousal will diminish over time as the player learns some coping mechanisms, for instance, fast routines for shooting the monster despite the surprising speed or the surprising location of the monster.

A film will create arousal related to the viewer's expectations of what will happen to the central protagonists. This combination of arousal and expectation is what is ordinarily called *suspense,* and it is mainly linked to first-time viewing. Video games also evoke suspense related to the outcome of local sequences as well as related to the final outcome of the game. But suspense in video games is interwoven with the interactive and repetitive nature of the game. The outcome in a given game is in principle just as uncertain the second time through as it is the first time. The player might, in the first playing, by chance shoot an important antagonist or by chance solve a problem, make a perceptual or motor mistake, or forget a step. The time factor in games characterized by dynamic interaction will often create differences in performance from one playing to another. Only by training will the player achieve such an expertise that the game will lose its suspense, and thereby its ability to arouse and stimulate the player. Suspense in video games is partly linked to explorative and dynamic coping, because, contrary to film suspense, video game suspense supports coping, not passive expectations.

I mentioned that the playing of a video game could be divided in three phases: challenge, mastery and automation. The player may have a strong experience of agency and free will in the first two phases. However, the way in which the game is controlled by the designer, and is therefore a "noninteractive" experience, may surface in the third, automated stage. In order to experience our exertion of agency and free will, we need to feel that we are not enacting some stimulus-response patterns. Not only do we need to have a choice between a series of different options, we also need to "feel" that they are real options. But even if a given game world has a series of different paths and options at a given moment, not all these options are equally valid. Often a game will have rather few optimal strategies. The final stage in playing a given game therefore consists in explicitly or intuitively learning these constraints and the optimal strategies of a given game world, just as our everyday may become a dull routine that carries out some automated optimal strategies that rule out a series of alternatives. This further underlines the fact that the experience of interactivity and agency is a subjective one that varies over time, not something that is a static feature of a given game. The experience of interactive agency demands a certain degree of unpredictability in order to guarantee challenge and salience, but also a certain degree of predictability in order to support active coping.

That video games are based on repetitive playing and on interaction has important consequences for the emotional experience in comparison with films. The player's emotional experience is a personalized one. When a viewer is observing, say, how a monster is approaching a character, the possible arousal in the form of fear is not linked to the personal coping potential of the viewer, the viewer has to vicariously identify with the coping potentials of the endangered film character. The viewer cannot personally come up with specific coping strategies; like the rest of the audience, the viewer can only hope for a positive outcome and eventually make some more personal predictions. But a player of a video game is personally responsible for the outcome of such a confrontation. It is the player's evaluation of his own coping potential that determines whether the confrontation with a monster will be experienced as fear (if the evaluation of his coping potential is moderate), despair (if he feels that he has no coping potentials), or triumphant aggression (if he feels that he is amply equipped for the challenge). This entails that the emotional experience will vary over time, because of the learning processes leading to a change in coping potentials. The first-time player of a game may feel despair, the more experienced player may feel a little fear, whereas the master will feel triumphant aggression. Furthermore, different players will have different emotional experiences, linked to their different expertise, although such devices, like options for playing the game on different levels of difficulty, make it easier for the unskilled player to get some of the emotional experiences of the more skilled. There is no such thing as preprogrammed levels of difficulty in film viewing, because the basic assumption in film viewing is that viewing is not an individualized experience, although some films may possess symbolic and enigmatic elements that are not accessible to everybody.

The interactive, output-directed nature of video games puts some constraints on the types of emotions that can be elicited by video games compared with films that are mainly input-driven, driven by the powerful screen representations that viewers passively receive. By its emphasis on motor control it is obvious that video games are mostly able to evoke those emotions that are supported by the sympathetic nervous system (fight and flight-related emotions). The typical emotions evoked by video games are related to active coping. The film experience is basically a passive one, although simulation of character actions can provide a strong active dimension to film. But many films are centrally aimed at evoking strong passive emotions, for instance, melodramas. The input-driven nature of film makes it easy to cue strong passive emotions, including experiences of fate, and they may evoke a strong autonomic outlet, like crying. In contrast, video games are based on acting out the emotions, and the games may therefore even create some kind of catharsis.[44]

Murray's vision of holodeck-like video stories implies stories that would also appeal to our active social skills and social emotions, like establishing friendship, exerting care, feeling jealousy, falling in love, and so on. Such stories would be more attractive to women, and the success of the doll-house game *The Sims* shows the market potentials for games that take some steps toward modelling the nonaggressive social world. There are, however, important technical problems that have to be solved before video games can have holodeck-like or filmlike stories. Some problems, like making programs that could make flexible, individualized, and context-dependent facial expressions and body language for the protagonists that could create empathy, love, or jealousy in the player, might be solved. But to make fully autonomous agents that function like real human beings presupposes a full AI model of humans.

Some video games also excel in evoking lyrical-associative experiences, closer to emotions supported by the parasympathetic nervous system. Games such as *Myst* and *Riven* and other adventure games are experientially based on series of audiovisual freeze-frames and pauses that the player can explore and seek out one by one. Part of the pleasure of such games is therefore not active control of the type exerted in dynamic interpersonal and inter-agency relations (like the control exerted in shoot-'em-up games in which the player in dynamic real time is confronted with monsters, etc.). On the contrary, the pleasure of such *Myst*-type adventure and mystery games is partly a series of associative and contemplative situations and feelings, in which the associative processing of the perceptual input is just as important as the motor output. Such static associations cue feelings, that is, general emotional states without specific objects or specific action tendencies, not emotions. Such "passive" feelings of a mismatch between grandiose input and blocked output[45] were called "sublime feelings" by the preromantic and romantic poets, and the quest for sublime feelings is one of the main parasympathetic reactions cued by video games, as an alternative to the dominant aesthetics of sympathetic control.

Because the story development in video games is driven by the player's motor action, its central story format is linked to a first-person perspective of the basic story experience. Video games may also be used as a vehicle for third-person stories, driven by curiosity. But third-person stories in the computer have some difficulties in synthesizing the function of player control and player agency, with the "passive" simulation of third-person actions, cued by visual stimuli. In films and novels (third) persons are infused with the life and agency by authors and characters, and most readers and viewers will attribute that life to the characters, not to the "storyteller." In the video game, it is the job of the player to create "life" in the third person, and failure to do so will create feelings of a mechanical lifelessness, eventually perceived as due to the designer and his or her system or as a feeling of insufficiency.

Conclusion

The basic narrative format is a way of arranging perceptions, emotions, cognitions, and motor actions (pecma), based on innate brain modules and with or without a linguistic representation. Narrative mechanisms predate language and even the linguistic forms are (also) cues for reactivations of the pecma-structures. The mental mechanisms are geared to the ecological niche of humans. Narratives presuppose living agents that act and experience in space-time, contrary to other formats of representations, like associative forms, prepositional forms, and so on, that are often linked to an "interior" mental niche. Features of the narrative first-person experience may be represented in different media that each have their specific affordances. In general, media representations (including language) afford discursive rearrangements and deviations from canonical forms. Film and video games afford first-person perceptions, video games afford motor interaction, written stories afford complicated deviations from canonical representations, and so on. The media forms are therefore not only representations but also forms that afford new activities (from circumventing internal memory constraints to enhancing the possibility already latent in fantasy of creating virtual actions and scenarios). Media forms also greatly enhance the possibilities of choosing different levels of representation, from ten-minute representations of the history of the universe to fine-grained visuo-motor simulations of actions. It may be difficult to make a lower limit to the phenomenon "narrative," although most would think that learning quite basic action patterns like those found in *Tetris* (which lacks an agent-in-time-space dimension) fall below the category of narrative.

The basic narrative format is linked to a living agent in a natural environment, and therefore does not presuppose any storyteller except the experiencing agent. Mediated representations may be experienced as "untold," as a simulation of an experiential sequence, but also as "told," as a communicative text. The last point of view also implies that the text may be understood as "art," as a specific communicative strategy among several possible strategies. The basic narrative format is linked to linearity, because significant actions and processes are based on linearity and irreversibility. The linear narrative forms are different from some "paratelic"[46] phenomena like dancing in which there is reversibility and in which there is no source-path-goal-schema, and different from associative structures as found in hypertexts with dense nonlinear links. Although a given instantiation of a video game is linear, a given game "world" affords many different instantiations. We may thus distinguish between a given game sequence that is linearly narrative and the affordances of the game world (and its representation in the player's mind) that might be called "meta-narrative" because the player envisions the individual game from a meta-perspective of possibly all the different options and trajectories within the game world. This meta-narrative stance is similar to art appreciation, because art appreciation is based on comparing a given choice of representation with other possible choices.

Video games provide personalized experiences that are based on playing (that is: pleasurable *repetitive learning* processes), backed up by emotions that change over time not only because of the events but also due to the development of the learning processes. The subjective experience of nonlinear choice is strongly enhanced by the repetitive nature of games that allow different lines of actions in different playings of the same game, contrary to film, which chooses one line of action and one narrative out of the virtual options. The experience of agency may over time be constrained by learning the way in which the game world is a designer construct, and thus provide an experience of automation or provide an experience of interacting with designer intentions.

Video games are furthermore mainly based on sympathetic, aversive emotions, due to their output-driven setup, contrary to films which are input-driven, and thus able to simulate parasympathetic emotions, but also to a certain extent able to simulate output-driven narratives, thus cueing sympathetic emotions.

Notes

1. Brenda Laurel, *Computers as Theatre* (Reading, MA: Addison-Wesley, 1993).
2. Hugo Münsterberg, *The Film. A Psychological Study* (New York: Dover, [1916] 1970).
3. See Torben Grodal, *Moving Pictures: A New Theory of Film Genre, Feelings, and Cognition* (Oxford: Clarendon/Oxford University Press, 1997).

4. See Kay Young and Jeffrey L. Saver, "The Neurology of Narrative," *SubStance* 30, Nos. 1–2 (2001): 72–84.

5. See Antonio R. Damasio, *The Feeling of What Happens: Body and Emotion in the Making of Consciousness* (New York: Harcourt Brace, 1999).

6. Torben Grodal, "Art Film, the Transient Body and the Permanent Soul," *Aura* VI, No. 3 (2000).

7. See Grodal, *Moving Pictures.*

8. See Damasio, *The Feeling of What Happens,* 188, passim.

9. A description of the prelinguistic basis of experiences and thinking may also be found in Gilles Fauconnier and Mark Turner, *The Way We Think: Conceptual Blending and the Mind* (New York: Basic Books, 2002).

10. See Ian Tattersall, *The Monkey in the Mirror* (New York: Harcourt Brace, 2001), and also Fauconnier and Turner, *The Way We Think.*

11. See Michael C. Corballis, *The Lopsided Ape: Evolution of the Generative Mind* (New York: Oxford University Press, 1991), Antonio R. Damasio, "Brain and Language," in *Mind and Brain: Readings from Scientific American Magazine* (New York: Freeman, 1993), and Fauconnier and Turner, *The Way We Think.*

12. See David Bordwell and Kristin Thompson, *Film as Art,* 6th ed. (New York: McGraw-Hill, 2001) and Grodal, *Moving Pictures.*

13. See David Bordwell, *Narration in the Fiction Film* (London: Methuen, 1986) and Grodal, *Moving Pictures.*

14. See Jean M. Mandler, *Stories, Scripts and Scenes: Aspects of Schema Theory* (Hillsdale, NJ: Lawrence Erlbaum, 1984).

15. See Torben Grodal, "Film, Character Simulation, and Emotion," in *Nicht allein das Laufbild af der Leinwand . . . ,* ed. Friss, Hartmann and Müller (Berlin: VISTAS, 2001).

16. See Grodal, "Film, Character Simulation, and Emotion."

17. See Fauconnier and Turner, *The Way We Think,* esp. chapter 11.

18. See Mandler, *Stories, Scripts and Scenes.*

19. See Joseph Anderson, *The Reality of Illusion: An Ecological Approach to Cognitive Film Theory* (Carbondale: Southern Illinois University Press, 1996).

20. Marie-Laure Ryan, "Beyond Myth and Metaphor—The Case of Narrative in Digital Media," *Game Studies* 1, No. 1 (July 2001). Available online at <http://www.gamestudies.org/0101/ryan/>.

21. See Roman Jakobson, "Linguistics and Poetics," in *Style in Language,* ed. Sebeok (Cambridge, MA: MIT Press, 1960).

22. See Grodal, *Moving Pictures* and "Film, Character Simulation, and Emotion."

23. For instance Marie-Laure Ryan, "Beyond Myth and Metaphor."

24. Janet Murray, *Hamlet on the Holodeck* (Cambridge, MA: MIT Press, 1997).

25. See Torben Grodal, "Video Games and the Pleasures of Control," in *Media Entertainment: The Psychology of its Appeal,* ed. Zillman and Vorderer (Mahwah, NJ: Lawrence Erlbaum, 2000).

26. Murray, *Hamlet on the Holodeck.*

27. Laurel, *Computers as Theatre.*

28. See Grodal, *Moving Pictures* and Torben Grodal, "Die Elemente des Gefühls. Kognitive Filmtheorie und Lars von Trier," in *Montage/av 9/1/00:* 63–98.

29. Bela Balazs, *Theory of the Film* (New York: Dover, 1970).

30. See Grodal, *Moving Pictures.*

31. Bordwell, *Narration in the Fiction Film.*

32. George Lakoff, *Women, Fire, and Dangerous Things: What Categories Reveal about the Mind* (Chicago: Chicago University Press, 1997).

33. Roger Callois, *Les jeux et les hommes* (Paris: Gallimard, 1958).

34. See Paul D. MacLean, "Ictal Symptoms Relating to the Nature of Affects and Their Cerebral Substrate," in *Emotion: Theory, Research and Experience,* Vol. 3, ed. R. Plutchik and H. Kellerman (New York: Academic Press, 1986), 61–90.

35. In the article "Film Futures," published in *Substance* 31, No. 1 (2002), David Bordwell has described a group of films that try out different options and different futures, thus telling stories that wind back to a possible point of bifurcation. The experience of such films may

however often change from a mimetic to a playful mode. The first version of the narrative is experienced in a more serious, "existential" mood by the viewers than the following versions, because the viewer feels the playful intentions of the addresser in version two and three (see Tom Tykwer, *Lola Rennt*). However, if the film's use of multiple futures is based on some supernatural premises, as in Harold Ramis's *Groundhog Day* or James Cameron's *Terminator II*, the viewer may accept alternative versions with the same kind of existential involvement, because they are not playful repetitions any more but consequences of supernatural laws.

36.   J. L. Bordewijk and B. van Kaam, "Towards a new classification of TeleInforation Services," *Inter-Media* 14, No. 1 (1986).
37.   Laurel, *Computer as Theatre.*
38.   Lakoff, *Women, Fire, and Dangerous Things.*
39.   See Ryan, "Beyond Myth and Metaphor."
40.   Grodal, *Moving Pictures.*
41.   Claude Bremond, "Le message narratif," *Communications* 4 (1964): 4–32.
42.   See David Bordwell, "Film Futures."
43.   Jesper Juul, "Games Telling Stories?," *Game Studies* 1, No. 1 (July 2001). Available online at <http://www.gamestudies.org/0101/juul-gts/>.
44.   See Grodal, "Video Games and the Pleasures of Control."
45.   See Torben Grodal, "Subjectivity, Realism and Narrative Structures in Film," in *Moving Images, Culture and the Mind,* ed. I. Bondebjerg (Luton: University of Luton Press, 2000), 87–104.
46.   See Grodal, *Moving Pictures.*

CHAPTER 7

As We Become Machines

Corporealized Pleasures in Video Games

MARTTI LAHTI

The way cultural discourses today, as well as our theories addressing those discourses (and stemming from them), imagine technologized bodies and subjectivities is clearly influenced by William Gibson's novel *Neuromancer* and, in particular, the term "cyberspace" that it introduced to our cultural vocabulary.[1] This has been particularly evident in writing about the Internet. Gibson's alluring fantasy of "meatless" subjects incorporated into a computer seems to resonate simultaneously, and powerfully, with both hopes and anxieties stemming from the Internet as a new medium shaping the public sphere. Interestingly though, and not surprisingly, considering how cumbersome a technology it was at the time, Gibson didn't have the Internet in mind when he coined the term cyberspace. Instead, he found an inspiration for it in video games:

> [In arcades] I could see in the physical intensity of their postures how *rapt* these kids were. It was like one of those closed systems out of a Pynchon novel: you had this feedback loop, with photons coming off the screen into the kids' eyes, the neurons moving through their bodies, electrons moving through the computer. And these kids clearly *believed* in the space these games projected. Everyone who works with computers seems to develop an intuitive faith that there's some kind of *actual* space behind the screen.[2]

Such a conceptualization of cyberspace is of interest to me, because it draws our attention to video games as a *paradigmatic* site for producing, imagining, and testing different kinds of relations between the body and technology in contemporary culture. As Sherry Turkle has pointed out in relation to the above quote, Gibson sees the player as already being subsumed by the computer, already as a cyborg.[3] Indeed, I will argue that video games epitomize a new cyborgian relationship with entertainment technologies, linking our everyday social space and computer technologies to virtual spaces and futuristic technologies. Games both rely on and thematize a contemporary sensibility and fantasy that Anne Balsamo, among others, has identified. In *Reading Cyborg Women,* Balsamo suggests that the "natural body" is being replaced or supplemented with its technologically enhanced other.[4] Games—in particular fighting, shooting, and racing games—are a symptomatic site of a confusion or transgression of boundaries between the body and technology that characterizes contemporary culture.[5] As Scott Bukatman has suggested, games "represent the most complete symbiosis generally available between human and computer—a fusion of spaces, goals, options and perspectives."[6] This symbiosis, I would argue, occurs primarily through the corporealization of the experience of playing, in the case of games. That is, they crystallize a new and complex relationship between corporeal experience (the body) and our subjectivity. Video games reside in that contemporary cultural juncture in which, according to Balsamo, "the body and technology are conjoined in a literal sense, where machines assume organic functions and the body is materially redesigned through the application of newly developed technologies."[7]

In this essay, I will explore connections between this cyborgian promise of various games, paradoxically articulated through a simultaneous disembodiment of vision and contrasting refocusing on corporeality. One of the most often repeated and taken-for-granted assumptions in much writing on "cyberspace" is revealed in a tendency to treat new media, games included, as machines to realize desires for bodily transcendence, that is, an "out-of-body" experience. For example, Margaret Morse writes: "For couch potatoes, video game addicts, and surrogate travelers of cyberspace alike, an organic body just gets in the way."[8] In contrast, I will demonstrate how games actually anchor our experience and subjectivity firmly in the body or in an ambiguous boundary between the body and technology. That is, video games invite us to retheorize bodily experience through the corporeal coordinates of our subjectivity. Morse ends her article, "What Do Cyborgs Eat?" from which the above quote is taken, by asking "How can cyborgs become meat?"[9] Ultimately, this essay offers an exploratory account of how that has indeed happened.

Being in the "Third Place"

According to Ted Friedman, computer games teach us to "[think] like the computer," a process which creates a sense of "self-dissolution," being "sucked in." He goes on to describe playing a game such as *Civilization II* as being in an "almost meditative state, in which you aren't just interacting with the computer, but melding with it."[10] Clearly, this emphasis on cognition applies to the turn-based strategy games that Friedman is concerned with, underlining computer games' attractive and addictive potential to immerse us in their technologically-created worlds. However, what Friedman's analysis ignores, partly because of his focus on this particular genre, is the bodily, almost noncognitive, dimension of the experience of being sucked into the computer.

One of the characteristics of video games throughout their history has been an attempt, with the help of various technologies, to erase the boundary separating the player from the game world and to play up tactile involvement. Indeed, much of the development of video games has been driven by a desire for a corporeal immersion with technology, a will to envelop the player in technology and the environment of the game space. That development has coincided with and been supported by developments in perspective and the optical point-of-view structures of games, which have increasingly emphasized the axis of depth, luring the player into invading the world behind the computer screen.

Early arcade and home video games, including classics such as *Computer Space, PONG, Space Race, Tank,* and *Space Invaders,* were mostly based on simple graphics, representing a flat, two-dimensional world seen from a distance and from above, a divine point of view. The player could perceive and identify the entire universe of the game all at once; and, correspondingly, the monitor (or frame) firmly demarcated the limits to the game world, underlining its distance from the player's real world. Other games such as *Asteroids* and *Pac-Man* popularized "wraparound" screens, where a character or a vehicle could leave the screen on one side and reappear on the other, a structure gesturing toward a continuous and limitless game world. This development was further reinforced by arcade and home video games— for example, platform games such as *Sonic the Hedgehog, Super Mario,* and *Donkey Kong*—that extended the game world to include other elements important for an immersive experience. These games coupled a strongly unidirectional screen movement from left to right with a need to react to stimuli emerging from offscreen space, within an increasingly detailed representational game world with more layers of graphic depth. Taken together with an option to scroll, as in games such as *Football* and *Defender,* this effectively erased the boundaries of the screen. Instead of limiting the game world itself, the monitor now set the limit as to how much of it a player could *see,* demarcating and identifying with her vision, while further emphasizing the potential endlessness of the game world. After all, a player of such games needs to be ever-conscious of the fact that her nemesis could reside just outside the visible field, ready and waiting to destroy her. The screen started to become more closely identified with the player's point of view (rather than the totality of the game's playable universe), thus setting the stage for what is probably the most important change in the history of video games, the introduction of a third dimension.

Until recent years, when personal computers' processors and graphics cards became powerful enough to handle complicated 3-D worlds, the development of video games was dominated by arcade games, whose profit was based in large part on creating an addictive experience that lured players to feed coins into a machine by drawing them into the game world. This experience was reinforced and enhanced by the introduction of the first games based on 3-D graphics, which further erased the boundaries between the player and played, convincingly feeding Gibson's remarked-on "intuitive faith that there's some kind of *actual* space behind the screen." Considering how early manufacturers introduced the first 3-D games, it seems clear that the development of game technology was indeed strongly influenced by an attempt to redirect the player's vision, to create a sense of looking and moving into this space behind the screen. Already in 1980, Atari released *Battlezone,* a vector graphics game that utilized one of the hallmarks of later 3-D games, a first-person point of view. This prominent feature of *Battlezone* exemplified its (new) genre as a first-person shooter, which was to become one of the most common genres of contemporary video games. And this attempt to identify a player's vision and point of view with the monitor wasn't restricted to arcade games, since the first-person point of view was found also in the *3D Monster Maze* (JK Greye Software, 1981) for the Sinclair ZX81 home computer, a game in which the player navigates through a black-and-white maze trying to avoid a Tyrannosaurus Rex.

However, it took another decade and the release of the first games using a 3-D game engine—such as *Howertank One* and *Catacombs 3D* (both id software, 1991) and in particular *Wolfenstein 3D* (id software, 1992; based on *Castle Wolfenstein* by Muse Software)—before 3-D games started to become common, and gradually dominated game markets. These were quickly followed by a series of 3-D hits such as *Doom* (id software, 1993), *Quake* (id software, 1997), *Tomb Raider* (Eidos, 1996), *Duke Nukem 3D* (GT Interactive, 1996), *Unreal* (GT Interactive, 1998), *Half-Life* (Valve Studios, 1998), and *Metal Gear Solid* (Konami, 1998), as well as their various reincarnations in sequels. The first of these introduced elements that later became standard solutions in 3-D games. These include an impression of a limitless game space with choice of direction in movement, a first-person point of view, movement into the depth-axis of the image and, relatedly, objects moving toward the player. In fact, objects requiring the player's reaction not only emerge from off-screen space, but can act—that is, shoot at the player in the case of *Wolfenstein 3D*—before even being "seen" or appearing on-screen.

These games regularly used a variety of techniques to register the visceral element of playing, that is, to imagine bodily sensations or consequences for the player otherwise indicated only as a viewing position, most prominently in the case of first-person shooters, a genre marked by the visual absence of a player's avatar. For example, damage done to the player's "body" is represented with a health meter, pained grunts, or the sounds of blows, or a flashing screen. We see "through the eyes of the monitor" what our body is supposed to feel and register. (A more recent and interesting example is found in the Nintendo 64 title *Perfect Dark,* in which kicking and punching "results in a momentary blurring of the screen should you get hit."[11]) Similarly *Wolfenstein 3D* introduced another representational element that stands in for the absent body and that has since become a standard in first-person shooters, namely, (a hand with) a gun at the bottom of the screen. As a representation of the player's hand (and/or weapon) as a sort of imaginary prosthesis, it links the player's body into the fictional world, again emphasizing a continuum between the player's world and that of the game.

Thus, video game history is characterized by a significant shift in perspective relations between the player and the field of play, from the vertical omniscience of the God's-eye-view, through a ground-level, third-person perspective along the horizontal axis, to a fully subjective perspective where character and player are unified into a first-person movement through the virtual space. One effect of this unification is the creation of a stronger experiential homology between the fictional world of the game and the real world, where virtual space begins to seem continuous with the player's space rather than sharply delimited by the frame of the monitor as I have been arguing. Our sense of movement and relation to the screen has thus similarly changed. 3-D games (for example *Doom* or *Quake*) brought with them a sense of limitless space opening behind the screen.

A number of games (such as Nintendo 64's *Super Mario,* or *Bushido Blade*) also allow the player to occupy the role of camera operator as well as character—selecting and shifting among various angles of view and from different proximities to the action. In this way, the player can control the flow of vision as well as being the agent of action. While in some ways mitigating a full mapping of player subjectivity into a first-person character point of view, this control of angle and distance of point of view nonetheless increases the illusion of the game environment's encompassing wholeness, creating a continuous virtual space for the player's virtual body to roam, extended through the apparatus of a kind of prosthetic vision. Overall, the flourishing of first-person point of view, including computer-generated "virtual zooms" and "tracking shots," in addition to a regular movement into the depth-axis of the screen, creates a sense of penetration into the computer and the represented world "behind" the screen, Gibson's cybernetic loop that ties us into the projected space. This effectively erases the boundary between a "real" and "virtual" world and creates a sense of delirium that makes up for the lack of bodily movement (found in its clearest form in flight simulators).

Furthermore, developments in game technology intensify this bodily dimension of our experience, heightening the impression of sensory immersion and a physical link to an imaginary environment with data gloves, joysticks with feedback mechanisms such as rumble packs, pedals and wheels, motion-sensing technology (for example, moving seats), and surround sound. They provide a tactile feedback from the computer to the body that literalizes the implied bodily sensations conveyed through visual and sonic effects used in earlier games such as *Wolfenstein 3D*. Such technologies fuse us with the computer by letting both the game world and the technological apparatus that brings it to us spread out of the monitor to encompass the space around the player, wrapping itself around her body. But this kind of desire for a cybernetic relation with the computer—and the related desire to cross the boundary that separates our real from the computer's imaginary world—doesn't only apply to recent games. On the contrary, a desire to use technological extensions to immerse us in the game world has been a distinguishing element of games' development from the very beginning. Already in 1967, when Ralph Baer and Bill Harrison were working on a prototype of a video game system that was to become the Magnavox Odyssey, they developed a toy gun that could be used to shoot dots on a monitor.[12] And indeed the Magnavox Odyssey, the first home video game system, included a light gun, too.

In general, this emphasis on tactile interaction has been especially important for arcade games, from which it has gradually spread to the home. In arcades, players can sit astride a motorcycle or stand on a pair of skis, feeling bumps and vibration through these apparati, and using their whole bodies to control the game world by, for example, leaning into the curves as they round corners or negotiate moguls represented on-screen. A most fascinating recent example is a Korean game called *Boon-Ga Boon-Ga,* in which the player's task is to spank various characters with a hand-shaped peripheral.[13] On the home front, consider the Thrustmaster Fighting Arena, a recent example of rather complicated technology, which is now being sold for home entertainment to replicate the arcades' corporeal experience. It is an interactive bodily control unit for various PlayStation fighting and boxing games, which is made up of a responsive mat and infrared sensors. According to the manufacturer, the mat and sensors replace the normal gamepad buttons as input mechanisms, conveying the player's real-world bodily movements for "the ultimate in realistic punching and kicking actions. Break the infrared beam and your on-screen character reacts in real time."[14] Clearly the notion of "realism" is based here on the tactility of playing and the player's real bodily experience, not on the level of verisimilitude of the representation on the screen; and by implication, the kind of pleasures that this technology is expected to intensify is corporeal in nature. It is a seamless loop between the computer (controller) and the player that promises the most intense experience for the player, as exemplified and underlined by the gaming magazine *Edge*, which in its review of the PlayStation2 game *Rez* (in a section suitably entitled "Good Vibrations") notes that, "Pitching DualShock's rumble capacity into the auditory and visual mélange proves hugely successful in immersing players of *Rez* into a suitably trance-like state." The review then bemoans the fact that European players do not have access to the ASCII Trance Vibrator unit available in Japan, which would "[boast] three to four times the vibrational power of the standard PlayStation2 controller."[15]

This delirium of virtual mobility, sensory feedback, and the incorporation of the player into a larger system thus tie the body into a cybernetic loop with the computer, where its affective thrills can spill over into the player's space. This desire is perhaps best exemplified by players' attempts to control the game world more fully with their own, empathetic bodily movement. By this I mean that familiar experience of, say, craning forward, trying to peer around corners by leaning left or right, or ducking as you desperately try to save your character—that is, yourself—from being annihilated. The urgency of being able to control your own body when playing is captured by a review of a PlayStation2 title, *Burnout*, called "one of the most addictive" games of recent times and a "valiant, much-needed adrenaline-filled syringe passionately thrust into the exhausted heart of the videogame racing community." In this review, players are warned against losing control, even for second: "[Try] not to blink. Blink and you'll almost certainly hit something."[16] This identification and immersive experience during the game play remains compelling, even addictive, because our surrogate body on the screen mirrors our desires and bodily experiences; it represents us. It is directly controlled and affected by us, and our (real bodies') actions, even involuntary ones (like blinking!) carry dire consequences for the game world. In this sense, our pleasure is based on blurring the distinction between the player and the character: we jump, fly, shoot, kick, and race when we are actually clicking the mouse or tapping the controller. And correspondingly, when we blink, our avatar dies or crashes.

This kind of utopian sense of liberation from real-life spatiotemporal constraints, central to the cyborgian promise of games, resonates with earlier mechanical thrill rides that according to Lauren Rabinovitz mobilized a similar double-desire: "The person surrendered to the machine, which, in turn, liberated the body in some fashion from its normal limitations of placement and movement in daily life."[17] That is, this process relocates and doubles our body in such a way that it is simultaneously and interconnectedly present in two places at once: The player's body is next to the computer screen or television monitor, but her avatar, the "I" or vision that was part of the body, is traveling through and in the virtual space of the game opening behind the monitor. That boundary experience of simultaneously being and not being there—or occupying that "third place" in the terms of Sony PlayStation2 ads—was acknowledged recently in an advance review of *StarCraft: Ghost,* which describes the ambiguous doubleness of the player's identity by using alternative pronouns: "[S]he/you must engage in a range of . . . missions."[18] Importantly, as Erkki Huhtamo has argued, these two forms of subjectivity and corporeality, the virtual and physical, are not mutually exclusive but continuous and complementary.[19] The monitor guides us into (a perceptual and corporeal) interaction with the computer and, as a technologized form of vision, it becomes a component and extension of the body; it replaces our body, or rather extends its capacities, and becomes both a representation and source of bodily experience, thus creating a hybrid condition resonant with the cyborg.

Considering that immersion into the fictional world and blurring the distinction between the player and the game world are such central, acknowledged, and celebrated parts of video games' pleasures, it comes as no surprise that they also function as a key appeal in the games' publicity. Indeed, the discourse around video games regularly interpellates us as a character in a game world, further blurring the distinction between us and the fictional space. To give just one example, a review of *Project Ego,* a forthcoming Xbox game, gives the following laudatory description of playing it: "[Y]our decisions should affect not only your appearance, but how the world around you reacts to your presence."[20] Our identification with the game world is based on the centrality of the body in two senses. First, the game world and various characters (our avatar included) react to our decisions and real corporeality (even when it's something as simple as clicking the mouse)—that celebrated "interactivity" of computer-based media. As Scott Bukatman has suggested, "[t]hrough the translation of percept into movement, the players' thoughts . . . are given their place in the world."[21] That is, the strong sense of bodily presence, so central to games, is based on this corporealization of perception, the translation of perception into bodily movement (in opposition to the immobility associated with cinema spectatorship, for example). Second, an important part of that interactivity is the ability to influence the way your avatar ("you") looks on the screen.

That is, the representation of an avatar's body forms an important dimension of our desire for immersion in the fictional world of a game. This becomes especially evident in first-person shooters, in which the player is regularly represented on the screen by something as minimal as a hand, gun, or other piece of equipment. However, even these games more often than not include introductory sequences during which the player gets to select what her screen double looks like, what weapons that character will carry or what kind of outfit s/he wears, and so on. This second order of interactivity—the representational presence of the body—seems to provide a sort of (ideological) framework for the first, corporeal identification and pleasure.

Kick-ass Experiences

Allucquère Rosanne Stone has labeled this kind of "cybernetic interaction," in which our pleasure is based on being in a loop with the computer, as "cyborg envy" and describes the seductiveness of its gender politics in the following fashion:

> There is also a protean quality about cybernetic interaction, a sense of physical as well as conceptual mutability that is implied in the exciting, dizzying physical movement within purely conceptual space.... This sense, which seems to accompany the desire to cross the human/machine boundary, to penetrate and merge, which is part of the evocation of cyberspace, and which shares certain conceptual and affective characteristics with numerous fictional evocations of the inarticulate longing of the male for the female, I characterize as *cyborg envy*.[22]

This envy exists not only as an affective or ontological quality in a generalized desire to merge, as described by Stone, but it can also take on a more directly representational form. Witness numerous fighting and adventure games in which the player can select an avatar from a matrix of characters of different gender and race, with an increasing number of them being female (as in *Mortal Kombat, Tekken, Battle Arena Toshinden, Bushido Blade, Resident Evil, Tenchu: Stealth Assassin, TimeSplitters 2*—not to mention that the only option in the *Tomb Raider* series is the famous Lara Croft). However, at the same time that such games invite the male player to "merge" with the female, the games simultaneously redraw the gendered boundary very clearly. While allowing him to play the female, it also asks him to disassociate himself from her and instead to take visual pleasure in looking at her, as the excessively eroticized feminine features of various characters often quickly reveal. In picturing our avatar on-screen as we play, such games thus also paradoxically demand something of a departure from 3-D gaming's purely subjective perspective (and lack of on-screen representation other than the hand/gun) of the gamer-character, a point to which I shall return later.

Many optimistic commentators have emphasized the utopian dimension of the possibility of leaving one's body behind—as well as the real-world social identities that have become grounded through it. For example, the *New York Times* critic J. C. Herz celebrated this cyborgian dimension of video games:

> One of the most compelling things about fighting games is how they play with ideas about the human body. . . . By selecting a different character, you alter your dimensions. With no more effort than a chameleon, you can change your skin.[23]

Changing one's skin, however, within the context of a fighting or shooting game, does not imply any experimentation with the types of real world social privileges that are linked to the skin, for example. Not just a choice among fully constituted characters, many of these games ask us to further specify—and exercise control over—the kind of the body we desire. We are lured into a supermarket of bodies and body-parts from which the player's representative, her virtual self, can be created and customized. Unhinged from contexts of social inequalities, the body is here aestheticized as variety itself, turning it into a mutable fashion statement, an adaptable task-oriented instrument, or a toy with which we can play.

The importance and attractiveness of being able to augment and upgrade the real body through customizing the represented body was captured by an anonymous writer, who describes a PC version of *Deus Ex* in a way that blurs the boundary between these two dimensions: "Even the *player's body* is customizable. More importantly, power-ups scattered throughout the game enable microscopic biomechanical upgrades which enable *you* to see in the dark, breathe underwater, or run faster."[24] Some game types offer various prostheses to choose from as well, where weapons, tools, and means of transport become an extension of the character, and a salient part of that character's bodily attributes for the player. In racing and flying games, for instance, we couple ourselves with machines by selecting a vehicle as an extension of us. This takes on a distinctly capitalist dimension in games like *Extreme Sports* where one must earn enough money to upgrade to new and better equipment in order to compete, with our purchases guided by the attributes assigned by the game to the character body we've chosen.

Games commodify our cyborg desires, our will to merge with and become technology. To be able to earn a more spectacular outfit, the player is invited to learn repetitive bodily movements and reactions. That is, like industrial work, fast fighting and shooting games are based on repetition of similar movements and their precise timing; our bodies have to develop a sort of prosthetic memory if we (our avatars) are to survive as we melt into electronic worlds. Indeed as Julian Stallabrass has suggested: "Computer games force a mechanization of the body on their players in which their movements and the image of their alter-ego provide a physical and a simulated image of the self under capital, subject to fragmentation, reification and the play of allegory."[25] They seduce us to take pleasure in a sort of Taylorian effectivity and the commodification of the mechanization of work and bodies, making it a pleasurable experience. Thus, what Ted Friedman has called "cyborg consciousness"—learning to internalize the logic of the program and "thinking *along with* the computer, becoming an extension of the computer's processes"[26]—can equally describe gaming's imposition of (real) corporeal discipline which is tied to and motivated by a set of (represented) bodily rewards, in the form of earned enhancements. In this understanding, "cyborg consciousness" informs and feeds the player's desire to spectacularize herself through the selection and control of represented bodily attributes.

This is further supported by the fact that games' interactivity makes us as players responsible for producing spectacular sequences. Various games reward successful continuous playing with spectacular cinematic sequences at the end of the game or by letting us unlock new characters, outfits, weapons, vehicles, or other equipment after finishing a level; and this is seen as an important source of pleasure, as exemplified by the following review of *Rollcage Stage II*, a PlayStation 2 game: "*Stage II* wouldn't be the success it is without its splendidly rewarding structure—nearly every triumphant achievement brings about new goodies."[27] Similarly, in *Civilization III*, reaching "Space Victory" is rewarded with a short computer-animated sequence of launching "your own" spaceship. During one level in *Rez*, you actually get to construct a female figure, piece by piece, if you successfully finish various shooting tasks.

Games, however, impose clear restrictions on our potential desire to toy with different bodies. They restrict our choice to a clearly differentiated and limited matrix of body types, to a shopping list of bodies marked as distinct and distinguishable representatives of various races, sexes, and nations. That is, games set limits to the mutability of the body. Rather than deconstruct or destabilize identities of raced or gendered belonging, such games invoke and reinforce a narrow set of highly codified, preexisting categories to be temporally inhabited as an easily assumed, ready-to-be-invaded vessel of the Other. At the same time, game menus promise an experience of exploring what it might feel occupying different electronic subjectivities and bodies by creating a range of alternate selves. They suggest that cyborgization is partially driven by a desire to try on different bodies, to trespass or toy with racial and sexual boundaries, underlining psychic and social structures motivating racial and sexual cross-dressing.

For white men, this becomes a safe way to try on being a different race or sex without the risk of relinquishing any social or cultural power associated with the white male identity in the real world. Identification, one must remember, is not simply a process of recognizing one's likeness in a screen representation. Rather, it is always about projecting oneself into a space defined by its otherness from the subject. The question is more one of the degree of alterity across which that projection can take place and what desires it answers to. It is crucial to recognize, in this regard, that the entire range of characters offered by such games share a single dominant quality, that is, the mastery in their field. If femininity for men has been associated with passivity and weakness, for instance, "trying on" femininity within the context of such games nonetheless remains a kick-ass experience.

Carol Clover has identified a similar process, what she calls a "play of pronoun functions," in describing modes of identification for horror cinema, or more specifically, slasher films.[28] Here, a largely adolescent male audience identifies across gender, shifting loyalties from a male killer to a "final girl" heroine, in part as a way of playing with what it would be like to be female, but an ultimately phallicized and triumphant female. Play with subject positions is not just across the pronouns he/she however, but, a shift in the camerawork's construction of a cinematic "I." From stalking female victims through the killer's eyes (and often his literal optical perspective rendered in extended subjective camerawork), horror films shift toward a presentation of the point of view of the "final girl," a combined victim-hero, as she eventually turns the tables on the killer. Shifting across such identificatory options, both in terms of on-screen embodiments and in terms of spatially positioned points of view, is the particular pleasure of slasher films for Clover. Video games offer a somewhat different but parallel "play of pronoun functions." There is an ambiguous double-effect in game-playing. Games have increasingly moved toward a fully subjective set of perspective-based relations, orienting the viewer to the action as oneself; yet they also have insisted on manufacturing increasingly exotic fantasy selves, defined sharply by categorical difference, otherness, from oneself. And games have done this by offering a simultaneous experience of disembodied perception and yet an embodied relation to technology.

I have suggested that, yes, on one hand, various games emphasize an immaterial and disembodied vision that explores a virtual landscape with relative freedom and liberates perception (and the body) in some fashion from its normal limitations of placement and movement in daily life. On the other hand, games respond to this liberated vision and out-of-body experience by locating knowledge and experience firmly in the familiar terrain of the body. They accustom us to the newness of new technologies by coupling the game world's cyborg bodies and subjectivities (reassuringly) with our own bodies, making the virtual and the physical complementary rather than mutually exclusive realms. Joysticks, game controllers, pedals, and various steering systems further foreground haptic interaction and simultaneously encapsulate players in a game world complete with bodily sensation.

In this context, games' importance lie in the fact that they challenge us to rethink audiovisual theories that have regularly articulated media spectatorship as a passive process that dematerializes the body and foregrounds a psychic or cognitive experience. But the body, too, is a site where sensory stimuli are registered. And increasingly, it is precisely the carnal pleasures of gaming that are being mobilized by producers and sought out by consumers. If something is left behind when we play, it is not the body. We may be toying with the body when we play, but we remain flesh as we become machines.

Acknowledgment

My deepest gratitude to Melanie Nash whose insightful and generous suggestion and criticism again helped considerably to focus my argument.

Notes

1. Alluquère Rosanne Stone credits this book as having created the "imaginal public sphere" for the "technologically literate and socially disaffected" groups in Silicon Valley and thus having provided a cornerstone for a "new community." See Alluquère Rosanne Stone, "Will the Real Body Stand Up? Boundary Stories about Virtual Cultures," in *Cyberspace: First Steps,* ed. Michael Benedikt (Cambridge, MA, and London: MIT Press, 1992), 95. Even though one may not quite agree with Stone's utopian tone, it would be hard to deny Gibson's centrality to the way contemporary discourse imagines technologized bodies and subjectivities.
2. In Sherry Turkle, *Life on the Screen: Identity in the Age of the Internet* (New York: Simon & Schuster, 1995), 265. Turkle is quoting Colin Greenland, "A Nod to the Apocalypse: An Interview with William Gibson," *Foundation* 36 (Summer): 5–9.
3. Turkle, *Life on the Screen: Identity in the Age of the Internet,* 265.
4. Anne Balsamo, *Technologies of the Gendered Body: Reading Cyborg Women* (Durham, NC, and London: Duke University Press, 1996).
5. See Stone, "Will the Real Body Stand Up? Boundary Stories about Virtual Cultures."
6. Scott Bukatman, *Terminal Identity: The Virtual Subject in Post-Modern Science Fiction* (Durham, NC, and London: Duke University Press, 1993), 196–197.
7. Balsamo, *Technologies of the Gendered Body: Reading Cyborg Women,* 2–3.
8. Margaret Morse, "What Do Cyborgs Eat? Oral Logic in an Information Society," *Culture on the Brink: Ideologies of Technology,* eds. Gretchen Bender and Timothy Druckrey (Seattle: Bay Press, 1994), 157.
9. Morse, "What Do Cyborgs Eat? Oral Logic in an Information Society," 189.
10. Ted Friedman, "*Civilization* and Its Discontents: Simulation, Subjectivity, and Space," in *On a Silver Platter: CD-ROMs and the Promises of a New Technology,* ed. Greg M. Smith (New York University Press: New York and London, 1999), 137.
11. "Perfect Dark," *Edge* 82 (March 2000): 27.
12. Rusel Demaria and Johnny Wilson, *High Score: The Illustrated History of Electronic Games* (McGraw-Hill/Osborne: Berkeley, 2002), 14.
13. "Spanking good coin-op fun," *Edge* 102 (October 2001): 17.
14. See <http://europe.thrustmaster.com/products>.
15. "Rez," *Edge,* 105 (Christmas, 2001): 75.
16. "Burnout," *Edge* 104 (December 2001): 70.
17. Lauren Rabinovitz, "Temptations of Pleasure: Nickelodeons, Amusement Parks, and the Sights of Female Sexuality,"*Camera Obscura* 23 (May 1990): 77.
18. "StarCraft: Ghost," *Edge* 118 (Christmas, 2002): 37.

19.   Erkki Huhtamo, "Encapsulated Bodies in Motion: Simulators and the Quest for Total Immersion," in *Critical Issues in Electronic Media*, ed. Simon Penny (Albany, NY: State University of New York Press, 1995), 177.
20.   "Project Ego," *Edge* 101 (September 2001): 30.
21.   Bukatman, *Terminal Identity: The Virtual Subject in Post-Modern Science Fiction*, 198–199.
22.   Stone, "Will the Real Body Stand Up? Boundary Stories about Virtual Cultures," 108.
23.   J.C. Herz, "Fighters Customizable for Combat," *New York Times*, July 22, 1999, D4.
24.   "Deus Ex," *Edge* 83 (April 2000): 35.
25.   Julian Stallabrass, *Gargantua: Manufactured Mass Culture* (London and New York: Verso, 1996), 89.
26.   Friedman, "*Civilization* and Its Discontents: Simulation, Subjectivity, and Space," 136.
27.   "Rollcage Stage II," *Edge* 82 (March 2000): 71.
28.   Carol Clover, *Men, Women, and Chain Saws: Gender in the Modern Horror Film* (Princeton, NJ: Princeton University Press, 1992).

CHAPTER 8

Hot Dates and Fairy-Tale Romances

Studying Sexuality in Video Games

MIA CONSALVO

"I'm always thinking about girls. I'm popular with ALL the ladies in Lindblum. Come to me if you have any girl trouble, ok?"

—Zidane to Vivi in *Final Fantasy IX*

"Only opposite-sex relationships qualify for a proposal of marriage."

—*The Sims* Instruction Manual: 57

Coinciding with the release of more adult-themed games such as *BMX XXX* (2002) that feature highly realistic female nudity, popular attention to games is beginning to broaden from solely considering violence to thinking about sex. But sex and sexuality have been integral (if subtextual) parts of many games, and their expression generally reifies conservative beliefs about heterosexuality and "proper" romance. For example, the Sony PlayStation game *Harvest Moon: Back to Nature* (2000), is rated E for everyone. The game is a farming simulation and features no violence of any type. The game gives "you" as the main character three years to bring your grandfather's farm back into shape. That involves growing seasonal crops, raising livestock, and keeping the property in good condition. However, an equally important part of the gameplay involves "getting a girl" and having her marry you. "You" are by definition male, and to properly advance in the game, you are encouraged to flirt with and date different female characters, in hopes that one will return your affections and agree to marry you and help out on the farm. And that's just a farming simulation game for "everyone." What do other (more mainstream) games have to say with regard to sex and sexuality?

Research that has focused on gender and race in games comes the closest to exploring these issues. Feminist researchers have started to systematically explore images of women in mainstream video games, and have found that representations of women and girls in games reapply many stereotypes of femininity and vulnerability found in more traditional media.[1] Likewise, research on masculinity and race has explored how certain games construct Asian men through tired and reductive stereotypes.[2] Yet, these female and male game characters do not exist in isolation from each other, but interact in varied situations. And these interactions are many times sexualized, usually with the presumption of heterosexual interests. Although this situation is not surprising, considering that a majority of the population identifies as heterosexual, it does demand to be studied, to better see how sexuality and sexual orientation are represented in games, and how heterosexuality is normalized and presented as a "regular" part of life, while queerer interactions are either absent, or made to appear deviant (and denigrated) to some degree.

These situations have become more explicit over the history of games. For example, the original *Donkey Kong* (1981) game featured the player as the male plumber Mario attempting to rescue Princess Zelda from the giant male ape. Admittedly, the true excitement of the game came from dodging barrels and climbing ladders to advance—there was no dialogue or interaction between characters. It was presumed that a "rescue the princess" theme was sufficient back-story to explain why someone would want to dodge barrels and climb ladders, and it worked.[3] The heterosexual nature of the theme (why would you want to rescue a princess? Who were "you" in the first place? Why was it a female that needed rescuing? Why was it a male doing the rescuing?) was implicit, and indeed very peripheral to actual gameplay. John Banks has correctly argued that exploring how games such as *Donkey Kong* perpetuate ideas about patriarchy through their representations merits attention, but, as Banks also argues, we must go beyond surface constructions to study how gameplay might perpetuate or even challenge such readings in different sorts of ways.[4]

This essay begins charting that territory, as it focuses on the construction and continuing refinement of sexuality as a part of characterization and storyline in games. It also explores the underlying presumption (in most games) that the player of the game desires a gaming experience where heterosexuality is seen as a social norm. The essay uses various theoretical approaches to studying sexuality in games, and suggests how studying both representations and gameplay are valuable.

This essay focuses on two examples while taking a multilevel approach. First, the essay considers representations of characters as they appear in the games—the narratives and history offered, visuals, and situations found (including character dialogue, subplots, appearance, etc.). This "surface" level and these elements must be explored to determine some of the implicit as well as explicit sexuality found in games.

However, as game theorists such as Janet Murray and John Banks note,[5] a game is not simply a text to be read, but an experience to be had—and so we must also consider the performative level of gameplay. Here things get much more complex. A human being is manipulating a character (or multiple characters) in a game, and is thus performing actions, and assuming a gender as well as a sexual orientation (to varying degrees), for an avatar. How a player's input alters or reinforces what is presented in the game—how static representations become dynamic—becomes much more complicated, especially as more queer readings arise, and the heterosexuality implied in the games either fails to matter/materialize, or can be subverted in interesting ways. There are several theoretical approaches that are useful in understanding these transgressive practices, including Sedgwick's formulations of male homosocial desire and its place (and displacement) in erotic triangles, an investigation of the idea of gay-window advertising (here, becoming gay-window gaming), explorations of abstract characters and the identifications they encourage, idealized heterosexuality, and considerations of the concepts "game" and "play" themselves. Putting together these approaches in exploring *The Sims* (2000) and *Final Fantasy IX* (2000) leads to multiple interpretations of gaming and sexuality.

This essay considers the following questions:

- How can we study sexuality in video games?
- What are some theories that could be useful in this exploration?
- Are there useful distinctions to be made between representations and gameplay?
- How is sexuality expressed in the games studied?

Living the Romance: *Final Fantasy IX*

The console game *Final Fantasy IX* was released in 2000 to economic and critical success.[6] *Final Fantasy IX (FF9)* is one of the most recent entries in a successful product line created by producer Hironobu Sakaguchi for Square Company Limited (*Final Fantasy X* for the Playstation 2 was released in January 2002). The *Final Fantasy* series is one of the best selling (and best known) in the industry, with more than 33 million units sold.[7] *FF9* is a role-playing game that is quite closed-ended, requiring the player to engage in a traditional "video game" style of play: exploring a world; fighting monsters; solving riddles; and ultimately getting to the "end" of the game. The plot of

FF9 is also highly traditional, employing warriors, princesses, castles, evil sorcerers, good magicians, and a battle to save the planet from the forces of evil.

The central character that the player "controls" throughout the game is Zidane, a young male of indeterminate race (but light complected and with a tail) who must battle his nemesis, Kuja, before winning the game and, also, the hand of Princess Garnet. Two approaches will be taken to better understand how sexuality is constructed and expressed in this game. The first approach examines the surface representation or romance between two of the main characters. This level approaches the game as a media product that idealizes compulsory heterosexuality, conceptualized by Adrienne Rich as a system that naturalizes male-female sexual relations and punishes women who attempt to deviate from this system.[8] The second approach studies gameplay, and how a player manages his potential desire for the main character, through recourse to Eve Sedgwick's theory of the erotic triangle, here reconfigured from screen theory to account for the activity of gameplay. Each approach yields a different understanding of how the game could be "read," and each provides valuable insight into the expression of sexuality in games.

The Literal Fairy-Tale Romance—Representing Ideal Heterosexuality

Adrienne Rich has written that feminists must study heterosexuality as a political institution in order to better understand how it is perpetuated in patriarchal societies.[9] One way it has been normalized is through media representations of the ideal heterosexual romance, shown as "the great female adventure, duty and fulfillment."[10] And, as Leena-Maija Rossi further explains, heterosexuality in mediated images or representations is often employed to help "evoke desire and identification" between characters and audiences.[11] Seen in this light, it is odd that a game sold mainly to males would have a romantic storyline contained within it,[12] but Rich addressed her arguments mainly to how women have been forcibly positioned as heterosexual subjects, and I argue that men have become the targets of such positioning as well. With that in mind, we can better analyze a central component of the *FF9* plot—the developing romance between Zidane and Garnet and the "naturalness" of heterosexuality for fantasy characters.

The game begins with computer-animated scenes, showing a beautiful young woman sitting alone in a castle, in a low-cut white dress. It is obvious that the game will concern her in some way, although at this time just how remains a mystery. More information is provided through the introduction of Zidane. As mentioned above, he is shown as a puckish character, ready to fight but with a charming quality. He is also quickly defined by his interest in girls—in the first few hours of gameplay, his dialogue with various characters demonstrates just how "girl crazy" he is—although this banter is usually presented in a humorous manner. To Princess Garnet, on knowing her for literally minutes, he says after she jumps off a high wall "wow, you're really athletic Princess. I think I'm falling for you." Later, when she has been kidnapped, he explains to a friend "yeah—what's there to think about! She's cute ... and she's in trouble. That's all that matters." Trying to finish the character Vivi's thought, "I was just thinking," Zidane offers "about a girl?" To Vivi's denials, Zidane elaborates: "I'm always thinking about girls. I'm popular with ALL the ladies in Lindblum. Come to me if you have any girl trouble, ok?" Even other characters occasionally get tired of his girl talk and ask him to "get your mind off girls for a second."

Zidane's dialogue at the beginning of the game goes a long way toward establishing his character as insistently heterosexual. Although his excessive girl talk prompts some characters to ask him to stop, the naturalness of his desire for girls is not questioned, but is instead usually reinforced by other characters as they react favorably to seeing beautiful women. The game architecture also reinforces Zidane's heterosexuality by allowing him to learn the ability "protect girls," which allows him/you to "take damage in place of a girl" during battles.[13]

While Zidane's heterosexuality is important, it would not function effectively if Garnet were not seen as potentially returning his affections. Although in the beginning she does not give overt indications, the game itself predicts a future union, and her actions also suggest that at the least, she too is heterosexual. For example, perhaps an hour in game time after the two have met (a disguised Garnet knocks down Zidane when she runs past him in the castle), Zidane has a flashback to this "meeting" which he and you view, while he states "maybe fate brought us together. Man I can't stop thinking about her." Even if Garnet herself doesn't realize it yet, she and Zidane have been "brought together" by fate—as they literally collide with each other.

Additionally, because Garnet is running away from the castle and her mother, she must take on an assumed identity and also change her speech and behaviors to appear more like a "commoner." In conversation with an old woman who is picking bugs off plants in a garden, she does not express the "normal" expression of distaste for them (as the old woman states "most girls hate oglops"), but then tries to "blend in" better and counts to three after which she screams and throws the oglop down. Garnet tries to blend in by acting more "authentically" like a girl, and as the woman states, girls hate bugs (oglops). A traditional position for girls is offered, and Garnet fulfills it. As the story progresses, she expresses her feelings for Zidane, also traditional, and which are ultimately fulfilled. Garnet works at being a "regular girl" and all that it implies. Part of that is heterosexuality, which is fulfilled as well.

The story of the romance in the game is idealized—it is a classic "star-crossed lovers" tale featuring a girl and boy thrown together by fate, forced to work together, separated temporarily by duty (Garnet must assume the throne when her mother dies), but ultimately reunited in a classic "happily ever after" scene. The pairing is also idealized in that one is royalty while the other is a thief, suggesting that these two are an unlikely match, but through the strength of their love, they manage to overcome all obstacles (including saving the world) to get to their happy ending. In this reading of the Garnet-Zidane romance, heterosexuality is shown as natural and preferable, with marriage being the logical conclusion to romance, and the theme of "love can conquer all" dutifully upheld. It's hard to get more idealized than that. However, that idealized romance may not be so trouble-free if gameplay is taken into account, as the next section suggests.

FF9, Identification, and the Erotic Triangle

FF9 is more than a representation of an ideal romance—it is a game to be played. And as stated before, the main character/avatar the player controls is Zidane. Yet, what is the nature of this relationship between the player and the game character/avatar? In traditional screen theories, spectators are thought to identify with on-screen characters. Yet, this identification can be troublesome, as it is often based on normative ideas about gender and sexuality, leaving female and gay spectators invisible, or in disruptive positions.[14] Furthermore, *FF9* is not a film, but an interactive game. Can the same theoretical positions be relevant? Research on the player-avatar relationship has been limited to explorations of avatar creation for (textual and graphical) Internet chat spaces, and beginning examinations of the player's level of interactivity in contemporary video games.[15] In addition, other theoretical approaches (from visual theory) concerning the level of abstraction of the character and the ability or desire of the player to then identify or care for that character are integrated. This essay draws links between these various approaches, in an attempt to begin investigating the potential for player-avatar "identification," and what this identification might mean for different sorts of players.

The cartoonist and visual theorist Scott McCloud has written about the abstract nature of cartoon characters, and how the lack of details in characters allow viewers to identify with them (more than they would with more detailed, photo-realistic characters), because it encourages the viewer to see or position "himself" in or as the character.[16] A visual or iconic abstraction is "a vacuum into which our identity and awareness are pulled . . . We don't just observe [it], we become it."[17] McCloud's argument fits with game characters and those who play them—as the characters provide (to varying degrees) a certain level of abstraction, which combined with the ability to control the character, encourages the player to identify with the character, to "become" the character during gameplay. For example, although in CGI cut-scenes in *FF9* Zidane is represented as more "realistic" (greater detail in facial features, active expressions of emotions, although still in a distinctively anime-style), during actual game play the avatar for Zidane is much more abstract or stripped down in level of detail. The greater simplicity of style found in the Zidane "controller avatar," while a technical necessity, also functions to give players a better opportunity to "insert" themselves into the role of Zidane, and identify with the character. Additionally, the history of the central character (such as Zidane) is generally left underdeveloped, especially in relation to other characters. That also gives the player more opportunity to insert himself into the character, and as the player-character identification is further collapsed, the player is given one more push to care about the future of the character.

Steven Poole takes a somewhat different approach to player-character identification, but ultimately argues the same point.[18] He believes that players are more attracted to recent, almost lifelike characters such as "Lara Croft" of the *Tomb Raider* series, over the abstractions of Pac-Man, but because these characters aren't "too real" either, the player comes to care for them and feel badly if they die. Structurally, the player is also encouraged to see the game through the eyes of this particular character, often seeing events from this particular perspective a majority of the time, and only occasionally from the perspective of other characters. Additionally, as Gary Fine found in his study of paper-and-pen role playing gamers, heavy players usually become invested in maintaining and advancing their characters, and also came to identify with their characters to various degrees, such that they would cheat to prevent the death of a favorite character, or refuse to play with other gamers that would not help protect the group.[19]

As mentioned before, one component of *FF9* is the romance between Zidane and Princess Garnet, including their flirtation, banter, and increasing intimacies. The player is allowed to initiate some of these moments as choices for action are sometimes given—for example, will Zidane respond to a question from Garnet in a sarcastic or a caring manner? Will he admit to other characters his feelings for Garnet? Through the choices offered within the game, the player is drawn into the storyline and potential romance, but the romance proceeds regardless of any active efforts the player-character may make, and assumes a pre-set heterosexual format. Yet, the (male) player is encouraged to care about the central (male) character, and this presents a potential problem.

Pretty Boys that Wear Lace—How Masculine is That?

The character of Zidane is pictorially represented as feminized in many ways—long hair, physically small in stature, clothes with lace, a lack of obvious muscles. Can the assumed male heterosexual player successfully identify with a feminized male character, without perhaps coming to care for or even desire the character too much? Gay male players may identify with and desire the character at the same time, but heterosexual players (allegedly) do not.[20] Likewise, how does the character of Zidane, presented in such a nonmasculine way, demonstrate that he is in fact still worthy of being the "normal" (heterosexual and male) hero of the game? One way to contain these tensions is through the insertion of the female love interest: Garnet. Thus, Zidane is saved from gayness through his continual romantic interest in Garnet, and the player is allowed to channel any potential feelings of desire for the character into Garnet as well, and reassure himself that he, too, is heterosexual and thus still in a privileged position.[21] This containment of (potentially) homosocial feelings and displacement of desire occur through the construction of an erotic triangle.

Eve Sedgwick writes of the problems of male homosocial desire (defined as nonsexual interest and affection between men) in contemporary society—how to manage its expression when there is such a strong disjunction between the homosexual and the homosocial for male social actors. One response is the strategic use of the erotic triangle, comprising two men and one woman. Sedgwick quotes Levi-Strauss in explaining that the woman serves as a "conduit of a relationship" between two men—such that although the two men (shown as buddies) are competing over a woman, their actual interest is in each other.[22] The woman is a convenient placeholder to secure their heterosexuality, even as they seek more or better fulfillment through their relationship with the other man (and this relationship is not expressly or even intentionally sexual). The classic example of this erotic triangle is found in the male buddy action movie, where two men, that are good friends, end up competing over a woman who is either single or the girlfriend of one of the males. The situation largely becomes one of one-upmanship as the two men try to compete for the woman, and their interactions become more intense as they vie for dominance. But ultimately they are not as interested in the relationship with the woman as they are in their relationship with each other—yet societal fears of being seen as homosexual lead the men to displace their feelings for each other into the safe area of friendly competition over a heterosexual love object. Sedgwick's model builds on feminist interrogations of patriarchal systems, where "woman exists only as an occasion for mediation, transaction, transition, transference, between man and his fellow men."[23]

Although the erotic triangle is generally applied to film or novel representations, I believe it can also be remediated to take gameplay into account. In many games, especially computerized role-playing games, a player is encouraged to identify with one central character that he/she controls for a majority of the game, even if there are other central characters present. The erotic triangle applies best to gameplay in which the intended player is male, and the central character played is also male—the dominant situation in games and gaming, according to the Interactive Digital Software Association.[24]

If the player-character, or player-Zidane, relationship is considered as the male/male part of the erotic triangle, then Garnet serves as the female component. No matter how play proceeds, Zidane and Garnet establish a conventional heterosexual romantic relationship, and the player is encouraged to insert himself into this budding relationship as well. Although Sedgwick postulates antagonism between the two male characters over the female, there is little of that evidenced in the player-Zidane connection. That is because the tensions generated in more conventional applications of the triangle are not necessitated in the game world—the ultimate goal of the game world is the collapse of distinctions between the player-Zidane, who will *both* get the girl in the end, after they have successfully saved the world from evil, and thus need not fear losing in any competition over a woman. Garnet thus serves a central function in gameplay—for as mentioned previously, the player is encouraged to identify closely with Zidane, to care for and wish to develop the character, if not take on the temporary identity of the character. The erotic triangle thus spatially collapses the two males into one, competing, very successfully now, for not only the princess but more importantly for the (normative) validation of masculinity—heterosexuality—that is conferred through this relationship.

And what if the player is a heterosexual female, or a gay male? Viewing the game (or playing the game) from these subject positions demonstrates how norms can be made visible and problematized. For example, a heterosexual female playing the character of Zidane is "forced" to flirt with another woman (character) as a regular part of gameplay. In this instance identification with the main character becomes much more difficult, and the erotic triangle collapses, unable to sustain the conflicting desires of the player-character combination. The flirtation dialogues within the game serve to remind the female player that she is not of the normative group hailed by the game—but is instead an interloper, doubly masquerading within the confines of the game. Thus, using the erotic triangle to examine gameplay can show how normative groups can successfully be "hailed" and comfortably inhabit the player-character role. Nonnormative players, however, collapse the erotic triangle and show how delicate subject positions can be—and how heterosexuality can play an important role in sustaining these positions. Yet, what would happen if games allowed players greater freedom to explore these same issues, rather than dictate a role to them?

"Playing" Games, Playing Queer?

Video games share similarities with other forms of electronic media, yet are also different from them in fundamental ways. Another way to understand sexuality in *FF9* (as well as games generally) is to look more closely at the concept of play. Johann Huizinga has written one of the most well known explorations of play in history and culture, and although Huizinga reads play into almost all aspects of human life (including warfare, politics, the law, culture and religious rituals) his outlines for play serve well here for understanding how the concept of play can be applied to games. He writes: "The disguised or masked individual 'plays' another part, another being. He is another being"[25] and play is "a stepping out of 'real' life into a temporary sphere of activity with a disposition all of its own."[26]

As argued earlier in this essay, the player of *FF9* is encouraged to identify with, or at least temporarily assume the identity of, another persona (Zidane), thus disguising him/herself for a fixed period of time. The rules of the game are different from those of real life, and the player is indeed "masked" through the layer of the identity/persona of the character she controls within the game. Another way to describe this space/time would be a period of liminality, where the player is *between* her "real" life and the life of the character on the screen. As the rules of real life are temporarily lifted, so are social expectations, at least for some players. Thus, "normative" aspects of identity may be played with—altered or rejected—because the experience is "only a game." Researchers studying social actors in online MUDs have remarked that these individuals often experiment with gender and race identity.[27] Alternative masks of gender, race, and sexuality also are offered in games, but unfortunately most of these masks are stereotypes or caricatures, such as Zidane, that do not stray far from the assumed identity of the game player. More open-ended games with less scripting of these elements may provide better masks or opportunities for experimentation or exploration. Unfortunately most games currently on the market do not provide a wide array of these "masks."

By examining surface representations as well as the gameplay of *FF9*, different ways of understanding the expression of sexuality and how players might respond to it are found. The game can be both a "literal fairy-tale" that portrays heterosexuality as a logical part of a happy ending, as well as a space for male players to potentially desire a male character, or care deeply for him. By examining *FF9* using the theory of the erotic triangle, the normative construction of the game as for male players is exposed. Straight female players are reminded of their "otherness" through the romance, and straight male players are encourage to displace any "wayward" desires onto the more acceptable object of Garnet. In this second examination, the game is not so simply a fairy-tale, and the clashing of sexualized roles becomes apparent. These "roles" also can be examined as "masks" that the player can put on to experiment with various identities, but current games, such as *FF9*, do little to challenge stereotypical understandings of the difference of others. So, various theories can give us different interpretations of games, and while they may not be in complete agreement, they do give us more sophisticated understandings of the experience of gaming. To that end, the next section takes up *The Sims*, and explores its approaches to sexuality through other theoretical methods.

A More Radical Sexuality: Studying *The Sims*

Will Wright created *The Sims* in 2000 for Maxis, and it was released to both critical and popular acclaim. The game has become the best selling PC game of all time, and has spawned five "expansion packs" (*Livin' Large, House Party, Hot Date,*[28] *Vacation,* and *Unleashed*), which have all been commercially successful (the game is available on the Macintosh platform as well).[29] Wright's previous creations include *SimCity,* which is one of the few games studied in depth by academic researchers. Ted Friedman and Scott Miklaucic have studied different editions of the game, and explored how ideological biases and the organization of "space" built into the game have limited its more radical potentials.[30] *The Sims* is also ripe for analysis, and especially for this essay, as the goal of the game is to develop a neighborhood of healthy and happy "simulated people" and watch them go about their daily lives. The player of the game can create individuals as well as families, build houses, encourage or discourage various social interactions, and engage in lots of vicarious consumption. The mechanics of gameplay, as well as what is and isn't allowed, are explained in the game manual, which also provides hints to help players create more interesting situations.

There is no "winning" in *The Sims,* and no end to the game. Actually, Wright has stated that *The Sims* isn't a game—instead, it's a "software toy," which makes it even more intriguing to examine.[31] Players can continue to "play God" until they tire of the activity, but with the continual stream of add-on activities, products, and situations for Sims to encounter (including alien abductions, roach infestations, and mechanical bulls to install in the living room), this tendency is forestalled.

The Sims is perhaps the most progressive game yet released concerning sexuality, making it a good candidate for study. For example, there are various options offered to the player, including having same-sex roommates kiss and sleep in the same bed, and opportunities for this couple to be offered a child by an adoption agency. However, only opposite-sex couples are allowed to get married (but their relationships can fail and Sims can "move out" if pushed far enough). So, *The Sims* in some ways challenges norms of heterosexuality but in other ways reaffirms them. Another interesting facet of the game is its particular positioning of the player, as more a "god" than any other character in the game world. That placement raises interesting questions about character identification and investment in gameplay.

The Instruction Manual: A Primer in Structured Polysemy

While it is impossible to know exactly how many players of *The Sims* (or any computer game) actually read the instruction manual, the manual does offer help for the beginning player and can serve as a reference tool during gameplay. Examining the manual comes the closest to studying strict "representations" in this essay, as the images and words are static, and although readers may choose to interpret them differently, they cannot be altered like images in the game can be. To aid in understanding these representations and the language used here, a semiotic approach is taken, which posits that meanings can be slippery and contested, even as dominant meanings and definitions can occur.

The manual is written in a light and humorous tone, probably in an attempt to keep the interest of the reader. The tone and language also suggest that it is the reader who is ultimately in charge of the direction of the game, even as the "rules" proscribe certain limits on player imagination and desire. The manual includes pictures to illustrate as well as keep the manual visually appealing.

Pictures in the manual are all black and white, and are mostly screenshots or segments of screenshots showing players how to use and understand the game interface. However, there are also semitransparent "background" images of various Sim characters on many of the all-text pages, serving mainly as decoration. Many Sims are pictured alone, yet some are in pairs, interacting in various ways. However, when Sims are shown in a potentially "romantic" pose (embracing, dancing slowly) the partnering is always male/female, with no same-sex couples pictured. The only same-sex partnerings show Sims arguing, talking, or playing together. Thus in a subtle way the "naturalness" of heterosexual relations is enforced through the use of certain images and the omission of others.[32]

When studying the text of the manual, the situation becomes more complicated and more interesting in what it signifies. For a majority of the text, a structured polysemy of meaning is present, as personal pronouns to delimit the gender or implied sexuality of Sims (as individuals or in pairs) are absent. So, the text makes statements such as "romance between Sims can occur if they're feeling well disposed toward one another as well."[33] The use of the nongendered terms "Sims" as well as "they're" allows the reader to infer a variety of possible pairings, including male/female; male/male and female/female. As Sender has argued, this type of polysemy allows gay readers to interpret the meaning as queer or open to "alternative" meanings, while homophobic[34] straight readers may only "see" the romance as "naturally" occurring between opposite-sex Sims.[35] Both readings are allowed through the use of vague signifiers, and both interpretations can be enacted during gameplay.

While structured polysemy is the dominant mode of signification for the manual, certain sections do move from loose signifiers to more concrete (and limiting) directives. And, tellingly, these instances occur in regards to sexuality and what ultimately the game does and doesn't allow. So, for example, "only opposite-sex relationships qualify for a proposal of marriage."[36] Here, rather than an ungendered "they" or "Sim" the manual's language limits connotations with words such as "only," "opposite-sex," and "qualify." It is clear to the reader that even if same-sex Sims can develop a romance, "they" cannot get married in the game as it is currently coded. Likewise, the manual explains that same-sex Sims can "move in" together, and will even be offered the chance to adopt a baby, but it is "nothing you can plan on."[37] But, for opposite-sex Sims, "if you give your sexy Sims' batteries enough charge on the Romance scale (think passionate kisses), a dialog box appears letting you choose for them to have a baby."[38] In the manual then, heterosexuality is coded as sexy, and straight Sims are offered a "choice" of a baby, while gay Sims aren't described as sexy and can't "plan on" having children. The text (and the game) allows for some development of family for both hetero and homo Sims, although the language used to describe both is quite different. And, the label for the family ("married" vs. "living together") differs as well. Although the resulting situations for "gay" and "straight" Sims are the same—cohabitation—it is important that the labels attached to each are different, suggesting either a qualitative difference or a lack of commitment for those that "live together" as opposed to getting married. Language choices are important here, and the manual is making a statement reflective of contemporary cultural unease over the issue of gay marriage. What makes this situation even more problematic, however, is that the game also allows individual Sims to get married multiple times—as the manual explains, marriage is more of an "event" than a "state" for Sims. So, in an odd way, polygamy is sanctioned in a way that gay marriages are not.

Finally, the manual makes an interesting move in conflating gender with biological sex, and reifying both as a primary signifier of identity. In the section on how to create new Sims, the manual explains "perhaps the best way to begin putting things in order might be by selecting a sex for your Sim-to-be—gender is a pretty basic constituent of self from which to build a personality."[39] In one sentence, sex and gender are conflated as the same thing, and are further signified as an element of identity so important that personality is built *upon* sex/gender, which becomes a primary "core" of the self. Feminist scholars such as Judith Butler have correctly challenged the sex/gender conflation, arguing that genders (and their constituent attributes) are assigned to sexed bodies in an artificial manner reliant (in part) on culture, history, and social systems.[40] Although sex and/or gender may be constituent elements of a "self," it is interesting that this particular choice for Sim-building is coded in, and another potentially core element—sexual orientation—is left absent in the Sim-construction process.

So, in reading the instruction manual for information about Sim sexuality, conflicting messages appear. While much of the language is deliberately vague, allowing readers to "read into" the text multiple meanings (if they desire), many important sections relating to sexuality and constructions of family are more structured, disallowing the polysemy of other sections and reinscribing normative heterosexuality. Semiotically, the manual provides more and less open signification, perhaps striving for some balance between the interests of gay as well as homophobic players.

Creating New Characters (Gender, Race, Appearance, Personality, and Other Factors)

Although players may initially use prefabricated characters when learning how to play *The Sims,* it is expected that most players will move beyond these stock characters, and start creating their own. Creation of "families" is a central component of the game and is quite telling in terms of normative expectations and choices. These choices can challenge or reinforce traditional ideas about gender, race and other identity norms.

To create Sims, players go to a "Create New Family" screen. Even if players intend to create only one individual Sim, this Sim is considered a "family." From a feminist perspective, the use of the term "family" evokes traditional structures, but in the game players are able to create any sort of family that they desire—one person, a heterosexual couple with or without children, a same-sex couple, a group of platonic adult men and/or women, or just about any combination. Thus, players can establish any unit of measurement they desire as a "family." However, each family is designated through one common last name—although in this case it does not automatically come from the father—and it can be any name the player wishes. However, that does limit the radical potential created by nontraditional families, at least to some degree.

After choosing a family or "household" name, the player then moves on to creating new Sims. Another screen appears where the player is invited to enter a first name for the new Sim, as well as create a personality based on five components ("neat"; "outgoing"; "active"; "playful"; "nice") that can be differently weighted, as well as choose whether the Sim is a child or adult; male or female; and with light, medium or dark complexion. Additionally, a box showing the potential Sim is displayed, and players can alter the appearance of their Sims—choosing different heads that have different hair colors and styles, show advanced age or youth, have various facial hair and/or features, and also choose different bodies, which have various clothing options. Thus, players are encouraged to experiment and customize their Sims, creating "individuals" that can be very different from one another in appearance as well as personality.

On the surface, this diversity is refreshing in a video game—very few other games offer players this variety in choosing the characters they will play, or in creating them. However, closer examination of these choices suggests that underneath the diversity, some traditional ideas about race and gender (if not sexuality) can still be found, however subtle. For example, when the dialog box for creating an individual Sim first appears, the default Sim that pops up is a light-complexioned male Sim that looks middle-aged and is dressed in white-collar work attire—a white shirt with a pocket protector and gray pants. Because the game encourages exploration and experimentation with Sim characters, it is likely that most players quickly move past this first option with little thought, yet the default image of the hegemonic white male showing up first does reinforce the traditional notion of white men being the "norm" in American society, from which all others then deviate.[41]

Additionally, although many choices are offered to the player in constructing a Sim, choices can be more or less limiting. There are sixteen bodies for women, five for children (both girls and boys) and eighteen bodies for men. There are various numbers of heads available—with fewer choices for darker-shaded "heads" than for the lighter-shaded ones. Bodies have their own sets of norms built in as well—no body is disabled or obese, with the majority being slim and toned. Only one male body is noticeably overweight, and none of the children's bodies are out of shape. A range of ages is reflected in heads and bodies, with some showing gray hair and spectacles, and others looking very youthful. Once set in motion, Sim characters never age (they may die of accidental death however), and children never grow up.

Importantly, when creating characters there is no "check off" box to code a Sim as gay, straight, or bisexual. Sexuality is defined within the game as an activity, rather than as an unchangeable aspect of identity. For Sims, being gay or straight is all about choice, rather than an innate preference. This could be interpreted as positive or negative. For many gay rights activists, for example, the implication that sexuality is "merely" a choice gives credibility to arguments that if homosexuality is optional, then individuals can opt "out" of that activity. For this group, seeing difference in sexuality as "innate" is politically necessary. By contrast, some might applaud the choice, as to suggest that any body is "innately" sexualized (or gendered) is essentialist and reductionist, and the product of social, cultural and historical conditioning, rather than biological structure. So—defining Sim sexuality as about choice (and variable choice—Sims can have multiple "lovers" of different sexes), rather than essence can be read as progressive and regressive by different groups.

Finally, it is important to note that Will Wright consciously chose to make available "gay relationships" for Sim characters, and has said so in interviews.[42] His stated intent was to allow players to be able to create families that "looked like their own families," although in the popular press it seems that many game reviewers are more interested in creating gay Sims simply out of curiosity than any need to better reflect "real life."[43] But whatever the intentions of players, the opportunity is present to have Sims display straight, gay, or bisexual behaviors, even if this doesn't remain part of their "core" identity.

All of these options and limitations regarding bodies, personality, behaviors, and actions suggest that diversity is an important aspect of the game, but that diversity must be limited. Even if diversity was limited only for financial or practical reasons, it is important to raise this issue, to better understand which options were ultimately considered necessary and which were expendable. It is also critical to note that I have analyzed the choices that are offered to players of the basic Sims game. This does not include add-on game updates, or player created options. Fans of *The Sims* have created numerous Web pages with scores of choices for modifying Sims—new clothing, heads, objects, and more. This does allow more customization, yet I limit this analysis to the basic choices offered every player in order to keep this analysis manageable.

Gay Window Gaming in *The Sims*

Analyzing gameplay can be challenging when the construction of characters (or creation of representations) is *part* of the gameplay. However, there are other theoretical tools that can help illuminate how playing with sexuality can be more liberating, as well as more isolating, in open-ended games such as *The Sims*. One concept or tool helpful for understanding sexuality and its expression in games is one borrowed from another medium and format: gay window advertising.

The term "gay window advertising" has been used in identifying advertising that is designed somewhat ambiguously to appeal to both "straight" and "gay" readers.[44] The ads typically used coded signs or symbols (an attractive man alone; rainbow colors; the color lavender; two women together but in a nonsexual way) to suggest to gay readers that they are included in the ad's appeal, but the codings are never so explicit that straight readers would "catch on" and see the ad as also appealing to gays. Thus, the ads succeed in addressing both gay and straight consumers, without the fear that straight consumers will be offended by the appeal to gays and lesbians.

However, while some people have praised these ads for finally acknowledging gay audiences and recognizing that gay people do indeed buy products, others have criticized them for continuing to hide explicit forms of gay sexuality and identity, and for bowing to entrenched homophobic assumptions about what heterosexual readers can "accept" in "their" media.[45] For both the positive and negative connotations associated with gay window advertising, I believe the concept can be applied to *The Sims,* to better explain how gay sexuality or identity is expressed in gameplay.

Although gayness is not a feature explicitly "coded in" to characters in *The Sims,* it is also *not* a feature omitted or forbidden, therefore "coded out." Although same-sex Sims cannot get married, there is no law (or code) forbidding them from sleeping together, or even living together. Indeed, if they live together long enough, they may even be "offered" a baby. There is clearly a range of opportunities for the player to create "gay" Sims, whether one or an entire neighborhood. And, although marriage is still off limits, there are no "hate crimes" in Sim-land to discourage gay Sims from stepping out of their (well-stuffed) closets, or even any reason for them to be *in* a closet to begin with.

This wider range of possibilities for the expression of sexuality, as well as sexual identification, is at least in some ways a more liberal approach to characters, games, and gameplay. Players are encouraged to create their own characters, however they choose—either in their own images or as far from them as possible. There doesn't need to be a "joyful wedding" to mark the "end" of the game; indeed there need be no end to the game. Additionally, as Henry Jenkins has written, some players of *The Sims* have found it to be a helpful tool in "play acting" certain situations, or coming to terms with real life problems.[46] So *The Sims,* at least for some players, and on some levels, can be transgressive and offer new ways of seeing a video game, and ways of characterizing and playing them.

To borrow from Sender, Wright has created a structured polysemy with *The Sims*, where a range of readings of the game are allowed "that are variously responded to by audiences, depending...upon the relevance of a given reading to their cultural identification."[47] So, gay-friendly gamers can create a gay Sim or gay Sim neighborhood, while homophobes need never see or encounter gay Sims in their own creations.

However, this creation of a "gay window" into gaming also can be limiting. Just as the game gives players control over the creation and interaction of characters, this control allows players to construct their own games as they prefer. Options not explored will not surface, at least in the game as it is currently constructed. Game designers make choices, and these choices have consequences. This is especially important to consider with *The Sims*, as its appeal is based in part on its attempts to accurately "model" human life. Thus, games such as *The Sims* can be judged on how well they model or challenge dominant social structures. These social structures, and how they are played out in the game, need to be critiqued for their correspondence to (or departure from) "reality."

So, it is important that players can create rich, whites-only neighborhoods, for example, and never have to "worry" about all the "poor, black Sims" displaced from this land. And while gay Sims will likely live peaceful and happy lives in one game, they probably won't exist at all in a majority of Sim-lands. Likewise, random characters in a game do not "come out" (that I have heard of or seen) as gay, lesbian, bisexual or even transsexual. Gayness *can* be coded out of existence for the homophobic player, creating a world where every Sim-person is "naturally" straight and does not transgress the stated rules of "normal" society. Homophobic players need never encounter a gay Sim in daily life, or even acknowledge their existence.

Homophobic players are not forced to read *any* of their Sims as gay, and because the "reading" or construction of a gay Sim depends on the volition of the player, homophobic players can choose to overlook or never consider the potential for gay Sims at all. And although gay players (and gay-friendly straight players) can create a more "realistic" simulation of their own lives, where gays are integrated into the fabric of everyday society, this interaction is strangely devoid of political consequences. Although gay life may be unproblematic in one Sim neighborhood, those interested in gay life and culture will have little to go on, as the networks of gay society (including gay bars, bookstores and coffeehouses, gay films, political action groups and the larger gay community) are not readily present or apparent in this still gay-friendly world.

The ability of players to create new "skins" for their Sims, and the ability to create and download new objects into the game offers potential hope for gay culture to be reflected in Sim-life, but currently it is more hope than reality.

Playing God/Mom

Finally, the perspective the player takes in *The Sims* is different than in *Final Fantasy IX*, in that the player does not take on the "identity" of any one character in particular, but is expected to create and manage multiple characters. While players can limit themselves to only playing one character, and playing multitudes would get out of hand, the general expectation is that players are responsible for at least a few Sim inhabitants. While allowing more options, such activities do limit the investment a player might have for any individual character, and characters' particular future in the neighborhood.

Furthermore, the game itself encourages a different way of thinking about the characters in the game. The game is structured for the player to be the "eye in the sky" rather than having a first or third person view of the action, such as what is found in the *Quake* or *Tomb Raider* games, respectively. In *FF9*, the player does not literally see the game world through Zidane's eyes (the view is generally a third-person overview), but by only being able to control one character (a majority of the time—occasionally the player can control another player, but only temporarily), a closer relationship with this one character can more easily be established. This device works to invest the player's energy into protecting Zidane and coming to care for his role in the world and his actions within it.[48] However, the structuring of *The Sims* is markedly different.

In *The Sims*, players can control any character they desire, by quickly switching among them and by zooming into and out of different houses. While players can develop "favorite" characters that they soon focus more playing time on, the ability to just as quickly "dump" or more literally "evict" characters (or families) does not force the same attachment that *FF9* does. You may hate Zidane, or even another peripheral character, but you can't kill, evict, or otherwise oust any of these characters from the game.[49] As Murray argues in regards to narrative, stories such as those in films may kill off favorite characters, and although viewers may be upset or enraged at the act, they must accept it, and in doing so they make an emotional investment in the film and its particular story. When games allow players to randomly change storylines, create and evict characters at will, and see the world through no particular set of eyes, such emotional investments may be harder to come by. That does not mean that players will *never* make these close attachments or fail to make interesting or difficult choices, only that they will be less likely to occur. Thus, *The Sims*, through a plethora of choices, ends up perhaps leaving the player with fewer investments, rather than more. And, in doing so, the players can choose to invest less emotional energy into caring about characters, gay or straight, since they are all so interchangeable. Game design has consequences, and while many choices can seem to be liberating, these choices can also be constraining in other ways as well.

By using different theoretical approaches to *The Sims,* varying interpretations of the game appear. The instruction manual for the game pictorially represents a narrow slice of Sim life, while the text has varying degrees of ambiguity, mostly relating to choices concerning sexuality and having children. The creation of characters within the game furthers the ambiguity, as sexual orientation is defined as an activity, rather than being coded as a core of identity. And, finally, the act of gameplay seems the most liberating, in that it allows players more options than the manual would suggest, and lets players create a world peopled by "queer" Sims unburdened with "essential" identities or sexualities. Yet, this same world might be absent for homophobic players, and these radical potentials would never surface.

Conclusions

This essay has explored how sexuality is expressed in two games, and has demonstrated how various theoretical approaches can yield different understandings of the same game. It shows that theories applicable to other forms of media can be adapted to the study of video games, and also points to the need for examining more than the surface level of representation in games. Additionally, while heterosexuality is often the dominant sexuality portrayed in games, this "representation" or "performance" can be subverted—both through the actions of the player and the structure of the game itself.

The example of *FF9* illustrates quite well traditional storylines in games, in which the idealized heterosexual romance is a highly traditional "fairy-tale"—suggesting that heterosexuality is natural and preferred, and romance between men and women (and boys and girls) is expected, desired, and to be sought out. Traditional ideas about men protecting women (who are constantly in need of rescue), and men pursuing women romantically, are played out in games like *FF9*. However, although highlighting the narrative vehicle of compulsory heterosexuality found in the game, analysis of this fairy-tale romance does little to help us understand the central motivations of the player—who is likely more concerned with the central actions of exploration, fighting, and general advancement.

Players of *FF9* are encouraged to care about the central character they play, through various devices such as abstraction encouraging identification and the perspective of the game world. However, with the normative male heterosexual player, that could present a problem if the player comes to care for the character "too much" and perhaps desire the character.[50] That tendency is forestalled or eliminated through the construction of an erotic triangle consisting of the player-character and Princess Garnet. However, the triangle points to the normative construction of the player as a heterosexual male—other subject positions create tension within the triangle, and would not function as successfully. Therefore, when taking gameplay into account (in conjunction with surface representations), sexuality as expressed in *FF9* is more complex, and might possibly allow for some "queer" readings, if the player of the game so desires it. That might be the case for some players, if when people engage in play, they put on various "masks" of identity and experiment with alternate rules (and discard social conventions), if only temporarily.

Players can also experiment with identity in other ways, and more fully, in other games such as *The Sims*. Although reading the "surface represen-tations" encountered in the instruction manual of *The Sims* gives players the idea that the game is somewhat conservative, in gameplay far more rad-ical potentials emerge. Gamers can experiment with the sexuality of their Sims to a degree far greater than in any mass market video game yet pro-duced. Sexuality for Sims is coded as an activity rather than a core aspect of identity, making almost any Sim potentially bisexual, homosexual, hetero-sexual, or even nonsexual. However, the radical potential of that sexuality is dimmed, because the expression of the sexuality requires activity on the part of the gamer. If players do not wish to challenge the presumed normative heterosexuality of their Sims, these potentials will likely not emerge, and the expression of queer sexualities, and explorations of queer identities, is submerged or ignored.

The two games examined in this essay are not meant to be representative of all video games, past or present. Instead, they are case studies for demon-strating how different theoretical approaches can fruitfully be applied to the study of games. They further demonstrate the importance of examining sexuality in games. While all games might not have overtly sexual themes, many games employ sexuality to some degree with characters and stories. Exploring more systematically how these varying sexualities are expressed is imperative, especially as the potential for more diversity in sexuality is arriving, through the success of *The Sims*. Sexuality is a component in many games, and going beyond the study of violence to consider sexuality and its expression will demand more theories to guide us.

Notes

1.   Nnedimma Okorafor and Lucinda Davenport, "Virtual Women: Replacing the Real." Paper presented at the annual meeting of the Association for Education in Journalism and Mass Communication, Washington, DC, August 2001.
2.   Jeffrey Ow, "The Revenge of the Yellowfaced Cyborg: The Rape of Digital Geishas and the Colonization of Cyber-Coolies in 3D Realms' *Shadow Warrior*," in *Race in Cyberspace*, eds. Beth Kolko, Lisa Nakamura and Gilbert Rodman (New York: Routledge, 2000), 51–68.
3.   J. C. Herz, *Joystick Nation: How Video Games Ate Our Quarters, Won Our Hearts, and Rewired Our Minds* (Boston: Little, Brown, & Company, 1997).

4. John Banks, "Controlling Gameplay," *M/C: A Journal of Media and Culture* 1, No. 5 (1998). Available online at <http://www.uq.edu/au/mc/9812/game.html>.

5. Janet Murray, *Hamlet on the Holodeck: The Future of Narrative in Cyberspace* (Cambridge, MA: MIT Press, 1998). Banks, "Controlling Gameplay."

6. Although there are some significant differences between computer, console, and arcade games, for this essay, the term "video game" is used to indicate all three when making general references to games. Arcade games were not chosen for this analysis because their style of play is quite different, requiring a player to master skills quickly and play games where there is little story or character development. This is because of the structure of arcade games, which are marketed on a per game basis. Game designers want a game that is over quickly to encourage replays. In contrast, console and computer games require a much larger upfront investment ($40–$60 instead of $1) and are thus expected to hold quite a bit of content to demonstrate their "value." This is why, for example, sixty-hour role-playing games are quite common as computer and console games but not as arcade games.

7. Skyler Miller, "The History of Square," *Gamespot.com* (2001). Available online at <http://www.gamespot.com/gamespot/features/video/hist_square/index.html>.

8. Adrienne Rich, "Compulsory Heterosexuality and Lesbian Existence," in *Feminist Frontiers IV,* eds. Laurel Richardson, Verta Taylor and Nancy Whittier (New York: The McGraw-Hill Companies, 1997), 81–100.

9. Rich, "Compulsory Heterosexuality and Lesbian Existence," 84.

10. Rich, "Compulsory Heterosexuality and Lesbian Existence," 92.

11. Leena-Maija Rossi, "Why Do I Love and Hate the Sugarfolks in Syruptown? Studying the Visual Production of Heteronormativity in Television Commercials," in *Conference Proceedings for Affective Encounters: Rethinking Embodiment in Feminist Media Studies,* eds. A. Koivunen and Susanna Paasonen (University of Turku, School of Art, Literature and Music, Media Studies, Series A, No. 49, 2001). Available online at <http://www.utu.fi/hum/mediatutkimus/affective/rossi.pdf>.

12. *FF9* is a console game, and according to the Interactive Digital Software Association, a majority of purchasers of console games are male. Interactive Digital Software Association, "Who Purchases Computer and Video Games?" (2001). Available online at <http://www.idsa.com/ffbox6.html>. Additionally, other research has found that more males (56 percent) than females (23 percent) have played games that fall under the genre of "role-playing games" (of which *FF9* is one), also suggesting that the audience for *FF9* is largely (although not solely) male. Mia Consalvo and Robert Treat, *Exploring Gameplay: A Survey of Game Players Preferences* (unpublished manuscript, 2002).

13. Throughout the game, the various characters have the opportunity to learn differing abilities—usually based on their identity (as thief, mage, or healer, for example). One of the first abilities Zidane learns is "protect girls," while other characters content themselves with learning magic spells such as "fire" or "cure."

14. Brett Farmer, *Spectacular Passions: Cinema, Fantasy, Gay Male Spectatorships* (Durham, NC: Duke University Press, 2000). Laura Mulvey, "Visual Pleasure and Narrative Cinema," *Screen* 16, No. 3 (1975), 6–18.

15. Lisa Nakamura, *Cybertypes: Race, Ethnicity, and Identity on the Internet* (New York: Routledge, 2002). John Suler, "The Psychology of Avatars and Graphical Space in Multimedia Chat Communities," *Chat Communication,* ed. Michael Beiswenger (Stuttgart, Germany: Ibidem, 1999): 305–344. James Newman, "In Search of the Videogame Player: The Lives of Mario," *New Media & Society* 4, No. 3 (2002), 405–422.

16. Scott McCloud, *Understanding Comics: The Invisible Art* (New York: Harper Collins, 1993).

17. McCloud, *Understanding Comics,* 36.

18. Steven Poole, *Trigger Happy: The Inner Life of Video Games* (London: Fourth Estate, 2000).

19. Gary Fine, *Shared Fantasy: Role-Playing Games as Social Worlds* (Chicago: University of Chicago Press, 1983).

20. Katherine Sender, "Selling Sexual Subjectivities: Audiences Respond to Gay Window Advertising," *Critical Studies in Mass Communication* 16 (1999), 172–196.

21. It is beyond the scope of this essay to investigate fully the genesis of video game characters, especially those of Japanese origin. But it is interesting to note that the Japanese have a category of anime and manga characters that are called "bishonen" which refer to feminine images of

young men or boys. These boys are pictured as nonthreatening, often with large eyes, flowing hair, physically very beautiful, and interested in love, emotions, and relationships. Typical consumers of these images include girls and women—and this genre is seen as not out of the ordinary in Japan. Many of these images have achieved "cross-over" success in products marketed to the west, including certain images of men, including Zidane, in games such as *Final Fantasy IX.*

22.   Eve Kosofsky Sedgwick, "Gender Asymmetry and Erotic Triangles," in *Feminisms: An Anthology of Literary Theory and Criticism,* eds. Robyn Warhol and Diane Price Herndl (New Brunswick, NJ: Rutgers University Press, 1993), 481.

23.   Susan Fraiman, "Geometries of Race and Gender: Eve Sedgwick, Spike Lee, Charlayne Hunter-Gault," *Feminist Studies* 20 (1994), 67, quoting Luce Irigaray, "Commodities Among Themselves," in *This Sex Which is Not One,* trans. Catherine Porter (Ithaca, NY: Cornell University Press, 1985), 193.

24.   Interactive Digital Software Association.

25.   Johan Huizinga, *Homo Ludens: A Study of the Play Element in Culture* (Boston: Beacon Press, 1950), 13.

26.   Huizinga, *Homo Ludens,* 8.

27.   Sherry Turkle, *Life on the Screen: Identity in the Age of the Internet* (New York: Simon & Schuster, 1995).

28.   This essay does not explore the characters, situations, actions, and objects from the five add-on expansion packs for *The Sims.* Although *Hot Date* would have provided interesting analysis, it was not available during the writing of this essay.

29.   Trey Walker, "*The Sims* Overtakes *Myst,*" *Gamespot.com* (2002). Available online at <http://www.gamespot.com>.

30.   Ted Friedman, "Making Sense of Software: Computer games and Interactive Textuality," in *Cybersociety: Computer-Mediated Communication and Community,* ed. Steve Jones (Thousand Oak, CA: Sage, 1995): 73–89. Scott Miklaucic, "Virtual Real(i)ty: *SimCity* and the Production of Urban Cyberspace." Paper presented at the annual meeting of the Association of Internet Researchers, Minneapolis, MN, October 2001. Available online at <http://www.english.uiuc.edu/miklauci/simcity1.htm>.

31.   Richard Rouse, *Game Design: Theory and Practice* (Plano, TX: Wordware, 2001).

32.   I here use the terms "natural" or "naturalness" in quotes to draw attention to how heterosexuality is consistently presented in contemporary mainstream society as either the logical or only choice in regard to sexual orientation or sexual activity. It is so "normal" that it is not even remarked on when it is represented, but is instead viewed as a regular, unremarkable facet of human existence. Centrally, however, the normative construction of heterosexuality as the only "real" sexuality is the area to which I wish to draw attention.

33.   Instruction Manual for *The Sims* (San Francisco: Maxis, 2000), 54.

34.   I use the term homophobic with some reservations, as the word literally means "fear of man." However, popular usage of the term has changed its meaning to fear or hatred of homosexuals, homosexual ideas, and related attitudes and behaviors. Precision in language is important for theoretical arguments, but currently there are no alternative words available that better capture the range of attitudes and behaviors I wish to address here.

35.   Sender, "Sexual Subjectivities."

36.   Instruction Manual, 57.

37.   Instruction Manual, 61.

38.   Instruction Manual, 59.

39.   Instruction Manual, 32.

40.   Judith Butler, *Bodies That Matter* (New York: Routledge, 1993).

41.   Robert Hanke, "Theorizing Masculinity With/in the Media," *Communication Theory* 8, No. 2 (1998), 183–203.

42.   Rouse, *Game Design.*

43.   Mark Boal, "Me and My Sims," *The Village Voice,* 2000, Available online at <http://www.villagevoice.com/issues/0013/boal.php>. Bill Stiteler, "The Sims," *Applelinks.com,* 2000. Available online at <http://www.applelinks.com/reviews/sims.shtml>.

44.   Sender, "Sexual Subjectivities."

45.   "Commercial Closet Association Mainstream Advertising Best Practices," The commercialcloset.org (2003), available on-line at <http://www.commercialcloset.org/cgi-bin/iowa/

index.html?page=best>. Suzanna Danuta Walters, *All the Rage: The Story of Gay Visibility in America* (Chicago: University of Chicago Press, 2001).

46. Henry Jenkins, "From *Barbie* to *Mortal Kombat*: Further Reflections." Paper presented at the conference *Playing by the Rules: The Cultural Policy Challenges of Video Games*, Chicago, IL, October 2001. Available online at <http://culturalpolicy.uchicago.edu/conf2001/papers/jenkins.html>.

47. Sender, "Sexual Subjectivities," 190.

48. Poole, *Trigger Happy*.

49. Once you begin advancing in *FF9* you have the ability to swap party members around, giving you the ability to "leave out" annoying members. However, this option is not available for Zidane—he always remains in the party and is the central character that the player controls. Additionally, although some other characters can be marginalized through neglect, this can come back to haunt the player later, as in some battles where certain characters are required. And if the player has neglected to advance (or "level up") all characters, that can cause greater difficulties.

50. Popular attention has been paid to male gamers that may desire the character Lara Croft from the *Tomb Raider* series for more than her athletic abilities. For example, it has been estimated that there are over one hundred fan websites devoted to Lara, and there was extensive media attention (for a video game) when rumors of a "nude patch" for Lara were alleged to be available on the Internet. "The Croft Times," *Newsweek*, November 10 1997. Available online at <http://www.cubeit.com/ctimes/news0094a.htm>. Additionally, websites such as "Planet Lara" often boast of selections of "hot pictures and photos" as well as "hot wallpapers" for free downloading. Chris Ridgeon, "Planet Lara: Where the World Revolves Around Lara." Available online at <http://www.planetlara.com/index.asp>.

CHAPTER 9

Video Games and Configurative Performances

MARKKU ESKELINEN
RAGNHILD TRONSTAD

Let's begin by pretending we are ignorant of what computer games are, and of how to study games in general. In Elliott M. Avedon and Brian Sutton-Smith's *The Study of Games,*[1] there's no suggestion that games are anything more or less than games. If one browses through the index of this classic book, comprising a century or so of Western game scholarship in a wide variety of fields and disciplines, concepts and entries such as story, drama, or narrative are nowhere to be found. It seems therefore safe to assume that in the early 1970s those rare individuals who took games and game studies seriously understood very clearly they were focusing on activities and structures that were at least as medium-independent as stories.[2] You can use chess as an example if you really must: it can be played against a computer and its AI, another player (or many players simultaneously), over postal and other communication networks, and with or without a physical board and pieces, the shape, size, and material of which are of no importance; or, in more contemporary terms, the coexistence of console, mobile, and PC versions of the same game.

Eleven years later, in *The Art of Computer Game Design,*[3] Chris Crawford first separated games from stories and then focused, among other things, on the differences between games and computer games (or more precisely among various game technologies[4]). He found half a dozen crucial benefits of the latter in the sense of extending and expanding game design possibilities. First, there's a greater responsiveness to the player's wishes. This is because "the computer is dynamic; it imposes little constancy on any element of the game."[5] Second, the computer can serve as game referee. Third, there's an advantage in real-time play, as "the computer is so fast that it can handle the administrative matters faster than the humans can play the game."[6] The computer is also able to provide an intelligent opponent and to limit the information given to the players in a purposeful way. And, finally, "the use of telecommunications for game play makes possible game structures that are out of the reach of other technologies. It allows us to create games with huge numbers of players."[7] To be sure, there were also many disadvantages and weaknesses the game designers had to struggle with: the poor I/O rate, single user orientation in the hardware design, and the harsh requirement of programmability.

In short, to borrow a relatively recent keyword from Jay David Bolter and Richard Grusin, it seems that to Crawford computer games were remediated games, and not remediated cinema as they mainly are to Bolter and Grusin.[8] This latter view is odd, given the fact that many computer and console games are modeled after preexisting games, sports, and competitive activities. Let us note in passing that such second-order games (especially the fighting and sports games, on the one hand, and many strategy games in debt to their board predecessors, on the other) make various narrativist approaches to computer games look even more ridiculous than they are on purely formal grounds. There also exist the all-too-obvious connections between many childhood games such as hide-and-seek and a wide variety of sneaking, chasing, and attacking activities in action-adventure games.[9]

It wasn't until the 1990s that various Monty Pythonesque approaches to media and especially "new media" gained more ground, bringing with them the assumptions that computer games are not games, but "something completely different," preferably narratives or drama or anything else that has a considerably higher cultural status than games.[10] This unproductive conceptualization may well have its roots in popular parlance referring to computer games as a medium or media. Usually these buzzwords are left undefined, perhaps to leave more room for other truisms, but still it is safe to say that there are two grave risks in applying the good old jakobsonian model of communication to computer games. First, it reduces computer games to a mere delivery channel for something more important or meaningful (as, rather curiously, stories or narratives are taken to be). Second, it implies there's a receiver or an audience somewhere, and we don't mean buyers and consumers. This masks very effectively the fact that games (unlike art) don't need audiences as an integral part of their "communication" structure. Consequently, the very idea of audiencelessness seems to be incomprehensible to most media scholars, as it tends to undermine the ready-made use value of approaches and theories borrowed from their favorite disciplines and scholarly fields of choice.

Still, it may say something about the general appeal of the art frame that even to Marshall McLuhan[11] and Chris Crawford games were art (or at least equivalent to art). If we were to take this far-reaching insight seriously for once, we'd first bracket all assumptions regarding the individual or collective value of computer games and any resulting babble about aesthetics. Instead, there's a more basic question to be asked: If games are art, then what kind of art are they, and what kind of already existing and well-established art forms might they resemble? The typical, usually implicit, answers include print novels and Hollywood cinema, which are odd choices, as these styles, genres, modes, and practices require only interpretative activity from their readers, spectators, and consumers.

In contrast to these kinds of traditional art, various performances, installations, kinetic and robotic art, to name only a few, may challenge their audiences using variable semiotic sequences. These kinds of arrangements require nontrivial effort and more than mere interpretative activity and engagement from the users, operators, and participants. Following Espen Aarseth,[12] we might call these forms different species of ergodic art. Now, there's no doubt that games and computer games are ergodic[13] if not art, because in games we have to produce, encounter, and respond to variable sequences of action. Of course, there is a crucial difference separating these practices from each other: in art we may have to configure in order to be able to interpret, whereas in games we have to interpret in order to be able to configure, and proceed from the beginning to the winning or some other situation.[14] Still, it might be possible to build a continuum from ergodic art to games or at least follow this hypothetical path in order to gain more detailed findings and more minuscule similarities and differences between different kinds of performances, actions, and live activities. This approach also allows us to avoid the pitfalls of transforming or forcing theories to suit objects running counter to their basic assumptions.

Keeping in mind what was said about the audienceless nature of games it is important to note that it is not difficult to find theories of actions, activities, and events without audiences in performance theory. A few years after McLuhan's breakthrough in *Understanding Media,* Allan Kaprow wrote about Happenings and suggested certain measures and precautions that should be taken, concluding that "it follows that there should not be (and usually cannot be) an audience or audiences to watch a Happening."[15] Some five or six years later, he drafted an un-artist for us in a paper,[16] the last section of which focuses on playing and gaming, preferring the former to the latter. And, a little later, he traced the tradition of artists using everyday models in their practices of un-art.[17] At this point participatory performances seem to dissolve into the situations, operations, structures, feedback structures, and learning processes encountered in our everyday routines, while the un-artist leaving the art frame behind turns herself into a player-educator opposing both competitive games and exhausted work ethics.[18] So, here we could see our first continuum, albeit a tentative one, emerging from performance and Happenings to gaming through playing.

There are also interesting parallels between computer games and robotic art. The early classics of the latter stress the themes of remote control, cyborg entities, and autonomous behavior.[19] All these we meet again when our avatar struggles against human or nonhuman adversaries in a video game. Also, the dialogic relations championed by Bakhtin (and Kac after him[20]) are markedly visible in games and sports. Two or more humans and a piece of equipment to be played with constitute a very different setting and situation than one human contemplating an object of art. It would be possible to build another continuum from static and permanent objects of art through responding kinetic or robotic entities and environments to toys, playthings, and equipment to be manipulated (game objects).

Ergodic Continuities

"Ergodic phenomena are produced by some kind of cybernetic system, i.e. a machine (or a human) that operates as an information feedback loop, which will generate a different semiotic sequence each time it is engaged."[21] This kind of system has a potential for actualizing itself differently every time it is used, thus also creating other than interpretative problems. In addition to the usual activity of constructing meanings, we must do nontrivial work to produce sequences of signs that are not necessarily shared by any other user. Thus the stable and continuous identity of the material foundation of the work of art is questioned, and we have to entertain the possibility that for every individual system we also have, to some degree, an individual medium. That necessitates yet another beginning for this essay.

Based on this condensed sketch of the ergodic, we can discern three categories of systems. First, systems that concretize and actualize themselves in the same sequences of signs every time. We are talking about traditional art here, be it a novel, a film, or a painting: the only thing we are asked to do is to interpret it, to experience it, and to give some meaning to it. All this is difficult enough, and will remain that way.

Second, systems that require nontrivial work from their user, reader, or spectator, and have the potential of manifesting themselves differently every time they are used. These we might call ergodic art, regardless of what kind of signs are produced, their source, their medium, or the spatial and temporal limits of their existence and appearance. We could counter the distinction between art and ergodic art by claiming that they are both interpretative practices; that whatever work we have to do in an ergodic labor camp we will do it in order to get something to interpret; we might have to configure and reconfigure the system to the best of our ability or curiosity, but our interests are ultimately interpretative. And that's probably true; the nontrivial work is usually not an end in and of itself. Or, at least, it is not very pleasurable if it is.

Third, we all know there are pleasurable systems and modes that are not dominated by interpretative interest. We're referring to games and computer games in particular. We have to interpret in games, but we do so in order to configure, in order to proceed from the beginning to the winning or some other situation. Games usually come with explicit goals, rules and instructions as to how to manipulate the equipment (whatever this is made of and capable of in terms of sound, vision, movement, and action). By situating ergodic (or interactive, if you want to go back to unspecified banalities) art in between well-established interpretative practices and games, certain conceptual benefits are gained, as we have moved here beyond the much hyped beyond and can enjoy the luxury of conceptual double vision.

When the safe and somehow manageable totality, be it coherent or not, vanishes from sight, the spectators and readers have to try very different strategies of comprehension, which may seem complicated if and when they do not know the limits and the functional principles of whatever they are encountering in the disguise of an artwork. There's no guarantee that the work works as it seems to work, or continues to work as it has worked so far, not to mention that it works as its manual or other paratext claims it works. Although the situation is usually far from being that extreme, these anamorphic and metamorphic works[22] still contain fundamental and irreducible possibilities for unreliability undermining the illusions of mastery and control inherent in static scriptons.[23]

From this perspective, computer games are interesting precisely because they domesticate the excess of both ordinary and avant-garde products and the fundamental potential for impermanence and unreliability inherent in new media objects. It would be tempting to generalize and argue that as long as we have systems with either one material level or several material levels with trivial mutual relations, narrative is the most powerful or popular arrangement that can be used in connecting them—but, whenever the relation of levels turns out to be arbitrary, the concepts of gaming and simulation will be more and more dominant or popular.[24] Despite the fact that computers can support, emulate, and modify whatever aesthetic tradition and convention there is (except perhaps the nonmediated performance), the most satisfying way of pacifying consumers facing potential insecurity will be computer games. They promise fun and pleasure in exchange for following and applying the rules. That's exactly what art sometimes promises to do, too, but what it rarely delivers.

So far we have been playing around with two common sense assumptions: games are audienceless and in playing games we have to deal with variable sequences of action. Now it is time to introduce our third modest observation: playing a game is a special kind of performance or activity among many others.

Theater, Performance, and Happenings

Art events that are today presented as "performance" refer to the experiments of artists in the 1960s and 1970s (mainly from the visual arts) to establish a nontheatrical Performance Art challenging traditional aesthetical notions of mimesis and representation. Performance Art aspired to be nonrepresentational. Nonmatrixed[25] acts and events were performed in "real time" in order to transcend the representationality of the Western theatrical performance tradition and obtain a sense of unmediated presence.[26]

Originating in the same aesthetical and political climate as Performance Art, the Happening was nevertheless a somewhat different phenomenon. Happenings were created and performed in order to transform the notion of art altogether: to break the barrier between art and life. Happenings weren't supposed to be "art," in the traditional sense of the term: "The Happening is conceived as an art, certainly, but this is for lack of a better word, or one that would not cause endless discussion. I, personally, would not care if it were called a sport."[27] Happenings had participants only—no audience. When performed in public places, Happenings would inevitably be witnessed by people, but these people were not to be addressed as an audience. They weren't to be included in the Happening in the sense audiences are included in other live art events, such as theater or Performance Art.[28]

Decades ago, Roland Barthes suggested that theater is a cybernetic art form,[29] because there is a real time feedback loop between the players and their audience. It is easy to expand that notion to cover other live arts as well and discern two different loops: a transactional one between the audience and the actors and an interactive one between the actors.[30]

The transactional feedback loop between performer(s) and audience is naturally nonexistent in Happenings.[31] In theater and Performance Art, however, there is such a feedback loop to be identified, allowing the audience members to affect—to a greater or lesser degree, dependent on what kind of role or "user function" they are allowed—the performance through their presence and responses. Early Western theater forms (such as, for instance, the French seventeenth- to eighteenth-century court theater) would often allow the audience to demand repetition of particularly compelling scenes, as well as omission of scenes they found boring. The conventions of the later bourgeois theater, however, implied a nonparticipatory audience, where the available responses were restricted to applauding/not applauding. This convention has had great impact on Western theater audiences in general. Being allowed merely minimal influence on the progression of the performance, the user function of audiences in theater and Performance Art is therefore usually limited to being interpretative. Sometimes, however, it may be explorative, too, as in the staging of plays with alternative endings such as Ayn Rand's *Night of January 16th* (1936).[32] Other marginal practices such as the court theater convention mentioned above, certain types of participatory performances in which the audience isn't totally merged into the performance, and popular forms such as "theater sport"[33] suggest that the ergodic continuum available to theater audiences may be extended even further.[34]

When it comes to the interactive feedback loop between performers, we will restrict ourselves to identify one main structural difference between certain performance practices and traditional theater. Theater, writes Kirby, is based on an information structure that is essentially cumulative: each element in the performance is organized in order to provide information, either by reflecting, explaining, or clarifying earlier information given.[35] In performances arranged this way, the performers will necessarily have to respond and react to each other's actions. (That is, of course, provided that there's more than one actor involved in the performance.) Other performance practices, however, will often have what Kirby calls a compartmented structure, which "is based on the arrangement and contiguity of theatrical units that are completely self-contained and hermetic. No information is passed from one discrete theatrical unit—or 'compartment'—to another. The compartments may be arranged sequentially . . . or simultaneously."[36] Now, the sequential arrangement of compartments does not necessarily affect the interactive feedback loop between the performers. But when the Happening or performance is simultaneously compartmented, the performers will also function as "discrete units," not passing or communicating anything between themselves. In simultaneously compartmented Happenings, therefore, the interactive feedback loop will be nonexistent as well.

Kaprow articulated the following guidelines on how to create a Happening:

1. The line between the Happening and daily life should be kept as fluid and perhaps indistinct as possible.
2. Themes, materials, actions, and the associations they evoke are to be gotten from anywhere except from the arts, their derivatives, and their milieu.

3. The Happenings should be dispersed over several widely spaced, sometimes moving and changing, locales.
4. Time, closely bound up with things and spaces, should be variable and independent of the convention of continuity.
5. The composition of all materials, actions, images, and their times and spaces should be undertaken in as artless and, again, practical a way as possible.
6. Happenings should be unrehearsed and performed by nonprofessionals, once only.
7. It follows that there should not be (and usually cannot be) an audience or audiences to watch a Happening.[37]

One similarity between Performance Art and Happenings as two avant-garde forms challenging traditional theater is that they were both nonmatrixed. Also excluding the audience from the performance situation, Happenings succeeded in moving one step further than Performance Art, away from the traditional notion of art toward the condition of un-art. Starting out as unique organized events, Kaprow's Happenings evolved into playful repetition of everyday routines. When these routines were sometimes documented and fed back to the art community, the Happening would still be situated within an art frame.[38] But when they weren't—when the Happening was performed in total privacy—this art frame was no longer present. With the art frame removed, the activities performed in these late Happenings as a form of un-art come quite close to what we otherwise would define as play.

Happenings, Play, and Games

Neither Happenings, play, nor games require an audience. Although some games—like soccer—will often include one, having an audience present is never a requirement in order to play soccer. This is one crucial difference between Happenings, play, and games on the one hand, and Performance Art and theater—where an audience is required—on the other.[39]

In *The Oxford History of Board Games,* David Parlett makes the distinction between formal and informal games, where the latter is "merely undirected play, or 'playing around.'" Formal games, by contrast, have "a twofold structure based on ends and means," where "means" refer to the agreed set of equipment used in the game, as well as to specific procedural rules that explain how to manipulate this equipment in order to produce a winning situation. Winning then defines the "end" of the game, "as termination and as object."[40]

Parlett's definition of formal games may function as a definition of games in general, or of games as opposed to play. His definition of informal games, by contrast, is too vague to be useful, especially as it suggests that there are no rules or regularities involved in play (or what he calls "informal games"). Instead of Parlett, we will use Gonzalo Frasca's distinction between ludus and paidia rules[41] to identify the relation of play to games. Frasca reserves the term "ludus" for games that produce winners and losers. Ludus rules are therefore rules that define a winning situation. Paidia rules are rules that define or restrict the process of playing; how the equipment may be manipulated. Both play and games will contain paidia rules, but only games will have the additional ludus rules.[42] In play, paidia rules and goals are often set by the player(s), while in games both ludus and paidia rules will usually be defined beforehand. In simulations such as *SimCity*—a paidia game, as it doesn't contain any ludus rules—there are paidia rules defined beforehand. However, the player is allowed to set her own goals.

In Happenings, the objective of the actions performed is completion, not (as in games) to reach a winning situation. Trivial work is required in order to complete the tasks; no obstacles or adversaries are involved. Instead of rules, there will be instructions, or a "scenario," as Kaprow prefers to call it.[43] The following examples of available activities in one of Kaprow's Happenings[44] are chosen to illustrate how the instructions to a Happening may sometimes nevertheless resemble ordinary paidia rules:

- On the shoulder of a stretch of highway, a fancy banquet table is laid out, food on the plates, money in the saucers. Everything is left there.
- People stand on bridges, on street corners, watch cars pass. After 200 red ones, they leave.
- Two people telephone each other. Phone rings once, is answered "hello." Caller hangs up. After a few minutes, other person does the same. Same answer. Phone clicks off. Repeated with two rings, three rings, four rings, five rings, six rings, seven, eight, nine, etc. . . . until a line is busy.
- On the street, kids give paper flowers to people with pleasant faces.[45]

However, in Happenings the rules are given,[46] while in play rules are self-assertive, established by the player.

Regarding the self-sufficiency of actions performed, play is a rather diverse category: usually actions will be performed in order to reach a particular goal, but sometimes the act of performing them will be sufficient in itself. Unlike in organized events, completion of the tasks is not a necessity in play. The work required may be trivial or nontrivial, depending on whether or not there are obstacles included.[47] Rules are usually defined by the player, as well as possible goals. (But if the goal defined implies a situation the player may either "win" or "lose," a ludus rule is added, in which case play turns into a game.)

Simulation video games are one example of paidia, or play, that involve goals and subgoals without implying any winning situation. As video games are always ergodic, simulations also require nontrivial work from the player. Nontrivial work of the configurative kind that is always required in order to play a video game constitute what we will later refer to as the player's "configurative performance" in the game.

In Happenings and certain forms of play, the tasks to be performed are trivial; and they do not involve adversaries or obstacles forcing the player to vary her actions in order to find a "right way" to carry them out either. In games, and especially in video games, the situation is different. Here the player needs to try out different solutions by varying her approaches, seeking the right combinations of actions that are required to overcome the obstacles and make progress in the game. Aarseth calls such obstacles in video games "aporias," analysing gameplay as a continuous chain of such aporias overcome and replaced by "epiphanies" (solutions). Based on this analysis, he identifies a threefold temporality in gameplay, consisting of event time, negotiation time, and progression time.[48]

The "difference" between play and "ordinary life" proposed by both Huizinga and Caillois has been much debated.[49] There are several ways of understanding this distinction, all of which may be applied to certain kinds of play and games but not to others. One is connected to rules and goals: in the game, the player is subjected to rules and sets himself goals that do not apply to his "ordinary life." That is to say, the game does not affect his life outside the game, and when the game is over, his "ordinary life" remains chiefly unchanged. Another way of understanding it is to connect it to the "fixed limits of time and place,"[50] setting an arena for play outside of which nothing that takes place within the game has any effect. A third is connected to make-believe, transforming the real time and place of play to an imagined time and place. Kirby's "matrixed performance" could be a result of such make-believe.

Role-playing games require that the players assume roles in accordance with the specific time and place that is assigned to the game-world. Even if not consciously acting, most actions of their representation in the game (their avatar) will nevertheless appear to the other players in the context of this matrix. Because of the "otherness" of the game-world, the not-acting convention of the nonmatrixed performance is impossible—or at least futile, in terms of effect—in any multiplayer video game in which there is an interactional feedback loop between players represented by avatars.

Despite the separateness of play and games from ordinary life, most—if not all—games may, however, have intended or unintended consequences that do affect the player's "ordinary life," too. The proposed line between play and life is therefore never absolutely fixed. On the contrary, offering the opportunity to play with this line—to stay within, negotiating, pushing it, transgressing it—may in fact be another characteristic typical of play and games, as well as of live art in general.

Risk and Investment

In November 2001, mobile phone users could subscribe to a project called "Surrender Control," created by Tim Etchells, author and director of the U.K.-based experimental theater group Forced Entertainment. "Surrender Control" lasted for five days, during which the participants were sent seventy-five SMS messages with instructions on how to behave, what to think or actions to perform. Following all the instructions—that is, "abiding by the rules"—would inevitably expose the participants to a certain social risk, as some of the messages involved touching and making eye contact with unknowing passers-by, or breaking, dropping, or stealing things.[51]

Video games seldom require the kinds of investment that put players at risk. Certainly, there is "risk" defined within the context of the game (or it wouldn't be a game) but not the kind of risk that may transgress the boundaries of the game and affect the player on a personal level.[52] Here the game's separateness from "ordinary life" resembles the separateness of the matrixed performance from the real world outside of it.

Frasca wrote an article addressing the lack of "seriousness" in computer games, arguing "current computer game design conventions have structural characteristics which prevent them from dealing with 'serious' content."[53] The two characteristics Frasca specifically points to are: (1) you can save games and try again if you're making a wrong move; and (2) death is reversible. In other words, you never really have to face the consequences of any of your actions. This, Frasca argues, makes games dealing with serious historical content (like the Holocaust) intolerable, no matter how "good" or "humanist" the intentions behind them.

As a solution to this Frasca suggests a game model that can only be played once, the OSGON (one-session game of narration). Here all choices will matter because there's no way the player can save or restart the game, and dying in the game means "game over."[54]

If the point with the OSGON is that the player should be forced to engage more seriously in the fate of his or her protagonist in the game, more than the mere monetary investment of having bought and paid for the game must be at stake. Naturally, if the character dies because of some foolish action of the player, and there is no way the character can be resurrected, or the game restarted, the consequences of the player's actions will be experienced as more serious than in games that can be restarted. However, it is not given that such consequence will have any moral impact on the player, or affect the player on a personal level, if the player is otherwise incapable of relating to the character's fate. For the OSGON to make sense, therefore, it is necessary that the players are also put at risk through personal, nonmaterial investment. This kind of investment could be accomplished by building up the player's sense of commitment to the game-world through identification with his or her character.[55]

Such commitment through identification is common in multiplayer role-playing games (MUDs and their graphical counterparts such as *EverQuest* and *Ultima Online*) in which a player can be associated with the same character over years. Although the player may start out thinking of her character as a medium for her own actions,[56] little by little the character will obtain its own "autonomous" identity—departing from that of the player—by accumulating properties, traits, and a history of its own within the game-world. This separate character identity will contribute to keeping the game-world within which the player is acting separate and matrixed. Nevertheless, it is always the player who makes all the decisions on behalf of the character.[57]

In the *TubMud*[58] quest *Havoc*, the fourth chapter contains obvious references to Nazi ideology, making Holocaust part of the (otherwise fictitious) system the character is on a mission to defeat. Suddenly there are slight changes in the scenario: from having established and upheld a fixed fictional frame safely addressing the identity of the character, the quest suddenly starts referring to the player.[59] Blurring the boundaries between the fictional game world and the real world of the player this way, the quest succeeds in questioning the identity of the player through the player's identification with the actions of her character. Becoming aware of herself and her role in the "game," she may come to realize what would in fact be the "real" consequences of her choices. *Havoc* is not an OSGON: if the player fails the first time, it can be redone. But the suspicious act of having failed when it mattered, including its implied Real Life consequence—if the choices in the game had been proposed to her for real—cannot be redone.

When substantial material investment is required in order to play a game, this may also contribute to breaking down the barrier between the game and ordinary life, making the game less matrixed and separated by introducing real consequences. Sometimes such material risk is included as an integral part of the game, such as in gambling, boxing, mountain climbing, or tightrope walking.[60] Not very surprisingly, subjecting oneself to extreme material risk was also a common technique used by Performance Art practitioners in the 1970s in order to keep the performance nonmatrixed.

One example of this is Marina Abramovic's "Rhythm 0" (1974), in which the artist displayed seventy-two objects—including a pistol—on a table and subjected herself to the audience for six hours, inviting them to use the objects on her as they pleased. Chris Burden's performances from the same decade are also worth mentioning:

> In "Prelude to 220" (also known as "110," 1971), Burden was strapped to a concrete floor in close proximity to a pair of water-filled buckets with submerged live electric wires; had the buckets been tipped over (which, obviously, didn't happen), electrical current might have traveled through the spilled water to Burden's body. In "220" (1971) Burden and three of his friends spent the night atop wooden step-ladders which were sitting in a pool of water containing a live electrical wire; had the participants fallen off the ladders (again, none did), they would have been electrocuted.[61]

In "Rhythm 0" and "Prelude to 220," the destinies of the artists were completely in the hands of the audience. As such, they approach games of chance, in which the player has no control of the outcome but must rely on Fortune. Lacking the monetary stake, it would be incorrect to equate these two performances with gambling. Still, the particular combination of chance and vertigo involved is characteristic also of gambling practices such as betting and roulette. (Or Russian roulette, even, if we want to equate at least what is at stake on the "losing" side.) Considering the lack of explicit, binding rules, though, these performances are less ludic and more paideic than both betting and roulette.[62] Then again, since the ludic side of Caillois's vertigo category is less concerned with rules than it is with the necessity of exercising skill and concentration in the process, the other performance described— Burden's "220"—must be placed on the opposite side of the scale. Assuming that it was concentration rather than pure chance that kept the four men from falling off the ladders, "220" will be ludic rather than paideic despite its lack of conventional "game rules."[63]

Different kinds of games and video games will require that the player assume different roles during gameplay. The live art examples discussed in this and the previous two sections illustrate possible player positions. Massively multiplayer online role-playing games are perhaps the most complex games in this respect, involving a wide variety of roles to assume. Before starting out, the player will read the manual and follow the instructions in order to create a character. Interacting with other players, she may act as a matrixed performer, as well as an interpretative or ergodic audience member. Many tasks will need testing and experimenting with varying sequences of action in order to be successfully completed. Competitive elements lead to situations of winning and losing, although the nature and complexity of such games seldom allow for a final winning situation. The game always continues, with or without the player.

The nonmatrixed performer is a contradiction in the context of role-playing games. Abstract games and games that do not involve interaction between avatars, however, may easily involve a nonmatrixed perfomer. And when the outcome of a game results in substantial changes with regards to the player's life outside the confines of the game, we may say that she assumes the position of the gambler as well.

The Distribution of Information and the Modalities of Action

Gaps. According to David Bordwell, narration is "the process whereby the film's syuzhet and style interact in the course of cueing and constraining the spectator's construction of the fabula."[64] Games contain other kinds of dominant cues and constraints: rules, goals, the necessary manipulation of equipment, and the effect of possible other players, for starters. This means that information is distributed differently (invested in formal rules for example), it is to be obtained differently (by manipulating the equipment), and it is to be used differently (in moving toward the goal).

In short, there are both ergodic and nonergodic flows at play in computer games, as there is both something to be interpreted (nonergodic state) and action to be taken (ergodic events, that is, changes of state) forming a feedback loop, where information is gained through action and further action is guided by information already gained. Consequently, we should concentrate on articulating the process whereby the game structure cues, guides, and constrains the player's activities (or gameplay). In other words, the focus should be on the player's configurative performance and on interests and expectations that dominate her use of information.

The model behind Bordwell's insights could be transformed to suit these purposes a bit better if we take our route away from the usual linearity of film to the nonlinear and ergodic phenomena that games consist of, through cybertext theory, letting it transform and expand the heuristic potential inherent in Bordwell's approach. That way, we can add nontrivial effort and action to his model of perception and cognition. Following Meir Sternberg,[65] Bordwell discerns a system of gaps between fabula and syuzhet; these can be temporary or permanent, diffused or focused, and flaunted or suppressed.[66] In the course of narration, these gaps are created, opened, and closed, and they regulate what the readers or spectators can know about the events depicted at any given time or specific point in the narrative. This could be called narrative design.

It should be noted that in linear and non- or only trivially-ergodic products such as books and films, the reasonable assumption is that given and received information meet at the specific and invariable points of the text. That's not the case with ergodic texts and games, and we have to discern and be aware of at least two types of metagaps. These are situated between given and received (or distributed and obtained) information and between received and applied (or used) information. We'll first take a more detailed look at the former gap and address both the combination of events and the dynamics of ergodic gaps. Then we'll shift our focus to the player's expectations and discuss them in terms of motivation, exposition, and orientation.

Whatever action-related gaps exist or can be said to exist in games are to be situated between means and ends, procedures and goals, between the necessary manipulation of the equipment and the objectives of this manipulation. We can now specify these relations by applying Aarseth's cybertext theory in order to produce a dynamic map of ergodic aporias.[67]

First, gaps are either static or dynamic. Static gaps are constant; they are always there between the player and her goal (or subgoal) and have to be encountered and overcome. Dynamic gaps are dependent on the player's actions in the sense that some of them can be avoided and the goal could still be reached.

Second, gaps are either determinate or indeterminate. They either function the same way every time or they don't. In the former case, the same response in the same situation will always produce the same result.

Third, gaps are either intransient or transient. Transient gaps can be overcome only within a given (limited) time; intransient gaps don't impose such constraints on the player.

Fourth, personal gaps are character specific, while impersonal gaps are not. In other words, every player has a chance to encounter the latter kind of gaps.

Fifth, random gaps are available all the time to the player, while controlled gaps are not. The latter may be dependent on the player's progress and skills.

Sixth, unlinked gaps are autonomous and linked gaps are necessarily connected to other gaps.

Finally, in addition to configurative gaps existing in every game (and without which there wouldn't be any game in the first place), there may be at least three other kinds of gaps in video games. First, interpretative gaps that can only be interpreted. Examples include permanent, temporal, and other kind of gaps in a backstory or cut-scenes. Second, exploratory gaps that need to be located through exploring and choosing paths; they are not immediately "there" to be encountered and are usually related to the basic architecture of event spaces every player must be or become familiar with (the sooner the better). Third, textonic gaps that are gaps the player can permanently add to the game structure.

Combinations. As games consist of open series of events rather than of closed sequences of events like narratives, we might try to apply Aarseth's heuristic functional typology[68] also to individual and semiautonomous strings and clusters of events instead of the totality of them. Then we would have a very different eventology at our disposal, capable of taking into account the combinatory nature of events in the bottom-up world of computer games, or, more generally, the ways games divide themselves into parts and sequences. A somewhat reduced version of this model is shown below combining four cybertextual variables with four temporal ones. In a more complete model, there should be similar spatial, causal, and functional relation types attached to modified cybertextual variables. As these parameters are types of connection and combination, it wouldn't in any way hurt to be familiar with certain well-documented oulipian objects and operations.[69]

In short, the player is there to manipulate the properties and relations of events and existents. These relations can be divided into four basic categories: temporal, spatial, causal, and functional.[70] Some of these relations are open to manipulation and others are not. And some of these configurable relations may be the strategically right or better ones to try out. Temporal relations can be further divided into the aspects of order, frequency (repetition), duration, speed, and simultaneity, and when we play we may want, in addition to various other possibilities, to change the order of certain events, or make them repeat themselves more or less often, prolong or shorten their duration, or make them appear simultaneously.

Event Types and Event Times.

	Order	Frequency	Duration	Simultaneity
Dynamics	static, intratextonic, textonic			
Determinability	determinate, indeterminate			
Perspective	personal, impersonal			
User function	configurative, interpretative, explorative, textonic			

Basically, the vertical categories deal with elements of constancy, chance, equality, and the tasks of the player, and the horizontal ones are categories for temporal connections between events. Static order is always there between two events, static frequency means an event will reoccur the same number of times, static duration is always the same, and static simultaneity implies the events in question always occur at the same time. In the intratextonically dynamic register, the order between events, and their repetition, duration and simultaneity can vary; and textonically dynamic order, frequency, duration, and simultaneity are all qualities that one or several players can add to the preexisting game structure. Determinability is here related to the consequences of the player's repeated actions. If his response to a given situation is exactly the same, the results (the resulting events) are also the same (in terms of their order, frequency, duration, or simultaneity) in determinate cases; in indeterminate cases they are not, as there is some random element at nontrivial work. Personal order is related to and dependent on the character or other player-representation, while impersonal order is not, in which case the order is the same to every player. Other temporal parameters can be tied to the character, too. Finally, configurative relations can be altered to suit the player's strategy, interpretative relations can only be interpreted like the information cut scenes give to the player, explorable temporal relations can be explored and tested in order to find the right or possible way to proceed, and textonic temporal relations can be permanently added to the game structure by the player.

Motivation. Game elements have to be motivated to the player except perhaps in the simplest of games. Traditional theories[71] give us four basic types of motivation: compositional, realistic, transtextual, and artistic. As we are not concerned merely with interpreting why some elements are there, the question to be asked should also concern the possible use of whatever event or existent is there to be manipulated by the player. In this matrix realistic devices hint that they function as their real life counterparts (they don't necessarily have to function similarly, however, as the expectations the players have can also be diverted or frustrated to build more accurate or complicated ones alongside the inevitable surprise effects), and transtextual ones as such devices do in other games of the same genre or in other "media." Compositionally motivated devices are there to fulfill some game specific reason (this is the most self-explanatory category), and artistic devices function as enigmas: we are sure they may be of good use but haven't quite figured out what this would be (which is the usual case with designed novelties or exceptions that have to justify themselves in the end—of the game or the player's patience.) Without the interplay between the various game devices and the schemata the player use to make sense of them, and the dynamics of fulfilled, frustrated, delayed, and diverted expectations, the player would have to face the most annoying learning curve—that of trial and error. This also may be the reason why we don't expect to see the equivalent of avant-garde artists emerging from the game designer community.

Exposition. The player's expectations could be discussed in terms of exposition, motivation and orientation. Exposition concerns here the initial layout of necessary and relevant information in relation to the beginning situation. It may be given in the very beginning (preliminary) or later (delayed), and it can be given in a lump (concentrated) or in several installments (distributed). This gives us three basic options for distribution: preliminary and concentrated, delayed and concentrated, and delayed and distributed.[72] The first option gives the player solid ground for jumping in; there's nothing much left to know after you know you should kill everything that moves in

Quake or how to arrange *Tetris* blocks. In the other extreme, in MMORPGs crucial information concerning the game world and the players' positions in it just keeps on coming. In many questlike games such as *Myst*, there wouldn't be much of a game without delayed and concentrated exposition giving you the crucial bits of information concerning the sons and their father.

Orientation. It is in the player's best interest to get familiar with the temporal, spatial, causal, and functional properties and relations of the game world or the event space. Some of these will obviously be described and clarified in the manual, but there's a practical limit to how detailed this information can possibly be. The depth and range of knowledge the player can have before starting the game naturally varies from game to game, but in most cases the orientation of the player toward the game world continues while the game is already on. We have already discussed models of exposition, so here the focus is more on the further orientation and the still rather general properties and relations that are useful to learn almost in any game.

Keir Elam's dramatological score[73] and especially its category of deictic orientation are useful in orientating our modest theoretical attempts. There are spatial, temporal, functional, activity, and person deixis[74] at play in his model. If we modify it a little we'll have the following twelve dimensions: singular or plural distal orientation toward the adversary (you, they); plural proximal orientation toward one's teammates (we); singular proximal orientation toward the player herself (I); orientation toward nonplayer characters (he); proximal orientation toward context (here); distal orientation toward elsewhere (there); proximal orientation toward context time (now); distal orientation toward other time (then); orientation toward current activity; orientation toward absent activity; orientation toward present object; and orientation toward absent object.

We can use these dimensions in at least three different respects. First, not all games contain or activate all these orientations. There may be no "elsewhere" outside the one arena; there isn't necessarily any other time to consider than that which goes on now ("then" means the game's over), and there might be no NPCs (nonplayer characters) or teammates. Second, and to apply the ancient formalist keyword, usually one of these dimensions dominates the other available ones at any given moment of the game. Third, these basic orientations can be combined with and further specified using more game-specific descriptions and distinctions such as Aarseth's game and cybertext typologies[75] and Jesper Juul's useful distinction between two elementary game structures.[76] Here's one suggestion of what every player may want or need to know in order to orient her activities in the game: the number of arenas (one or several), access in terms of movement (random or controlled); access in terms of vision (random or controlled); finality (end or no end); transience (transient or intransient); game structure (emergence or progression[77]); type of causality (determinate or indeterminate); number of players (one, two or several); perspective (personal or impersonal); character status (static or dynamic); and quality of adversaries (capable of learning or not).

Philosophies of Action. If we wanted to continue specifying the player's orientation even further (as a series of tasks and subgoals), we'd study the availability of certain intertwined modalities of action to find out what is possible, necessary, prohibited, permitted, or obligatory to do in the game, and what the players do or could know, believe, or wish regarding those action schemes or schemata. In other words, the basic gaps here are between the deontic[78] and alethic[79] possibilities for action in the game and the player's epistemological,[80] doxastic,[81] and boulomaeic[82] attitudes. It is clear that in more open-ended (playlike) simulations with no defined or binding goals there's much more room for boulomaeic modalities than in most action games. The beginning situation is always a combination of knowledge and beliefs as seen from the player's perspective. Gradually the former will replace the latter, and if it manages to do so completely, we might consider the game exhausted and not replayable any more.[83] It's also evident that the more the game also constitutes and accommodates a community of players the more there will be need for various etiquettes in the interaction between the players. And, needless to say, the more dominant the aspect of community-building and role-playing, the more complex the scope, width, flexibility, and interplay of modalities.

So after all, behind every ludology and narratology there is (or should be) some kind of philosophy of action. The problem is that these general philosophies are not very detailed; that is, they are good for nothing if not modified. Still, let's try. There's "an agent, his intention in acting, the act or act-type produced, the modality of the action (manner and means), the setting (temporal, spatial, and circumstantial) and the purpose."[84] These six (or seven if we separate manner and means) elements produce fifteen (or twenty-one) mutual basic relations to be studied, as it is precisely the distribution of these relations (and the action schemes within them), on the one hand, and the system of gaps, on the other, that makes the game.

Here we can't go very much into detail, but the direction sketched above might be worth taking if one is interested in locating game-specific features and developing a more thorough conceptual understanding of game design and gameplay. The rough idea is that these six or seven interacting sides of action form a feedback loop or more to the point a series of loops where they constantly affect each other all the way from the beginning to the end of the performing or playing or gaming sessions. These relations can be hierarchic or of equal importance; static or dynamic; permanent or temporary; and more or less determined by each other. While a systematic study of these relations and their distribution in games and game genres calls for another paper[85] or book, it is rather safe to say that some of these relations (and the arrangements within them) are always more interesting, intriguing, challenging, dominant, or important than others.

Pleasure

Ultimately, it is necessary to balance every approach loaded with modal logics and other formalizations of calculation with pleasure and excess oriented perspectives to take the joys of playing better into account. It is or should be a well-known fact that after codes and structures, Barthes[86] moved into the realm of pleasure to make sense of what readers actually do while reading, something that can't be reduced to grammars and codes. We are encountering a similar problem with games, although it is clear that the game is its rules, to which it could be reduced as a system of means and ends (unlike narratives, the so-called rules and grammars of which are metaphorical constructions of the most simplistic of conventions). Still, there's a limit to formalizations, as they don't say much about the player's experience and deeper motivations. Ironically and polemically, Barthes described four ways to connect the reading neurosis with the hallucinated form of the text. It might be too straightforward and moralistic, too, to jump right away into combining the gaming perversion with the hallucinated functioning of the game, but it also might be just the right direction to go for those to whom the word *game* has ceased to be a four-letter word.

It might also be possible to bring Caillois's model into the finer details of computer games and gaming as a kind of basic typology for describing the orientation, combination, articulation, and characteristics of events. It is not uncommon to find events and series of events that contain *agôn* [competition], *alea* [chance], *ilinx* [vertigo] and *mimicry* [simulation] oriented aspects, so these types mix much better with each other than Caillois would like us to think.[87] Especially so if we do the usual trick and reduce those categories to their main experiential attractions: competition (winning through struggling), maximum anticipation (waiting to be thrilled or surprised, exposing oneself to chance), losing (perceptional and/or bodily) control, and role-playing (impressing and influencing others). When these are required or need to be endured it is *ludus* or a game; if they can be chosen (and enjoyed) at will it is *paidia* or playing.

In gaming, the player enters a feedback loop in which she's both subject and object of her own action. The pleasures of activity are combined and merged with the pleasures of passivity, and their dynamic balance is what is essential in grafting or inducing addictive experiences. Once again, we'd need to consult and experience various forms, techniques, and patterns of pleasurable action and addiction instead of the usual academic-scholastic arts and encyclopedias of interpretation, but that calls for another occasion, a game perhaps.

Notes

1. Elliott M. Avedon and Brian Sutton-Smith, *The Study of Games* (New York: Wiley, 1971).
2. To take but one example, this could be shown to be the case in Jacques Ehrmann's deconstructive reading of Huizinga and Caillois. See Jacques Ehrmann, "Homo Ludens revisited," *Yale French Studies* 41 (Game, Play, Literature), ed. Jacques Ehrmann (1968), 31–57.
3. Chris Crawford, *The Art of Computer Game Design* (1982). Available online at <http://www.vancouver.wsu.edu/fac/peabody/game-book/#game>.
4. In retrospect, one may suspect that thorough conceptualisations of differences and similarities between various game technologies would perhaps have lead to more productive results than the still ongoing prattle about computer and video games as an interactive medium.
5. Crawford, "The Art of Computer Game Design," Chapter 4.
6. Crawford, "The Art of Computer Game Design," Chapter 4.
7. Crawford, "The Art of Computer Game Design," Chapter 4.
8. Jay David Bolter and Richard Grusin, *Remediation: Understanding New Media.* (Cambridge, MA: MIT Press, 1999), 97–98.
9. In the April 2002 issue of *Edge* magazine, game designer Miamoto is quoted as having derived the sneaking aspects of *Metal Gear Solid* from his childhood experiences of hide and seek. See also Steven Poole, *Trigger Happy* (London: Fourth Estate, 2000), 176.
10. It is quite understandable that the industry benefits from these kinds of loose definitions when it has to face ill-informed moral panics, especially in societies more willing to see the roots of violence in computer games than in their own Dickensian social and educational infrastructures. And as with any other offer an average academic can't refuse the benefits are mutual: there's a huge illiterate demand for diluted adaptations of literature and film studies 101s. As we know, there was violence in Homer, too; not to mention the complex game that made Gilgamesh who and what he was.
11. See Marshall McLuhan, *Understanding Media: The Extensions of Man* (London: Sphere Books, 1964).
12. Espen Aarseth, "Aporia and Epiphany in *Doom* and *The Speaking Clock*: Temporality in Ergodic Art," in *Cyberspace Textuality*, ed. Marie-Laure Ryan (Bloomington and Indianapolis: University of Indiana Press, 1999), 31–41.
13. In ergodic literature, nontrivial effort is required to allow the reader to traverse the text, that is, the user has to do something else in addition to interpreting: choose paths or alternative actions, configure the signifiers or add his own programming, and so on. See the section on Ergodic Continuities, and Espen Aarseth, *Cybertext. Perspectives on Ergodic Literature* (Baltimore and London: The Johns Hopkins University Press, 1997).
14. See Markku Eskelinen, "The Gaming Situation," *Game Studies* 1, No. 1 (July 2001). Available online at <http://www.gamestudies.org/0101/eskelinen.hml>.
15. Allan Kaprow, "The Happenings Are Dead: Long Live the Happenings," in *Essays on the Blurring of Art and Life* (Berkeley and Los Angeles: University of California Press, 1996), 64.
16. Allan Kaprow, "The Education of the Un-Artist, Part II," in *Essays on the Blurring of Art and Life* (Berkeley and Los Angeles: University of California Press, 1996), 110–126.
17. Allan Kaprow, "The Education of the Un-Artist, Part III," in *Essays on the Blurring of Art and Life* (Berkeley and Los Angeles: University of California Press, 1996), 130–147.
18. See Kaprow, "The Education of the Un-Artist, Part II," 120–126.
19. See Eduardo Kac, "Origin and Development of Robotic Art," *Art Journal* 56, No. 3 (*Digital Reflections: The Dialogue of Art and Technology,* Special issue on Electronic Art) ed. Johanna Drucker (1997), 60–67. Available online at <http://www.ekac.org/articles.html>.

20. In Eduardo Kac, "Negotiating Meaning: The Dialogic Imagination in Electronic Art," in *Proceedings of Computers in Art and Design Education Conference* (Middlesbrough, Tees Valley, UK: University of Teesside, 1999), n.p. Available online at <http://www.ekac.org/articles.html>.

21. Aarseth, "Aporia and Epiphany in *Doom* and *The Speaking Clock:* Temporality in Ergodic Art," 32–33.

22. Aarseth, *Cybertext*, 178–182.

23. Cybertext theory makes a useful distinction between textons (strings of signs as they are in the text) and scriptons (strings of signs as they are presented to users). The mechanism by which scriptons are generated or revealed from textons is called a traversal function, which in turn can be described as the combination of seven variables (dynamics, determinability, time, perspective, access, links, and user functions) and their possible values. See Aarseth, *Cybertext*, 60–63.

24. Cybertext theory is most of all about the cybernetic production (and consumption) of signs and the unique dual materiality of that production. This uniqueness stems from potentially arbitrary relations between two separate material levels (the storage medium and the interface medium) and leads to a heuristic typology of texts into which Aarseth is capable of situating every textual object from *I Ching* to MUDs based on how its medium functions, but independently of what that medium is. See Aarseth, *Cybertext*, 40, 60–63.

25. Matrixed and nonmatrixed performance: matrixed performance is when the time and place established on stage differs from the time/place of the spectators—when the performers impersonate fictional characters in traditional theater for instance. The nonmatrixed performance, by contrast, takes place in the same time and place as its audience, and no "acting" is involved—only nonmatrixed "acts" of the nonmatrixed performer. See Michael Kirby, "Acting and not-acting" in *A Formalist Theatre* (Philadelphia: The University of Pennsylvania Press, 1987), 3–20.

26. However, since a theatrical frame is often created and imposed on the performance by the spectator regardless of the efforts of the performer to evade any fictional situation, to exorcise representionality from the performance situation once and for all turned out to be impossible. Audiences will always try to contextualize—to search the "meaning behind"—and they will gladly create and impose a fictional framing on the performance themselves if they aren't presented with one. Performance Art as a nonrepresentational art form eventually disappeared. Today's performance events are usually less concerned with avoiding representionality, placing themselves somewhere in between Performance Art and traditional theater: approaching the old form but without sharing its ideology. (For an analysis of Performance Art as originally a "function," then a "genre," see Josette Féral, "What Is Left of Performance Art? Autopsy of a Function, Birth of a Genre," *Discourse* 14, No. 2 [1992], 142–162.)

27. Allan Kaprow, "Excerpts from 'Assemblages, Environments & Happenings,'" in *Happenings and Other Acts*, ed. Mariellen R. Sandford (London and New York: Routledge, [1966] 1995), 236.

28. Some—for instance, Michael Kirby—seems to include events with audiences in their definitions of Happenings. Kaprow, however, is unambiguous on this point: "A Happening with only an emphatic response on the part of a seated audience is not a Happening but stage theatre. Then, on a human plane, to assemble people unprepared for an event and say that they are "participating" if apples are thrown at them or they are herded about is to ask very little of the whole notion of participation.... I think that it is a mark of mutual respect that all persons involved in a Happening be willing and committed participants who have a clear idea what they are to do. This is simply accomplished by writing out the scenario or score for all and discussing it thoroughly with them beforehand. In this respect it is not different from the preparations for a parade, a football match, a wedding, or religious service. It is not even different from a play.... There is an exception, however, to restricting the Happening to participants only. When a work is performed on a busy avenue, passersby will ordinarily stop and watch, just as they may watch the demolition of a building. These are not theatregoers and their attention is only temporarily caught in the course of their normal affairs. They might stay, perhaps become involved in some unexpected way, or they will more likely move on after a few minutes. Such persons are authentic parts of the environment" (Kaprow,

"Excerpts from 'Assemblages, Environments & Happenings,'" 240–241). Because the definition we are using for Happenings is based primarily on Kaprow's work, also his later developments of the form (whether it is now called "un-art," "activities," or "participatory performances") will be included in it.

29. Roland Barthes, "Literature and Signification," in *Critical Essays*, trans. Richard Howard (Evanston: Northwestern University Press, [1963] 1972), 261.

30. See Keir Elam, *The Semiotics of Theatre and Drama* (London: Routledge, 1980), 87–97.

31. Lacking an audience, the Happening also avoids having a theatrical framing imposed on it by the meaning-seeking spectator, and can thereby more easily remain within a nonmatrixed domain.

32. See Aarseth, *Cybertext*, 10.

33. "Theater sports" are contests in improvisation, partly directed by the audience. The audience also will sometimes function as judge in these contests, deciding what team or actor wins. (Another example of competitive theater is the Greek drama—origin of Western classical theater—which was written and performed as part of a contest.)

34. However, fitting these practices into the established cybertextual categories of explorative, configurative, and textonic user functions is problematic and would require a more thorough investigation of them. Perhaps also the ergodic will need to be divided differently when applied to live arts.

35. Michael Kirby, "Happenings: An Introduction," in *Happenings and Other Acts*, ed. Mariellen R. Sandford (London and New York: Routledge, [1965] 1995), 4–5.

36. Kirby, "Happenings: An Introduction," 5.

37. Kaprow, "The Happenings Are Dead: Long Live the Happenings," 62–64. Once, in the early stage of his practice, while experimenting with formalist structures to create a particular Happening, Kaprow encountered a problem concerning his assigned material. The everyday items and situations he wanted to make use of were simply too associative to be subjected a formalist structuring. A formalist approach, he realized, requires "a substance that is at once stable and general in meanings.... [A]bstract shapes such as circles and squares, the raising and lowering of an arm that does nothing else. The impact of the imagery, the 'what' is not as important as the intricacy and subtlety of the moves the imagery is put through" (Kaprow, "Excerpts from 'Assemblages, Environments & Happenings,'" 243.) However, using such material would inevitably turn the Happening into "art," loading the otherwise simple situations with some undefined aesthetic "meaning." Somehow, video games today present us with a similar (although reversed) "problem": being already too domesticated as expressions of popular culture, perceiving them as art is far from obvious. Jodi's (Joan Heemskerk and Dirk Paesmans) modification of *Wolfenstein* is an interesting example in this respect of how a game originally displaying recognizable situations is transformed into art simply by estranging the imagery: in Jodi's version, all objects are replaced by geometric forms, the Nazis being triangles "shouting incomprehensible nonsense in German" (Tilman Baumgärtel, "Alle Nazis werden Dreiecke," *Die Zeit* 16 (2002). Available online at <http://www.zeit.de/2002/16/Kultur/200216_computerspielkun.html>).

38. Kaprow makes a distinction between "artlike art" and "lifelike art" where the latter is "often indistinguishable from ordinary living" (Richard Schechner, *Performance Theory* [London and New York: Routledge, 1988], 288, note 23).

39. Caillois stresses the role of the spectator in games of simulation (*mimicry*): "The rule of the game is unique: it consists in the actor's fascinating the spectator, while avoiding an error that might lead the spectator to break the spell" (Roger Caillois, *Man, Play, and Games*, trans. Meyer Barash [New York: Schocken Books, 1979 (1958)], 23). However, this rule can be valid only where mimicry is ludic. In Caillois's definition, mimicry reaches is most ludic form in theater and spectacles, while his examples of more paideic forms of mimicry are phenomena that do not necessarily require an audience.

40. David Parlett, *The Oxford History of Board Games* (Oxford: Oxford University Press, 1999), 3.

41. It should be noted that although they are named after Caillois's concepts of "ludus" and "paidia," Frasca's terms have different implications.

42. See Gonzalo Frasca, *Videogames of the Oppressed: Videogames as a Means for Critical Thinking and Debate* (Master thesis, Georgia Institute of Technology, 2001), 7–11. Available online at <http://www.ludology.org>.

43. Richard Schechner, "Extensions in time and space. An interview with Allan Kaprow," in *Happenings and Other Acts*, ed. Mariellen R. Sandford (London and New York: Routledge, [1968] 1995), 222.

44. "Self-Service" (1967), a Happening that spanned four months, and included participants in three different cities. Thirty-one activities were selected out of a bigger number; each city getting its share of "available activities." The participants had to perform at least one of the activities available in his or her city, preferably all of them.

45. Quoted from Allan Kaprow, "Self-Service," in *Happenings and Other Acts*, ed. Mariellen R. Sandford (London and New York: Routledge, 1995 [1968]), 230–234.

46. Much like in rituals where rules are also "given by authority." See Schechner, *Performance Theory*, 13.

47. Examples of play that do not (necessarily) involve goals and require trivial work only could be swinging, or counting-out rhymes (from Caillois's classification in *Man, Play, and Games*, 36).

48. See Aarseth "Aporia and Epiphany in *Doom* and *The Speaking Clock*: Temporality in Ergodic Art," 37.

49. Ehrmann, for instance, attacks this supposed difference from almost every possible angle in "Homo Ludens Revisited," although not very productively.

50. Cf. Johan Huizinga, *Homo Ludens. A Study of the Play Element in Culture.* (Boston: The Beacon Press, [1938] 1955), 9–10; and 28.

51. This same kind of risk may also be present in the form "invisible theater," in which a group of actors arrange and enact fictional—but apparently genuine—situations in an everyday context (for instance, in the metro). The audience (other people traveling with the metro) is unknowing of the situation being staged. One crucial difference between "invisible theater" and Happenings is that the situations enacted in "invisible theater" is in fact addressed to the unknowing spectators: to provoke them into thinking or reacting. (See Augusto Boal, *Games for Actors and Non-actors*, trans. Adrian Jackson [London and New York: Routledge, 1992], 6–16.)

52. Except perhaps the risk Aarseth pointed to in the beginning of *Cybertext*, that is always involved when encountering ergodic works: "the risk of rejection.... Trying to know a cybertext is an investment of personal improvisation that can result in either intimacy or failure." Aarseth, *Cybertext*, 4.

53. Gonzalo Frasca, "Ephemeral Games: Is It Barbaric to Design Videogames after Auschwitz?" In *Cybertext Yearbook 2000*, ed. Markku Eskelinen and Raine Koskimaa (Saarijärvi, Finland: University of Jyväskylä, Research Centre for Contemporary Culture, 2001), 172.

54. A problem that remains unsolved with the OSGON is that not even the end of a game would probably be accepted by the critics as being "serious" enough to represent "serious" content.

55. Another apparent restriction with the OSGON is that it requires that the players master the rules and conventions of the game beforehand—that they already know how to play—as it is otherwise only annoying to lose one's only chance while still testing out the equipment (this way, however, the OSGON definitely puts the player at risk, but in the more material sense of the term).

56. Thus, initially approaching the game world in a more or less nonmatrixed state.

57. In performance theory, the relationship between performer and character is expressed as the character being "not-me, but also not-not-me."

58. Available online at <telnet morgen.cs.tu-berlin.de 7680>.

59. This late introduction of direct references to the player's history—adding the element of "seriousness" to the game—also works reflexively, framing her previous actions (which were performed within the context of an apparently safe and fixed fictional matrix) differently.

60. Competitive games can introduce an element of "seriousness" simply by making the outcome of it an issue for betting, as winning or losing a serious amount of money would affect most "ordinary lives."

61. Sam McBride, "Sing the Body Electronic: American Invention in Contemporary Performance," *Sycamore* 1, No. 3 (Fall, 1997), 2. Quoted from the web version. Available online at <http://www.unc.edu/sycamore/97.3/electron.html>.

62. Cf. Callois's classification of games (Caillois, *Man, Play, and Games*, 36).

63. This is also the case with another life-risking performance of Abramovic's, "Rest Energy," made in cooperation with Ulay in 1980, the description of which goes as follows: "Standing across from one another in slanted position. Looking each other in the eye. I hold a bow and Ulay holds the string with the arrow pointing directly to my heart. Microphones attached to both hearts recording the increasing number of heartbeats. (Marina Abramovic)." Quoted from <http://www.werkleitz.de/events/biennale2000/E/katalog/abramovic_ulay.html> [11.10.2002], where there's also an illustration to be found.

64. David Bordwell, *Narration in the Fiction Film* (Madison: University of Wisconsin Press, 1985), 53.

65. Meir Sternberg, *Expositional Modes and Temporal Ordering in Fiction* (Baltimore: Johns Hopkins University Press, 1978).

66. Bordwell, *Narration in the Fiction Film*, 54–55.

67. Such aporias are formal obstacles, not semantic ambiguities: "These three temporal levels [event time, negotiation time and progression time] may be regarded as aspects of a single dynamic: the basic structure of any game, which is the dialectic between aporia and epiphany. In narratives, aporias are usually informal structures, semantic gaps that hinder the interpretation of the work. In ergodic works such as *Doom*, the aporias are formal figures, localizable "roadblocks" that must be ovecome by some unknown combination of actions. When an aporia is overcome, it is replaced by an epiphany: a sudden, often unexpected solution to the impasse in the event space. Compared to the epiphanies of narrative texts, the ergodic epiphanies are not optional, something to enhance the aesthetic experience, but essential to the exploration of the event space. Without them, the rest of the work cannot be realized" (Aarseth, "Aporia and Epiphany in *Doom* and *The Speaking Clock*: Temporality in Ergodic Art," 38).

68. Aarseth, *Cybertext*, 60–63.

69. Warren F. Motte, ed., *Oulipo: A Primer of Potential Literature* (Illinois: Dalkey Archive Press, [1986] 1998), 49–51.

70. Eskelinen, "The Gaming Situation."

71. See Boris Tomashevsky, "Thematics," trans. Lee T. Lemon and Marion J. Reis, in *Russian Formalist Criticism*, eds. Lee T. Lemon and Marion J. Reis (Lincoln and London: University of Nebraska Press, [1925] 1965) , 61–95, and Bordwell, *Narration in the Fiction Film*.

72. Bordwell, *Narration in the Fiction Film*, 56; Tomashevsky, "Thematics," 72–73; and Sternberg, *Expositional Modes and Temporal Ordering in Fiction*.

73. Elam, *The Semiotics of Theatre and Drama*, 185–191.

74. Elam, *The Semiotics of Theatre and Drama*, 26–27.

75. See Espen Aarseth "Dataspillets diskurs—mellom folkediktning og kulturindustri," in *Perifraser* (Bergen, Norway: University of Bergen, Dept. of Comparative Literature, 1995), 315–342; and Aarseth, *Cybertext*, 60–63.

76. Jesper Juul, "The Open and The Closed: Games of Emergence and Games of Progression," in *CGDC Conference Proceedings*, ed. Frans Mäyrä (Tampere, Finland: Tampere University Press, 2002), 323–330.

77. "The history of computer games can be seen as the product of two basic game structures, that of emergence (a number of simple rules combining to form interesting variation) and that of progression (separate challenges presented serially" (Juul, "The Open and The Closed: Games of Emergence and Games of Progression," 324).

78. More precisely: deontic modalities of obligation (must), of nonobligation (need not), of prohibition (must not), and of permission (may). See Elam, *The Semiotics of Theatre and Drama*, 189.

79. More precisely: alethic necessity (positive and negative), possibility and impossibility, probability and alethic possibilities in terms of interrogation and hypothesis. See Elam, *The Semiotics of Theatre and Drama*, 189.

80. Modalities of knowing and not knowing.

81. Modalities of believing and not believing.

82. Modalities of wishing/wanting and not wishing/wanting.

83. See Ragnhild Tronstad, "Performing the MUD Adventure," in *Digital Media Revisted* eds. Gunnar Liestøl, Andrew Morrison, and Terje Rasmussen (Cambridge, MA: MIT Press, 2003), 215–237.

84. Elam, *The Semiotics of Theatre and Drama*, 121. In the context of games, means refer to equipment, and manner to the specifics of rule-based behavior addressed above. Purposes can be replaced with goals. Agents, their intentions, acts, and settings are self-explanatory.
85. For a fuller treatment and transformation, see Markku Eskelinen, "Six Obstacles in Search of a Theory" (forthcoming).
86. Roland Barthes, *The Pleasure of the Text*, trans. Richard Miller (New York: Hill and Wang, 1975 [1973]).
87. Caillois, *Man, Play, and Games*, 71–80.

CHAPTER 10

Simulation versus Narrative
Introduction to Ludology

GONZALO FRASCA

Academic video game studies have known an incredible development during the last couple of years. Slowly, academic interest has shifted from the early do-games-induce-violent-behaviors studies toward analyses that acknowledge the relevance of this new medium. Several international conferences on game studies took place in 2001, plus the publication of *Game Studies,* the first peer-reviewed online journal on the field.[1] In 2002 and 2003, the number of conferences and workshops kept growing steadily. After an early start as a subset of digital text studies, video game studies is finding its own academic space. Probably the most promising change comes from a new generation of researchers who grew up with computer games and now are bringing to this new field both their passion and expertise on this form of entertainment.

So far, the traditional—and most popular—research approach from both the industry and the academy has been to consider video games as extensions of drama[2] and narrative.[3] While this notion has been contested (especially by Espen Aarseth[4]) and generated a sometimes passionate debate, the narrative paradigm still prevails. My goal in this essay is to contribute to this discussion by offering more reasons as to why the storytelling model is not only an inaccurate one but also how it limits our understanding of the medium and our ability to create even more compelling games. The central argument I will explore is that, unlike traditional media, video games are not just based on representation but on an alternative semiotical structure known as simulation. Even if simulations and narratives do share some common elements (characters, settings, and events) their mechanics are essentially different. More important, they also offer distinct rhetorical possibilities. Therefore, my strategy will be to explore a particular topic and show how games and narratives provide authors with essentially different tools for conveying their opinions and feelings. In addition to this, I will explore how the concept of authorship fits within two different genres of simulation, *paidia* and *ludus*. In order to accomplish this, it will be necessary to introduce some concepts of ludology, the still-nascent formal discipline of game studies.

What is Ludology?

Ludology can be defined as a discipline that studies games in general, and video games in particular. The term is not new and it has been previously used in relation with non-electronic games, particularly among the board gaming community. In 1999, I pointed out the lack of a coherent, formal discipline that dealt with games as one of the reasons why researchers were looking for theoretical tools in literary and film theory and narratology.[5] Since then, the term "ludologist" grew in popularity among the game academic community to describe someone[6] who is against the common assumption that video games should be viewed as extensions of narrative. Personally, I think this is quite a simplification. Of course, we need a better understanding of the elements that games do share with stories, such as characters, settings, and events. Ludology does not disdain this dimension of video games but claims that they are not held together by a narrative structure. Nevertheless, it is important to keep in mind that ludology's ultimate goal is not a capricious attempt to unveil the technical inaccuracy of the narrative paradigm. As a formalist discipline, it should focus on the understanding of its structure and elements—particularly its rules—as well as creating typologies and models for explaining the mechanics of games. However, formalism is not the flavor of the month in these posteverything times. Certainly, formal approaches are limited—and ludologists should always keep that in mind—but they are probably the easiest way to uncover the structural differences between stories and games. I personally see this structural approach as a first, necessary step in video game studies, which we will definitively outgrow once it helps us to better grasp the basic characteristics of video games.

Simulation versus Representation

Representation is such a powerful and ubiquitous formal mode that it has become transparent to our civilization. For millennia, we have relied on it for both understanding and explaining our realities. This is especially true with a particular form of structuring representation: narrative. Some authors, such as Mark Turner,[7] even state that narrative mechanisms are cognitive structures deeply hard-wired into the human mind. It is because of its omnipresence that it is usually difficult to accept that there is an alternative to representation and narrative: simulation.

Simulation is not a new tool. It has always been present through such common things as toys and games but also through scientific models or cybertexts like the *I-Ching*. However, the potential of simulation has been somehow limited because of a technological problem: it is extremely difficult to model complex systems through cogwheels. Naturally, the invention of the computer changed this situation.

In the late 1990s, Espen Aarseth revolutionized electronic text studies with the following observation: electronic texts can be better understood if they are analyzed as cybernetic systems. He created a typology of texts and showed that hypertext is just one possible dimension of these systemic texts, which he called "cybertexts." Traditional literary theory and semiotics simply could not deal with these texts, adventure games, and textual-based multiuser environments because these works are not just made of sequences of signs but, rather, behave like machines or sign-generators. The reign of representation was academically contested, opening the path for simulation and game studies.

Scientists have traditionally used simulation for explanatory purposes and particularly for predicting the behavior of complex systems. Treatises abound on simulation theory but generally they provide an approach that is too technical and goal-oriented for our task of understanding it as an alternative to representation. What follows is a working definition that I distilled from combining elements of semiotics with several computer simulation theory essays.[8] I removed any references to the computer, since simulation can exist in nonelectronic devices such as traditional toys. This definition is provisory; it does not aim to be exhaustive and it will certainly change as we increase our understanding of simulation semiotics or "simitiocs." Therefore: "to simulate is to model a (source) system through a different system which maintains (for somebody) some of the behaviors of the original system." The key term here is "behavior." Simulation does not simply retain the—generally audiovisual—characteristics of the object but it also includes a model of its behaviors. This model reacts to certain stimuli (input data, pushing buttons, joystick movements), according to a set of conditions.

Traditional media are representational, not simulational. They excel at producing both descriptions of traits and sequences of events (narrative). A photograph of a plane will tell us information about its shape and color, but it will not fly or crash when manipulated. A flight simulator or a simple toy plane are not only signs, but machines that generate signs according to rules that model some of the behaviors of a real plane. A film about a plane landing is a narrative: an observer could interpret it in different ways (i.e., "it's a normal landing" or "it's an emergency landing"), but she cannot manipulate it and influence how the plane will land since film sequences are fixed and unalterable. By contrast, the flight simulator allows the player to perform actions that will modify the behavior of the system in a way that is similar to the behavior of the actual plane.[9] If the player increases the power variable on the simulator, the simulated plane will move faster through the virtual sky on the computer screen. As we will later see, video games are just a particular way of structuring simulation, just like narrative is a form of structuring representation.

To an external observer, the sequence of signs produced by both the film and the simulation could look exactly the same. This is what many supporters of the narrative paradigm fail to understand: their semiotic sequences might be identical, but simulation cannot be understood just through its output.[10] This is absolutely evident to anybody who played a game: the feeling of playing soccer cannot be compared to the one of watching a match. Apparently, this phenomenological explanation is not as evident as it may seem. As Markku Eskelinen argues, "Outside academic theory people are usually excellent at making distinctions between narrative, drama, and games. If I throw a ball at you I don't expect you to drop it and wait until it starts telling stories."[11] This problem might be because we are so used to see the world through narrative lenses that it is hard for us to imagine an alternative. But it may also be true that it is easier to try to apply narratology, which most researchers are already familiar with, than starting from scratch from a whole new approach. Also, because both the public and the media production industry are already extremely proficient in consuming and creating narratives, the temptation to constrain games to this existing channel may be too high. Video games imply an enormous paradigm shift for our culture because they represent the first complex simulational media for the masses.[12] It will probably take several generations for us to fully understand the cultural potential of simulation, but it is currently encouraged from different fields, such as the constructionist school of education and Boalian drama. One of the most interesting cognitive consequences of simulation is its encouragement for decentralized thinking,[13] which may in the long-term contest Mark Turner's claim of a "literary mind" by introducing the possibility of an alternative "simulational" way of thinking.

For several years, I have tried, with mixed success, to expose my nonnarrative theory of games to both researchers and designers by isolating the structural formal differences between the two. In this essay, I will propose a complementary approach based on their rhetoric characteristics. For my argument, I will assume that video games are capable of conveying the ideas and feelings of an author. My claim is that simulations can express messages in ways that narrative simply cannot, and vice versa. Sadly, our current knowledge of simulation rhetoric is extremely limited but I am confident that it will develop in the near future. Interestingly, it may not be through the game industry—that has been quite conservative since the marketing people took over the show, encouraging cloning over originality—but, rather, through *advergames*. *Advergaming* is one of the new buzzwords that are popular among e-marketers. According to *Wired*'s Jargon Watch,[14] an *advergame* is: "A downloadable or Web-based game created solely to enable product placements." I am not fully satisfied with this definition, since it clearly denotes the problems of shifting from a representational paradigm to a representational one. In my opinion, "product placement" is probably the most straightforward and obvious form of *advergaming*. Instead, this genre's key lays in modeling—not simply representing—the product or a related experience in the form of a toy or game. Many *advergames* are still satisfied to show an image of the product or its brand logo within the game instead of trying to convey experiences that are related to what is being sold. While I am a big supporter of the concept of the video game designer as an auteur, and it is true that many of them do use the medium to express their thoughts, their main goal remains to entertain. Advertisers, by contrast, use entertainment as a means but not as an end. What they want is to promote their brands and products and, because of this, they see in games a tool for persuasion. This puts them in an extremely privileged position for realizing that the potential of games is not to tell a story but to simulate: to create an environment for experimentation. An agency can place an ad in a magazine to enumerate the set of gizmos in a new car, but images, sound and text are not enough if they want their audience to be able to play around with them. In such a case, a simulated environment provides an experience that traditional advertising cannot deliver. As *advergaming* grows in popularity, it will hopefully also spread the idea that games may not just be a form of entertainment. Gaming literacy will some day make players aware that games are not free of ideological content and certainly *advergames* will play a role in this education because they have a clear agenda.

Game Rhetoric: Freedom of Speech, Freedom of Play?

On Friday, April 19, 2002, senior U.S. District Judge Stephen Limbaugh rejected a request against a St. Louis ordinance passed in 2000 that limited the access of minors to video game arcades.[15] According to the Associated Press, Limbaugh reviewed four games and found "no conveyance of ideas, expression, or anything else that could possibly amount to speech. The court finds that video games have more in common with board games and sports than they do with motion pictures." One week later, CBS reported that former wrestler and Minnesota governor Jesse Ventura was considering the use of video games for political propaganda.[16] Obviously, Ventura's campaign committee did regard games as a form of speech. Political video games are not new—a great example is the popularity of amateur anti-Osama online games[17] that were posted after September 11—but until now they have almost always relied on parody. If Ventura had gone through with his proposal,[18] he would have broken into new rhetorical ground, because electoral propaganda is one of the most visible examples of ideological speech.[19] Because of Ventura's status as a pop icon, his games would have probably been related to the action genre (he is supposed to be a tough guy, after all). However, political video games would probably shine with more dynamic, exploratory genres such as real-time strategy or simulators. Simulation has been used, with different degrees of complexity, to showcase urban dynamics (*SimCity*) or South-American dictatorships (*Trópico*).[20] It would not be surprising if in the near future politicians tried to explain their plans on tax or health reform through simulation. As Ted Friedman has pointed out,[21] Marx's *Capital* would make a much better simulator than a film.

Even if *advergames* are likely to be the Petri dish for simulation rhetoric, the example that I will propose is closer to art than to marketing. This is because most advocates of the narrativity of games always compare them to novels, films, or drama. So, I will suggest a topic that has both known success in traditional narrative and is as distant as possible from today's commercial video games: a worker's strike. In the late nineteenth century, Emile Zola wrote *Germinal*,[22] a novel about a strike held by mine workers in the north of France. At the end, the workers are defeated. All their efforts were in vain; their fight was not able to change their miserable work conditions. In the late twentieth century, Ken Loach described in his film *Bread and Roses*[23] a similar story about janitors in Los Angeles. The story ends differently: the janitors are victorious, even if their leader, an illegal immigrant, is deported back to Mexico.

Traditional storytelling normally deals with endings in a binary way. When Zola wrote *Germinal* he faced two options: the strikers could win or lose.[24] He opted for the second one, probably for conveying the idea that the social revolution was going to be a hard task. By contrast, Loach seems more optimistic. He depicts these oppressed janitors who stood up for their rights and were able to obtain better working conditions, even if their leader failed on a personal level. Narrative rhetoric is a well-lubricated tool. As we can see in these two examples, it allows authors to state that even a defeat could mean hope and even victories cannot be attained without losing something. Both storytellers are arguing that change is possible. However, neither of them is telling us to what degree that change is possible. We learn that workers may fail or win, but diegetic media is not able to break its inherent binary structure. Narrative authors or "narrauthors" only have one shot in their gun—a fixed sequence of events.[25] At most, they could write five or six different stories describing strikes, so the reader could make an average and decide the probabilities that workers have to succeed. But traditional narrative media lacks the "feature" of allowing modifications to the stories, even if exceptions happen in oral storytelling and dramatic performances. In such media, it is always possible for an audience to go through several iterations of a story. In a game, going through several sessions is not only a possibility but a requirement of the medium. Games are not isolated experiences: we recognize them as games because we know we can always start over. Certainly, you could play a game only once, but the knowledge and interpretation of simulations requires repetition.

Unlike narrative, simulations are not just made of sequences of events, they also incorporate behavioral rules. Imagine that we designed *Strikeman,* a real-time strategy game in the tradition of Ensemble Studio's *Age of Empires* in which you could play the role of a labor organizer. Your goal would be to have the most workers join your strike and then deal with its organization and implementation. Unlike what would happen in storytelling, the sequence of events in a simulation is never fixed. You can play it dozens of times and things would be different. In one session, the boss could call the police and repress your workers. In another game, you may have to deal with spies infiltrated into your organization or another worker may contest your leadership and try to sabotage your actions. Games always carry a certain degree of indeterminacy that prevents players from knowing the final outcome beforehand. To paraphrase Heraclitus, you never step in the same video game twice.

Let's focus on two characteristics of such a game. First, the result of the strike is in part a consequence of your performance as a labor leader. This may seem obvious—we like to believe that we are responsible of the consequences of our actions—but it is not a feature available in storytelling. After all, as we learned from classical Greek drama, stories and fate go together. No matter how badly literary theorists remind us of the active role of the reader, that train will hit Anna Karenina and Oedipus will kill his father and sleep with his mother. Similarly, the strike in *Germinal* is going to be a failure because the narrauthor decided beforehand that it should be that way. Nevertheless, simulation authors or "simauthors" can also incorporate different degrees of fate (through hard-coded events, cut-scenes, or by manipulating pseudo-random events) into their games. Victory is partly because of the player's performance but other things are beyond her control. The software could randomly slip in constraints (like an infiltrated saboteur), making your goal more difficult to reach. The simauthor always has the final word: she will be able to decide the frequency and degree of events that are beyond the player's control.

Second, imagine that we had a library of different simulations dealing with strikes, designed by different simauthors from different cultures and ideologies. Even assuming that all simulations would incorporate a winning scenario, some would be much difficult than others, depending on how they were programmed. Some might depend more on chance while others would define their outcome based solely on the player's performance. Whoever designs a strike simulator that is extremely hard to play is describing his beliefs regarding social mechanics through the game's rules rather than through events. Simulations provide simauthors with a technique that narrauthors lack. They are not only able to state if social change is possible or not, but they have the chance of expressing how likely they think it may be. This is not just by stating info (for example, "the probability of winning is 93 percent") but, rather, by modeling difficulty. This technique is also transparent: it is well hidden inside the model not as a piece of information but as a rule. Narrative may excel at taking snapshots at particular events but simulation provides us with a rhetorical tool for understanding the big picture.

Aristotle on the Holodeck

I previously described stories as being heavily associated with the concept of fate. This idea is the backbone behind the Marxist drama school, developed by Bertolt Brecht and more recently expanded by Augusto Boal. Marxists argue that Aristotelian drama and storytelling neutralize social change because they present reality as an inexorable progression of incidents without room for alterations. Boal's answer to this problem can be found in his corpus of drama techniques, the Theater of the Oppressed,[26] which combines theater with games in order to encourage critical debate over social, political, and personal issues. The forum theater, one of his most popular techniques, reenacts the same play several times by allowing different audience members to get into the stage and take the protagonist's role. This short play always depicts an oppressive situation and the audience is encouraged to participate by improvising possible solutions to the problem that is being staged. Boal's ultimate goal is not to find an actual solution to the crisis—even if sometimes the technique actually accomplishes this—but, rather, to create an environment for debating not just through verbal communication but also through performance. Forum theater perfectly fits the definition of simulation:[27] it models a system (the oppressive situation) through another system (the play).[28]

Video game designers have searched for decades for a way of bringing together the pleasures of stories and "interactivity." As Lev Manovich states,

"Interactive narrative remains a holy grail for new media."[29] Brenda Laurel, a long-time advocate of interactive stories' feasibility has recently defined them as "a hypothetical beast in the mythology of computing, an elusive unicorn we can imagine but have yet to capture."[30] Nevertheless, Boal was able to create a non-computer-based environment that combines a high degree of freedom for participants while creating a compelling experience. However, Boal's success is probably due to the fact that he took a different path than the one suggested by Laurel in her now classic *Computers as Theater*. Laurel, as well as most "interactive narrative" supporters, focuses on Aristotelian closure as the source of the user's pleasure. The biggest fallacy of "interactive narrative" is that it pretends to give freedom to the player while maintaining narrative coherence. The pleasure in Boalian drama is given not by its seamless three-act structure but by the opposite: the ability to interrupt and modify it. Simulations are laboratories for experimentation where user action is not only allowed but also required. Coherence from session to session is simply not a requirement in the game world. The gratification for Boalian actors is not the one of the professional actor but rather the one of the child who plays make-believe. The child is constantly adapting his fantasy to different changes, without the grown-up's obsession with closure. Certainly, simulation challenges narrauthors because it takes away their source of power: the ability to make statements through sequences of causes and effects. To use a metaphor, narrauthors "train" their stories so they will always perform in an almost predictable way.[31] By contrast, simauthors "educate" their simulations: they teach them some rules and may have an idea of how they might behave in the future, but they can never be sure of the exact final sequence of events and result. The key trait of simulational media is that it relies on rules: rules that can be manipulated, accepted, rejected, and even contested. Narrauthors have executive power: they deal with particular issues. On the other hand, simauthors behavore more like legislators: they are the ones who craft laws. They do take more authorial risks than narrauthors because they give away part of their control over their work.

Chances are that Aristotle's famous lost book of Poetics was not about video games, but the fact is that Aristotelianism is also present in the world of games. There are different typologies of games, which can generally be useful even if they usually do not comply with the formal rules of scientific taxonomy. Roger Caillois's game categorization of *alea, agôn, ilinx,* and *mimicry* is one of the best known.[32] However, I do not find this classification extremely useful as its groups constantly overlap. Instead, I prefer Caillois's distinction between *paidia* and *ludus,* which describes the difference between "play" and "game."[33] *Paidia* refers to the form of play present in early children (construction kits, games of make-believe, kinetic play) while *ludus* represents games with social rules (chess, soccer, poker). Although Caillois describes these categories through examples, he does not provide a strict definition. It is common to think that *paidia* has no rules, but this is not the case: a child who pretends to be a soldier is following the rule of behaving like a soldier and not as a doctor. In a previous essay, I have suggested[34] that the difference between *paidia* and *ludus* is that the latter incorporates rules that define a winner and a loser, whereas the former does not.

Structurally, *ludus* follows the same three-act rule behind Aristotelian stories. *Ludus* sessions go through a first act in which the rules are acknowledged, a second act in which players perform, and, finally, a third act that concludes the game and draws the line between victors and losers. Accordingly, the same terms that the Marxist drama school uses in its critique of Aristotelian theater could be applied to *ludus*. *Ludus* games provide an "organic whole," a closed product that can only be explored within a secluded set of rules defined by the author. Certainly, just as it happens in narrative, the reader/player is free to participate within those limits and this is where the pleasure of reading/playing resides. Even so, *ludus* remains ideologically too attached to the idea of a centralized author. By contrast, *paidia* games are more "open-ended" than their *ludus* counterparts.

In both drama and games, the Aristotelian/*ludus* approaches are definitively the most widely popular and perfected. We are all familiar with "Hollywood endings" and the generally manicheist philosophy behind industrialized narratives. In a similar way, *ludus* provides us with two possible endings: winning and losing. The popularity of this formula is almost surely because of the simplicity of its binary structure. However, this is also its most important limitation. Certainly, *ludus* works great within worlds built around dichotomies. This explains, in part, why current computer games have so much trouble in trying to escape from the fantasy and science-fiction realms. In other words, the binary logic found in *ludus* stands out when delivering games set in fairy-tale-like environments, where things are generally black or white. When you move onto other topics such as human relationships, suddenly distinctions are not so clear-cut. Only *paidia,* with its fuzzier logic and its scope beyond winners and losers, can provide an environment for games to grow in their scope and artistry.

The choice between *paidia* and *ludus* structures is ideologically essential for a simauthor because both carry different agendas. The simulated world in *ludus* games seems more coherent because the player's goals are clear: you must do X in order to reach Y and therefore become a winner. This implies that Y is a desired objective and therefore it is morally charged. Saving the world, rescuing a princess or destroying the alien menace are all classic examples of *ludus* goals. By stating a rule that defines a winning scenario, the simauthor is claiming that these goals are preferable to their opposite (letting the world crumble apart, leaving the princess behind, and sharing our living space with the aliens). *Ludus* is the simulational structure of choice for modernist simauthors: these designers have moral certitudes (Mario is good, the monsters are bad). Clearly defined goals do not generally leave much room neither for doubts nor for contesting that particular objective. Not surprisingly, all military games are *ludus* because they do not admit options that break its binary logic (friend or foe, dead or alive, with us or against us). Based on this, it would seem that *paidia* is a less modernist technique aimed at designers who have more doubts than certitudes. Well, this is only partly true. Any *paidia* game, such as *SimCity*, leaves its main goal up to the player who can build any kind of city she wants (the biggest, the most ecological, the prettiest, etc.). In other words, *SimCity* is not necessarily forcing players to model their cities to resemble New York, Tokyo, or Paris. However, even if the designer left out a winning scenario (or a desirable urban structure) ideology is not just conveyed through goal rules. A more subtle—and therefore more persuasive—way to accomplish this is through what I will call "manipulation rules." These rules are opposed to goal rules in that they do not imply a winning scenario. The following is a list of manipulation rules from different games: "you cannot touch the ball with your hands unless you are the goalkeeper" (soccer); "pawns can only move forward" (chess); "fruits will give you extra score" (*Ms. Pac-Man*). As all simulations are constrained, limited approaches to (real or fictional) systems, designers have a limited amount of manipulation rules. In the *SimCity* example, the designer could convey his ideology by adding or leaving out manipulation rules that deal with, say, public transportation, racial issues, or ecology. In other media, such as cinema, we have learned that it is essential to discern between what is shown on the screen and what is being left out. In the realm of simulation, things are more complex: it is about which rules are included in the model and how they are implemented. For example, films can be analyzed on how they portray certain minority groups. A game like *The Sims* does showcase characters from different races, genders, and ages (you can even get a tool to design your own character, selecting from different body structures and skin colors). However, the way that *The Sims*'s designers dealt with gay couples was not just through representation (for example, by allowing players to put gay banners on their yards), they also decided to build a rule about it. In this game, same-gender relationships are possible. In other words, homosexuality is really an option for the players and it is included in the simulation's model. However, we could perfectly imagine a conservative game where the designers would have ruled out same-gender relationships. Homosexuality is not the goal of *The Sims*, just a possibility. By incorporating this rule, the designers are showing tolerance towards this sexual option but we could hardly say that they are encouraging it (in order to proselytize, for example, a rewarding *ludus* rule could be implemented where players could be rewarded by their homosexual behavior).

So far, we can distinguish three different ideological levels in simulations that can be manipulated in order to convey ideology. The first level is the one that simulation shares with narrative and deals with representation and events. This includes the characteristics of objects and characters, backgrounds, settings, and cut scenes. For example, a simple switch of character skins could turn *Quake* into a deathmatch between Israelis and Palestinians. (Actually, there is a pro-Palestinian first-person shooter, *Under Ash,* available at <http://www.underash.net/emessage.htm>). Here the rules of the game remain unchanged: only the characters and settings are modified. However, on an ideological level, this game completely differs from the original.

The second level is the one of manipulation rules: what the player is able to do within the model. In same cases, certain manipulation rules state a possibility. In others, they are necessary to attain a level three goal. For example, in *Grand Theft Auto III* (*GTA III*) it is possible to shoot prostitutes in order to get money after having sex with them. Even if many people were disgusted by this possibility, it is essential to point out that this is not the goal of the game. Rhetorically, a game where you may kill sexworkers is very different from a game where you must kill them in order to win. Most *paidia* games work within this level.

The third level is the one of goal rules: what the player must do in order to win. It deals with what the author states as mandatory within the simulation. While it is possible to have fun in *Super Mario* without rescuing the princess, the player cannot win unless he accomplishes this goal. Games with goal rules provide both a personal and social reward: whoever reaches the end of a game will be recognized as a good player. On this third level, simauthors funnel through all the available actions and encourage some that will lead to the winning scenario.

At first, it would seem that these three levels are enough for a basic description of how ideology works within simulation. However, there is at least one extra one. The fourth ideological level is the one that deals with meta-rules. Certain simauthors do allow players to contest the model's built-in assumption by giving different degrees of freedom to partially modify the three levels that I have just described. A meta-rule is a rule that states how rules can be changed. Many games include editors that allow players to build "mods" or modified versions of the original games. Other games are open-source and can be changed on their source code level. Some only allow you to do cosmetic changes while others permit more drastic modifications. Still, it is important to keep in mind that meta-rules do not imply neither the death of the author nor the player's freedom. Indeed, meta-rules are rules and as such they are present in the game because the author wanted them to be there. In other words, it is the author's decision to make the source code or editing tools available to the player. Certainly, a simauthor who allows her public to alter her work is quite different from the traditional idea that we have of the role of the narrauthor. Nevertheless, with or without meta-rules, the simauthor always has the final word and remains in charge because total player freedom is impossible since it would imply that no rules are unchangeable and therefore the game could literally become anything.

I have just suggested a typology of simulation rules (manipulation rules, goal rules, and meta-rules) that can help us to better understand how the designer's agenda can slip into the game's inner laws. However, this typology is not exhaustive and could certainly be expanded (for example, by analyzing the ideological role of the interface rules or by examining the nuances between games which have both winning and losing scenarios and those where you can only lose). I am convinced that it will take us a long time to grasp the potential of simulation as opposed to narrative, mainly because we are so familiar and proficient with the latter. Simulation contests our notions of authorship and also the boundaries that we are used to apply to works of art.

In the Rules of the Rose is the Rose

In his poem "The Golem,"[35] Borges tells the story of the rabbi of Prague who, after long permutations, is able to find the key word that holds the secret of life. A monster, the Golem, is created, but the process involves more than magic words. Borges describes how the rabbi modeled his puppet and then trained him, like an ancient virtual pet, into the mysteries "of the Letters, Time, and Space." The Golem learned very much like an expert system. But in this pessimistic view (similar to the myth of Frankenstein) this "simulacrum," as Borges calls it, fails to reproduce the human soul. Certainly, simulation has its limitations, just like representation. Simulation is only an approximation and even if narrauthors may feel threatened by it, it does not announce the end of representation: it is an alternative, not a replacement.[36]

For the first time in history, humanity has found in the computer the natural medium for modeling reality and fiction. Simulation, in both its *paidia* and *ludus* flavors, provides a different—not necessarily better—environment for expressing the way we see the world. It is common to contrast narrative and drama because the former is the form of the past, of what cannot be changed, while the latter unfolds in present time. To take the analogy further, simulation is the form of the future. It does not deal with what happened or is happening, but with what may happen. Unlike narrative and drama, its essence lays on a basic assumption: change is possible. It is up to both game designers and game players to keep simulation as a form of entertainment or to turn it into a subversive way of contesting the inalterability of our lives.

Representation and narrative may still hold a lot of tricks in their bags, but the promise of the yet unexplored field of simulation and games is so vast and appealing that some of us can hardly wait to start experimenting with it. Whoever slowly walked back home after buying a long-awaited video game knows exactly the kind of excitement that I am talking about.

Notes

1. See <www.gamestudies.org>.
2. Brenda Laurel, *Computers as Theater* (London: Addison Wesley, 1993).
3. Janet H. Murray, *Hamlet on the Holodeck: The Future of Narrative in Cyberspace* (New York: Free Press, 1997).
4. Espen Aarseth, *Cybertext. Perspectives on Ergodic Literature* (Baltimore: Johns Hopkins, 1997).
5. Gonzalo Frasca, "Ludologia kohtaa narratologian," *Parnasso* 3 (1999), 365–371. Also published as "Ludology Meets Narratology: Similitudes and Differences Between (Video)Games and Narrative." Available online at <http://www.ludology.org>.
6. Particularly part of the *Game Studies* journal crew, including Espen Aarseth, Markku Eskelinen, Jesper Juul, Aki Järvinen, and myself, among others.
7. Mark Turner, *The Literary Mind* (Oxford: Oxford University Press, 1998).
8. Gonzalo Frasca, *Videogames of the Oppressed: Videogames as a Means for Critical Thinking and Debate* (Master's thesis, Georgia Institute of Technology, 2001). Available online at <http://www.ludology.org>.
9. The accuracy of the simulated model, just as it happens in traditional representation, depends on the observer. A simple flight simulator could be very sophisticated for an amateur but dismissed as simplistic by an expert pilot.
10. Espen Aarseth, *Cybertext. Perspectives on Ergodic Literature.*
11. Markku Eskelinen, "The Gaming Situation," *Game Studies* 1, No. 1 (July 2001). Available online at <http://www.gamestudies.org/0101/eskelinen/>.
12. Toys and games (particularly board games) are indeed previous examples of simulational media. However, their models cannot match the complexity of the ones generated with computers.
13. Mitchell Resnick, *Turtles, Termites, and Traffic Jams* (Cambridge, MA: MIT Press, 2001).
14. See <http://www.wired.com/wired/archive/9.10/mustread_pr.html>.
15. "St. Louis County's regulations on video games upheld," *The Nando Times* (April 25, 2002). Available online at <http://www.nando.com/technology/story/379154p-3030283c.html>.
16. Ashley H. Grant, "Jesse "Video Game" Ventura," *CBS News.com*, April 26, 2002. Available online at <http://www.cbsnews.com/stories/2002/04/26/politics/ main507378.shtml>.
17. For a collection of Osama games, see <http://www.newgrounds.com/collections.osama. html>. While political games have not yet caught massive attention, games based on news and political events are also a great field for experimenting with game rhetoric. Personallay, I especially enjoy the challenges created by this new genre -which I propose to call *newsgaming*- that combines the characteristics of political cartoons with video games.
18. Ventura later decided he would not run for reelection, so we may never see his political video games.
19. The closest antecedent would be Augusto Boal's use of his game/theatrical techniques— which are nothing but computer-less simulations—for his political campaign as a legislator in Rio de Janeiro. For more information on this unique and fascinating project, see Augusto Boal, *Legislative Theater* (London: Routledge, 1999).
20. While this simulation is definitively a parody, its extreme use of clichés and simplification are a clear example of a colonialist attitude in video game design. Having grown up myself during a dictatorship in Uruguay, I find the game insulting. I would not object to a simulation that dealt with issues such as torture or political imprisonment if it aimed at understanding

politics and sociology. In this case, however, it is simply used for entertainment, which is nothing short of disgusting. Alas, I guess South American oppressed are not yet a powerful lobby in the land of political-correctness.

21. Ted Friedman, "The Semiotics of Sim City," *First Monday* 4 (1999). Available online at <http://www.firstmonday.dk/issues/issue4_4/friedman/>.

22. Émile Zola, *Germinal* (Paris: Hatier, 2001).

23. Ken Loach, *Bread and Roses* (Studio Home Entertainment, 2001).

24. It would be possible for the author to create an "open" ending that would rely on the reader's imagination to decide what happened to the strikers. But again, it is the author and not the reader who ultimately decides the use of this form of ending.

25. The fixed sequence that I am referring to is the one of the actual events. The events as told can be rearranged in nonlinear ways through techniques such as flash-forwards and flashbacks. This is the difference between story and discourse, a distinction widely accepted in narratology.

26. Augusto Boal, *The Theater of the Oppressed* (New York: TCG, 1998).

27. Boal even describes the original forum theater play as a "model" or "antimodel."

28. For a more extensive analysis among Boal's drama, games, and video games, see Frasca, 2001.

29. See <http://www.pause-effect.com/reviews.html>.

30. Brenda Laurel, *Utopian Entrepreneur* (Cambridge, MA: MIT Press, 2001), 72.

31. Again, while the reader's interpretation is not predictable, the mechanics of the narration remain inalterable.

32. Roger Caillois, *Les jeux et les hommes: Le masque et le vertige* (Paris: Gallimard, 1967).

33. Unlike English, French and Spanish only have one term for referring to both "play" and "game." Nevertheless, I still use Caillois's terms, because of the different meanings that English attributes to "play," which can both be a noun or a verb.

34. Gonzalo Frasca, "Ludologia kohtaa narratologian."

35. Jorge Luis Borges, *Ficciones* (Buenos Aires: Emecé, 1971).

36. Actually, I have suggested in my work *Videogames of the Oppressed* (following Aarseth's ideas) that simulation and representation only differ in a matter of degree. But for the sake of clarity during these early days of ludology, it may be safer to consider them as different.

CHAPTER 11

From Gamers to Players and Gameplayers

The Example of Interactive Movies

BERNARD PERRON

For any film scholar who has begun to take an interest in video games, what is commonly referred to as the interactive movie seems a natural place to start. No other multimedia product came closer to crossing the threshold that separates the worlds of film and video games. However, a film scholar who commences research on this premise will be both disconcerted and disappointed, for many reasons.

In the early 1990s, following on the heels of laserdiscs, CD-ROMs were able to store digitized video, and thence became the standard, most widely distributed support for computer data. The interactive movie, which flourished in this technological environment, is not easy to categorize. The first popular game named as such, *The 7th Guest* (1992), is more a puzzle game with few live-action[1] cut-scenes. In that sense, to begin with the bestselling *Myst* (1993), a lot of games have embedded video clips that serve as informative sequences or simple transitions but they are not called interactive movies for all that.[2] What is more, in his 1995 lecture "The Challenge of the Interactive Movie," Ernest W. Adams noted that the term refers to a variety of games, from "a kind of space flight shoot-'em-up, with little bits of video in between" (*Wing Commander III: Heart of the Tiger*, 1994) to a graphic adventure (*Under a Killing Moon*, 1994), or from "a one-pass-through sort of game" (*Critical Path*, 1993) to a movie in movie theaters where the audience votes on how they want the plot to go (*Mr. Payback*, 1995).[3] Also, curiously enough, the video games section of *All Media Guide* (*AMG*) considers digital video not as a technology but as a mode of presentation, confusedly listing "Adventure" as the game's genre and "Interactive Movie" as the game's "style" for *The Dame Was Loaded* (1995), *Star Trek: Borg* (1996) or *The X-Files Game* (1998), and so on. By contrast, the style of the live-action video game *Phantasmagoria* (1995) is characterized as a "Third-Person Graphic Adventure."[4] The expression is no longer used by *AMG*, but a few years ago, the style of *The Beast Within: A Gabriel Knight Mystery* (1995), another live-action game by Sierra similar to *Phanstamagoria*, was called "first person/cinematic adventure." As Adams said, all kinds of weird stuff here.

Obviously, games using live-action video rely on narrative and film conventions that could be analyzed. But for someone studying film, those aspects of the interactive movie are not of great interest. Even if a game such as *Urban Runner* (1996) claimed to have a script as good as a Hitchcock movie, interactive movies look much like B-grade films. The general plotline revolves around fighting some sort of evil spirit in order to save the world, save people your avatar knows, or save the avatar himself. All the genre clichés are used in order to facilitate the gamer's participation.[5] Except in longer, elaborate cut-scenes that still show nothing aesthetically new, the mise en scène and the montage are pretty basic. The rhythm and pace of the action is continually interrupted in order to make more of the gamer's decisions. As far as photography is concerned, live actors are usually shot in front of a blue or a green screen. Because 3-D computer graphics of those games (and of this period) are not photorealistic and lighting on actors does not always match the backgrounds, the virtual environments really look like layers added afterward.[6] From Chris Jones himself playing the detective he has created in the *Tex Murphy* series, to numerous unknown B-grades actors, the acting in interactive movies is very noticeable, but not for good reasons. Even when big name stars *are* involved, the result is often dubious.[7] On the whole, as Celia Pearce straightforwardly stated, "It is almost impossible to match the production, acting, and writing quality of film in a CD-ROM. Misguided attempts to do so have yielded such eminently unmemorable experiences as the *Johnny Mnemonic* game, whose mediocrity was rivaled only by the film on which it was based."[8]

Indeed, the film scholar will rapidly find that the media convergence between film and game was not well received in video game circles. For instance, even if *Phantasmagoria* was one of the top sellers of 1995, *Computer Games Magazine* called "this hotly-anticipated game 'overblown, unintentionally hilarious and incredibly dull,' labeling it a 'disaster.' "[9] The interactivity of interactive movies is described as selective, branching-type, or menu-based.

Most importantly, it is a closed interactivity in which "the user plays an active role in determining the order in which already-generated elements are accessed."[10] The interactivity in question is in fact an illusion.

> While the ideology of a self-selected narrative and open-ended storyline suggests freedom and choice, this is precisely what interactive cinema strives to conceal. The user colludes with being a "player", whose freedom can be summed up as: "you can go wherever you like, so long as I was there before you"—which is of course precisely also the strategy of the "conventional" story-teller (or narrational agency) whose skill lies in the ability to suggest an open future at every point of the narrative, while having, of course, planned or "programmed" the progress and the resolution in advance.[11]

Like the interactive narrative in general, the interactive movie is seen as an oxymoron. It is not possible to tell a story by putting the storytelling in the hands of the spectator. And the linearity of a story is going against the nonlinear nature of a game. Daniel Ichbiah has perfectly summarized this duality:

> . . . the genre "interactive movie" has lost its letters of nobility and its evocation arouses as much enthusiasm as an eruption of acne. It would seem that neither genre, cinema or game, really win with this mixture. When the gamer sees the action interrupted in order for him to choose the sequence of the movie, a share of what made *thrillers* interesting—the continuity—fails. And those who like the elation obtained by good gameplay lose patience when filmed sequences last forever.[12]

In the cyclical organization of the game, viewing is privileged over acting in the interactive movie. But playing a game is not about viewing a movie with a joystick in hand.

After all is said and done, the failure of the interactive movie seems to be total. But it need not be so if we look the other side of the picture. Interactive movies demonstrate that it is not always pertinent to try to "repurpose" the analytical and theoretical tools of other fields, in this case film studies, when studying video games. It is certainly not the film or the narrative part that is worth examining. Any researcher interested in video games should concentrate on the game aspect. One can never emphasize enough the importance and pertinence of Gonzalo Frasca's call for a ludology, a "discipline that studies games and play activities,"[13] and video games in particular. I'm following such a course here. From this perspective, the gameplay of the interactive movie makes itself conspicuous. As rudimentary and ultimately dull for the video game connoisseur as it might be, it still necessitates a particular activity in order to transcend the movie. This essay will analyze and characterize this activity, and more specificly the kind of player it necessitates. The reason is simple: "not only play taken as such refers to the player, but there is no play without a player. Play implies the playing."[14] Since my thinking is very much motivated by one of the last interactive movies produced, *Tender Loving Care* (1999), my analysis of this game will be much longer. However, as with any inductive reasoning process, my specific observations lead to a broader theory.[15]

A Question of Attitude

If, as Huizinga wrote at the beginning of *Homo Ludens: A Study of Play-Element in Culture*, "any thinking person can see at glance that play is a thing on its own,"[16] it is not so easy to define the scope of this "own." "Play" and "game" are used in various contexts, looked at from a wide range of points of view and studied by many disciplines. But when we talk about play in general, and Huizinga pointed it out right after the comment I have just quoted, it should never be forgotten that, "in acknowledging play you acknowledge mind, for whatever else play is, it is not matter."[17] It is the player's state and presence of mind that determine this free activity and make acceptable the given though arbitrary rules. The fun of play is the fun of the player. This is one of the fundamental characteristic of play and games. Furthermore, in his famous book *Les jeux et les hommes* (translated *Man, Play, and Games*), it is the player's attitude that Roger Caillois uses as a principle of classification capable of subsuming the multitude and infinite variety of games. He then proposes

> a division into four main rubrics, depending upon whether, in the games under consideration, the role of competition, chance, simulation, or vertigo is dominant. I call these *agôn, alea, mimicry*, and *ilinx*, respectively. All four indeed belong to the domain of play. One *plays* football, billiards, or chess (*agôn*); roulette or a lottery (*alea*); pirate, Nero, or Hamlet (*mimicry*); or one produces in oneself, by a rapid whirling or falling movement, a state of dizziness and disorder (*ilinx*).[18]

Still, for Caillois, this classification does not cover the entire universe of play. That's why he will place those four types of game on a continuum between two opposite poles.

> At one extreme an almost indivisible principle, common to diversion, turbulence, free improvisation, and carefree gaiety is dominant. It manifests a kind of uncontrolled fantasy that can be designated by the term *paidia*. At the opposite extreme, this frolicsome and impulsive exuberance is almost entirely absorbed or disciplined by a complementary, and in some respects inverse, tendency to its anarchic and capricious nature: there is a growing tendency to bind it with arbitrary, imperative, and purposely tedious conventions, to oppose it sill more by ceaselessly practicing the most embarrassing chicanery upon it, in order to make it more uncertain of attaining its desired effect. This latter principle is completely

impractical, even though it requires an ever greater amount of effort, patience, skill, or ingenuity. I call this second component *ludus*.[19]

By doing so, Caillois introduces the bipolarity of the range of games accepted, according to French specialist Michel Picard,[20] by all human sciences and widely used, for example by Picard himself in his analysis of reading, and myself regarding the playful dimension of cinema,[21] Andrew Darley in his study of new media genres,[22] and Frasca when he looks at video games. These two modes of activity are differentiated by the term "play" in the English language, referring to the mode deploying itself freely in a way that is conceived as it unfolds like in the creative playing of a child,[23] and by "game," which is the mode defining itself by rules that order its course. Following the definitions of French philosopher André Lalandé, while keeping with Caillois's terminilogy, Frasca defines the two activities as follows:

> Paidia is "*Prodigality of physical or mental activity which has no immediate useful objective, nor defined objective, and whose only reason to be is based in the pleasure experimented by the player.*"
>
> Ludus is a particular kind of *paidia*, defined as an "*activity organized under a system of rules that defines a victory or a defeat, a gain or a loss.*"[24]

This fundamental duality allows one to delineate the particular forms that the gameplay can take and the playful or ludic activity this latter institutes. I am, here, more interested in the player's experience and the attitudes he or she may have. Contrary to Frasca, though these two English terms are often used until now without differentiation, I will still refer to play/player and game/gamer, for reasons that will follow. The pertinence of such utilization becomes apparent the moment one perceives that the two extremities discussed here are contained within the term "gameplay" itself.

It is also important to note that the attitude of the player is taken to be a consciously chosen one. As Jacques Henriot has shown, "distance is the initial form of play."[25]

> To play, it is necessary to know how to enter into the game. To enter in the game, it is necessary to know that it is a game. There must be, therefore, on the part of the one that starts to play, a preliminary comprehension of the sense of the game. The ludic attitude, as with all attitudes, is taken on. As with all attitudes, it is understood.[26]

The player then knows that the rules of a given game (or even of play, as we'll see) will limit his moves. But he accepts those by playing. More important, maybe, the ludic attitude implies "an intention of illusion"; illusion (*in-lusio*) meaning nothing less than beginning a game, recalls Caillois. Again, interactive movies demarcate this boundry clearly. The player knows his or her choices might be very limited and that his or her freedom will be controlled in some ways but will act as if these were not. The "as if" is referring to the *mimicry,* the role-playing considered to be the heart of the video game's experience. In that sense, the clarification made by Janet Murray is really important:

> The pleasurable surrender of the mind to an imaginative world is often described, in Coleridge's phrase, as "the willing suspension of disbelief." But this is too passive a formulation even for traditional media. When we enter a fictional world, we do not merely "suspend" a critical faculty; we also exercise a creative faculty. We do not suspend disbelief so much as we actively *create belief.* Because of our desire to experience immersion, we focus our attention on the enveloping world and we use our intelligence to reinforce rather than to question the reality of the experience.[27]

The pleasure of playing also depends on "being played." Marshall McLuhan, among others, has observed: "A game is a machine that can get into action only if the players consent to become puppets for a time."[28]

The Gamer

In the video game industry, the player is called a "gamer" (usually designated as either casual or hardcore). Accordingly, in order to make a clear distinction, it would be preferable to talk about "movie games" instead of "interactive movies"[29] when talking about those live-action video games[30] (and talk in particular about 2-D movie games, which refers to full-motion video arcade games that were called interactive movies). Seen in a ludic perspective, this delineates, straight off, an activity and an attitude toward it.

The gamer of a movie game has to feel he is part of the movie; that he is in the movie. That's where the fun lies. As we know, not only is the gamer lead to identify himself with the main stereotyped character—Tex Murphy, for instance—but this character becomes his surrogate in the diegetic universe, the avatar. Therefore, the gamer is bound to the rules and limits of the game universe and of the gameplay. Caught in a branching structure pattern, more or less complex due to the limitations of the live-action video and more or less random in what could happen next, the gamer remains a pathfinder. The task is clear: explore the diegetic space of the game in order to find various rooms or locations where he will meet people and collect clues, objects and/or tools that will be useful to unfold the plot and kill the evil spirit. For example, Tex Murphy will have to get a silver dollar from Rook, the owner of the pawnshop in front of his place, in order to get in the place where he'll be able to play a game for the ticket that will finally bring him to the Moon Child space station he has to destroy. To play is also to bind oneself, as Henriot would say.

The action of the movie game generally organizes itself in shot-reverse shot combinations in order to leave room for decisions: the avatar is shown (shot), then the things he can look at and use or the places he can go to (reverse shot); a choice is made and the avatar is shown enacting this choice (shot), and so on. In the third-person perspective, the avatar is left immobile in a medium or wide shot. Moving the mouse over the image will make the cursor change or produce a highlight. This indicates that an action can be made. A click on that object or direction will show the avatar enacting the action. As was noted, the interactivity of the movie game is menu-based. It is not always as explicit as a dialogue box. Rather, the branching points and the menus are hidden within the picture. Choosing one exit over another will begin a new sequence of action or kill the avatar (*Johnny Mnemonic,* 1995). Moving the cursor over the image reveals the (menu of) objects the gamer has to choose from. In an adventure game, this will create other explicit menus, such as an inventory (*The Dame Was Loaded*) or a series of icons at the bottom of the screen (*The X-Files Game*).

It goes without saying that movie games (and a great majority of video games) lean toward the *ludus* pole. Although *ludus* is considered a pole that can amalgamate the four game rubrics, Caillois nevertheless distinguishes it from *agôn*:

> The difference from *agôn* is that in *ludus,* the tension and skill of the player are not related to any explicit feeling of emulation or rivalry: the conflict is with the obstacle, not with one or several competitors.[31]

Except for the first live-action arcade shooting games such as *Mad Dog McCree* (1990) and a few other live-action video games with the same shooting arcadelike episodes (such as *Eraser Turnabout* and *Hardline,* both from 1996), movie games are far from being about competiton (*agôn*) of the shoot-'em-up against computer-controlled opponents or against other hardcore gamers style.[32] The gamer toils much more to get through a zigzag narrative. Through problems, puzzles, tests, examinations, and/or simple questions, the gameplay's main purpose in an adventure game is to control the progression of discovery of a causal chain of events. In Caillois's terms, more embarrassing chicaneries render the gamer increasingly uncertain of attaining his desired effect. The stake is to get to the end of the adventure, that is, to win the game. But this will depend on the performance of the gamer. Thus, movie games require an amount of effort, patience, skill, or ingenuity. The gamer has to reflect, make decisions, and perform certain actions until he or she finds success. Tex Murphy might for instance try more than once to win the game he has to play in order to stay alive and get his ticket to the Moon Child. Those purposely tedious moments recall the *ludus* element of the game: "... the pleasure experienced in solving a problem arbitrarily designed for this purpose also intervenes, so that reaching a solution has no other goal than personal satisfaction for its own sake."[33] The gamer goes for the challenge. Considered too easy to traverse, movie games were not greatly respected by experienced adventurers. But the fact that movie games were and are still not well regarded by the video game connoisseur allows one to take a look at the person who plays outside the territory of those enthusiasts expert in the realm of video game playing.

The Player

It is imperative we distinguish those "movie games" from the "interactive movies" that might not fit the usual marketing appellation of the video game industry. For instance, *Tender Loving Care* (1999), designed by Rob Landeros and directed by David Wheeler, who fathered the movie *The 11th Hour* (1995) together, and *The 7th Guest* (1993), created by Landeros on his own, does not fit the broad description of the "movie game" I have just outlined. The concept is something quite different, a concept that Landeros and Wheeler revived with slight changes in *Point of View: An Interactive Movie* (2001). Because I could not see how this would attract and satisfy a gamer, I had to discern the attitude and the state of mind of the person who would play it. To pursue my argument, I will therefore refer not to a gamer but to a player when talking about the interactive movie. *Tender Loving Care* helps clarify this distinction.

Tender Loving Care is one of the last productions to try to mix live-action video with a certain amount of gameplay. It is also one of the first interactive movies to be made available on standard DVD format,[34] inaugurating the trend of releasing arcade and PC games such as *Sherlock Holmes, Consulting Detective* (1999, a movie game from 1991), *Mad Dog McCree* (2001) and *Dragon's Lair* (2002, the famous arcade 2-D movie game from 1983) for normal DVD players, which are seen as another—possible[35]—gaming platform. There are two ways to see this adaptation: as a way to attract movie viewers to the interactive gaming world, or a way to make the interactive concept break into movie DVD rental and sales. Although the degree of storytelling and gameplaying may vary, *Tender Loving Care* is certainly more a story and less a game. If *The 7th Guest* had more gameplay time than movie time, the inverse is true here. The player literally views the movie with the remote in hand. There is no complex branching structure behind it. As Landeros describes it: "TLC doesn't branch, it bulges."[36] The narrative is linear but punctuated by slight differences: short scenes are added or removed, lines of dialogue change, scenes are done in different ways, or, and it is certainly a dimension on which the designers have played, erotic scenes are more or less explicit. Yet, those differences depend on gameplay section choices, rudimentary and of limited number[37] as they may be.

But let me describe the opening of the interactive movie. Arriving in front of a house for sale, Dr. Turner, a psychiatrist played by John Hurt, looks around and then speaks directly to the camera. He tells the player that something strange happened in the house. Even if Dr. Turner was close to all the protagonists in this event, it is as much a mystery to him as it is for anyone. Then, he addresses the player: "Perhaps you can help. A fresh eye and an uncluttered view. And maybe together we can reassemble the happenings and have a better understanding of what took place. We can only hope." The events to be understood concern a couple, Michael and Allison Overtone. The first scene shows the arrival of Kathryn Randolph, a nurse/therapist coming to live with the couple for a while in order to nurse Allison, who acts as if their young daughter, an only child—dead in a family car accident—is still alive. Michael shows Kathryn her room. The psychiatric nurse, who was recommended to the couple by Dr. Turner, is so eager to meet her patient that she forces Michael out of the room by walking toward him while starting to get undressed. When the room's door closes, Dr. Turner reappears and initiates the three phases of gameplay.

First, there is an exit poll consisting of four to nine questions. While giving his own thoughts and theories about what's going on, Dr. Turner asks that players give their opinions on some of the things they have just seen (Was it a good idea to make Jody's room look "lived-in"?—I agree, I disagree, or I have no opinion; Do you believe Michael has ever been unfaithful?—Yes, No, or I have no opinion, etc.) and their impressions about the characters (Dr. Turner is hiding something.—I agree, I disagree, or I have no opinion; Which of the following best describes the way Kathryn appeared in the (nurse) uniform?—Angelic, Seductive, Powerful, Sinister, or Professional; etc.). He also addresses intimate and provocative questions to the player (A term that might describe my own sexuality would be?—Repressed, Average, Healthy, or Overpowering; How do you feel in the company of highly intelligent people?—Intimidated, Stimulated, Superior, Humiliated, or Comfortable ; etc.). Once these first questions are answered, the player is free to explore the Overtone's House, rendered in 3-D,[38] by choosing a room and navigating through arrow keys: looking at what's around the house, books, magazines, and TV or radio programs; rummaging in the character's private belongings such as diaries, e-mails, letters, professional files, Kathryn's commentaries on her microcassette recorder, and so on; and encountering characters who will directly share their feelings and thoughts.[39] When the player has terminated this exploration, he or she must then look for a spiral figure that will start a TAT, standing for "Thematic Apperception Test." The first time, Dr. Turner prepares the player. He says: "Sit back and clear your cluttered mind. Let your thoughts go free, and leave your inhibitions behind." Then he shows some paintings, photographs, or drawings and asks between fourteen to twenty-nine questions about them and about the player themselves. Since it is a personality test, the questions are incredibly varied (Who is watching her (a painting showing a woman seen in a room through a window)?—A Passerby, A Peeping Tom, A Killer, The Artist, or Me; The artist who painted this (an abstract painting)—Is insane, Has a unique vision, Has some "issues" to deal with, Is a genius; If I was stuck behind the lines in enemy territory, I would most want to have—A gun, A white flag, A map, or A cyanide capsule; The best game to play at a birthday party is—Pin the tail on the donkey, Hit the piñata, Pass the orange, Croquet, or Spin the bottle; etc.). Curiously, Steve Ramsey, a reviewer from *Quandary Computer Game Reviews* said about this TAT: "When you have had enough exploring, you must find the hotspot that generates the Thematic Apperception Test (TAT) (Dr. Turner will tell you where to look.) You "leave" the game and the good doctor shows you images and asks you questions, again some of them quite intimate."[40] But in fact, as we'll see, this is a fundamental part. Once the test ends, the movie resumes and the next story episode (lasting between four to ten minutes!) will be altered by all the answers given. This process will be repeated fifteen times during the interactive movie in order for the player to get to one of the four main endings.

The events, into which the player has to look, have already taken place. The whole dichotomy between story and discourse or narrative (between *histoire* and *récit* in French) then keeps its significance. One knows that interactivity unfolds at that very moment. When the gamer interacts in a game, it is always in the here-and-now. It's real time. What is happening can be changed, that is the story, but not the order, duration, or frequency of this happening. The gamer is cut off from all the narrative possibilities of the discourse, the main reason for the presence and existence of the cut-scenes. Not being able to occur at the same time, interactivity and storytelling are well separated in *Tender Loving Care*. Contrary to the gamer of movie games, the player remains outside the diegetic world. Position is reaffirmed by questions asked and direct address to the camera that calls on and reminds the player that he is watching. The same strategy is used in the interactive movie *I'm Your Man* (1998, originally released in 1992[41]), in which the three main protagonists question the player about what branch the action, placed in the present this time, should take. The role of the player is to react to story episodes, not to enact them. *Tender Loving Care* is not based on the action of players, but on *re*actions. As opposed to the gamer who has at the same time to find out details about his avatar (for example, the agent the gamer embodies in *The X-Files Game* has "forgotten" his password to log into the FBI system right at the beginning of the game[42]), the diegetic world and the plot, the player of

Tender Loving Care concentrates on his perception of the main characters. They all seem to hide something. What really are Kathryn's intentions? What is her relationship with Dr. Turner? Is Michael the loving husband he seems to be? This set of questions the player is being asked or asks of himself or herself during the gameplay sections is different from those of a gamer who must figure out how to get out of a room they've just entered (as at the beginning of *Urban Runner* for example).

Relying on the standard and basic DVD menu structure, the idea of the questionnaire in *Tender Loving Care* truly shows that the interactive movie (and interactive narratives in general) is more about hyperselectivity than interactivity, more about multiple choices (even true/false in movie games where a bad choice kills your avatar) than developed and open-ended answers. The questionnaire conceals neither the significance nor the range of choices. It is about controlling the unfolding of the movie, not the things inside the diegetic world. The player is capable of commenting *on* the movie, not intervening *in* the movie. As to Landeros and Wheeler's own aims, their production "provide[s] a form of gameplay in [a] non-game experience."[43] This is the whole point, the material is more about a play experience.

Having based the gameplay on the reactions rather than on the actions of the players, Landeros and Wheeler did not have to script the interactor. They did not have to ask themselves what to do so that the player would be correctly positioned when the dramatic climax would be ready to take place. Actually, the only place where the player controls action is during their exploration of the house. The potential of the interactive process of navigation is then exploited. This phase, which allows one to take a look behind the scenes of the drama and to seek clues there about the characters, is the sole situation left for the gamer who, moreover, sees it that way.[44] But it is not an obligatory phase. The effort demanded by the gameplay of the interactive film is really not huge. It concerns choosing among certain options. Rewards are not exceptional compared to the video game that offers substantial rewards; access to a superior level, to a best arsenal, to a best score, and so on. In *Tender Loving Care,* the rewards are always only other film sequences. The only appraisal players will have is a more or less detailed psychological profile of themselves at the end.[45]

It is clear that interactive movies, as opposed to movie games, lean toward the *paidia* pole. This mode of playful activity deploys itself freely. To return to Caillois's definition, an indivisible principle, common to diversion, turbulence, free improvisation, and carefree gaiety is dominant. *Paidia* manifests a kind of uncontrolled fantasy. As we have seen, at the beginning of the first TAT, Dr. Turner tells the player "to clear your cluttered mind, to let your thoughts go free and leave your inhibitions behind."

He thus institutes a free play in which the player has to let themselves go. There will be no hard thinking, no wrong answers, subsequently no need to cheat to be able to continue (but end codes might be needed by someone who wishes to see all endings). In addition, it is possible for the player to change their manner of answering in the course of the play, going from a conservative one (answering that heaven is a beautiful place, and not an harem or a golf course) to a more shameless one (confessing that one likes watching other people have sex). Besides, as few reviewers have noted, the logic behind the questionnaire of *Tender Loving Care* is really not obvious.[46] In Caillois's classification, this refers to the *alea*, the game of dice. To use another definition of the word "play" as in "a wheel has some play in it," meaning that it's rather loose, we would say that "there is play" between the player's answers to the questionnaire. The player knows that the gameplay section actualizes the narrative, but does not know how. The distinction is made by Wheeler himself; *Tender Loving Care* is "an adventure in which the choices are subliminal and intuitive as opposed to deductive or rational. Subconscious as opposed to solution-oriented."[47] The TAT is based directly on random access. But this randomness is not negative. In this case, "the purpose of interactivity is to keep the textual machine running so that the text may unfold its potential and actualized its virtuality."[48] One knows the questions of the TAT hide the computer codes, codes that will determine the way the next story episode will unfold. By answering the questionnaire, the player sets up one of the few possible outcomes and one of the endings. As in *The Sims* (2000), there is no total control over the results of player management. "Furthermore, the impossibility of impact on the cinematic is one of the sources of our pleasure in it. . . . Our distress will not influence [the characters'] behaviour."[49] That's why, despite what Steve Ramsay said about the TAT not being part of the game, it is a fundamental part of the gameplay. Since the player must choose one answer, without foreseeing the cause-and-effect relationship between choice and action, the player may let his or her fantasies reign.

After this analysis of *Tender Loving Care*, it is necessary to introduce some shades of gray into this somewhat stark notion of free play. According to Andrew Darley, who studied video games along with digital cinema and special venues attractions, the genres of visual digital culture cannot lean toward *paidia* or early or "ideal" manifestations of playing.

> Not only are they [the certain kinds of rudimentary play principle in operation in the genre of visual digital culture] further removed from the direct (imaginative and physical) control of the player, but they are also to an increasing extent mechanised (made more mechanistic) by their inscription in the expressions and genres in questions. The element of creative control and imaginative

spontaneity that is attached to true play—"child's play"—is diluted. . . . Another way of putting this might be to say that the play principles in the forms of visual digital culture have been subjected to further processes of instrumentalisation.[50]

Obviously, players are not free in the sense that they may do anything they want, and this is even more true in games as closed and structured as an interactive movie. We are indeed far from the anarchic side associated with Caillois's *paidia* and the pure creativity at the heart of Winnicott's child playing. We are still talking about games. The type of game that is generally referred to as most faithfully approximating the liberty and the creativity of this pole is the MMORPG, in which players personify characters inhabiting a virtual universe that they themselves make evolve. But, by contrast, it is necessary to take into account the fundamental distance or detachment of play. As Darley says, after the McLuhan quote I've mentioned, and others, "it is not incorrect to say that it is the spectator who is 'played with.' "[51] In a ludic perspective, players know they are playing and being played. But that does not change the attitude they're invited to have and the illusion they maintain. Faced with the alternatives presented, restricted though they may be, the player selects the one preferred. It is not necessary to contemplate at length to decide if Kathryn is manipulative in *Tender Loving Care* or if one is going to follow a character escaping by a window or return with another to the party in *I'm Your Man*. The course undertaken to that point can influence decisions, as the actions of the characters will have predetermined effects, but one is not obliged to uphold a considered judgment. The player is making improvised decisions as they are required. The interactive movie interrupts itself only momentarily.[52] It does not remain blocked at a given stage because the player missed an element, a clue or some information. What is more, in Grahame Weinbern's conception of interactive cinema, while the player has some control over what is onscreen, being able to change the stream by freely touching the screen of *Sonata* (1991/1993) for example, the movie itself does not stop at all.[53] But still, the player has to make a decision within a regulated structure. This is fundamental. Like Frasca so relevantly pointed out, play, like games, is also predicated on strict rules: a child, for example, does not play an aircraft's pilot the same way he or she plays a doctor. This is not, therefore, what distinguishes the two types of playful activity, but: "Games have results: they define a winner and a loser; play does not."[54] The player does not play to win or lose or to get a better score. There is no such result. The player does not have to cheat to get to the end. They may be disappointed, but they never lose. If the movie game is like a puzzle, the interactive movie is more a game of construction and editing. It is largely for this reason that interactive cinema in theater does not function. The procedure of the vote introduces an *agôn* dimension to the improvised behavior of the player, who is more often frustrated at not seeing the movie progress through the turns chosen.

The Player in a Game

The dividing line between *paidia/ludus* or play/game is not as trenchant as it has been presented thus far. Following Henriot, it is necessary to extend the assessment. "We thus have, if one wants to apprehend the "play" phenomenon in its totality, to discern the share of play that enters into the performance of a game."[55] The gamer would then, in the game, take the attitude of a player. It is tempting to introduce the term "playgamer" to refer to this gamer acting as a player in a game, but since the attitude is comparable, I do not think it is necessary.

In her study of the multilinearity and open-form narrative of the movie game *Phantasmagoria*, Angela Ndalianis exposes, in a way, the change of attitude:

> If linearity and character motivation traditionally associated with Hollywood cinema are not the player's predilection (or if the player simply can't work out how to access all options present in the game design), it is possible to produce a narrative that has more in common with art cinema and avant-garde cinema forms of narration and nonnarration. In the case of bad game play, not only is it possible to miss entire portions of narrative action (thereby creating narrative gaps), but it is also possible to focus on actions that are in no way concerned with unraveling a narrative.[56]

The player of Ndalianis is, to begin with, a gamer who is supposed to find the cause-and-effect structures of *Phantasmagoria* and to follow the main character Adrienne's motivation, which is to kill the demon that possesses her husband Don. The gamer becomes a player by going away from these lines of Hollywood narrative form, following Ndalianis's examples, to make Adrienne wander aimlessly around the house and in town, make her eat in the kitchen or look at herself in the numerous mirrors littered around the house, go to the bathroom, comb her hair, put on makeup, or go to the toilet. It is by leaning toward the *paidia* pole, by the simple enjoyment of the doing of the gameplay and of the possibility to play with the movie that the player's activity loosens up the linear and causal relations of the action or focuses on "nonincidents" that undercut the narrative concerns. This produces, according to Ndalianis, art cinema narrative form and avant-garde cinema nonnarrative structures.

Once again, the obvious flaws and limitations of movie games are revealing. Compared to the gamer who will leave the game only upon arriving at the end of its course (unless they are unable to and quit), the player will put an end to activity when they've had enough. The often quoted assertion of Stuart Moulthrop that describes the reading experience of hypertext applies here: "You are done when it is over for you."[57] But clearly, the player of *Phantasmagoria* would quite rapidly get tired of the little subversive games. That is explained in Frasca's accurate distinction:

> If *ludus* can be related to narrative plot, *paidia* can be related to the narrative settings. The ability to perform *paidia* activities is determined by the environment and the actions. By environment we mean the space where the player is (real, as in a school playground, or virtual, as in a videogame). The environment includes topology, objects, and other characters.[58]

Movie games are more about narrative plot than about environment. The live-action avatar can only do the actions that have been filmed (comb her hair as Adrienne). Nor does the virtual environment of movie games have the power of fascinating fabulous 3-D scenery. For instance, because there are no monsters, zombies, or enemies running after you, anyone playing one of the games of the *Myst* series generally ends up wandering around the island for the sake of the graphics, thus forgetting the goal of the search for a while. Moreover, one can see the evolution of video games by underlining the analogy used by the designers of *Grand Theft Auto III* (2001): "For the first time, players are put at the heart of their own gangster movie, and let loose in a full-realized 3 dimensional city, in which anything can happen and probably will."[59] We are here far from the linearity and light randomness of the movie game. And in the cyclical organization of the game, acting is now privileged over viewing. Referring to Janet Murray's description of digital environments, *Grand Theft Auto III*'s Liberty City is as interactive (procedural and participatory) as immersive (spatial and encyclopedic).[60] What makes the success of such a driving-shooting-action-mission-simulation game is that there is as much for the gamer that has to accomplish specific missions to do as there is for the player who wants to wander the city and just go on committing various criminal acts. And with *Grand Theft Auto III,* we truly find the turbulence, free improvisation, anarchic play, frolicsome and impulsive exuberance associated with *paidia.*

The Gameplayer

Insofar as it is possible to act like a player in a movie game, it would be possible to play like a gamer during an interactive movie by, for example, trying to go through every gameplay section of *Tender Loving Care* within a minute or to find the right combination of answers in order to get the most explicit erotic scenes.[61] But there is a much more important gamer's attitude to underline.

In showing that *Phantasmagoria* could lead to the production of other types of cinema, Ndalianis notes without underscoring it that this production came from "bad game play." From this angle, the share of play that enters in the performance of a game could be understood in the light of Winnicott's observations of the child's positive social attitude toward playing: "This attitude must include recognition that playing is always liable to become frightening. Games and their organization must be looked at as part of an attempt to forestall the frightening aspect of playing."[62] Aside from the social fear that shoot-'em-ups and video games arouse in general, this highlights the notion of control and regulation. The attitude of the player in a game, we should repeat, cannot transform itself into the pure play of a free child playing. There are rules to follow. The *ludus,* noted Caillois, disciplines the *paidia.* Nevertheless, thoses rules can be perverted or transgressed. For instance, in *The X-Files Game,* if your avatar is pointing a gun at a colleague, they'll unavoidably tell you not do that or ask what's the matter with you. If you shoot, your avatar will be seen in the traditional photo session before going to jail and that will make the game end. If you decide to shoot the wall instead, or handcuff anyone for fun, your superior will reprimand you and ask for your badge. But those transgressions do not lead very far in movie games. However, they're becoming more and more eclectic. Espen Aarseth has described perfectly the change in question:

> The fourth layer of the model, the user, is of course external to the design of the cybertext but not to its strategy. In the early adventure games, this strategy assumed an ideal reader, who would solve all the riddles of the text and thereby extricate the one definite, intended plotline. Eventually, this strategy changed, and now the reader's role is becoming less ideal (both in a structural and a moral sense) and more flexible, less dependable (hence more responsible), and freer. The multiuser, programable cybertext instigates a more worldwise, corruptible reader; a Faust, compared to the Sherlock Holmes of the early adventure games.[63]

Beyond simple cheating, taking the attitude of being a cheater, the gamer will try to take all possible advantage of the gameplay. He will test the limits of the game. It will not be a question of playing the game but of playing freely *with* the game. The attitude that characterizes the two poles of the range of games will, so to speak, merge in what we might call a gameplayer, a meta-player that will literally make their own game of the game. The gameplayer can drop the mandatory missions in *Grand Theft Auto III* and concentrate on specific actions that, compared to those of *Phantasmagoria,* can look like real challenges that can be achieved or not. It might not be possible to swim at the beaches of Liberty City, but there plenty of other things to do. For example, the gameplayer can try by all means to get inside the Bush Stadium of Staunton Island by flying over it or by piling up cars in order to get over the frontage or to become a sniper hidden and waiting in ambush on the roof of a building to kill the most possible people for the purpose of raising the wanted level and triggering some sort of counterattacks by the police and the army. As the gamer who will post his walkthrough of a game, the gameplayer will show his "gameplay tricks." As an example, the gameplayers playing with *Halo* (2001) all take advantage of the procedural authorship of the digital environment that creates a world of possibilities.[64] Some are putting bodies in trees, others making vehicles jump over a hill or get to areas not yet documented or reached.[65] Some tricks take even weeks to accomplish.[66] The gameplayer uses a great amount of effort, skill or ingenuity to win a challenge that they have set for themselves of their own free will.

Coming to Terms

A new field of study often relies on neologisms in order to create its own terminology. The new words then allow us to talk more precisely about the aspects and concepts related to it. In the case of ludology, it might be relevant to do so, but it might also be important to clarify the utilization of terms already in use. As Seymour Chatman assumed in his book *Coming to Terms: The Rhetoric of Narrative in Fiction and Film,* from which I derived the title of my conclusion:

> . . . every discipline needs periodically to examine its terms. For terms are not mere tags: they represent—in some sense, even constitute—a theory. By scrutinizing its terms, we test and clarify the concepts that a theory proposes. Through that clarification we can better decide whether they help or hinder our work.[67]

The term "gamer," which dates from 1620–1630, according to the *Oxford English Dictionary,* refers to "one who hunts game."[68] It is associated with two other words that, ultimately, have greater bearing on the subject, the "gamester" and the "gamner," both of which define a player at any game. In Samuel Johnson's *A Dictionary of English Language (1755),* the term "gamester" is defined as the "one who is vitiously [*sic*] addicted to play."[69] But there is no mention of "gamer." Nowadays, video games have popularized the usage of this latter term, as "gameplay." In the same way, the study of games and video games in particular is actually putting the emphasis on the bipolarity of the range of games. Therefore, studying video games might bring a better understanding of ludic attitudes and lead to a more rigorous utilization of the terminology. For instance, to be precise, we should talk about the gamer of a chess game, whether on traditional board or on computer. Whether hardcore or casual, the gamer enjoys the challenge and wants to win the game. Otherwise, this might be a coincidence coming under the general utilization of the term, although the observation is really not based on a scientific survey as I did not look to a great number of interviews. Will Wright, creator of the *SimCity* series and *The Sims*, really does talk more about the players than the gamers of his *paidia* video games.[70] What makes *Grand Theft Auto III* a great video game is that it is designed for all gamers, players, and gameplayers.

Obviously, the distinction between players, gamers, and gameplayers that I've just made works perfectly in many languages but not in English. To resort, for example, to these English words instead of only "joueur" in French stresses right away the type of attitude and activity at stake. But, as these terms are used without distinction and consideration in English, and as outside hardcore academic theoretical thinking "player" remains the common word used to refer to someone who engages in some game, it might be necessary—and it is easily enough done—to rereplicate their meaning by associating them with Caillois's increasingly well-known poles. As we would talk about *paidia* and *ludus* video games, we would then talk about the *paidia* player, the *ludus* gamer and the *ludus* gameplayer. However, it is certainly one of the tasks and goals of ludology to discipline the free and anarchic use of play and games related terms.[71]

Notes

1. Since full-motion video (FMV) is also applied to 2-D and 3-D animation games such as *Blade Runner* (1997), for instance, I prefer to refer to live-action video in order to make it clear I'm talking about movies.

2. However, since video games are largely compared to cinema, *Myst* is, for instance, considered to be an interactive movie by Jay David Bolter and Richard Grusin in *Remediation: Understanding New Media* (Cambridge, MA: MIT Press, [1999] 2002), 96. By contrast, in showing that video games are strongly seen as the extension of narrative, Gonzalo Frasca notes that "recent games such as *Metal Solid Gear 2* do really try to look and behave like an 'interactive movie.'" See "Simulation 101: Simulation versus Representation" (2001). Available online at <http://www.ludology.org/articles/sim1/simulation101.html>.

3. Ernest W. Adams, "The Challenge Of The Interactive Movie," *1995 Computer Game Developers' Conference*. Available online at <http://www.designersnotebook.com/Lectures/Challenge/challenge.htm>.

4. Here's how those two kinds of "style" are described by the video games section of *AMG* (<http://www.all.game.com>): (1) "The Interactive Movie uses full-motion video as a means to tell the story. In general, these titles require the user to make certain decisions that will help determine which subsequent video clips will be seen. Wrong choices will typically end the game, while correct choices will have the adventure continue until it is eventually completed"; and (2) "The Third-Person Graphic Adventure has traditionally been one of the most popular styles of adventure games, and it involves guiding a character (who is always visible on the screen) through a number of graphic settings that help illustrate the story. Many games in this style feature groups of words somewhere on the screen that can be strung together to form commands. These words are then selected through the use of an input device such as a mouse or joystick."

5. As Janet Murray said: "The more filmic CD-ROMs rely on later formulaic genres such as the murder mystery or the horror film. Genre fiction is appropriate for electronic narrative because it scripts the interactor. When I begin a CD-ROM murder mystery, I know I am supposed to question all the characters I meet about what they were doing at the time of the

murder and keep track of all the suspects' alibis. I will use whatever primitives I am given (navigation through the space, conducting an interview, picking up pieces of evidence and looking at them under a microscope, etc.) for enacting these prescribed scenes. In a Western adventure I can be counted on to try to hoot at the bad guys, and in a horror story I will always enter the haunted house. I perform these actions not because I have read a rule book but because I have been prepared to do so by exposure to thousands of stories that follow these patterns." In *Hamlet on the Holodeck: The Future of Narrative in Cyberspace* (New York: The Free Press, 1997), 192.

6. For technical insights on the use of FMV, as for critical and historical perspective on the subject, see Ben Waggoner and Halstead York, "Video in Games: The State of the Industry," *Gamasutra.com* (January 3, 2000). Available online at <http://www.gamasutra.com/features/20000103/fmv_01.htm>.

7. Take, for instance, this critic of *Ripper* (1996): "The game's most famous cast member, Christopher Walken, is inexcusably bad as Detective Vincent Magnotta—a cop with a violent past and a personal connection to the Ripper. After Walken's convincing and powerful cinematic performances in movies such as *The Deer Hunter* and *The Dead Zone*, this largely amateurish portrayal makes you wonder what could have led to such a debacle. Did he know his lines before he stepped in front of the camera? Was the budget so tight that there was only one take of each scene? Did the director misread the script as much as Walken did? Does Walken consider acting in an interactive project a small-time gig with an unimportant audience?" Jeffrey Adam Young, "Ripper," *Gamespot.com* (January 5, 1996). Available online at <http://www.gamespot.com>.

8. Celia Pearce, "Story as Play Space: Narrative in Games," in *Game On: The History and Culture of Videogames*, ed. Lucien King (New York: Universe, 2002), 115.

9. *Computer Games Magazine* 120, November 2000, 70.

10. Lev Manovich, *The Language of New Media* (Cambridge, MA: MIT Press, 2001), 40.

11. Thomas Elsaesser, "Digital Cinema: Delivery, Event, Time," in *Cinema Futures: Cain, Abel or Cable?*, eds. Thomas Elsaesser and Kay Hoffmann (Amsterdam: Amsterdam University Press, 1998), 217.

12. Daniel Ichbiah, *La saga des jeux vidéo* (Paris: Éditions Générales First–Pocket, 1997), 287. Freely translated.

13. Gonzalo Frasca, "Ludology Meets Narratology: Similitudes and Differences between (Video) Games and Narrative" (1999). Available online at <http://www.jacaranda.org/frasca/ludology.htm>.

14. Jacques Henriot, *Le jeu* (Paris: Synonyme—S.O.R., [1969] 1983), 89. Freely Translated.

15. Since I first wrote the present essay, I have used the same theoretical framework to study the interactive movie, hypervideo, "wovie" (an combination of "web" and "movie") and movie game in a more general perspective. Therefore, while making now a revision, I would like to note that some passages found here have been reused and rewritten to fit in this French essay. See Bernard Perron, "Jouabilité, bipolarité et cinéma interactif," in *Hypertextes. Espaces virtuels de lecture et d'écriture*, eds. Denis Bachand and Christian Vandendorpe (Québec: Nota Bene, 2002).

16. Johan Huizinga, *Homo Ludens. A Study of the Play-Element in Culture* (Boston: Beacon Press, [1938] 1955), 3.

17. Johan Huizinga, *Homo Ludens*, 3.

18. Roger Caillois, *Man, Play, and Games*, trans. Meyer Barash (New York: The Free Press of Glencoe, [1958] 1961), 12. Original french edition: *Les jeux et les hommes* (Paris: Nrf Gallimard, 1958).

19. Roger Caillois, *Man, Play, and Games*, 12–13.

20. Michel Picard, "La lecture comme jeu," *Poétique* 58 (March 1984): 253–263. Freely Translated.

21. Bernard Perron, *La Spectature prise au jeu. La narration, la cognition et le jeu dans le cinéma narratif* (Ph.D. thesis, Université de Montréal, 1997).

22. Andrew Darley, *Visual Digital Culture: Surface Play and Spectacle in New Media Genres* (London and New York: Routledge, 2000).

23. Authors like Donald Woods Winicott or Henri Atlan are preferring to use the term "playing" to emphasize the creativity of this mode. See Winnicott, *Playing and Reality* (New York: Basic Books, Inc., 1971) and Henri Atlan, "L'homme-jeu (Winnicott, Fink, Wittgenstein)," in *À tort et à raison* (Paris: Seuil, 1986), 261–293.

24. Frasca, "Ludology Meets Narratology. Similitudes and Differences Between (Video)Games and Narrative."

25. Henriot, *Le jeu*, 79. Freely Translated.

26. Henriot, *Le jeu*, 83. Freely Translated.

27. Janet Murray, *Hamlet on the Holodeck. The Future of Narrative in Cyberspace*, 110.

28. Marshall McLuhan, "Games: The Extensions of Man," in *Understanding Media: The Extension of Man* (New York: McGraw-Hill Books Company, 1964), 238.

29. Indeed, this is indicative of the secondary status accorded to video games, as this makes them sound as though they are aspiring to be movies.

30. Among others, Frank Beau made the distinction in "Joueur versus spectateur," *Cahiers du cinéma* 502 (May 1996): 14.

31. Callois, *Man, Play, and Games*, 29.

32. It is not my subject, and this certainly asks for deeper thoughts, but the shoot-'em-up experience gives the impression that it fits in Caillois's fundamental relationship *mimicry-ilinx*. Even though *mimcry* and *ilinx* presume a world without rules, like the forbidden relationship *agôn-ilinx* since the blind fury the vertigo can cause is a negation of controlled effort and of any ruled environment, the latter description given by Caillois answers the vision and fear people have about this type of game: "The alliance of *mimicry* and *ilinx* leads to an inexorable, total frenzy which in its most obvious forms appears to be the opposite of play, an indescribable metamorphosis in the conditions of existence. The fit so provoked, being uninhibited, seems to remove the player ... far from the authority, values, and influence of the real world ..."(In Callois, *Man, Play, and Games*, 75–76.) In our complex and advanced society, the fear of this *mimicry-ilinx* relationship would also be explained by the fact that it's a remainder of more primitive societies. "May it be asserted that the transition to civilization as such implies the gradual elimination of the primacy of *ilinx* and *mimicry* in combination, and the substitution and predominance of the *agôn-alea* pairing of competition and chance? Whether it be cause or effect, each time that an advanced culture succeeds in emerging from the chaotic original, a palpable repression of the powers of vertigo and simulation is verified. They lose their traditional dominance, are pushed to the periphery of public life, reduced to roles that become more and more modern and intermittent, if not clandestine and guilty, or are relegated to the limited and regulated domain of games and fiction where they afford men the same eternal satisfactions, but in sublimated form, serving merely as an escape from boredom or work and entailing neither madness nor delirium." (In Callois, *Man, Play, and Games*, 97.)

33. Callois, *Man, Play, and Games*, 29.

34. It is also available on CD-ROM or DVD-ROM.

35. The failure of the NUON-enhanced DVD player (2000) that wanted to become an alternative gaming platform demonstrates that the technological convergence goes more in one-way: DVD movie playback toward game consoles (as the PS2 and Xbox can play DVDs).

36. Gloria Stern, "What Interactive Media Needs Is TLC: Gloria Stern Talks to Rob Landeros and David Wheeler,"*Hollywood Interactive Network* (1997). Available online at <http://hollywoodnet.com/Stern/cyberflicks10.html>.

37. As a matter of fact, the gameplay opportunities being limited to the ends of chapters, the number of questions are as numerous in the first sections as they are in the last. And, yet, beyond the fact that it kept alive the interactivity, it stands to reason that the number should have been less numerous while the suspense was intensifying toward the end.

38. He'll also be able to explore Dr. Turner's office on two occasions. This option has not been repeated in *Point of View: An Interactive Movie,* in which there is no chance to navigate in the apartment of Jane, the main protagonist. However, at the end of each chapter, if he wants, the player will be able to explore some private belongings and other relevant things (around five each time), and/or to encounter the characters that give their thoughts at the given point in the movie (around five each time). Those explorations and encounters that wish to change the player's point of view on the action are really limited and without great repercussions.

39. That is the case in the first exploration if the player visits Kathryn's room. Kathryn speaks into a microcassette recorder, her back to the viewer. She then turns and looks at the camera startled: "Who ... who are you? ... And what are you doing in my room? ... Oh. Oh wait a minute I see ... You're the ... uh ... viewer, right? ... Huh ... I didn't realize you could just

sneak up on me like that. I'll have to be more careful, (she grins). . . . Never know what I might be doing . . . Well, I have to meet my patient now. You're probably going to snoop around my room aren't you? Guess there's nothing I can do about it. Oh well, you probably won't find anything too incriminating (she flashes another grin) . . . I hope." She leaves.

40. Steve Ramsey, *"Tender Loving Care," Quandary Computer Game Reviews* (February 2001). Available online at <http://www.quandaryland.com/2001/tlc.htm>.

41. *I'm Your Man* is, with the already mentioned *Mr. Payback,* a production of Interfilm. It was released in few theaters with a three-button joystick that let the audience collectively but, with a "majority rule," decide directions the movie would take. Marketing itself as "the first interactive movie on DVD," it is available since 1998 for home playing.

42. Ernest Adams takes the problem of amnesia as one of the three very serious problems of interactive storytelling. In "Three Problems for Interactive Storytellers," *Gamasutra.com* (December 29, 1999). Available online at <http://www.gamasutra.com/features/designers_notebook/19991229.htm>.

43. Randy Sluganski and Tom Houston, "Interview with Rob Landeros et David Wheeler," *JustAventure.com* (1999). Available online at <http://www.justadventure.com/Interviews/Landeros_and_Wheeler/Landeros_and_Wheeler_Interview.shtm>.

44. For instance, François Taddei describes this phase this way: "Then you will be able to explore freely the surroundings (the house of the couple, the psychiatric clinic) so as to accumulate clues allowing to better understand the emotions lived out the characters." In "Tender Loving Care," *Les Productions 640Kb inc* (May 1999). Available online at <http://micro.info/chronique/chronique.php?Id=123>. Freely Translated.

45. It is, depending on which version is played, the CD-ROM or the DVD-ROM or the DVD video. Because computers can store a great deal of data, the former version provides a much more detailed analysis.

46. For instance, demonstrating that he played the movie only once, Tim Belehrad wrote: "The path of the film, along with plot and character development and even the ending, *are said* to be affected by your answers," in *"Tender Loving Care* is first look at interactive cinema," *The Advocate Online* (September 17, 1999). Available online at <http://www.theadvocate.com/enter/story.asp?StoryID=1613>, my emphasis. This reviewer's example speaks for itself: "It's fascinating and hard to put this thing down—and depending on your responses scenes may unfold differently. For example, there's a scene near the beginning in which Kathryn is undressing in her room, in view of Michael. On the DVD, she appeared naked briefly, while on a subsequent trip through the CD-ROM version she kept her bra on during that scene (which made us wonder which questions we'd answered wrong!)." In "Tender Loving Care and I'm Your Man on DVD: Empowering Movies Put You in the Action," *Technofile.com.* Available online at <http://www.technofile.com/dvds/tlc_yourman.html>. Steve Ramsey went further and wrote: "Unfortunately, there was no cause and effect that was immediately discernible between my answers and the action, and as I watched each scene of the movie I had to take it on faith that my answers were affecting what was happening. In other games, if I use an inventory item to open a door and then tell my character to enter, there is a simple and apparent connection between what I have done and what happens on the screen; in this game the connection is invisible, and whilst it may be far more sophisticated, I felt somewhat detached from the whole thing. You are not asked questions like 'should Michael enter Katherine's room,' nor can you reload a scene and answer the questions differently to see the immediate effect (the game automatically saves when you exit and picks up where you left off next time you play). Only by playing the game again can you observe any differences." In Steve Ramsey, *"Tender Loving Care."*

47. Randy Sluganski and Tom Houston, "Interview with Rob Landeros et David Wheeler."

48. Marie-Laure Ryan, *Narrative as Virtual Reality. Immersion and Interactivity in Literature and Electronic Media* (Baltimore and London: The Johns Hopkins University Press, 2001), 205.

49. Grahame Weinbren, "In the Ocean of Streams of Story," (Interactive Cinema) *Millennium Film Journal* 28 (1995), 19.

50. Andrew Darley, *Visual Digital Culture,* 172.

51. Andrew Darley, *Visual Digital Culture,* 173.

52. However, the player who wishes to quit during playing on DVD Video is given a Session code of eighteen digits that he will have to use to continue the story from the point he left off.

53. Grahame Weinbren, "In the Ocean of Streams of Story."

54. Frasca, "Ludology Meets Narratology: Similitudes and Differences between (Video)Games and Narrative."

55. Henriot, *Le jeu,* 51. Freely Translated.

56. Angela Ndalianis, ""Evil Will Walk Once More": *Phantasmagoria*—The Stalker Film as Interactive Movie?," in *On a Silver Platter. CD-ROMs and the Promises of a New Technology,* ed. Greg M. Smith (New York: New York University Press, 1999), 106–107.

57. Stuart Moulthrop and Sean Cohen, "About the Color of Television" (October 1996). Available online at <http://raven.ubalt.edu/features/media_ecology/lab/96/cotv/cotv_about.html>.

58. Frasca, "Ludology Meets Narratology: Similitudes and Differences between (Video)Games and Narrative."

59. See info at <http://www.rockstargames.com/grandtheftauto3/flash/main.html>.

60. Murray, *Hamlet on the Holodeck. The Future of Narrative in Cyberspace,* 71.

61. "(A)s soon as the *paidia* player determines a goal with winning and losing rules, the activity may becomes a *ludus.*" In Frasca, "Ludology Meets Narratology: Similitudes and Differences between (Video)Games and Narrative."

62. Winnicott, *Playing and Reality,* 50.

63. Espen Aarseth, *Cybertext: Perspectives on Ergodic Literature* (Baltimore and London: Johns Hopkins University Press, 1997), 105.

64. "Authorship in electronic media is procedural. Procedural authorship means writing the rules by which the texts appear as well as writing the texts themselves. It means writing the rules for the interactor's involvement, that is, the conditions under which things will happen in response to the participant's actions. It means establishing the properties of the objects and potential objects in the virtual world and the formulas for how they will relate to one another. The procedural author creates not just a set of scenes but a world of narrative possibilities." In Janet H. Murray, *Hamlet on the Holodeck: The Future of Narrative in Cyberspace,* 152–153.

65. See, among others, <http://halo.bungie.org/tipsntricks/tricks.html>. Thanks to Carl Therrien for the references.

66. "*The Bottom of Halo* with FrogBlast. This took me two weeks to figure out and pull off, after I had the initial idea of turning on the light bridge AFTER getting the banshee. Hopefully, other people can complete this in a single day, following the instructions below. It's probably the most complicated trick to set up, and the easiest to actually perform (you don't even have to move while going down.) Skip to the bottom if you want to see the videos of getting to the bottom of Halo, and exploring the bottom. Continue reading if you would like a detailed description of how to do it. Click on the link directly below if you need help, and would like to see movies of the steps listed below. Enjoy!:)." See <http://yuan.ecom.cmu.edu/utfoo/mission/bottomhalo.htm>.

67. Seymour Chatman, *Coming to Terms: The Rhetoric of Narrative in Fiction and Film* (Ithaca, NY, and London: Cornell University Press, 1990), 1.

68. *The Oxford English Dictionary* (Oxford: Clarendon Press, 1989).

69. Samuel Johnson, *A Dictionary of English Language (1755)* (Hildesheim: G. Olms, 1968).

70. For instance, the word "gamer" is not to be found in Celia Pearce's long interview with Wright. See "Sims, BattleBots, Cellular Automata, God and Go: A Conversation with Will Wright by Celia Pearce," *Game Studies* 2, no 1 (July 2002). Available online at <http://www.gamestudies.org/0102/pearce/>.

71. Research for this essay was funded by a grant from the Social Sciences and Humanities Research Council of Canada and one from le Fonds québécois de la recherche sur la société et la culture.

CHAPTER 12

Interactive Storytelling

CHRIS CRAWFORD

The problem of interactive storytelling on the computer has attracted mountains of erudite commentary, floods of creative energy, and little in the way of significant results. To date, not a single interactive storyworld that commands wide respect has been created. Despite lots of talk and effort, all we have to show for our efforts are grandly hyped variations on old techniques. Among these are the following.

Noninteractive Stories with a Façade of Interactivity

These projects begin life as static, noninteractive stories. The authors expend vast efforts making their story cosmetically impressive. Somewhere along the way, they attempt to add interactivity in the form of a few buttons that introduce some minor variations in the story. The result, of course, is not interactive storytelling; it is a linear story with a few buttons tacked on. Such efforts should have long since been discredited, but the youth of the field and the lack of shared expertise permits these evolutionary dead ends to continue spontaneously appearing out of the muck. The passage of time and the development of a corps of experienced workers should put an end to such travesties.

Adventure Games Dressed Up as Stories

The efforts described above are based on the original text adventure game *Adventure* (1976), by William Crowther and Donald Woods, which was pioneering a quarter of a century ago. These days, it's a bit dated. But the adventure game genre is well-understood and there are plenty of development environments readily available. Moreover, the basic structure of an adventure game is so simple as to be immediately comprehended by the beginner. This has led to a large amateur community of artists intent on creating interactive storyworlds using adventure games as their platform.

The results, however, have not realized the grand dreams. The problem lies in the basic nature of the adventure game: it's really a puzzle system. The central architecture of an adventure concerns "rooms" and "objects." The player wanders among the rooms, finding objects that can be applied to solve puzzles in other rooms. The player spends most of his time shuttling between rooms, finding objects that give access to more rooms that contain more objects . . . you can see where this goes. Adventure games offer many fascinating, tortuous, obscure puzzles, but there's nothing narrative in their architecture, and so the attempts to infuse interactive narrative into the genre have failed. There are plenty of adventures that include an intrinsic storyline; one of these is the huge hit *Myst* (1993). While there's plenty of narrative in the game, none of it is interactive. Moreover, what interactivity there is lies far from the narrative. The puzzles that one solves in *Myst* have nothing to do with the story; it's as if two completely different media were grafted onto a single CD.

Computer Games Alternating with Stories

Since computer games are such a successful genre, quite a few companies have attempted to enhance their products by building a story into the game. The first attempts in this direction were commercially successful if only for their novelty value, and every few years somebody comes along with an interesting new twist that sells. But these products fall well short of interactive storytelling—they are more accurately termed "games alternating with stories." The basic structure at the outset relied on "cut-scenes"—nongame scenes that moved the story forward. Visualize a comic book cut up into separate frames that are copied to the screen between gameplay episodes and you have a clear image of the structure. More recently, cut-scenes have been more tightly integrated into the gameplay by using the same graphic engine for both displays. This creates an impression of more seamless integration, but architecturally the structure remains unchanged. The story itself is noninteractive, and the game itself lacks dramatic content. You interact with the nonnarrative game, then see some non-interactive story, then interact some more with the game, then see more story, and if you alternate between the two fast enough, it becomes an "interactive story"—right?

These three approaches are, at heart, attempts to plug interactive storytelling into a medium that has no architectural slot into which the storytelling might be plugged. Whereas the authors of such works have often produced excellent examples of their genres, the storytelling component always seems tacked on, and seldom offers any significant interaction.

Branching Storytrees

Another common approach assumes that an interactive storyworld consists of a core plot with some variations. The designer defines an initial state for the storyworld, then defines each of the dramatic branchpoints in the storyworld. Each branchpoint in turn leads to a number of different dramatic states, which have their own branchpoints, and so on.

The scheme is easy to understand and simple to implement. For this reason, the great majority of beginners to interactive storytelling attempt to build such a system. Their results always disappoint because of the geometric explosion of the branching tree. In just a few steps, the tree grows astronomically large, and the designer must specify thousands of different situations. When the designer compromises by building a storytree with only a few hundred situations, the result is always disappointingly boring.

World Simulators

These arise from the current hype concerning "emergent behavior." This concept, developed by workers in the fields of chaos theory and self-organizing systems, is a sound and valuable technique for studying certain forms of thermodynamically unstable complex systems. Unfortunately, it has been vulgarly paraphrased into simple-minded nonsense: build a really complicated, messy system, let it run for a while, and see if anything interesting comes out. The fervent belief is that, if one merely creates a sufficiently rich simulation of the real world, it will take on a life of its own and spontaneously generate "narrative life." Workers who pursue this approach seldom offer a clear notion of precisely what they expect to obtain; their approach is characterized more by hope than deduction. The notion is little different from that of medieval alchemists who vainly mixed various odds and ends in the hope of generating a living being. All they got for their efforts was a stinking mess, which is about what their modern counterparts obtain.

One of the few well-executed efforts in this field is the groundbreaking computer game *The Sims*, which simulates daily life. Characters move around the rooms of their home, make dinner, wash the dishes, go to the bathroom, sleep, and carry out all manner of other intensely undramatic activities. Sad to say, *The Sims* does not come close to achieving true interactive storytelling. It concerns itself with housekeeping, not drama. The characters keep track of their basic biological needs, but emotional needs, which I consider to be of paramount importance, are not given much attention. The game has been a huge commercial success, and despite my unfairly acerbic characterization, it does occasionally show a tiny spark of narrative life. Unfortunately, its central concerns are of such a mundane nature that these dramatically interesting moments are cherished more for their rarity than their dramatic power.

As the reader may infer from my jaundiced assessments of these strategies, I do not consider any of them to offer much hope of achieving true interactive storytelling. If we are to achieve interactive storytelling, we must concentrate all our energies on two factors: interactivity and storytelling. None of the cited approaches make that effort. Fortunately, we have accumulated a grand repository of expertise in storytelling. Since earliest times, each culture has developed and nurtured its core stories in the form of mythology.

Interactivity, however, remains little-understood. Many seem to have difficulty understanding the concept of interactivity. I define interactivity to be "a cyclical process in which two actors alternately listen, think, and speak to each other." A good conversation provides the ideal example of rich interactivity. Other definitions abound; most make essentially the same points. A few of the definitions I have seen are truly idiotic; the worst of these was: "By definition, the things people do on computers have always been interactive."[1]

Worse, interactivity is little-appreciated. Interactivity is not some secondary attribute like color balance or stereo imaging quality. Interactivity is the sum and substance of the entire revolution that has been shaking our society for the last few decades. We don't refer to the Industrial Revolution as the "Steam Engine Revolution" and we don't refer to the Agricultural Revolution as the "Plow Revolution," and two hundred years from now they won't call this the "Computer Revolution"—it will be known as the Interactivity Revolution. None of the other attributes that people concentrate so much energy on are particularly new or revolutionary. We've had graphics since the first cave drawings. Sound generation has been around for a long time, too. Animation is more recent, but it's still a century old. The integration of sound, graphics, and animation has been around since the first talking movies. And the accumulation and management of large amounts of information has been with us since the first libraries. The only factor that is truly new and revolutionary about the computer as a medium is interactivity, and there should our efforts be directed. The failure to direct their efforts toward interactivity and storytelling explains the failure of the above-cited strategies.

How to Proceed toward Interactive Storytelling

The first and foremost question in all interactive design is, "What does the user do? What kinds of choices can he make?" For interactive storytelling, the first-cut answer is simple: the user must be able to make dramatically interesting choices. Unfortunately, the universe of dramatic choices is stupendously large, and so rich and varied that no simple coding system exists that permits us to represent it manageably. We could never fit the universe of dramatic choices into a computer, nor can I imagine a conceptual scheme whereby such a universe could be expressed.

We must therefore devise a scheme for pruning away dramatic options, reducing the list of options to something manageable. We can prune our options globally, by figuring out the broad list of dramatic options that would be available to the player at any point in the storyworld. We also can use local pruning, which is specific to the immediate situation in which the player finds himself. Thus, global pruning has us ask questions such as, "Would we ever want a character to be able to fall in love with a much younger person?" Local pruning would have us ask questions such as, "If the girl spurns the guy's attempted kiss, what options should he have?"

Note that this line of thinking forces our hand on the matter of input and output. We cannot have a free-form language entry system because the player cannot use free-form input. In other words, the player cannot be allowed to type in any text (or speak anything into a microphone). The player must instead choose from a list of dramatic options we make available to him. This is nothing more than standard menu-driven input, which is easy to implement and process.

Consider, for example, a hypothetical interactive storyworld in which the player romances a beautiful girl. Suppose that the player has wined and dined the girl, and they are now comfortably ensconced in a suitably private location. Finally, let's suppose that the player desires to caress her face. The range of ways that a player could declare his intentions is staggering: "I want to fondle Mary," "I put my hand on her cheek," "My hand slides across her shoulder towards her cheek," "Placing my hand on her face, I smile into her eyes." The computer cannot possibly understand that all these actions are essentially the same. A much better solution is to boil it all down to a single option: "I caress her cheek."

Some object that this is too great a constraint to place upon the player; players should be free to express their creativity, to input choices not anticipated by the storybuilder. While this certainly represents a noble goal, it is out of the question; free-form input from the player requires an infinitely large set of dramatic options. Moreover, the laws of drama do not permit arbitrary behavior; they constrain the actions of characters in stories to a tiny set of choices. Romeo discovering the apparently dead Juliet does not have the option to say, "Bummer. I think I'll go play badminton." When Captain Kirk bravely declares, "Ignore the danger—we'll risk the whole ship to save that crewman!" there is no dramatic force in the universe that will cause the Enterprise to be destroyed. In the universe of narrative, the laws of drama are as adamantine as the laws of physics in the real world. An interactive storytelling system that incorporates such laws naturally and automatically constrains the player's options without appearing intrusive or overbearing.

The Fundamental Laws of Drama

Can such laws be elucidated? Can we formulate and express such laws, and render them in computable form? For the short term, the answer is most certainly "no", but we have firm foundations on which to build. We already possess a great deal of concrete knowledge about narrative. Most of that knowledge takes the form of a great many rules of thumb; our task is to find the higher-level abstractions lurking behind all those rules. Some of those abstractions are, of course, impossibly abstruse. This should not deter us; the most abstract forms of physical law are expressed in terms understandable only to a few specialists, but we are nevertheless able to use these laws. Moreover, these most abstract physical laws are based on centuries of experience with less abstract laws. It will be centuries before we achieve a Unified Field Theory of Narrative; for now, we can be proud of achieving much less grandiose results.

Some of the basic laws of drama are easily constructed. For example, the concept of space in drama is very different from its analog in physics. Unlike physical space, dramatic space is not continuous but discrete, divided up into units known as "stages." A stage is an isolated physical space in which actors interact with one another. Actors occupying different stages are unable to directly interact. Modern cinema has expanded the notion of the stage by clever techniques such as the split-screen telephone call, the offstage telephone call, and action that is inferred by the audience from events that occur just outside the field of view of the camera. Nevertheless, the basic functional notion of the stage remains intact: it is an enclosed, discrete region in which actor interaction takes place.

Dramatic time also behaves differently. It proceeds in fits and starts. While important action is underway, dramatic time moves at the same pace as physical time. However, between dramatically significant events, dramatic time shrinks to nothing. We can jump a day, a week, a year, any time interval that the story demands. Dramatic time is event-driven, not clock-driven.

The Fundamental Components of One Dramatic Universe

What are the basic constituents of a dramatic universe? In the physical universe, we list such components as mass, energy, momentum, distance, force, and so forth. What are the corresponding elements of a dramatic universe? It is much too early to answer so fundamental a question definitively. However, I can offer as a working model the system of components that I have created for my own technology, which I call the "Erasmatron."[2] The basic components of the Erasmatron's dramatic universe are listed below. I have not included a great many minor components or components whose function is primarily housekeeping.

Actors

An actor is the most important component of any narrative. The Erasmatron provides for a variety of actors. Some of the attributes that each actor possesses are:

> Name
> Gender
> Active: an active actor is normal; an inactive player is not yet, or no longer, part of the story
> Conscious: this allows actors to be unconscious on stage
> Location: the stage occupied by the actor
> Timidity, Magnanimity, Gullibility, Pride, Integrity, Dominance, Loquacity, Greed, Sensuality, Volatility: These are personality traits that can be used in formulae for decision making. For example, a character with a large value of Timidity would be more likely to respond to a challenge by backing down. A character with little Gullibility will be less likely to accord trust to another character. A character with great Volatility can change moods more readily than a character with a low value of Volatility

Verb

A verb is an action that could be taken by actor. These are some of the attributes associated with verbs:

> Audience: constraints placed on the execution of the verb because of the presence or absence of other actors. For example, most characters won't engage in sexual activity unless they are in private. Similarly, an actor can't show off unless there is an appropriate audience
> Time To Prepare: how long it takes to set up the action
> Time To Execute: how long it takes to carry out the action

Stages

Stages are simple: they are merely the locations on which actions take place. Thus, stages have no dramatically important attributes. This reflects the traditions of drama; consider how seldom a playwright specifies anything about the attributes of the stage, or how readily a play can be carried out in the most minimal of stages. Clearly, stage attributes are not central to narrative.

The Erasmatron provides the storybuilder with a set of "blank attributes" that can be customized to fit any special requirements the storybuilder might have. For example, if the protagonist's hay fever is important to the narrative, a storybuilder can specify the pollen density for each stage.

Events

An event is any action taken by any actor. Events are comprised of:

>Subject: the actor performing the event
>Verb: the action performed
>Direct Object: the actor on whom the verb was performed
>Location: the stage on which the event took place
>Time: the clock-time when the event took place
>Causal Event: the event that this event is a response to ("before")
>Consequent Event: the last event that was a response to this event ("after")
>Knowledge: a table showing which actors know about this event. This is a simple Boolean variable—an actor either knows about this event or does not know about it
>Fallacious: whether this event actually happened, or is merely a lie
>Secret: whether knowledge of this event is meant to be kept secret by the original source of knowledge about it

In addition, each event has a set of secondary objects that can be used to specify additional information. For example, if the event is "Tom gave Mary the apple," Tom is the subject, Mary is the direct object, gave is the verb, and the apple is a secondary object. This system can handle large, complex sentences, such as "Tom gave Mary the apple in return for Mary telling Tom the secret about Jane."

Props

Props are physical objects. Props can be acquired by actors, concealed, or moved around. Props have just a few attributes, such as weight and value. In most stories, the physical attributes of props are not of much significance; occasionally, however, the story must take such factors into account. For example, the story might require a character to choose among several objects, because they are too heavy for all to be carried. Such situations, of course, seldom play a crucial role in the story.

Custom Components

Each of these various components also can have "custom components" defined and assigned by the storybuilder. Suppose, for example, that a storybuilder is designing a storyworld in which some stages are inside buildings, while others are outside, and the difference is significant to the storyworld. In this case, the storybuilder could assign a new component to the stages, perhaps called Outside. It would be a Boolean variable with the value *true* for a stage that is outside and *false* for a stage that is inside. Or, perhaps the storybuilder wants to take into account the age of each actor; a new variable called Age can be assigned to each actor that will permit the age of each actor to be assigned and factored into the storyworld calculations.

Some Other Laws of Drama

The Erasmatron storytelling engine contains a great many other laws of drama; here are a few of them.

Actors will remain on a stage so long as something is happening there. If nothing is happening, they will wait for a while and then seek another stage. If they have a plan to execute, they will move to the stage most likely to permit them to carry out their plan, taking into account such factors as the presence or absence of other characters, and so forth. If not, then they will seek out a stage for which they have a high value of "Territoriality," as defined by the storybuilder. Thus, some actors will tend to congregate around, say, a bar, while others might be more likely found at the shopping mall, and others at the horse barn. This doesn't prevent a beer-swigging chap from making an appearance at the mall; it's just more likely that he'll find his way to the bar.

Knowledge of events is initially confined to those who directly witnessed it. However, actors tend to share knowledge of events with other actors. The propensity to divulge such information depends on a number of factors. An actor's intrinsic Loquacity plays a large role, as does his Affection for and Trust in the interlocutor. The sensation-value of the news item is also important—actors tend to more readily reveal sensational news. However, an actor does take into account the likely emotional reaction of the listener before revealing news. If the revelation is likely to diminish the listener's goodwill toward the speaker, or someone the speaker cares for, then the speaker is less inclined to blab.

Actors also can reveal news with the proviso that it remain a secret, in which case the listener will be less inclined to pass the knowledge on to others. Of course, if the news is sufficiently sensational, and the actor in question has high Loquacity, then the secret might well be passed on.

Lies are just as important a component of drama as the truth. Actors can concoct fallacious events and then spread the news of them—thereby lying. These lies can then spread through the grapevine in exactly the same manner as true stories. Indeed, a worthy lie is sufficiently sensational to spread rapidly through the grapevine, reaching the entire cast in due course.

The only safeguard against lies and the broaching of secrets is the ability of the victim of these actions to track down and confront the source of the problem. Actors who are disturbed by or skeptical of some piece of information can demand of their source, "Who told you that?" in which case the source can reveal their own source, misdirect the questioner to a false source, or evade the question. With luck, the questioner can at least discover those who bear him/her ill will or who cannot be trusted.

Universal Laws and Local Laws

Some of the laws of physics are universal; they are true everywhere and all the time. Other laws turn out to be specific to a particular set of circumstances. For example, "What comes up must come down" is a reliable law of physics so long as one remains on the surface of the earth; those rare objects that attain escape velocity of 25,000 mph fall outside this law. Nevertheless, it is a good and useful law for most human experience. An example of a highly localized law would be "Cars left outside overnight won't start in the morning"—which applies only in winter in cold climates.

In much the same way, some fundamental laws of drama are universal, applying to all stories, while others are specific to a particular story. The laws cited above are all universal laws, but every particular story has its own particular laws of drama. For example, *Star Trek* stories have a law of drama that guarantees that foolish risks taken in pursuit of noble ends will seldom yield unhappy results. In some other stories, such as tragedies, foolish risks are the source of catastrophe.

My Erasmatron addresses this distinction by permitting the storybuilder to design his own laws of drama. These laws do not supercede the universal laws built into the Erasmatron storytelling engine; the Erasmatron's laws are designed to leave undefined a great many matters that are in the purview of the storybuilder. Thus, the Erasmatron maintains a two-level system for its storytelling laws. The fundamental laws are built into the engine. Laws that are specific to the story are defined by the storybuilder. The dividing line between what is universal and what is local is difficult to position. Too many universal laws constrain the creativity of the storybuilder; too few force the storybuilder to engage in too much busywork keeping track of and controlling petty details. I worked out the tradeoffs by collaborating with a science fiction novelist, Laura J. Mixon,[3] who used the Erasmatron to build a storyworld. The balance needs further refining, but it seems roughly correct.

Tools

Theoretically, a physicist could discover the laws of the universe using nothing more than a ruler, a clock, and scales. In practice, such an approach would be impossibly tedious. Exploring the laws of physics requires laboratory equipment and special tools. In the same way, exploring the laws of drama requires its own set of tools. The dearth of such tools explains why so little progress has been made in tackling the problems of interactive storytelling.

It should thus come as no surprise that I have spent more time developing the Erasmatron tools than the storytelling engine itself. The Erasmatron provides an entire development environment, complete with a scripting language, self-checking tools, tools for testing the behavior of verbs in isolation or in combination with other verbs, tools for grouping verbs functionally or by characteristics, and tools for tracing the behavior of the engine as it operates. The lesson I have learned from all this work is that anybody contemplating building an interactive storytelling technology must carefully consider not just the available performance of the system but also the creation of tools that will give full and easy access to the engine by the storybuilder. Without such tools, an engine is useless.

The most important lesson to arise from the development of the Erasmatron is the importance of good user interface design for nontechnical people. The designers of complex software seem to believe that the complexity of their software diminishes rather than intensifies their responsibility to design a good user interface. While it is certainly incumbent for storybuilders to familiarize themselves with technical concepts, especially the fundamentals of programming, the fact remains that the tools for interactive storytelling should relieve the user of the most tedious technical responsibilities.

A word on the fundamental concept of "tool" is in order here. A tool is not a magical device for solving any problem; it represents a considered tradeoff between generality and power. For example, a shovel is a good general-purpose tool for a wide variety of applications, but a bulldozer can move more dirt. The bulldozer cannot be used for gardening or trimming the lawn; it can do much more work in a much narrower set of applications. Theoretically, we could solve all the problems of interactive storytelling using C++ as our tool, but this would be akin to using a spoon when a bulldozer is needed; C++ as a tool can be used on almost any problem, and makes every problem difficult. Therefore, any storybuilding tool we build *must*, by its very nature, impose constraints upon the user in order to make the task less tedious. It does so by imposing a model of narrative structure upon the user. Every model excludes some details deemed to be minor in order to achieve greater clarity. The Erasmatron represents one set of tradeoffs, and is built on a model of "storyness" that represents my own compromise between my limited understanding of narrative, the limitations of the hardware, and the needs of the storybuilder.

The core of the Erasmatron lies in its scripting language. This language is used by the storybuilder to specify the results of particular actions, and to determine which choices a character will make in response to each event. I believe that I have succeeded in building a scripting language that is both powerful and accessible. A number of innovations lay behind this scripting language.

First, syntax errors are impossible in this language. A syntax error arises when the programmer makes an error in entering the program code. A missing semicolon, an out-of-place comma, or a simple typo will result in a "compiler error." Most such errors are easy to pick out, but for beginners they can be terribly demoralizing, and they continue to plague old pros. A few types of syntax error can introduce hidden bugs and wreak havoc with the program. All in all, syntax errors are to programming as insects are to a picnic: inevitable, irksome, and occasionally disruptive.

I therefore resolved to banish syntax errors entirely from my scripting language. I had only to replace traditional keyboard code entry with a simple point-and-click system. All four hundred of the basic words of the language are organized in a menu structure that makes them easily accessible. The trick was to organize the menus in a vertical stack along the left edge of the window, as in Figure 12.1.

Thus, the storybuilder does not type in the commands of the language; s/he selects them for inclusion in the code. The syntax of the language is built into the menu system: if a word doesn't belong in the selected location, then the menu item will not be available to the storybuilder. S/he simply *cannot* enter a bad command; the software won't permit it.

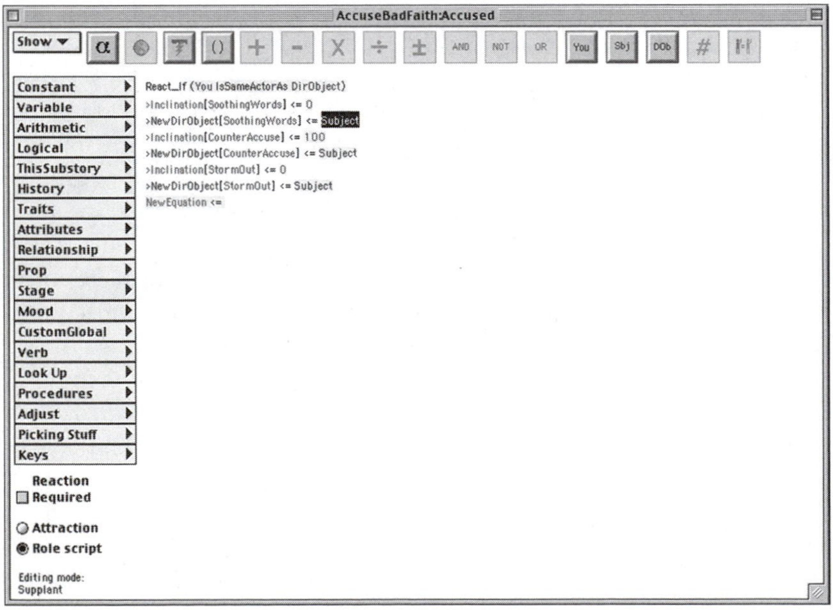

Figure 12.1. Erasmatron screen.

One contributor to this system is the concept of "hard typing." Every value, every number, every usable element in the Erasmatron scripting language is defined by its "type" and "value." The value is immediately understandable; we say that an actor's Timidity is 27 or his Affection for another actor is 55, or that he is located at Stage #43, or is holding Prop #19. The concept of type exists to differentiate apples from oranges, so to speak. An actor can pick up an object of type Prop, but not something of type Stage. An actor can punch another actor, but not a Verb. Thus, hard typing serves to clarify the relationships among all the numbers running around in the scripting language. There are exactly eight data types in the scripting language, and each type is displayed in its own characteristic color:

Actor	blue
Stage	brown
Prop	pink
Verb	green
Event	orange
Group	purple
Number	red
Boolean	black

The second important concept in the design of the language is "no busywork." For example, most programming languages have lots of special requirements that can be tedious and subversive. For example, if you wish to use a new variable, you must declare it at the beginning of the procedure in which it is used. In the heat of programming, with half a dozen mathematical requirements bouncing inside your head, it's easy to overlook this bit of programming trivia. You must initialize most variables before using them; failure to do so is a common source of error for beginning programmers. The total load of all this busywork can be a major distraction. Programmers must slip into an alternate state of consciousness in which they internalize the myriad special busywork requirements of their language. It's not healthy for the soul.

My solution to this problem required extensive programming on my part, but the results are impressive. Whenever the storybuilder creates anything new, the Erasmatron immediately creates all the necessary baggage required to make it run. It is impossible to build a storyworld that is catastrophically incomplete; at all times, every single component of the storyworld has everything it needs to function without crashing.

There is, however, an inescapable constraint on this automagical process: the Erasmatron cannot fill in all the blanks for the storybuilder. For example, consider the following situation: the storybuilder has just added a new function to a line of script. This function is "EventHappened"; it's quite useful because it can tell you if a specified event has previously occurred. For example, suppose that the storybuilder is working on the verbs for a fistfight and doesn't want the combatants to repeat themselves. If an actor has punched his opponent, he shouldn't punch him again, lest the story bog down in an endless loop of actors punching each other. The storybuilder can put the "EventHappened" function into a line of code so that, if the event "I punched the other guy" has taken place in the last five minutes, then the actor will refrain from using the verb "Punch." The function itself will appear on the screen as follows:

EventHappened (<u>Subject</u>, <u>Verb</u>, <u>DirObject</u>, <u>TimeRecency</u>)

Note the four values inside the parentheses: they serve to specify the exact event that the storybuilder wishes to refer to. The underlining indicates that the Erasmatron has not filled in these blanks (how could it possibly guess what belongs in those slots?); it requires the storybuilder to do so. Thus, when the Erasmatron cannot make a reasonable guess as to what belongs in a slot, it fills the slot with an underlined prompt indicating the nature of what goes into that slot.

The third important concept in the scripting language is "no crashable code." It is always possible to write a script containing nonsensical values. For example, consider a situation in which a maiden must either choose a husband or enter a nunnery. Suppose that, during one case, all the eligible men have marched off to war and been killed. There is nobody available to choose. Most programming languages would require the programmer to anticipate this possibility and write special code to deal with it. This kind of defensive thinking clogs up the creative process. The Erasmatron has a better system, which I call "Poison." Whenever any such nonsensical situation arises, the storytelling engine simply "poisons" the associated verb, skipping over it. The engine doesn't become befuddled and issue an error message to the player; it simply skips over the problem and continues operation. This makes the storyworld less exciting, because fewer dramatic possibilities are explored, but it keeps the story moving. Thus, the storybuilder is not burdened with keeping track of every odd possibility for failure; the engine will take care of it.

There is much more to tell about the Erasmatron, but this is not the right place for a complete description of a complex technology.[4]

Conclusions

Interactive storytelling is a Holy Grail that has attracted the attentions of many knights, but remains out of our reach. I have no doubt that someday somebody will attain this Grail, but the current scatterbrained and ad-hoc methods being used fall well short of what is needed. The Erasmatron provides us with a preliminary example of the kind of technology we will need. Its model for storytelling is solid and supports a goodly range of dramatic possibilities. It is equipped with a scripting language more appropriate to the needs of the non-technical artist than we see elsewhere. However, it falls well short of the minimum requirements; it is still too difficult to use. Considerably more effort will be necessary to achieve true interactive storytelling. I urge the reader to make that effort.

Notes

1. Ray Kristof and Amy Satran, *Interactivity by Design* (Mountain View, CA: Adobe Press, 1995), 1.

2. The name plays homage to my personal hero, Desiderius Erasmus of Rotterdam, the first media superstar in history. Erasmus wrote the first original smash hit book, *The Praise of Folly*, and followed it up with a number of other bestsellers, such as the *Adagia* and the *Colloquies*. His influence was profound, and continues today in some aspects of our educational system as well as in a great range of expressions such as "crocodile tears," "a man for all seasons," "to start from scratch," and many more.)

3. She is the author of *Glass Houses* (1992), *Burning the Ice* (2002), and coauthor of *GreenWar* (1997).

4. More details on the Erasmatron and its underlying technologies can be found on my website: <http://www.erasmatazz.com>.

CHAPTER 13

Gametime

History, Narrative, and Temporality in *Combat Flight Simulator 2*

PATRICK CROGAN

This essay examines the relationship between narrative and interactive elements in Microsoft's *Combat Flight Simulator 2: WW II Pacific Theater* (2000). I will argue that this game and this game genre, the flight simulator, are most valuable in this light for what they can tell us about a central question concerning the electronically mediated cultural milieu in which computer games are increasingly prominent. This question concerns the nature of computer interactivity and its transformative potential in contemporary audiovisual culture. While critical work on this question must address games as one of the major forms of computer usage, I will argue further that computer games such as *Combat Flight Simulator 2* crystallize a key tendency of the wider audiovisual entertainment culture. What we will see is that in the process of superseding narrative form by rendering it secondary to the prerogatives of interactive interface design, computer-mediated interactivity tends toward a construction of temporal experience that can best be understood as a transformed narrative operation.

My approach to *Combat Flight Simulator 2* (*CFS2*) in this essay will adopt a theoretical perspective that is oriented to the question regarding war's relation to peacetime cultural practices such as games and other audiovisual media included under the rubric of "entertainment." From this perspective, the experience of time that is a product of the design of this military-inspired flight simulation game will be considered for what it can reveal of war's impact on computer games and the wider "entertainment revolution" with which they have been associated.[1] The flight simulator game genre is a particularly apt object for this project, not only because it frequently takes military combat as its subject (as is the case with *CFS2*) but also because it is the direct descendant of computerized flight simulation developments that have been so crucial in the history of computer-generated imaging and simulation.[2] As James L. Davis noted in his contribution to a special issue of *Aerospace America* on flight simulation, the image generator component designed initially in the course of military flight simulation research is the "heart of any [computer-based] visual system," including computer-aided design (CAD) software, multimedia and animation packages, and computer games.[3] In a similar vein, Erkki Huhtamo has stated that "the flight simulator became one of the basic models for interactive media, especially after interactive visualization capabilities were added."[4] This means that flight simulation gaming offers a "replay" of the passage of military-driven technological innovations into the heart of contemporary computer visualization and simulation.

This question of war's relation to peacetime and its audio-visual cultural forms is indeed a large one. It exceeds the scope of this essay with its aim of exploring a specific feature of computer games through a detailed consideration of a particular flight simulation game. My approach to the theorization of computer games is informed by my orientation to this broader question concerning war, however, and it will become apparent that my discussion of flight simulation takes its place as an aspect of my response to this question. Consequently, it is appropriate at the outset of my discussion to formulate some central themes of my approach to the question of war and audiovisual culture.

War, Pure War, and the Military-Entertainment Complex

As both Manuel De Landa and Friedrich Kittler have demonstrated in their contributions to *Ars Electronica: Facing the Future, A Survey of Two Decades,* war has been a driving force of and pervasive influence on European civilization and, consequently, world history, since at least the early Modern period.[5] For Kittler, moreover, since the Napoleonic campaigns telecommunications and information systems have become themselves more than an adjunct to the conduct of warfare, they became "conceivable as weapons systems" themselves.[6] This militarization of communication and information technologies had an impact not only on the conduct of war but also on the nature of the radical transformation of western European social forms in the wake of the French revolution and the birth of the modern democratic state.

Kittler and De Landa each make the point that not only has war produced major organisational and technological innovations that have flowed into civilian society but also, in the process, has overflowed into peacetime social existence, contaminating the distinction between the somewhat nebulous but generally unquestioned categories of "war" and "peace." As Kittler has argued, this overflowing is a phenomenon widely acknowledged in social theory and cultural studies but one whose consequences are under explored.[7] Along with Kittler and De Landa, Paul Virilio is one of the few theorists to have examined this phenomenon in depth in his work. One of his key concepts, "pure war," describes the passage of war out of the spatial, temporal, and formal parameters that regulated its relation to peace.[8] Pure war names a mutated form of war that exists in a "pure" state of permanent preparation for and anticipation of actual warfare. In his view, this growing influence of pure war has transformed both war and peace and rendered increasingly problematic the maintenance of an unequivocal conceptual opposition between the two terms.

Virilio characterizes pure war as a key tendency of Western modernity and postmodernity, one which is increasingly apparent since the Cold War era.[9] In the nuclear age, the anticipation of total war infected peacetime with the logistical demand of maintaining a permanent state of preparation for absolute conflict. Logistics is a central concept in Virilio's articulation of the pure war tendency. In general usage, logistics is associated with the economic, supply, and transport considerations taken into account by military planning staff in their preparations for conducting war or for maintaining standing armed forces. Manual De Landa defines logistics as "the art of assembling war and the agricultural, economic, and industrial resources that make it possible."[10] The term also has gained a wider usage in describing labor and resource supply management and deployment outside of a narrow military context. For Virilio, however, while logistics first arose as an issue for military planning in the nineteenth century, its subsequent development and increasing significance in the twentieth century's armed conflicts resulted in an unanticipated accident, namely, the initiation of the pure war tendency. In *Pure War*, Virilio describes logistics as a dynamic system of "vector" coordination:

> [L]ogistics is not only food. It's also munitions and transportation. . . . The trucks bringing ammunition and the flying shells bringing death are coupled in a system of vectors, of production, transportation, execution. There we have a whole flow chart which is logistics itself.[11]

The logistical management of a system of vectors requires a translation of economic activity, systems of transportation, and armed conflict into an abstract and dynamic model of reality. This process of translation produces an informational "space"—the flow chart—in which logistical challenges are anticipated and mapped out in order to be resolved. Virilio argues that logistics has an ever-increasing impact on statecraft and military thought in the post–World War II period.[12]

Through the ascendancy of the logistical orientation, the dynamic tendency of "pure war" becomes increasingly integral to economic, political, and cultural activity. In *War and Cinema: The Logistics of Perception*, Virilio examines the close relationship between the development of cinematic and military technology.[13] This is apparent from the inception of cinema, he argues, in such phenomena as the immediate coupling of the film camera to the latest, fastest vehicular technology such as trains and aircraft in both early film entertainments (actualities, travelogues, thrill films) and military operations (strategic reconnaissance, artillery targeting, and damage assessment). *War and Cinema* speculates on the implications of this ongoing affinity between war and the most significant vision machine of the first half of the twentieth century for understanding modern audiovisual culture.

Chief among the major technological developments of the latter half of the twentieth century is the rise of computer technology, the engine driving contemporary information society and its proliferating audiovisual culture. The importance of military imperatives in the history of the development of electronic computing is widely acknowledged. Moreover, the history of computer gaming is a privileged instance of this history of influence, with theorists and commentators citing, among other things: the influence of war gaming simulations in think tanks such as the Rand Corporation on the rise of Systems Analysis; the primary role played by U.S. Department of Defence funding of university research into computer-generated imaging; the significance noted above of the development of real time audiovisual flight simulation for the United States Air Force by Ivan Sutherland; and the increasing cross-fertilization between military and private enterprise gaming and computer-imaging teams in the 1990s known as the "military-entertainment complex."[14]

This last term, coined by mainstream commentators such as J. C. Herz to describe recent developments in the computer games industry, acknowledges the pedigree of the close relationship between private enterprise and military organizations in its allusion to the military-industrial complex. Herz cites declining U.S. Federal budget appropriations for military research in the 1990s for the increased interaction between military and commercial "imagineers."[15] She also points out that gaming and computer simulation have been integral to U.S. military research and training programs for a long time. As Birgit Richard has argued, however, the military-entertainment complex represents a challenge to the assumed hegemony of military organizations in the area of technological innovation. Whereas "military simulators—the American SIMNET and applications like flight simulators—were considered to be the genesis of commercial video games up to the end of the 1980s," Richard argues that since then the flow of software and networking innovations has to a significant extent reversed direction.[16] Richard discusses two games, the artificial life simulator, *Creatures 2.0* (Cyberlife Technology, 1997), and the first-person shooter, *Doom 1.9* (id Software, 1994), which have followed this path from commercial release to military appropriation and adaptation. In the case of *Creatures*, the artificial lifeforms called "Norns" have been used by the British Ministry of Defence in experimental work on developing advanced pilotless fighter aircraft. The U.S. Marine Corp Modelling Simulation Management Office has adapted *Doom 1.9* for the purposes of tactical combat training exercises. Richard lists other games and 3D animation applications that are also of interest to the U.S. military.[17]

Richard says that "the interdependence of game-playing and warfare develops in two stages: first, an abstracted model of individual combat is transposed into the sphere of game-playing; in a second step, the model of artificial warfare represented here becomes a measure for real combat."[18] She argues that the games are "neutral" in themselves inasmuch as they abstract conflict and its implications in a playful staging of symbolic death with no material consequences. Their redesign by the military for the modeling of tactics and weapons systems for producing actual physical death represents a corruption of their "innocence": "*Creatures* and *Marine Doom* show that the process of simulation in the form of reality models is becoming a two-edged sword."[19]

Richard's claim about the innocent neutrality of the simulation of reality in computer gaming is problematic, because it does not take account of the massive significance of war and its logistical imperatives in the history of computer simulation and computer technology generally. She reiterates here the instrumental assumption about the value neutrality of the technological tool with respect to its potential human user. My approach, on the contrary, takes this assumption as itself an element of the logistical mutation I wish to examine here. That is to say, the neutrality of the simulation of reality in computer games needs to be considered in logistical terms. The process of abstraction involved in this neutralization makes a key contribution to the transformative dynamic driving the ongoing elaboration of the logistical flow chart. This is why, beyond the narrow economic explanation offered by Herz, the military-entertainment complex proliferates as the computer simulation of reality becomes more compelling and more central to our audiovisual milieu. Contrary to Richard, it represents not so much a loss for the military in its failure to remain at the cutting edge of research in computer technology, but a major leap forward in the merging of the military and the domestic spheres in the realm of audiovisual cultural forms. The two-way traffic between computer gaming and military simulation in the military-entertainment complex signposts a significant moment in the pure war tendency, one in which a further stage of the merger between the spheres of military and domestic activity and concerns is reached. The recently released online first-person shooter/real-time strategy game, *America's Army: Operations* (U.S. Army/Department of Defense, 2002), a game designed and hosted by the U.S. Department of Defense, eloquently illustrates this merger. Conceived as both a recruitment aid and as a propaganda work for the new, interactive media, the game is marketed on the basis of its superiority to commercial combat-based games because of the firsthand expertise of its game design consultants.[20] No longer reliant on a monopolistic control of developments in computer technology, the military appropriates innovations such as massively multiplayer game networking and incorporates these in its ongoing expansion into the domestic sphere.

Combat Flight Simulator 2 and Pearl Harbor

With this expansion of the military-entertainment complex in mind, let us turn to Microsoft's *CFS2*. What will be of most interest is the way in which it abstracts the historical events of the airwar in the Pacific from 1942 to 1944 in order to simulate a reality for gameplay. My particular focus will be on the game's construction of an experience, or, rather, a matrix of experiences of time and the way that history functions as part of this matrix. In this construction of time out of narrative and interactive solicitation of the gamer can be glimpsed a central element of the logistical transformation in play in games and audiovisual cultural forms more generally. As Lev Manovich has argued, computer games perfectly manifest the logic of the algorithm that is a core component of what he calls the "ontology of the computer."[21] In this ontology, "The world is reduced to two kinds of software objects that are complementary to each other—data structures and algorithms."[22] In the way they set the player a well-defined task, computer games exemplify the logic informing the predominant modality of computer interaction: "execute the algorithm in order to win."[23] The algorithm provides a means for mobilising the information held in the database structure. Manovich says that,

> for better or worse, information access has become a key activity of the computer age, and calls for the elaboration of an "info-aesthetics"—a theoretical analysis of the aesthetics of information access as well as the creation of new media objects that "aestheticize" information processing.[24]

New media objects such as computer games innovate forms of information processing that have implications for understanding contemporary culture, for they participate in what Manovich calls the "transcoding" of the computer ontology into other spheres of cultural activity.[25] My discussion of *CFS2* examines the logistical nature of its aestheticization of information processing.

In *CFS2*, the information database is drawn from major historical events, namely, those arising from the "Pacific War" of 1941–1945. The "Single Mission" and "Campaign" modes of gameplay have as their temporal and geographical parameters major events in the airwar in the Pacific theater from early 1942 to late 1944. The "Single Missions" are reconstructions of actual missions flown by Japanese and U.S. navy "aces" in the Pacific War, for instance, "Aces—Iwamoto's Mission" is introduced in the "Mission Briefing" window as follows:

> On November 17, 1943, IJN [Imperial Japanese Navy] ace Tetsuzo Iwamoto escorted dive-bombers from Rabaul on a strike against Cape Torokina on Bouganville. In the course of the mission he tangled with Navy Corsairs (of VF-17 squadron) for the first time, and claimed two of them shot down over Empress Augusta Bay. Now you will fly Iwamoto's mission.

Campaign mode involves playing a whole sequence of missions based on the major conflicts in the Pacific war after the commencement of hostilities at Pearl Harbor and up until late 1944 as the U.S. forces took control of islands in the Marianas.[26] The first mission flown as a U.S. Navy pilot is on February 1, 1942 over the Marshall Islands and the last is over the island of Tinian in the Marianas. The campaigns comprise sets of missions based on the major battles of the Pacific War, such as the Battle of the Coral Sea, the Battle of Midway, the Solomons Islands campaign, and so on. These mission sets are separated by "cinematics" or "cut-scenes," short prerecorded animated sequences that introduce the next phase of the campaign. They take the form of a graphically illustrated journal of an anonymous pilot combatant that relates his personal experience of the war as it unfolded. "Cut-scenes" are a common convention in a number of computer game genres including role-playing games (RPGs) and adventure games as well as flight sims and other military campaign simulations in which gameplay progresses from one scenario and locale to another or from one level to the next.

The other modes of gameplay—"Free Flight," "Quick Combat," "Training Missions," and "Multiplayer"—all occur somewhere over a map of the Pacific area, the spatial delimitation of which reflects the same sequence of historical events. This map and the menu of possible missions available and aircraft to fly are subject to optional modification by means of additional scenarios that can be either purchased from game design firms or downloaded as shareware from enthusiastic amateur programmers. And if the player has the time to learn the complex "Mission Builder" program that is packaged with the game, he or she can design missions to add to the list of available single missions. The design of *CFS2* to make it amenable to various modifications or "mods" by players ("end users" in game design parlance) is a widespread feature of game software today. Some "mods" play with the historical consistencies of *CFS2*, for instance, the incorporation of anachronistic aircraft models such as jets or biplanes from other Microsoft Flight Sim games, or the addition of different icons or "skins" for the pilot figure visible in the objective ("spot") view of the action, such as the Osama Bin Laden "skin" that appeared in many forms for different games shortly after September 11, 2001. Many modifications of the original game, however, supplement *CFS2*'s coverage of significant air campaigns in the Pacific War. One such "mod" is "In Defense of Australia," a downloadable "freeware" campaign based on air actions involving Japanese and Australian forces over Papua New Guinea in 1942.[27] It was reviewed on the official Microsoft *CFS2* website, the unnamed reviewer noting that "additional campaigns like this can also help to fill in the gaps in the historical representation of World War II."[28]

The Microsoft Games Division team set out to create a compelling and hence profitable game by envisaging gameplay as play in and with a reconstruction of historical temporality drawn from the narrative modes of more traditional media such as historical discourse, historical archives, war films, and documentaries. The game's manual is further evidence of this. It is packed with photos and reproductions of maps and other documents from the war such as illustrations from the period and numerous quotations from diaries, flight instruction manuals, and the like. It has a chapter with summaries of the major conflicts, another with biographies of the most famous aces and "key players" of the conflict, and extensive listings of aircraft specifications and details of other vehicles and equipment simulated in the game. In the "Acknowledgements" section the contributions of veteran naval aviators, Bob Campbell and Mike Weide, and "two living legends of the air war in the Pacific, Saburo Sakai and Joe Foss" are noted under the heading "Historical Advisers."[29]

As a task-driven, interactive form, *CFS2* re-deploys narrative but does not therefore abandon it, something that is made most apparent by the structuring role the "cut-scenes" fulfill in providing a progression through the extended Campaign mode of gameplay. Moreover, as Manovich claims, the employment of the gamer in a goal-directed task "makes the player experience the game as a narrative."[30] There is, nevertheless, a crucial transformation effected in this refiguring of narrative experience, one that is especially apparent in *CFS2*'s repurposing of historical narrative to perform a supporting role in the staging of gameplay. There is a significant parallel between what happens to narrative in *CFS2* and in the recent feature film, *Pearl Harbor* (directed by Michael Bay, 2001), a work that also draws on the history of the airwar in the Pacific. It is worth exploring this parallel in some detail here as a way of elaborating the specific features of the computer game's transformation of narrative temporality in the context of a wider phenomenon of the "transcoding" of computer-based logics, or, rather, logistics, of imaging and simulation in contemporary media representation.

Like *CFS2*, *Pearl Harbor* reconstructs historical events as a form of audiovisual entertainment. The marketing strategies that supported the film's release correspond closely to the packaging of *CFS2* as an historical work. As is customary with major commercial film releases, a flood of publicity releases from Touchstone Pictures and video and television programming accompanied the film's release. These featured interviews with veterans from the December 1941 attack.[31] The film's website is an archive of this marketing material. It includes a section entitled "The Documentary," which amounts to an oral history project focusing on both the Pearl Harbor attack and the making of the film as a record of the event.[32] The user can download short clips of interviews with veterans of Pearl Harbor and the later Doolittle bombing raid on Tokyo also featured in the film. Interviews with representatives of the U.S. Navy Office of Information and Department of Defense are also available concerning the consultation process the film production company entered into with various military and veterans' organizations and the extensive support the U.S. Navy lent to the production.

Both film and game, as mainstream audiovisual cultural productions, invest a great deal in presenting themselves as authenticated reconstructions of major historical events. As entertainment forms that incorporate fictional elements with these reconstructions, they do not purport to be "official" or "proper" historical projects. Nevertheless, the stakes are high for any media work setting out to portray "Pearl Harbor" in an American cultural context, given that it occupies such a crucial position in the mainstream historical narrative explaining U.S. involvement in World War II and legitimating its conduct of that war. This is perhaps why *CFS2*'s simulation of the Pacific theater conflict does not commence with the Pearl Harbor attack, leaving a significant gap in its "historical representation." Another reason for this absence and for that of the air campaign's climactic nuclear conclusion might be that the game is better able to situate the player in the midst of the war in the Pacific. Without the reconstruction of its beginning or end, the Pacific theater conflict can be experienced in gameplay less as a predetermined history and more as a series of contingent moments. *Pearl Harbor*, by contrast, does portray the attack as its central subject. It then reaffirms the predominant "victory narrative" of American history by also narrating the story of the famed Doolittle raid over Tokyo of July 1942, so that the film concludes by pointing ahead to the ultimate victory over the Japanese through air power.[33]

Although *Pearl Harbor* was overall a box office success domestically and internationally (including in Japan, where it reached No. 3 in box office ratings during its release), it was largely panned by mainstream film reviews.[34] Criticism of the film centred on the poverty of the character development and interaction in the central narrative thread involving a contest between two U.S. Army Air Force pilots for the affections of an Army nurse. The film was dismissed by most reviewers as a special effects movie that failed to rise above the presentation of its Computer-generated Imaging-driven spectacle of airborne death and destruction. The relevance of this dismissal to our discussion is highlighted in a particularly scathing critique of the film by David Thomson. In "Zap Happy: World War II Revisited," Thomson pronounces the ultimate condemnation of *Pearl Harbor* when he likens it to a video game. The film is, he says, "not just a colossal bore, but a defamation of popular history that leaves you in despair for cinema."[35] The defamatory nature of the film is identified with the loss of the "complexity of our history," which occurs when "the kids in the audience and the kids in charge have spent two decades playing video combat games."[36]

The comparison of *Pearl Harbor* to video games is a recurring motif in Thomson's broader attack on special effects-dominated films for the deleterious effect they are having on the cinema. Further on, Thomson identifies the "essential Bay shot" in *Pearl Harbor* as the

> POV [the "point of view" shot] of the bomb that falls on the Arizona; it has all the gravitational zest, and the denial of damage or tragedy, that's built into the trigger-jerking spasms of video games. What that means is a *mise en scène* that concentrates on preparing charges, mixing the explosive brew to get the right blend of amber and scarlet in the fireball, and making sure that every extra knows the art of being lifted off his feet and brought down on some union-approved mattress.[37]

For Thomson, *Pearl Harbor*, along with other special effects films that are preoccupied with presenting combat sequences, signals the "defeat [that] narrative has yielded up to technology" in the terrain of the representation of the reality of armed conflict.[38] *Saving Private Ryan* (directed by Steven Spielberg, 1998) and *Pearl Harbor* are the two recent World War II films he cites as part of this trend.[39]

Thomson employs a common stereotype of video gaming to condemn *Pearl Harbor*, namely, that gaming induces an uncomplicated but addictive sensory-motor engagement that deemphasizes intellection. Although this stereotype is open to challenge, Thomson's use of it here does provide, nevertheless, a means for identifying an important parallel between special effects films such as *Pearl Harbor* and computer games.[40] The shot he singles out in affirming the gamelike mise-en-scène of the film, the point of view shot of the falling bomb, could only have been achieved with the aid of computer-generated imaging (CGI). It does indeed resemble a virtual "shot" one could see in a computer game such as *CFS2*. The "Views" options in Flight Sim and other simulation games include a variety of points of view from which action can be seen and a weapon's-eye-view is usually one of these options ("Bomb/rocket" view in *CFS2*). In some flight sims, such as Graphic Simulations Corporations' *FA-18 Hornet Strike Fighter*, this weapon perspective duplicates that of the weapon itself, reproducing the now-famous automated vision of destruction celebrated in media coverage of "smart bomb vision" during the U.S.-led allied assault on Iraq in the Gulf War of 1991. In other games such as in *CFS2*, it is more like the shot in *Pearl Harbor*, a kind of "over the shoulder" shot of the weapon or a tightly framed, objective tracking shot of its trajectory.

In any case, *Pearl Harbor*'s citation of this kind of vision is only achievable by means of digital visual effects. Bay's audiovisual combat spectacle presents extraordinary views of the action such as the bomb POV and shots that portray aerial dogfighting maneuvers in a way that is not possible with a real camera. In doing so, it also stages the imaging power of contemporary digital visual effects as part of the film's spectacle. As Angela Ndalianis has observed, special effects films are highly reflexive films that foreground their effects as spectacles to be both enjoyed by the spectator and marveled at as technical achievements. These films "perform for an audience, and the performance centers around special effects technology and its illusionistic potential."[41]

Thomson says that the bomb POV shot "has all the gravitational zest, and the denial of damage or tragedy, that's built into the trigger-jerking spasms of video games." Like video gameplay, argues Thomson, the film is characterized by the weightlessness of its representation of grave human events. The impossibility of recording in live action the free fall of a bomb in this manner says something crucial to Thomson about Bay's digital aesthetic. For Thomson, the "essential Bay shot" is both literal proof of *Pearl Harbor*'s inauthenticity and a leitmotif of the constitutive lack of narrative *gravitas* in its restaging of such a significant historical subject as war.

Thomson's critique of the film draws on a notion of narrative as a key form of the cultural interpretation of spatiotemporal experience. As Christian Metz outlined in his "Notes Toward a Phenomenology of the Narrative," a narrative produces an ordering of events into a closed temporal sequence.[42] This ordering "unrealizes" the events inasmuch as they are not experienced in and as this order in reality.[43] The narrative structuring of events (real or fictional) into a temporal sequence is the ground of narrative significance for the semiologist Metz. The historiographer and narratologist Hayden White extends this view by arguing that this structuring of events in time is an interpretative process, one in which the significance of the events narrated arises from the connections that are constructed between them in the formation of the whole sequence. The phenomenologist Paul Ricoeur describes this process as a "configurational arrangement which makes the succession of events into significant wholes that are the correlate of the act of grouping together."[44] For Ricouer, the nonchronological "configurational dimension" of narrativity combines with the chronological "episodic dimension" in the narrative in which events are experienced successively. Through the configurational act of plotting, a pattern is elicited from succession.[45] While it is through this plotting that the possibility arises for a judgment to be formed concerning the significance of the events narrated, Ricoeur insists on the importance of "following a story" in the episodic dimension for the constitution of this possibility. Indeed, he argues that "there is no story if our attention is not moved along by a thousand contingencies."[46] For White, the significance produced by the arrangement of events is ultimately ethical in nature. "Could we ever narrativize without moralizing?" asks White at the conclusion of "The Value of Narrativity in the Representation of Reality."[47] The narrative produces time as a meaningful sequence of events that has ethical significance.

Although we have been focusing on the prominence of the visual effects in *Pearl Harbor*, the film can be viewed as a conventional narrative that produces the temporal ordering of events into a meaningful, ethical sequence in the manner I have just outlined. A common period film scenario plots the character arcs of three individuals that are played out against the backdrop of larger historical events. This melodrama of romantic discord first provides a thematic reflection of the wider historical tale of treachery and destruction and is then resolved by way of submission to the needs of the greater good— the personal competition between the two friends for the love of one woman dissolves in a consensus of cooperation between all three in the face of the fight for national survival that overwhelms their private lives.

In a way that parallels the function of the representation of history in *CFS2*, this conventional storyline in *Pearl Harbor* operates in what I would call a secondary register. That is to say, it functions as a supplement to the main operation of the film, namely, to stage the intense, extended battle scenes, chief of which is the Pearl Harbor attack sequence which lasts for approximately forty minutes. It provides a narrative "motivation" for these special effects spectacles and a way of punctuating their presentation. This is the central plank of most of the critical condemnations of the film—that the effects do not serve the narrative but, rather, the reverse occurs. While this is a quite common accusation leveled against effects films and even the action movie genre more generally, it is not my concern here to enter into this debate about the ethical value of effects films and the legitimacy of defending conventional narrative against other modes of filmmaking that privilege spectacle over narrative substance. It should be noted, however, that in a film such as *Pearl Harbor,* the stakes of this debate are seen to be particularly high because of the cultural significance and value placed on the historical events it depicts.

The "secondarization" of traditional narrative function is in no small part a result of the production pipelines of the computer-based imaging processes that dominate these films. *Pearl Harbor* is a signal film in this regard. Michael Bay said of his film that "our goal is to stage the event with utmost realism."[48] The digital effects sequences are the key means of achieving this goal. Their planning and coordination is paramount in the making of the film. Digital visual effects have to be combined with live-action sequences and "practical" effects (effects done on set during the shoot). Shooting schedules have to be devised with this coordination in mind. In "War Effort," Barbara Robertson details the major elements that had to be created digitally, namely, the airplanes and their flightpaths, smoke, fire, and related weapons effects, airplane crashes and ship explosions, and human figures.[49] Live-action shots must be planned and executed precisely to facilitate their contribution to the final digitally enhanced live-action image synthesis that is the goal of the production. The whole process of creating the effects and combining them with the live-action footage has to be conceived in advance as a complex flow chart or "pipeline" for the coordination of the different timelines of various procedures with the sequential demands of image composition and sound production. Live-action material is taken up as but one pathway within this pipeline. There is, I would argue, something of the logistical impulse animating the way the pipeline takes precedence over the live-action "shoot," formerly the privileged moment of the film production process—conventionally described as a three-stage progression from "preproduction" to "production" to "postproduction." Digital visual effects technology has, through the requirements it imposes on all aspects of a film's creation, effectively rendered this conventional understanding of filmmaking obsolete. The production of the effects demands that all other aspects of the production be treated as tasks whose execution must be planned in advance and managed in terms of preset priorities calculated to facilitate the creation of the digitally enhanced images.

The presentation of the resultant effects becomes the primary function of the film, and their staging celebrates this accomplishment. The bomb POV shot discussed above is one excellent example of this display of the unique power of digital imaging to "get" such a shot. Others include similar weapon's-eye-views from a torpedo's perspective and aerial dogfighting scenes that show planes being hit and damaged by bullets in a way that has not been possible except by resorting to archival footage of actual damage and destruction to aircraft in combat. Another such shot occurs later on in the Pearl Harbor sequence during the air attack on Haleiwa Airfield. A U.S. P-40 aircraft attempts to take off when it is destroyed by enemy fire. The shot involves a low-angle point of view from the runway surface as the damaged plane advances toward the camera. In what is actually a practical effect, the plane explodes and debris and smoke overwhelm the point of view. The shot includes a digital element, the addition of the trajectory of tracer bullets advancing right up to the camera position. The shot of the destruction is held longer than usual, registering the impact of the debris on the "eye" of the spectator and the ability of the film's production process to composit digital and practical effects into this "overwhelming" view of deadly destruction.

Pearl Harbor's conventional storyline supports the film's staging of the sequence of effects. After Manovich, the resulting sequence may be called a form of narrative inasmuch as it evinces a temporal progression from event to event. Its purpose, however, is no longer the interpretative construction of temporality outlined by narrative theorists such as Metz and White. This transformed narrative is no longer a mechanism for plotting events into ordered and significant relations—an intepretation machine—but another kind of operation. Narrative becomes the plotting of a trajectory of tasks to accomplish. The pattern produced out of the succession of events is the outcome envisaged in the charting of the film's production pipeline. The digital effects film theatricalizes the achievement of these tasks as its principle operation.

Gametime

If, in *Pearl Harbor,* conventional narrative has become a supplement to the film's effects display, in games such as *CFS2,* narrative is by design always already "secondary" to the interactive mode of user engagement. It supports the presentation of a task or a whole sequence of tasks the user must undertake (instant combat, training missions, networked play against other users, whole campaigns of twenty or so sequenced missions). Manovich states that a computer game is designed to immerse the player in the diegetic space of the game and for that purpose methods similar to those of conventional film and literary narratives are mobilized accordingly.[50] The primary object of playing the game, however, involves learning the game's algorithm in order to win. For Manovich gameplay amounts to a form of zero-degree narrative experience realized by constructing a temporal sequence of play in an illusionistic mise-en-scène that has this linear, teleological character. This narrative arranges the time the player spends in a feedback loop with the game's computer model into a story of sorts, one of personal discovery. The game's "secondary" narrative, in the case of *CFS2,* the history of aerial combat in the World War II Pacific theater, provides a contextual frame that enhances the player's illusory immersion in the game world.

Whether or not narrative is the most appropriate term for this characterization of the user's experience of gameplay is debatable. New media theorist Espen Aarseth, whose work is influential in the emerging terrain of computer games studies, prefers to characterize computer games as instances of what he calls "ergodic discourse." He elaborates the notion of the ergodic as a way of specifying the difference of various traditional and new media works from the conventional narrative form of temporalization. In "Aporia and Epiphany in *Doom* and *The Speaking Clock*," he explains the logic informing his appropriation of this term as follows:

> The word "ergodic" is appropriated from physics, and it is constituted by the two Greek words *Ergos*, "work," and *Hodos*, "path or road," and in this context it is used to describe a type of discourse whose signs emerge as a path produced by a non-trivial element of work. Ergodic phenomena are produced by some kind of cybernetic system, i.e., a machine (or a human) that operates as an information feedback loop, which will generate a different semiotic sequence each time it is engaged.[51]

The ergodic work is a form of interactive machinery that does not equate with the narrative configuration of a predetermined linear order. The ergodic work generates multiple sequences of events, so that what the interactor experiences is "one actualization among many potential routes within what we may call the event space of semio-logical possibility."[52] Aarseth states in another text on this topic that, while ergodic discourse is constitutively different from narrative discourse, ergodic forms will contain elements of narrative to some degree.[53] Computer games such as *CFS2* and the first-person shooter, *Doom,* that he takes as his subject in the essay noted above, would be ergodic works in these terms.

In this analysis, the ergodic core of these games is the interactive, goal-oriented gameplay. Each time play commences anew, the gamer actualizes one of many potential routes through the simulated event space. In *Doom,* the player takes on a first-person perspective of the game's virtual world and attempts to survive frequent deadly attacks by a variety of monsters while navigating labyrinthine environments in levels of increasing complexity and difficulty. Aarseth examines *Doom* to articulate his theory of ergodic temporality. "It is *Doom*'s raw, minimalist event space," he says, "that makes it particularly relevant as an illustration in the analysis of ergodic time."[54] More so than in narrative forms, which privilege the time of the tale and its telling, ergodic time concerns the "time of the audience," or, in this case, the gamers.[55]

Ergodic time unfolds on three levels according to Aarseth. The first is the "event time" determined by the controlling program in which the player reacts to the challenges put forward by the game and/or acts to preempt those challenges. The next level is a time of knowledge acquisition and "takes place on a level outside the game's event time."[56] Its form may vary structurally from game to game. Some games, like *Doom,*

> explicitly acknowledge the need for a "negotiation time" level, by letting the user "save" their progress (i.e., start over from a certain state of affairs, instead of at the beginning), in order to repeat difficult actions. Other games [like *CFS2*] must be played repeatedly to gain the necessary experience that will allow a successful progression.[57]

If the second level of "negotiation" comes to an end, the third level of temporalization is experienced, one in which the game is perceived as a complete sequence from beginning to end. This level would correspond to the quasi-narrative of achievement Manovich identifies with the tasking function of computer games.

Aarseth argues that these different temporal engagements with the ergodic work can be thought of as aspects of a "single dynamic: the basic structure of any game, which is the dialectic between aporia and epiphany."[58] This dynamic is a problem-solving process—an aporia, literally, a "nonroad," is thrown up by the game in order to be negotiated by the player. Reflection on the challenge posed by the aporia in the "negotiation time" outside of actual play alternates with experimental repetition of the aporetic encounter until a solution to the problem is found. The product of this alternation between the first two forms of gametime is an epiphany, that is, "a sudden, often unexpected solution to the impasse in the event space."[59] The third level of ergodic time, the quasi-narrative experience of a completed temporal sequence, is attained when all the game's aporias have been overcome. This, Aarseth calls "ergodic closure," something that games typically require but that is not essential to the operation of ergodic discourse in other forms.[60]

For Aarseth, the way computer games conjure an event space of aporias and epiphanies evokes the prenarrative, fundamental structure of all experience "from which narratives are spun."[61] Leaving aside an examination of this formulation of the underlying structure of experience in its transcendant generality—a task beyond the scope of this essay's focus on modes of temporalization in computer games—I would propose that the aporia/epiphany dynamic Aarseth identifies as the basis of computer gametime enacts the logistical principle Virilio has described as a driving force of the pure war tendency. Computer games model problems in anticipation of their solution by the player. If ergodic discourse requires the user to work, then gameplay is a form of training. Gametime is the process of learning the solution(s), as Manovich indicates when he says the player's goal is to master the game's algorithm. Attaining the third level of gametime, that of the experience of the game as a completed temporal sequence, is a function of successfully anticipating all the eventualities of the event space.

Training was and is the primary rationale driving the military development of simulation. If in general training is future-directed to the extent that it is about developing proficiencies in order to better execute some task, military training is about improving skills so that one may survive to attain a level of control over the "event space." This control allows one to prevail by destroying or otherwise negating the threat of the enemy. As a combat-based flight sim game, *CFS2* draws directly on this tradition of developing a lethal anticipation of events in its gameplay. Events are encountered in order to be preempted, that is, literally "acquired" in advance in the manner in which one refers to target "acquisition" by "smart bombs." To recall, logistics names for Virilio a process in which things are transformed into potential resources for military appropriation, but that in pure war has exceeded its conventional military framework of pertinence and comprehensibility. The mode of temporalization in *CFS2* and other computer games is one avenue in which this overflowing is apparent. Gametime is that of the transformation of events (in an "event space") into potential resources for the execution of a controlling procedure or algorithm. Ergodic closure is reward for the foreclosure of eventuality.

As I discussed earlier, flight sims are a "basic model" (to use Huhtamo's description) for interactive media. Simulator technology was developed from the 1930s in order to train pilots more safely and less expensively. It served a logistical purpose in the strictly military sense of the term, namely, the economical and efficient provision of resources (in this case, trained pilots) for war or for the preparation for war. As Virilio points out in *War and Cinema,* one of the outcomes of the permanent and massive preparation for war in the era of pure war was the rise of a veritable industry of simulation. Stimulated further by the energy crisis of the 1970s, this industry—and I would add this includes the emergence of commercial computer games in the same period—disseminated the logistical principle of anticipating problems affecting resource needs.[62] This continued and extended the influence of the massive military investment in the computerized and computer-assisted modelling of all aspects of war on the development of mainstream computer culture.[63]

The ergodic temporality of computer games as Aarseth characterizes it enacts the anticipatory function of computer simulation. The game design amounts to the staging of a set or sequence of potential problems and providing the player with the means for completing a flow chart of solutions. The "event space" in which these problems are situated becomes a function of this flow chart. In discussing what he calls the "navigable space form" so pervasive in computer media, Manovich cites the importance of Virilio's work in identifying its military origins.[64] In it, says Manovich, space becomes "something traversed by a subject, a trajectory, rather than an area."[65] It is a "medium" through which the gamer (as the model of the computer user) encounters a number of key elements that are constitutive of the problems being modeled and the work required to deal with them. In *CFS2*, these include the player's aircraft; his or her weapons and fuel provisions; the aircraft carrier or airstrip where the mission may originate and conclude (depending on the game mode being played); members of the player's flight, other "friendly" aircraft and other units such as ships and ground vehicles; enemy aircraft and other units; damage effects on the player's aircraft (and avatar, the virtual pilot); and elements of the milieu such as cloud, sun glare, and topography. The world amounts to a dynamic matrix in which the interaction of the player with configurations of these elements can be played out to advance the plotting of the flow chart of possible outcomes of the gametime.

The inclusion of "DIY" mission-building software with the game, now a common feature of flight and other simulation gaming, supplements the player's training in the processes involved in coordinating the interplay of all these elements in the design of gameplay. For Aarseth, this is an index of the "postindustrial culture" in which "game design becomes part of game play, and the distance between the makers and users becomes less."[66] I would add that it further indicates that audiovisual entertainment in contemporary "postindustrial" culture involves play with and around the increasingly central logistical impetus that orders that culture today. As Manovich has pointed out, computer gaming is a playful modality of computer use in the computer age. Computer usage involves "cognitive multitasking—rapidly alternating between different kinds of attention, problem solving and other cognitive skills."[67] This is a central aspect of computer culture in which one's interface with a computer is more or less the same for a variety of different functions:

> At one moment, the user might be analyzing quantatitive data; the next, using a search engine, then starting a new application, or navigating through space in a computer game; next perhaps, using a search engine again, and so on.[68]

For Manovich, the "temporal oscillation" between interactive gameplay and the experience of the noninteractive elements of gaming (such as the "cutscenes" that introduce the diegetic space of a game described above) is best understood ultimately in the framework of this switching between "different mental sets" required in the multitasking milieu of computer culture.[69] Gametime operationalizes the space-time of virtual worlds in order to play (with) multitasking.

For Virilio, the pure war tendency's logistical transformation of the world is more than anything else an accident of the speed race of modern technology, and in particular, weapons technology. Anticipation is foresight, that is, it is a form of speed through which one sees into the future, so that one comes to be in advance of events. Virilio has analyzed the absolute demand of modern technological war for this kind of foresight, realized in the "logistics of perception" that has dominated weapons technology from the rise of airpower to the subsequent developments in what he calls the "arms of communication" and the recent U.S. military doctrine of "global information dominance."[70] In *War and Cinema,* Virilio describes the anticipatory function of electronic surveillance and satellite reconnaisance as leading to the reconstitution of battlefield space-time "*in which events always unfolded in theoretical time*" (Virilio's italics).[71] This theoretical time amounts to a relativist, contingent chronology whose function is the plotting of vectors of "repressive response" over the terrain. Space is "derealized" in favour of its reappearance in and as the simulated "relief" of this flow chart of vectored movements. Flight simulation, and the computer games that have been modeled on its influential example, extend and generalize this process of rendering events in "theoretical time." Gametime allows for the leisurely refinement of "theoretical time" in the ergodic iteration of the encounter with event-problems until, in the end, the gamer prevails over them.

As the reanimation in computer gametime of the airwar in the Pacific—albeit one that modestly, or perhaps, with false modesty, avoids the ultimate acts in that theater of operations—*CFS2* highlights the continuity between the deterrent impulse of pure war logistical processes and the ultimate expression of the theory of airpower, the nuclear bombing that ended the war in the Pacific. Nuclear deterrence was born out of the "proof" of the hypothesis that a war could be won through the use of strategic bombing alone if it were sufficiently devastating to the enemy. This hypothesis had developed out of reflection by combatants on various sides on their experience in World War I (1914–1918). As Philip K. Lawrence has argued in *Modernity and War: The Creed of Absolute Violence,* it was especially embraced by the allied powers of the United Kingdom and the United States, which put its premises into practice in World War II. Lawrence's account of the reasons for this turns on the appeal airpower had for the instrumental discourses of modernity that dominated social and technological developments in these most "advanced" of Western liberal democracies. Lawrence states that "[m]odernity seeks to colonise the future; its watchword is control."[72] Airwar was enthusiastically promoted by its supporters as the most effective means for attaining that control in the context of armed conflict.

Airwar answers to a dream of remote control, one that particularly suited the United States and the United Kingdom's geographical positioning and their desire to prosecute war at a distance from home territory. Strategic bombing, even in a total war context, helped to distance citizens in the West from the moral consequences of war. The terrible killing and destruction of strategic bombardment were rationalized by proponents of the theory of airpower such as the American veteran William Mitchell as the necessary means for bringing about a more rapid conclusion to hostilities.[73] Airpower could wreak destruction far more quickly, it was theorized by the Italian airman Giulio Douhet, obviating the need for a traditional, land-based military conflict by compelling surrender.[74] Its potential to foreclose on the eventuality of land-based military conflict was "tested" with the nuclear attack on Japan. Its "success" opened the nuclear arms race and the pure war trajectory toward a generalized logistical anticipation of every contingency in the permanent preparation for absolute war.

Virilio has traced the subsequent development of this trajectory in the years since the collapse of the Soviet Union in his recent texts. *Desert Screen: War at the Speed of Light* discussed the Gulf War in terms of a new era of global deterrence no longer anchored by the "fatal couple" of opposing superpowers. The manner in which it was conducted and stage managed as a media event indicated the dominance of a logistical approach to global politics. The Iraqi military threat was virtually eliminated in advance of the ground engagement by means of massive air superiority and total control over Iraqi radar and communications networks.[75] This allowed the air campaign to be conducted in a manner resembling a simulation exercise or laboratory experiment. Indeed, the war, he states, resembled in many respects a televised arms expo in which the latest weapons could be demonstrated in a derealized space visible in the weapon's-eye views and in the charts and maps of the daily media briefings conducted by the U.S. Military.[76]

In *Strategy of Deception,* Virilio discusses this post–Cold War period in terms of a mutation of the doctrine of nuclear deterrence under the pressure of

> a growing threat of nuclear, chemical and bacteriological proliferation in countries concerned to forearm themselves on a long-term basis against the effects of an attack involving weapons of mass destruction and yet not able to employ high-precision weapons remotely guided from space.[77]

This proliferation of weapons of mass destruction under the impetus of an anticipatory logic of forearming is the necessary accident in Virilio's terms of the legacy of the theory of airpower, carried forward by the pure war logistical tendency. The resultant "unbalance of terror" is something which the illusion of precision weapons and remotely controlled conflict "sadly caused us to forget," says Virilio, namely, "the fact that aero-spatial war goes hand in hand with extremes of destruction and *the imperative need for an absolute weapon,* whether it be an atomic or neutron device, or chemical/bacteriological agents."[78]

Flight sims, along with the other computer games using three-dimensional graphics and indeed the interactive media forms based on the navigation of virtual space developed in flight simulation, disseminate this anticipatory impulse in and through mainstream audiovisual culture. Their mode of temporalization, characterized by Aarseth as an ergodic, path-finding experience, is a function of their design as anticipation machines. Gametime is about training for the day when the whole sequence of challenges can be overcome and the player can prevail over the event space, anticipating the advent of the game's narrative of achievement. It answers a logistical demand for control in a contemporary milieu in which, as Virilio reminds us, the anticipatory deterrence of threatening contingency goes "hand in hand" with its proliferation.

Manovich argues that the concept of narrative developed in relation to literary and traditional media works might be "too restrictive" for new media. Instead, he paraphrases Tzvetan Todorov's characterization of "minimal narrative" as the "passage from one equilibrium to another (or, in different words, from one state to another)."[79] In the logistical "narrative" of gametime, the end state is one of *prevalence,* literally, one of superiority, of effective dominance over the events encountered in the game. To "win" the game is to prevail in this sense, that is, by discovering and perfecting the means to control the events in advance of the encounter with them.

This minimal narrative does not function like the "interpretation machine" of conventional narrativity. To recall my examination of *CFS2* and *Pearl Harbor,* the historical framing of *CFS2* functions to support the minimal, logistical emplotment of event-problems by providing a coherent, significant storyline that facilitates the player's engagement with the fictional gameworld. Like the secondariness of *Pearl Harbor's* conventional period film storyline to its project of staging a sequence of spectacular audiovisual effects, the story of an individual's involvement in larger historical events is only a supplement to the prerogatives of gametime. If computer gaming encourages the "temporal oscillation" Manovich associates with multitasking, however, perhaps *Pearl Harbor* could be seen as producing a similar oscillation between narrative time and the intensive experience of the spectacular effect. The supplementarity of the narrative might be best understood in terms of a transcoding of multitasking from computer usage into the experience of the filmic medium.

This is to say that, as Jacques Derrida has shown, the supplement is never "only a supplement." Its exteriority to the thing it supplements is never simply in the manner of a pure surplus. It also replaces something, namely, the identity of the supposedly self-sufficient entity to which it is added as an optional extra. This means the supplement "insinuates itself *in-the-place-of;* if it fills, it is as if one fills a void."[80] In doing so, it alters the ensemble of which it forms part and is therefore never purely extraneous or inessential. Historical narrative, in filling the interpretative void of computer game and digital effects film, replaces what is lacking in their "minimal" narratives of the execution of a controlled sequence of events, whether they be game challenges or effects displays. The resultant form is not simply a minimal narrative that Manovich describes which would be devoid of "higher level" significance. It is a mutated temporalization that is perhaps best perceived in the way it refigures the classic task given to historical discourse—the prevention of history repeating itself.

According to this task, historical discourse is meant to produce a significant and ethical recounting of the destructive or negative events of history so that they themselves will not be repeated in the same way (or, conversely, it should render a comprehensive understanding of the great achievements of the past so that they become instructive models for the present). Clearly, an anticipatory logic is operative in this characterization of the historian's task. The historian's recollection of the past in the "configurational dimension" of narrative temporality—to recall Paul Ricouer's term for the way the narrative "construes significant wholes out of scattered events"—is a repetition of the events that is ultimately future-directed. This posture is crystallized in the ethical project that history (and all narrative) serves.[81]

The logistical gametime I have analyzed in this essay deemphasizes the ethical positioning of the user/audience in favor of the demands of training for control. The gamer "repeats history" in order to develop his or her control over events. He or she experiences them "ergodically," that is, as so many challenges modeled in the event-space. Ergodic time prevails over the arrival of the event so that it always arrives in the familiar form of an aporia to be negotiated in play, even when it is encountered for the first time. "Inside" a story, however, in the "episodic dimension" of the time of its telling, events happen as contingent, uncontrolled, and *as yet* lacking in their ultimate comprehensibility or resolution.[82] As Ricoeur has argued, this experience of the uncontrolled alterity of events is inseparable from and co-constitutive—with the "nonchronological" configurational dimension—of the ethical potential of narrativity because there is no story without the encounter with contingency at each moment of the story's unfolding in time. In gametime, the unrealized potential of preemptive control over the event is the principal (but not necessarily sole) configurational horizon of the episodic dimension. The tendency is toward a minimal ethics of prevalence over the event's contingency in the ergodic foreclosure of the "Game over," a time anticipated in the closing of each feedback loop between aporia and epiphany.

Notes

1. See Steven Poole, *Trigger Happy: Video Games and the Entertainment Revolution* (New York: Arcade Publishing, 2000).
2. See my "Logistical Space: Flight Simulation and Virtual Reality," in *The Illusion of Life 2*, ed. Alan Cholodenko (Sydney: Power Publications, forthcoming) for an extended discussion of the history of flight simulation and its impact on computer imaging systems.
3. James L. Davis, "Virtual Systems: Generating a New Reality," *Aerospace America* 31 (August 1993), 33.
4. Erkki Huhtamo, "Encapsulated Bodies in Motion: Simulators and the Quest for Total Immersion," in *Critical Issues in Electronic Media*, ed. Simon Penny (Albany, NY: State University of New York Press, 1995), 174.
5. Friedrich Kittler, "On the History of the Theory of Information Warfare," and Manuel De Landa, "Economics, Computers, and the War Machine," in *Ars Electronica: Facing the Future. A Survey of Two Decades*, ed. Timothy Druckrey (Cambridge, MA: MIT Press, 1999).
6. Kittler, "On the History of the Theory of Information Warfare," 174.
7. Kittler, "On the History of the Theory of Information Warfare," 174.
8. Paul Virilio and Sylvere Lotringer, *Pure War*, trans. Mark Polizzotti and Brian O'Keefe (New York: Semiotext(e), 1997).
9. For a consideration of Virilio's employment of the notion of the tendency, see Patrick Crogan, "The Tendency, The Accident and the Untimely: Paul Virilio's Engagement with the Future," in *Paul Virilio: From Modernism to Hypermodernism and Beyond*, ed. John Armitage (London: Sage Publications, 2000).
10. Manual De Landa, *War in the Age of Intelligent Machines* (New York: Zone Books, 1991), 105.
11. Virilio and Lotringer, *Pure War*, 16.
12. De Landa states that logistics achieves dominance over the other two main branches of military theory, strategy and tactics, so that "modern tactics and strategy would seem to have become special branches of logistics" (*War in the Age of Intelligent Machines*, 106).
13. Paul Virilio, *War and Cinema: the Logistics of Perception*, trans. Patrick Camiller (London: Verso, 1989).
14. On Systems Analysis, see De Landa, *War in the Age of Intelligent Machines*, 101–105; on Defence Department funding of CGI, see Howard Rheingold, *Virtual Reality* (London: Martin Secker and Warburg, 1991), 79; on Ivan Sutherland's work on flight simulation for the military, see Ken Pimental and Kevin Teixeira, *Virtual Reality: Through the New Looking Glass* (New York: Intel/Windcrest/McGraw-Hill Inc, 1993), 35; and on the "military-entertainment complex," see J. C. Herz, *Joystick Nation: How Videogames Ate Our Quarters, Won Our Hearts, and Rewired Our Minds* (Boston: Little, Brown and Company, 1997) 197–213, and Lev Manovich, *The Language of New Media* (Cambridge, MA: MIT Press, 2000), 277.
15. Herz, *Joystick Nation*, 199. This situation no longer holds due to enormous increases in U.S. military budget appropriations in the wake of 9–11.
16. Birgit Richard, "Norn Attacks and Marine Doom," in *Ars Electronica: Facing the Future: A Survey of Two Decades*, ed. Timothy Druckrey (Cambridge, MA: MIT Press, 1999), 339–340.
17. Richard, "Norn Attacks and Marine Doom," 340.
18. Richard, "Norn Attacks and Marine Doom," 341.
19. Richard, "Norn Attacks and Marine Doom," 342.
20. See the America's Army website, <http://americasarmy.com>. At the time of writing, the home page was advertising the imminent release of a second game, *America's Army: Soldier*, a role play genre game.
21. Manovich, *The Language of New Media*, 223.
22. Manovich, *The Language of New Media*, 223.

23. Manovich, *The Language of New Media,* 223.

24. Manovich, *The Language of New Media,* 217.

25. Manovich, *The Language of New Media,* 214. The principle of transcoding, described by Manovich as "the migration of computer-based forms back into culture at large," is a key concept in his study of new media forms and their impact on contemporary culture.

26. The decision by the Microsoft Games division team not to model the attack on Pearl Harbor as part of the mission package is curious, but perhaps understandable from a marketing point of view. It has not stopped Microsoft licensing a third party, JustFlight, from designing for *CFS2* a set of add-on missions based on the Pearl Harbor attack and on hypothetical alternative scenarios. Indeed, since the release of *CFS2* in 2000, and of Bay's film in 2001, several flight sims of the Pearl Harbor attack have been released commercially.

27. See the "Chaps Squadron" website at <http://www.chapshq.com>.

28. See the Official *Microsoft Combat Flight Simulator 2* website. Available online at <http://www.microsoft.com/games/combatfs2/articles_RAAF.asp>.

29. *Microsoft Combat Flight Simulator 2: World War II Pacific Theater Pilot's Manual* (Microsoft Corporation, 2000), 3. Consideration of the "packaging" of a computer game (in such elements as the manual, the literal packaging of the software, or the accompanying media marketing) is irrelevant in the view of Markku Eskelinen, who argues in "The Gaming Situation" (*Game Studies* 1, no 1 (July 2001), available at <http://www.gamestudies.org/0101/eskelinen/>) that computer games studies must concentrate on theorizing the gaming experience in order to delineate what makes games a unique form of practice. Any narrative constructions employed in creating the game's goals and rationalizing gameplay are not worth examining from the point of view of this project. Eskelinen states that "in this scenario stories are just uninteresting ornaments or gift-wrappings to games, and laying any emphasis on studying these kinds of marketing tools is just a waste of time and energy" ("The Gaming Situation"). Eskelinen's paper appears in the first issue of *Game Studies* and articulates the desire of the emerging field of work on computer games to establish its legitimacy as a distinct theoretical discipline, particularly in relation to traditional media studies and their focus on the analysis of narrative structures in cultural "texts." While its efforts to sketch out a functionalist approach to computer games that draws on certain phenomenological methodology and on the tradition of formalist game studies are worth close consideration, Eskelinen's paper insists on rather than satisfactorily demonstrates the irrelevance of narrative elements to understanding computer games. The extent to which narrative and historical elements pervade the design of computer games and structure the experience of gameplay cannot be simply dismissed in any legitimate project to theorise the nature and significance of computer games. The attempt to characterize the specificity of computer games must address their extensive appropriation and modification of elements from other media forms.

30. Manovich, *The Language of New Media,* 222.

31. Most notable among these supporting media works is the *National Geographic*-produced documentary, *Beyond the Movie: Pearl Harbor* (2000), distributed as television programming on the *National Geographic* Channel and subsequently released as a videotape. See the *National Geographic* website for further details, <http://plasma.nationalgeographic.com/pearlharbor/ngbeyond>.

32. See the official *Pearl Harbor* website at <http://video.go.com/pearlharbor/>.

33. See Tom Engelhardt, *The End of Victory Culture: Cold War America and the Disillusioning of a Generation* (Amherst: University of Massachusetts Press, 1998), for a detailed account of the "victory narrative" of American history. *Pearl Harbor's* production history of close cooperation with the U.S. military winds the clock back to the days of the early Cold War that Engelhardt describes in which U.S. forces were tantamount to coproducers of many films and television programs.

34. Japanese box office records are cited from Stephen Cremin's online *Asian Film Bulletin* no. 79 (July 21–22, 2001), available via e-mail subsription to <aflbulletin@mac.com>. With regard to the critical reception of *Pearl Harbor,* see, for example, Geoffrey Macnab, "*Pearl Harbor,*" *Sight and Sound* 11, No. 7 (July 2001), 49, and Macnab, "Bunk, But Unlikely to Bomb," *The Independent,* 23 March 2001, 12, Neil McDonald, "Swashing and Buckling," *Quadrant* 45, No. 7 (July 2001), 85–89, Ian Buruma, "Oh! What a Lovely War," *The Guardian,* May 28, 2001, Supplement 2–3, and Ed Rampell, "Pearl Divers Toy with Reality," *Variety* 292, No. 11 (April 30, 2001), 1.

35. David Thomson, "Zap Happy: World War II Revisited," *Sight and Sound* 11, No. 7 (July 2001), 34–37.

36. Thomson, "Zap Happy," 35.

37. Thomson, "Zap Happy," 35.

38. Thomson mentions *Star Wars* and *Starship Troopers* in this regard (36).

39. Thomson also criticizes Terence Malick's *The Thin Red Line* on other grounds, namely, for its "arty evasions" of the reality of combat experience (36). In contrast to these, Thomson discusses a number of films and literary works in compiling a catalogue of elements present in "the ideal war film," including *Men in War, Catch-22* (the novel), and *From Here to Eternity* (the novel and its filmic adaptation). The reading and watching of these "is a way of retrieving the actual experience of men who fought, died, or survived" (37).

40. Anyone who has spent many dozens of hours learning to play complicated flight sim games such as *CFS2* or adventure, role-playing or strategy games like *Blade Runner* (Westwood, 1998), *Civilization* (Microprose, 1990), *Age of Empires* (Microsoft, 2000) and *The Sims* (Electronic Arts, 2001) would immediately affirm that this stereotype is far from accurate in characterizing gameplay in many cases. Playing *CFS2*, the game that corresponds most closely to the war films that Thomson concerns himself with, involves learning basic flying techniques, tactical combat manouevres, and requires management of communications and coordination with other pilots (real or virtual). This is in addition to the extensive amount of historical material and information that is provided for the gamer to "learn" and to explore. Indeed, J. C. Herz observes in *Joystick Nation* that flight sim games are generally marketed to an older, male, age group, one that is perceived to have a particular predilection for the historical materials and technical details that go into the game design and packaging (211–212).

41. Angela Ndalianis, "Special Effects, Morphing Magic, and the 1990s Cinema of Attractions," in *Meta Morphing: Visual Transformation and the Culture of Quick-Change,* ed. Vivian Sobchack (Minneapolis: University of Minnesota Press, 2000), 259.

42. Christian Metz, "Notes Toward a Phenomenology of the Narrative," in *Film Language: A Semiotics of the Cinema* (New York: Oxford University Press, 1974).

43. Metz, "Notes Toward a Phenomenology of the Narrative," 21–24.

44. Paul Ricoeur, "Narrative Time," *Critical Inquiry* 7, No. 1 (Autumn, 1980), 179. For an extended analysis of narrative and temporality see Paul Ricouer, *Time and Narrative,* 2 vols. (Chicago: University of Chicago Press, 1984–1985).

45. Ricoeur, "Narrative Time," 178.

46. Ricoeur, "Narrative Time," 174.

47. Hayden White, "The Value of Narrativity in the Representation of Reality," *Critical Inquiry* 7, No. 1 (Autumn, 1980), 5–23. See also Hayden White, *The Content of the Form: Narrative Discourse and Historical Representation* (Baltimore: The Johns Hopkins Press, 1989).

48. Bay quoted in "Pearl Harbor: More or Less," *Air Power History* 48 (Fall 2001), 39.

49. Robertson, "War Effort," 22.

50. Manovich, *The Language of New Media,* 215. Manovich says that:

> Web sites and hypermedia programs usually aim to give the user efficient access to information, whereas games and virtual worlds aim to psychologically "immerse" the user in an imaginary universe. It is appropriate that the database has emerged as the perfect vehicle for the first goal while navigable space meets the demands of the second. It accomplishes the same effects that before were created by literary and cinematic narrative. (215)

51. Espen Aarseth, "Aporia and Epiphany in *Doom* and *The Speaking Clock:* The Temporality of Ergodic Art," in *Cyberspace Textuality: Computer Technology and Literary Theory,* ed. Marie-Laure Ryan (Bloomington: Indiana University Press, 1999), 32.

52. Aarseth, "Aporia and Epiphany," 32.

53. Espen Aarseth, *Cybertext: Perspectives on Ergodic Literature* (Baltimore and London: The Johns Hopkins Press, 1997), 5. Aarseth establishes the ground of his distinction between narrative and ergodic work in this text by insisting on the material differences between the ergodic work and the narrative textual form. He argues that, while an ergodic work, or what he terms a "cybertext," "is a machine for the production of a variety of expression," a nonergodic work is given in the single form of a "linear expression" (3). The work done by

the user of this nonergodic form is "trivial," for example, "eye movement and the periodic or arbitrary turning of a page" (2). Consequently, the "semantic ambiguity of a linear text" should not be confused with the "variable expression of the nonlinear text" (3).

Aarseth's argument here contributes to the response of new media theory to the claims by literary and traditional media theorists that interactivity was not invented by new media work but rather, is intrinsic to the process of reading and interpreting texts of any form. Manovich provides an insightful commentary on the insistence on the material difference of new media seen in Aarseth and other proponents of the specificity of new media interactivity. In *The Language of New Media* he calls this the "myth of interactivity" and accounts for it as the continuation of a "literal interpretation" of interactivity that is "a structural feature of the history of modern media." The literal interpretation of interactivity is just the latest example of a larger modern trend to externalize mental life, a process in which media technologies—photography, film, VR—have played a key role. Manovich attributes the trend to the instrumentalist vision of technological development and its desire for the objectivization and "standardization" of all processes (57).

54. Aarseth, "Aporia and Epiphany," 37.
55. Aarseth, "Aporia and Epiphany," 37.
56. Aarseth, "Aporia and Epiphany," 37.
57. Aarseth, "Aporia and Epiphany," 37.
58. Aarseth, "Aporia and Epiphany," 38.
59. Aarseth, "Aporia and Epiphany," 38.
60. Aarseth, "Aporia and Epiphany," 39. To illustrate this point Aarseth discusses a "poetic generator" software creation, John Cayley's *The Speaking Clock*, as an alternative ergodic form, which has a more open-ended function, namely, the creation of a potentially interminable series of poetic articulations.
61. Aarseth, "Aporia and Epiphany," 39.
62. Virilio, *War and Cinema*, 86–87.
63. For a survey and critique of the extensive employment of war gaming by the U.S. military and military-industrial complex in the 1950s and 1960s, see Andrew Wilson, *The Bomb and the Computer: Wargaming from Ancient Chinese Mapboard to Atomic Computer* (New York: Delacorte Press, 1969).
64. Manovich, *The Language of New Media*, 278.
65. Manovich, *The Language of New Media*, 279.
66. Aarseth, "Aporia and Epiphany," 37.
67. Manovich, *The Language of New Media*, 210.
68. Manovich, *The Language of New Media*, 210.
69. Manovich, *The Language of New Media*, 210–211.
70. On the arms of communication, see Paul Virilio, *Desert Screen: War at the Speed of Light*, trans. Michael Degener (London: The Athlone Press, 2002). The Gulf War marked the point, argues Virilio, at which the "arms of communication [satellites, radar/communications-jamming and electronic countermeasures, automated missiles and anti-missile systems, etc.] prevail for the first time in the history of combat over the traditional supremacy of arms of destruction" (113–114). Virilio's later text, *Strategy of Deception*, translated by Chris Turner (London: Verso, 2000) examines the NATO campaigns in the former Yugoslavia in terms of a more recent shift in U.S. military doctrine toward the achievement of "global information dominance" (17). The "information war" against Serbia was conducted with the "arms of communication" such as smart bombs and electronic countermeasures, but extended beyond a "war of [electronic] images" to a "policing of images," which mobilized the information flows from satellites and other monitoring devices along with the interruption of media and telecommunications transmissions inside Serbia and Kosovo (20). Information dominance allows for the restriction of information flows within and out of the enemy territory, and—so it is hoped—a corresponding deterrence of adverse political-strategic ramifications of the military campaign.
71. Virilio, *War and Cinema*, 59.
72. Lawrence, *Modernity and War*, 62.
73. Lawrence, *Modernity and War*, 70.
74. Lawrence, *Modernity and War*, 72.

75.   Virilio, *Desert Screen,* 113. This campaign was the model for the conduct of the more recent operations in Afghanistan against the Taliban regime and the Al Queda organization.

76.   Virilio, *Desert Screen,* 108:

> The war just suspended in the Near East will have been marked by such a significant number of innovations of every sort (strategic and tactical) that it must be seen henceforth as a conflict of pure experimentation, a *promotional war,* where the technological aspects prevails over the political and economic aspects, the consequences in these domains being very much open to debate.

77.   Virilio, *Strategy of Deception,* 4.

78.   Virilio, *Strategy of Deception,* 7.

79.   Manovich, *The Language of New Media,* 264.

80.   Jacques Derrida, *Of Grammatology,* trans. Gayatri Chakravorty Spivak (Baltimore: The Johns Hopkins University Press, 1976), 144.

81.   Ricoeur, "Narrative Time," 178.

82.   Slavoj Žižek argues that this is so even when the story is familiar. He makes the point in "Virtualization of the Master," in *Being On Line: Net Subjectivity,* ed. Alan Sondheim (*Lusitania* 8, (1997)), that "to the horror of the official ideology of interactive story-telling, I read a story in order to learn what 'really' happened to the hero (did he 'really' win over the coveted lady, etc.), not in order to decide about the outcome" (186). This is so even when the story is well known. For Žižek, narrative serves the function of reaffirming the power of the Symbolic Order to make the real meaningful, something which is achieved in and through each and every iteration of narrative temporalization of space-time. Interactive forms that privilege the control of the user to refashion his or her experience of the media work threaten the stability of this symbolic ordering of experience with consequences not foreseen by the proponents of the emancipatory potential of the new media.

Appendix
Home Video Game Systems
The First Thirty Years (1972–2001)

MARK J. P. WOLF
BERNARD PERRON
DAVID WINTER

This list, although extensive, is certainly not exhaustive. We have tried to be as complete as possible, but by no means are all existing systems listed here. After the invention of General Instruments' AY-3-8500 chip in 1975, and its release in 1976, there were hundreds of companies producing *PONG* imitations, many of which have long since gone out of business. Many of their early game boxes and manuals do not even list copyright dates, making precise dating difficult. Examples of these companies, from Europe and America, include: Acetronic, APF, Creatonics, Hanimex, ITMC, Rollet, Secam, Soundic, Radofin, and so on. A few of these companies' systems appear at the end of the list. Another system is not listed here because it was integrated into a piece of furniture; a TV set built by Magnavox, model 4305, had a built-in color *PONG*-like system, based on a General Instruments chip, and the controllers connected directly to the TV set. Also, home computers are generally not listed here, except for a few that were game oriented to the point that they were marketed as gameplaying machines (for example, the Texas Instruments 99/4A, which had game slots and cartridges made for them). The systems are presented by their manufacturer, their name and their model.

This list was compiled mainly from a variety of sources on the World Wide Web. Of particular interest regarding earlier systems are Greg Chance's

History of Home Video Games Homepage, a great resource for which we are extremely thankful (<http://208.240.253.18/>), and David Winter's *PONG-story* website (<http://www.pong-story.com>), an excellent source of information on early PONG-type games.

Home Video Game Systems

1972   Magnavox Odyssey 1TL 200

1974   Videomaster Home T. V. Game (VM 577)
Magnavox Odyssey (export version)

1975   Executive Games Television Tennis (35)
First Dimension Video Sports (FD 3000)
Magnavox Odyssey 100 (model 7010)
Magnavox Odyssey 200 (model 7020)
Philips Tele-Spiel ES 2201
Sears Tele-Games PONG (model 25796)
Videomaster Home TV Game (model VM 577,
   Bronze metal case version)
Videomaster Olympic Home T.V. Game (model VM3)
Videomaster Rally Home T.V. Game (model VM4)
Universal Research Video Action (VA2)
Zanussi Ping-O-Tronic TV Game

1976   Allied's Name Of The Game (A-100)
APF Electronics Inc. TV Fun (401)
Atari PONG C-100
Atari Super PONG C-140
Atari PONG Doubles C-160 (never released)
Atari Super PONG Ten C-180
Binatone TV Gaming Unit (same as Entex Tele-Pong)
Coleco Telstar (6040)
Coleco Telstar Classic (6045)
Coleco Telstar Ranger (6046)
Entex Tele-Pong (3047)
Fairchild/Zircon Channel F
First Dimension Video Sports (model 76)
General Home Products Wonder Wizard 7702/04/05/06
Magnavox Odyssey 300 (model 7500)
Magnavox Odyssey 400 (model 7516)
Maganvox Odyssey 500 (model 7520)
Mestron Fernseh Spiel TVG 2006

Microelectric Systems Ricochet (model MT-1A)
National Semiconductor Adversary (370)
Orelec PP-2000
Occitane (SOE) Match Robot (Occitel 2)
Occitane (SOE) Occitel
Radio Shack TV Scoreboard 60-3051
Radio Shack TV Scoreboard 60-3052
RCA Studio II
Ridgewood GAMATIC 7600
Sears Tele-Games PONG IV (model 99717)
Sears Tele-Games Speedway
Sears Tele-Games Speedway IV (model 99748)
Sears Tele-Games Super PONG (model 99736)
Sears Tele-Games Super PONG IV (model 99737)
Superlectron TV Challenger 2000
Unisonic Tournament 100
Unisonic Tournament 150
Unisonic Tournament 200
Universal Research Video Action 3 (VA3)
Universal Research Indy 500 (Video Action 4) S-100
Videomaster Superscore Home T. V. Game (model VM 8)

1976/1977   Academy Video Game (D-5654)
APF Match 405
APF TV FUN 401A
APF TV FUN 405
APF TV FUN 405A
APF TV FUN 442
APF TV FUN Sportsarama 402
Asaflex Video Sports
Audiosonic Home's TV Set PP-600
Binatone Colour TV Game (01-4931)
Binatone TV Master MK IV (01-4974)
Binatone TV-TRON (01-4982)
Bingo TVG 203
Bingo Video Game HI-1012
Blaupunkt TV-Action
Boots Audio TG100
Canadian Tire Corp. Video Sports (84-6072)
CIT Alcatel Visiomatic 101
Club Exclusiv 2000 (made by Interton)
Coleco Telstar Alpha Europa

Coleco Telstar Regent (6032)
Commodore T.V. Game 3000H
Concept 2000 Spectrum 6 (1025)
Concept 2000 TV+4 (1004)
Conic Video Game TVG 102-4
Creatronic Bi.Bip 4
Creatronic Bi.Bip 8
Dayya Corp. Marume 2000 (VM-90C)
DDR TV-Spiele
Derby Master 777-JS
Diasonic (model HVG-220)
Digitek TV Game 2001
E&P 4 Electronic TV Sport Games EP800
Electrophonic Pro-Sports TVG-1001
Enterprex Color Home Video Game Apollo 2001
Enterprex Color Home Video Game Apollo 2004
Gemini 7640
Granada Video Sports
Grandstand Adman 3000
Grandstand Adman TVG-2600 MK II
Grandstand Match of the Day 2000
Gulliver Triple Challenge (BG7701)
Hanimex 666 (S-N, S-P, etc.)
Hanimex 888
Hanimex 7771
Hanimex TV Scoreboard 888G
Heathkit GD-1380
Heathkit GD-1999
Hit-Go
Hometronics Telecourt (HVG-220)
Honeybell Video Sports Color (model Honeybell-55)
Intel Super-Telesport (D-688/36)
Intel TV Sport 1004
Interstate 1104
Interstate 1199
Interton Video 2400
Interton Video 2800
Interton Video 3000
Interton Video 3001
ITMC Telejeu
K-Mart S Four Thousand S 4000
K-Mart SC Eight Thousand SC 8000

Korting Tele-Multi-Play 825/042
Korting Tele-Multi-Play 825/336 (8000)
Lloyds TV-Sports 801 (E801)
Markint 4a
Markint 6 96
Markint Tele-Sports
Markint TV Sports 2002
Match Color
Match Spectrum 6
MBO Tele-Ball V
MECCA TV Game EP 460
Montgomery-Ward Telstar Video World Of Sports (6042)
Nintendo TV-GAME 6 (CTG-6V)
Novex Colour Video Sports Game (TV 9006)
Novoton TJ-142
Occitane (SOE) OC4 (orange)
OPL Optim Sport
Packel Instrument TV Sport
Palladium Tele-Match 4000
Philips N20
Philips N30
Philips Tele-Spiel Las Vegas ES2203
Philips Tele-Spiel Las Vegas ES2204
Philips Tele-Spiel Las Vegas ES2208
Philips Tele-Spiel Las Vegas ES2218
Philips Tele-Spiel Travmunde ES2207
Pizon-Bross Visiomat 11
Poppy Tele-Spiel 9009
Prinztronic Tournament II Deluxe 600002
Prinztronic Tournament VM8
Radio Shack TV Scoreboard (model 60-3055)
Radio Shack TV Scoreboard (model 60-3056)
Radio Shack TV Scoreboard (model 60-3057)
Radio Shack TV Scoreboard (model 60-3060)
Radio Shack TV Scoreboard (model 60-3061)
Radofin Electronic TV Game XM-017-D?
Radofin SC Eight Thousand SC 8000
Radofin Tele-Sports
Radofin Tele-Sports Mini (513)
Ricochet ElectronicSuper Pro MT-4A
Roberts Paddle IV IV
Roberts Sportrama 8 36

Samdo GM-402
Santron Home T.V. Game TG-101
Sanwa Tele-Spiel 9009
Sears Hockey-PONG 99721
Sears Hockey-Tennis 99722
SEB Telescore 750
Sennheiser TV Game TVG-96
Sheen Colour Video Sport 106C
Sheen Video Sport 104
Sonesta Hide-Away TV Game
Sportel
Sportron 105
Superlectron Fernsehspiel (model TVC-3000)
Syrelec Videosport 2
Tandy TV Scoreboard 60-9001
TCR Video Sport 600
Tele-Match Concert Hall IV (8800)
Tele-Match Television Computer Game (3300R)
Teleng Colourstars
Tempest Video Game
Thomson Jeu Video JV 1T
TV Challenger TVC-3000
Ultrasound 9010
Unimex Mark V and V-C (color)
Unisonic Sportsman (Tournament 101)
Unisonic Tournament 1000
Unisonic Tournament 2000
Unisonic Tournament 2501
Universum Color Multi-Spiel 4004S
Universum Tele-Sports
Universum TV Multi-Spiel
Universum TV Multi-Spiel 2004
Univox 41N
Venture Electronics Video Sports VS-1
Venture Electronics Video Sports VS-5
Venture Electronics Video Sports VS-7
Video 4000-EX (DX-506)
Windsor TV Game EP500
Windtronics Video Game (D-5614)

1977   Atari Stunt Cycle C-450
Atari Super PONG PRO-AM C-200
Atari Super PONG PRO-AM TEN C-202

Atari Ultra PONG C-402(S)
Atari Ultra PONG Doubles C-402(D)
Atari Video Computer System 2600
Atari Video Pinball C-380
Coleco Telstar Alpha (6030)
Coleco Telstar Arcade (6175)
Coleco Telstar Colormatic (6031)
Coleco Telstar Combat (6065)
Decca Sports TV Game Colour
Decca Sports TV Game Monochrome
DMS Tele-Action Mini (same as Radofin
    Tele-Sports Mini)
Gamatic (model 7704)
JCPenney Video Sports
Magnavox Odyssey 2000 (model 7510)
Magnavox Odyssey 3000 (model 7511)
Magnavox Odyssey 4000 (model 7530)
Nintendo TV-Game 15
Olympos Electronic Gamatic 7706
Philips Odyssey 2001
Sears Tele-Games Hockey-PONG (model 99721)
Sears Tele-Games Hockey-Tennis II (model 99733)
Sears Tele-Games Hockey-Tennis III (model 99734)
Sears Tele-Games Motocross (model 99729)
Sears Tele-Games Pinball Breakaway (model 99704)
Sears Tele-Games PONG Sports II (model 99707)
Sears Tele-Games PONG Sports IV (model 99708)
SEB Telescore 750
TCR Video Sport 7705
Videomaster Strika 2 Home T.V. Game (VMV8)
Videomaster VisionScore Home T.V. Game (VMV1)
Videomaster Colourshot Home T.V. Game (VMV2)
Videomaster Colour Score Home T.V. Game (VM-11)

1977/1978   Binatone TV-Master MK 6 (01-4907)
Binatone TV-Master MK 10 (01-4834)
Continental Edison (model JV-2703)
Interstate (model 1110)
Interton Video 2501
Lloyds TV-Sports 802
Lloyds TV-Sports 813
Philco/Ford Tele-Jogo II
Radiola T-02

Roberts Rally IV and Volley IV
Roberts Rally VI and Volley VI
Roberts Rally X and Volley X
Sheen 406-6
TEC FS-204
Unisonic Olympian 2600
Video Stellar

1978   Bally Professional Arcade (*renamed Bally Astrocade in 1982*)
Coleco Telstar Colortron (6135)
Coleco Telstar Gemini
Coleco Telstar Marksman (6136)
Magnavox Odyssey^2
Philips Odyssey 2100 (G7513/01)
Philips Videopac G7000
Videomaster ColourScore II Home T.V. Game (VMV6)

1978/1979   Asaflex Video Sports 2000
Binatone Colour TV Game 4 Plus 2 (01-4850)
Binatone TV-Master MK 8
Grandstand Adman Colour TV Game 3600 MK III
Grunding Tele-Spiel 1
Harvard Mini Color TV Game H-5
Hanimex Electronic TV Game 677CP
Ingersoll XK 600B
Intel TV Sport 2004
Intercord TV Games TVS-5
Klervox Jeu TV TVG-6
Match Match Color
MBO Tele-Ball VIII (443)
Occitane (SOE) OC 5000
Polistil Video Games V.G. 2
Polycon C-4016
Poppy Tv-Game Fernseh Spiel TVG-4
Prinztronic Tournament Mini
Prinztronic Videosport 600
Prinztronic Videosport 800-Color
RIL Robot
Saft-Leclanché TV 8 Sports (electronically the
    same as SOE OC 6000)
Sands Color TV Game C2600
Scomark 4 Sports Tele

SEB Telescore 751
SEB Telescore 752
Sinoca T.V. Game
TCR Video Sport 7801 (104)
TV 18 18 Spannende Videospiele C-4016
TV 2018 Color 18 Spannende Videospiele (240 1/2)
Universum Color Multi-Spiel 4010
Universum TV Multi-Spiel 2006
Univox 61N

1979   Mattel Intellivision
Milton Bradley Microvision
Texas Instruments TI-99/4 Home Computer
   (*see 1981, Texas Instruments 99/4A Home Computer*)
Videomaster Colour Cartridge Home T. V. Game

1979/1980   Grandstand Sports Centre (model 5000)
Grandstand Sports Centre (model 6000)

1980   APF M1000 / MP1000 / Imagination Machine

1981   Entex Select-A-Game
Radofin Colour TV Game
Universum Color Multi-Spiel (model 4106C)
Univox Tele-Sports 6
Texas Instruments 99/4A Home Computer
   (had a game cartridge slot)

1982   Adman Grandstand
   (*the European Fairchild Channel F System II, see 1976,*
   Fairchild Channel F)
Audiosonic Color TV Game (model PP-160)
Atari 5200
Bally Astrocade (*see 1978, Bally Professional Arcade*)
ColecoVision
Emerson Arcadia 2001
Entex AdventureVision
GCE/Milton Bradley Vectrex
ITMC SD-043
Poppy Color Video Game (model 9012)
Rollet Robot (model 4302)
Zircon Channel F II (*see 1976, Fairchild Channel F*)

1983   Bentley Compu-Vision 440
Coleco ADAM (*see 1982, ColecoVision*)

DMS Tele-Action (model GMT513)
Mattel Aquarius
Mattel Intellivision II (see 1979, Mattel Intellivision)
Nintendo Famicom (*Short for "Family Computer." Released in Japan in 1983, and in the United States in 1985 as the NES*)
Philips Videopac+G7400 (*see 1978, Philips Videopac G7000*)
Ultravision Video Arcade System

1984 *Year of the great video game industry crash.*
RDI Halcyon (home laserdisc game system)

1985 INTV System III (*see 1979, Mattel Intellivision*)
Nintendo Entertainment System (NES) (*released in Japan in 1983 as the Nintendo Famicom*)

1986 Atari 7800
Sega Master System (SMS)

1987 Atari XE Videogame System
Commodore C64 GS
Mattel Captain Power
Worlds of Wonder Action Max

1988 NEC PC Engine
(*The Japanese version of the TurboGrafx-16; see 1989, NEC TurboGrafx-16*)

1989 Atari Lynx (*formerly known as the Portable Color Entertainment System*)
Konix Multi-System
NEC TurboGrafx-16
Nintendo Game Boy
Sega 16-bit Genesis System (*also known as Sega Megadrive*)

1990 NEC Turbo-Express (*see 1989, NEC TurboGrafx-16*)
Sega Game Gear
Sega Master System II (*see 1986, Sega Master System*)
SNK Neo-Geo

1991 NEC PC-Engine Duo (*see 1989, NEC TurboGrafx-16*)
Super Nintendo Entertainment System (SNES) (*also known as Super Famicom NES*)

1992 3DO (*FZ10 and FZ1 3DO / Goldstar 3DO*)
Philips CD-I

1993 Atari Jaguar
Commodore Amiga CD-32

Goldstar 3DO
Panasonic 3DO Fz-1
Pioneer LaserActive CLD-A100

1994   Nintendo Super Game Boy
        Sega 32X (*see 1989, Sega Genesis*)

1995   Nintendo Virtual Boy
        Nintendo 64 (*N64, also known as Ultra 64, released in Japan*)
        Panasonic 3DO Fz-10
        Sega Nomad (*see 1989, Sega Genesis*)
        Sega Saturn
        Sony PlayStation

1996   Nintendo 64 (*N64 - released in US*)
        SNK Neo-Geo CDZ (*see 1990, SNK Neo-Geo*)

1997   Tiger Game.com

1998   Nintendo Game Boy Color
        SNK NeoGeo Pocket (released in Japan)
        Tiger game.com Pocket Pro

1999   Sega Dreamcast (*also known as Katana and Black Belt*)

2000   Nintendo Pikachu Nintendo 64
        Nintendo Pokémon Pikachu 2 GS
        Sony PSOne
        Sony PlayStation 2
        VM Labs NUON-enhanced Samsung DVD player (*also
            known as Project X*)

2001   Microsoft Xbox
        Nintendo GameCube (*also known as Dolphin*)
        Nintendo Game Boy Advance (*also known as Atlantis*)
        VCSp (*portable version of Atari 2600, homemade design*)

Other Systems (Years Unknown, 1976—1984)

Acetronic MPU-1000
Acetronic MPU-2000 / Radofin / Prinztronic
Audio Sonic MP1202 (Radofin, Prinztronic, Hanimex, Acetronic)
Conic M-1200
Granada ColorSport VIII (model CS 1818)
Hanimex (model TVG-8610)
Ingersoll mini TV Game (model XK 400)
ITT / Ideal Color Tele-Match Cassette

ITT / Ideal Color Tele-Match Cassette 2
ITT / Ideal Tele-Match Cassette
Monarch
NICS Electronics Systema TV-BOY
Ormatu 2001
Palladium Tele-Match
Philips P2000T
Philips Videopac G7200
Sears Tele-Games Gunslinger II
Sears Tele-Games Jokari
Siera Videopac G7000
Skylark Video Sports (model 124)
Sony MSX
Starex 501
Tandy TV Scoreboard (model 60-9005)
Universum Color Multi-Spiel (model 4014)

Bibliography

Aarseth, Espen. "Computer Games Studies, Year One." *Game Studies* 1, No. 1 (July 2001). Available online at <http://www.gamestudies.org/0101/editorial.html>.

———. "Aporia and Epiphany in *Doom* and *The Speaking Clock*: Temporality in Ergodic Art." In *Cyberspace Textuality,* edited by Marie-Laure Ryan, 31–41. Bloomington and Indianapolis: University of Indiana Press, 1999.

———. *Cybertext. Perspectives on Ergodic Literature.* Baltimore and London: The Johns Hopkins University Press, 1997.

———. "Dataspillets diskurs—mellom folkediktning og kulturindustri." In *Perifraser,* 315–342. Bergen, Norway: University of Bergen, Dept. of Comparative Literature, 1995.

Adamo, Sue. "Hollywood is Game," *Film Comment* 19, No. 1 (January/February, 1983), 40–41.

Adams, Ernest W. "Three Problems for Interactive Storytellers." *Gamasutra.com* (December 29, 1999). Available online at <http://www.gamasutra.com/features/designers_notebook/19991229.htm>.

———. "The Challenge Of The Interactive Movie." *1995 Computer Game Developers' Conference.* Available online at <http://www.designersnotebook.com/Lectures/Challenge/challenge.htm>.

Althusser, Louis. "Ideology and Ideological State Apparatuses (Notes toward an Investigation)." In *Mapping Ideology,* edited by Slavoj Žižek, 100–40. London: Verso, 1994.

Anderson, Craig A., and Karen Dill. "Video Games and Aggressive Thoughts, Feelings, and Behavior in the Laboratory and in Life." *Journal of Personality and Social Psychology* 78, No. 4 (April 2000): 772–790. Available online at <http://www.apa.org/journals/psp/psp784772.html>.

Anderson, Joseph. *The Reality of Illusion. An Ecological Approach to Cognitive Film Theory.* Carbondale: Southern Illinois University Press, 1996.

Anstey, Josephine, and Dave Pape. "Animation in the Cave." *Animation World Magazine,* April 1, 1998. Available online at <http://mag.awn.com/index.php3?ltype=search&sval=Animation+in+the+Cave&article_no=532>.

Atlan, Henri. "L'homme-jeu (Winnicott, Fink, Wittgenstein)." In *À tort et à raison.* Paris: Seuil, 1986, 261–293.

Au, Wagner James. "Dispatches from the Future of Gaming : Page 3: Will Wright Speaks ... To Arnold Schwarzenegger?" *Gameslice.com* (2001). Available online at <http://www.gameslice.com/features/gdc/index3.shtml>.

Avedon, Elliott M., and Brian Sutton-Smith. *The Study of Games.* New York: Wiley, 1971.

Avital, Tsion, and Gerard C. Cupchik. "Perceiving Hierarchical Structures in Nonrepresentational Paintings." *Empirical Studies of the Arts* 16, No. 1 (1998), 59–70.

Backiel, Al. "Dinner with Bob Polaro: An interview by Al Backiel." Available online at <http://www.digitpress.com/archives/arc00054.htm>.

Balazs, Bela. *Theory of the Film.* New York: Dover, 1970.

Balsamo, Anne. *Technologies of the Gendered Body: Reading Cyborg Women.* Durham, NC, and London: Duke University Press, 1996.

Banks, John. "Controlling Gameplay." *M/C: A Journal of Media and Culture* 1, No. 5 (1998). Available online at <http://www.uq.edu/au/mc/9812/game.html>.

Barab, Sasha, Michael Barnett, and Kurt Squire. "Developing an Empirical Account of a Community of Practice: Characterizing the Essential Tensions." *Journal of the Learning Sciences* 11, no 4 (2002) : 489–542.

Barker, Chris. *Cultural Studies: Theories and Practice.* London: Sage, 2000.

Barthes, Roland. *The Pleasure of the Text.* Translated by Richard Miller. New York: Hill and Wang, [1973] 1975.

————. *Elements of Semiology.* London: Cape, [1964] 1967.

Baudrillard, Jean. *Le Paroxyste indifférent.* Paris: Grasset, 1997.

Baudry, Jean-Louis. "Ideological Effects of the Basic Cinematic Apparatus." In *Movies and Methods,* Vol. 2, edited by Bill Nichols, 531–542. Berkeley: University of California Press, 1985.

Bauman, Zygmunt. *Dwa szkice o moralnosci ponowoczesnej.* Warszawa: Instytut Kultury, 1994.

Baumgärtel, Tilman. "Alle Nazis werden Dreiecke," *Die Zeit* 16 (2002). Available online at <http://www.zeit.de/2002/16/Kultur/200216_computerspielkun.html>.

Beau, Frank. "Joueur versus spectateur." *Cahiers du cinéma* 502 (May 1996), 14.

Bechar-Israeli, Haya. "From <Bonehead> to <cLoNehEAd>: Nicknames, play and identity on Internet relay chat." (Play and Performance in Computer Mediated-Communicaton) *Journal of Computer-Mediated Communication* 2, No. 1 (1995). Available online at <http://www.ascusc.org/jcmc/vol1/issue2/bechar.html>.

Belehrad, Tim. "*Tender Loving Care* is first look at interactive cinema." *The Advocate On-line* (September 17, 1999). Available online at <http://www.theadvocate.com/enter/story.asp?StoryID=1613>.

Bell, A. G. *Games Playing with Computers.* London: Allen and Unwin, 1972.

Bernstein, Charles. "Play it Again, Pac-Man." In *The Medium of the Video Game,* edited by Mark J. P. Wolf, 155–168. Austin: University of Texas Press, 2001.

Blanchet, Michael. *How to Beat the Video Games.* New York: Simon and Schuster/Fireside, 1982.

Boal, Augusto. *Legislative Theater.* London: Routledge, 1999.

————. *The Theater of the Oppressed.* New York: TCG, 1998.

————. *Games for Actors and Non-actors.* Translated by Adrian Jackson. London and New York: Routledge, 1992.

Boal, Mark. "Me and My Sims." *The Village Voice,* 2000. Available online at <http://www.villagevoice.com/issues/0013/boal.php>.

Bolter, Jay David. *Turing's Man: Western Culture in the Computer Age.* Chapel Hill: University of North Carolina Press, 1984.

Bolter, Jay David, and Richard Grusin. *Remediation: Understanding New Media.* Cambridge, MA: MIT Press, [1999] 2000.

Bonitzer, Pascal. "Partial Vision: Film and the Labyrinth." Translated by Fabrice Ziolkowski. *Wide Angle* 4, No. 4 (1981): 56–63.

Bordewijk J. L., and B. van Kaam. "Towards a new classification of TeleInforation Services." *Inter-Media* 14, No. 1 (1986): 16–21.

Bordwell, David. "Film Futures." *Substance* 31, No 1 (2002).

————. *The Cinema of Eisenstein.* Cambridge, MA: Harvard University Press, 1994.

————. *Narration in the Fiction Film.* Madison: University of Wisconsin Press, 1985. Other edition: London: Methuen, 1986.

Bordwell, David, and Kristin Thompson. *Film Art.* 6th Edition. New York: McGraw-Hill, 2001.

Bordwell, David, Janet Staiger, and Kristen Thompson. *Classical Hollywood Cinema.* New York: Columbia University, 1985.

Borges, Jorge Luis, *Ficciones.* Buenos Aires: Emecé, 1971.

Bransford, John D., and Daniel Schwartz. "Rethinking transfer: A simple proposal with multiple implications." *Review of Research in Education* 24: 61–101. Edited by A. Iran-Nejad and P. D. Pearson. Washington, DC: American Educational Research Association, 1999.

Bransford, John D., A. L. Brown, and Rodney R. Cocking. *How People Learn: Brain, Mind, Experience, and School.* Washington, DC: National Academy of the Sciences, 1999.

Branston, Gill. "Why Theory?" In *Reinventing Film Studies,* edited by Christine Gledhill and Linda Williams. London: Arnold, 2000.

Bread and Roses. Directed by Ken Loach, Studio Home Entertainment, 2001.

Bremond, Claude. "Le message narratif." *Communications 4* (1964): 4–32.

Brinton III, Joseph P. "Subjective Camera or Subjective Audience?" *Hollywood Quarterly* 2 (1947): 359–366.

Buckwalter, Len. *Video Games.* New York: Grosset and Dunlap, 1977.

Buchsbaum, Walter H. and Robert Mauro. *Electronic Games:Design, Programming, and Troubleshooting.* New York: McGraw-Hill, 1979.

Bukatman, Scott. *Terminal Identity: The Virtual Subject in Post-Modern Science Fiction.* Duke University Press: Durham and London, 1993.

Burnham, Van. *Supercade: A Visual History of the Videogame Age 1971-1984.* Cambridge, MA: The MIT Press, 2001.

"Burnout," *Edge* 104 (December 2001), 70–71.

Buruma, Ian. "Oh! What a Lovely War." *The Guardian,* May 28, 2001, Supplement 2–3.

Butler, Judith. *Bodies That Matter.* New York: Routledge, 1993.

Cahiers du Cinéma (Aux frontières du cinéma) Hors-série (April 2000).

Cahiers du Cinéma (Jeux vidéo) Hors-série (September 2002).

Caillois, Roger. *Les jeux et les hommes. Le masque et le vertige.* Paris: Nrf Gallimard, 1958. Other editions : Paris: Gallimard, 1967; *Man, Play, and Games.* Translated by Meyer Barash. New York: Schocken Books,1979. Polish edition : *Gry i ludzie.* Translated by Anna Tatarkiewicz and Maria Zurowska. Warszawa: Volumen, 1997.

Cassell, Justine, and Henry Jenkins. "Chess For Girls? Feminism and Computers Games." In *From Barbie to Mortal Kombat: Gender and Computer Games,* edited by Justine Cassell and Henry Jenkins, 2–45. Cambridge, MA: MIT Press, 1998.

Castells, Manuel. "Materials for an Exploratory Theory of the Network Society." *British Journal of Sociology* 51, No. 1 (January/March 2000): 5–24. Available online at <http://sociology.berkeley.edu/public_sociology/castells.pdf>.

Castronova, Edward. "Virtual Worlds: A First-Hand Account of Market and Society on the Cyberian Frontier." *CESifo Working Paper Series* (December 2001). Available online at <http://papers.ssrn.com/sol3/papers.cfm?abstract_id=294828>.

Catmull, Ed. *A Subdivision Algorithm for Computer Display of Curved Surfaces.* Ph.D. Thesis, University of Utah, 1974.

Chatman, Seymour. *Coming to Terms: The Rhetoric of Narrative in Fiction and Film.* Ithaca, NY and London: Cornell University Press, 1990.

Clover, Carol. *Men, Women, and Chain Saws: Gender in the Modern Horror Film.* Princeton, NJ: Princeton University Press, 1992.

Cohen, Scott. *Zap: The Rise and Fall of Atari.* New York: McGraw, 1984.

Collot, Milena, and Nancy Belmore. "Electronic Language: A New Variety of English." In *Computer-mediated communication: linguistic, social and cross-cultural perspectives,* edited by Susan C. Herring, 13–28. Amsterdam: John Benjamins Publishing Company, 1996.

Comolli, Jean-Luc, and Jean Narboni. "Cinema/Ideology/Criticism." In *Movies and Methods,* vol. 1, edited by Bill Nichols, 22–30. Berkeley: University of California Press, 1976.

Computer Games Magazine 120 (November 2000): 70.

Consalvo, Mia, and Robert Treat. *Exploring Gameplay: A Survey of Game Players Preferences.* Unpublished manuscript, 2002.

Consumer Guide. *The Complete Book of Video Games.* New York: Warner Books, 1977.

Consumer Microelectronics: Electronic Video Games. Creative Strategies Inc., 1976.

Corballis, Michael C. *The Lopsided Ape: Evolution of the Generative Mind.* New York: Oxford University Press, 1991).

Cowie, Elizabeth. *Representing the Woman: Cinema and Psychoanalysis.* Minneapolis: University of Minneapolis Press, 1997.

Crawford, Chris. *The Art of Computer Game Design.* 1982. Available online at <http://www.vancouver.wsu.edu/fac/peabody/game-book/#game>. Other edition: Berkeley: McGraw-Hill/Osborne Media,1984.

Crogan, Patrick. "Logistical Space: Flight Simulation and Virtual Reality." In *The Illusion of Life 2,* edited by Alan Cholodenko. Sydney: Power Publications, forthcoming.

————. "The Tendency, The Accident and the Untimely: Paul Virilio's Engagement with the Future." In *Paul Virilio: From Modernism to Hypermodernism and Beyond,* edited by John Armitage, 161–176. London: Sage Publications, 2000.

Cubitt, Sean. *Digital Aesthetics.* London: Sage, 1998.

Demaria, Rusel, and Johnny Wilson. *High Score: The Illustrated History of Electronic Games.* McGraw-Hill/Osborne: Berkeley, 2002.

Damasio, Antonio R. *The Feeling of What Happens. Body and Emotion in the Making of Consciousness.* New York: Harcourt Brace, 1999.

————. "Brain and Language." In *Mind and Brain. Readings from Scientific American Magazine.* New York: Freeman, 1993.

Darley, Andrew. *Visual Digital Culture: Surface Play and Spectacle in New Media Genres.* London and New York: Routledge, 2000.

Davis, James L. "Virtual Systems: Generating a New Reality." *Aerospace America* 31 (August 1993), 26–34.

Dayan, Daniel. "The Tutor-Code of Classical Cinema." In *Movies and Methods,* Vol. 1, edited by Bill Nichols, 438–450. Berkeley: University of California Press, 1976.

De Landa, Manual. "Economics, Computers, and the War Machine." In *Ars Electronica: Facing the Future. A Survey of Two Decades,* edited by Timothy Druckrey, 319–325. Cambridge, MA: MIT Press, 1999.

————. *War in the Age of Intelligent Machines.* New York: Zone Books, 1991.

Deleuze, Gilles, and Félix Guattari. *Mille plateaux.* Paris: Éditions de Minuit, 1980.

Derrida, Jacques. *Of Grammatology.* Translated by Gayatri Chakravorty Spivak. Baltimore: The Johns Hopkins University Press, 1976.

"Deus Ex," *Edge* 83 (April 2000), 34–35.

Durlach, Nat, and Mel Slater. "Presence in Shared Virtual Environments and Virtual Togetherness," *Presence: Teleoperators & Virtual Environments* 9, No. 2 (2000): 214–217.

Engelhardt, Tom. *The End of Victory Culture: Cold War America and the Disillusioning of a Generation.* Amherst: University of Massachusetts Press, 1998.

Ehrmann, Jacques. "Homo Ludens revisited," *Yale French Studies* 41 (Game, Play, Literature), edited by Jacques Ehrmann (1968), 31–57.

Elam, Keir. *The Semiotics of Theatre and Drama.* London: Routledge, 1980.

Elsaesser, Thomas. "Digital Cinema: Delivery, Event, Time." In *Cinema Futures: Cain, Abel or Cable?,* edited by Thomas Elsaesser and Kay Hoffmann, 201–222. Amsterdam: Amsterdam University Press, 1998.

Engestrom, Y. *Learning By Expanding: An Activity-Theoretical Approach to Developmental Research.* Helsinki: Orienta-Konsultit Oy., 1987.

Eskelinen, Markku. "500 words on 'Game Design as Narrative Architecture' by Henry Jenkins." In *First Person,* edited by Pat Harrington and Noah Frup-Waldrop. Cambridge, MA: MIT Press, 2002. Available online at <http://www.kolumbus.fi/mareske/failurologyjenkins.html>.

————. "The Gaming Situation," *Game Studies* 1, No. 1 (July 2001). Available online at <http://www.gamestudies.org/0101/eskelinen.hml>.

Farmer, Brett. *Spectacular Passions: Cinema, Fantasy, Gay Male Spectatorships.* Durham, NC: Duke University Press, 2000.

Fauconnier, Gilles, and Mark Turner. *The Way We Think. Conceptual Blending and the Mind.* New York: Basic Books, 2002.

Fencott, Clive. "Presence and the content of Virtual Environments" (1999). Available online at <http://web.onyxnet.co.uk/Fencott-onyxnet.co.uk/pres99/pres99.htm>.

Féral, Josette. "What Is Left of Performance Art? Autopsy of a Function, Birth of a Genre." *Discourse* 14, No. 2 (1992): 142–162.

Fine, Gary. *Shared Fantasy: Role-Playing Games as Social Worlds.* Chicago: University of Chicago Press, 1983.

Fraiman, Susan. "Geometries of Race and Gender: Eve Sedgwick, Spike Lee, Charlayne Hunter-Gault." *Feminist Studies* 20 (1994): 67–95.

Frasca, Gonzalo. "Ephemeral Games: Is It Barbaric to Design Videogames after Auschwitz?" In *Cybertext Yearbook 2000,* edited by Markku Eskelinen and Raine Koskimaa, 172–182. Saarijärvi, Finland: University of Jyväskylä, Research Centre for Contemporary Culture, 2001.

———. "Simulation 101: Simulation versus Representation" (2001). Available online at <http://www.ludology.org>.

———. *Videogames of the Oppressed: Videogames as a Means for Critical Thinking and Debate.* Master's thesis, Georgia Institute of Technology, 2001.

———. "Ludologia kohtaa narratologian." *Parnasso* 3 (1999): 365–371. Also published as "Ludology Meets Narratology: Similitudes and Differences between (Video)Games and Narrative." Available online at <http://www.ludology.org>.

Freud, Sigmund. *Beyond the Pleasure Principle.* New York: Bantam Books, 1959.

Friedman, Ted. "*Civilization* and Its Discontents: Simulation, Subjectivity, and Space." In *On a Silver Platter: CD-ROMS and the Promises of a New Technology,* edited by Greg M. Smith, 132–150. New York: New York University Press, 1999.

———. "The Semiotics of Sim City." *First Monday* 4 (1999). Available online at <http://www.firstmonday.dk/issues/issue4_4/friedman/>.

———. "Making Sense of Software: Computer games and Interactive Textuality." In *Cybersociety: Computer-Mediated Communication and Community,* edited by Steve Jones, 73–89. Thousand Oaks, CA: Sage, 1995.

Gabriel, Évelyne Esther. *Que faire avec les jeux vidéo?* Paris: Hachette, 1994.

Gauntlett, David. "Anthony Giddens: The theory of structuration." Extract of *Media, Gender and Identity: An Introduction.* London and New York : Routledge, 2002. Available online at <http://www.theory.org.uk/giddens2.htm>.

Geertz, Clifford. "Deep Play: Notes on the Balinese cockfight." In *Interpretation of Cultures.* New York: Basic Books [1972] 1973.

Goodman, Robert L. *How to Repair Video Games.* Blue Ridge Summit, PA: Tab Books, 1978.

Grant, Ashley H. "Jesse 'Video Game' Ventura." *CBS News.com,* April 26, 2002. Available online at <http://www.cbsnews.com/stories/2002/04/26/politics/main507378.shtml>.

Graser, Marc. "H'W'D Can't Crash Vidgames (motion pictures inspired by video games)." *Variety,* August 9, 1999. Available online at <http://www.findarticles.com/cf_0/m1312/12_375/55578478/print.jhtml>

———. "New Playground for Studios," *Variety,* May 17, 1999. Available online at <http://www.findarticles.com/cf_0/m1312/1_375/54701191/print.jhtml>,

Greenfield, Patricia Marks. *Mind and Media: The Effects of Television, Video Games, and Computers.* Cambridge, MA: Harvard University Press, 1984.

Greenland, Colin. "A Nod to the Apocalypse: An Interview with William Gibson." *Foundation* 36 (Summer), 5–9.

Grodal, Torben. "Film, Character Simulation, and Emotion." In *Nicht allein das Laufbild af der Leinwand . . . ,* edited by Friss, Hartmann and Müller. Berlin: VISTAS, 2001.

———. "Art film, the Transient Body and the Permanent Soul." *AuraVI,* No. 3 (2000).

———. "Video games and the pleasures of control." In *Media Entertainment: The Psychology of its Appeal,* edited by Zillman and Vorderer. Mahwah, New Jersey: Lawrence Erlbaum, 2000.

———. "Subjectivity, Realism and Narrative Structures in Film." In *Moving Images, Culture & the Mind,* edited by I. Bondebjerg, 87–104. Luton: University of Luton Press, 2000.

———. "Die Elemente des Gefühls. Kognitive Filmtheorie und Lars von Trier." *Montage/av 9/1/00,* 63–98.

———. *Moving Pictures. A New Theory of Film Genre, Feelings, and Cognition.* Oxford: Clarendon/Oxford University Press, 1997.

Grzegorek, Tomasz. "Tozsamosc a poczucie tozsamosci. Proba uporzadkowania problematyki." In *Tozsamosc czlowieka,* edited by Anna Galdowa, 53–70. Krakow: Wydawnictwo Uniwersytetu Jagiellonskiego, 2000.

Hannah, Valerie. "Switching on Teleworking." *The Electronic Herald,* April 10, 2002. Available online at <http://www.theherald.co.uk/business/archive/10-4-19102-0-9-52.html>.

Hanke, Robert. "Theorizing Masculinity With/in the Media." *Communication Theory* 8, No. 2 (1998), 183–203.

Heim, Michael. "The Essence of VR." In *The Metaphysics of Virtual Reality.* New York: Oxford University Press, 1993.

Heiserman, David L. *How to Design and Build Your Own Custom TV Games.* Blue Ridge Summit, PA: Tab Books, 1978.

Henriot, Jacques. *Le jeu.* Paris: Synonyme—S.O.R., [1969] 1983.

Herman, Leonard. *Phoenix: The Fall and Rise of Video Games.* 2nd ed. Springfield, NJ: Rolenta Press, 1997.

Herz, J. C. "Fighters Customizable for Combat," *New York Times,* July 22, 1999, D4.

————. *Joystick Nation: How Video Games Ate Our Quarters, Won Our Hearts, and Rewired Our Minds.* Boston: Little, Brown, 1997.

Higuinen, Erwan, and Charles Tesson. "Éditorial: Cinéphiles et Ludophiles." (Jeux Vidéo) *Cahiers du Cinéma* Hors-Série (September 2002), 5.

Huizinga, Johan. *Homo Ludens. A Study of the Play Element in Culture.* Boston: The Beacon Press, [1938] 1955.

Huhtamo, Erkki. "Encapsulated Bodies in Motion: Simulators and the Quest for Total Immersion." In *Critical Issues in Electronic Media,* edited by Simon Penny, 159–186. Albany, NY: State University of New York Press, 1995.

Ichbiah, Daniel. *La saga des jeux video.* Paris: Éditions Générales First-Pocket, 1997.

Interactive Digital Software Association. "Who Purchases Computer and Video Games?" (2001). Available online at <http://www.idsa.com/ffbox6.html>.

Irigaray, Luce. "Commodities Among Themselves." In *This Sex Which is Not One.* Translated by Catherine Porter. Ithaca, NY: Cornell University Press, 1985.

Iser, Wolfgang. *The Fictive and the Imaginary.* Baltimore and London: The Johns Hopkins University Press, 1993.

Jakobson, Roman. "Linguistics and Poetics." In *Style in Language,* edited by Sebeok. Cambridge, MA: MIT Press, 1960.

Jenkins, Henry. "Games, the New Lively Art." In *Handbook of Computer Game Studies,* edited by Jeffrey Goldstein and Joost Raessens. Cambridge, MA: MIT Press, forthcoming.

————. "Games as Narrative Architecture." In *First Person,* edited by Pat Harrington and Noah Frup-Waldrop. Cambridge, MA: MIT Press, 2002.

————. "Power to the Players. Why video games need the protection of the First Amendment." *Technology Review* (June 7, 2002). Available online at <http://www.technologyreview.com/articles/wo_jenkins060702.asp>.

————. "From *Barbie* to *Mortal Kombat*: Further Reflections." Paper presented at the conference *Playing by the Rules: The Cultural Policy Challenges of Video Games.* Chicago, IL, October 2001. Available online at <http://culturalpolicy.uchicago.edu/conf2001/papers/jenkins.html>

Jenkins, Henry, and Kurt Squire. "The Art of Contested Spaces." In *Game On: The History and Culture of Video Games,* edited by Lucien King, 64–75. New York: Universe, 2002.

Johnson, Samuel. *A Dictionary of English Language (1755).* Hildesheim: G. Olms, 1968.

Juul, Jesper. "The Open and The Closed: Games of Emergence and Games of Progression." In *CGDC Conference Proceedings,* edited by Frans Mäyrä, 323–330. Tampere, Finland: Tampere University Press, 2002.

————. "Games Telling Stories?" *Game Studies* 1, No. 1 (July 2001). Available online at <http://www.gamestudies.org/0101/juul-gts/>.

Kac, Eduardo. "Negotiating Meaning: The Dialogic Imagination in Electronic Art." In *Proceedings of Computers in Art and Design Education Conference,* n.p. Middlesbrough, Tees Valley, UK: University of Teesside, 1999. Available online at <http://www.ekac.org/articles.html>.

————. "Origin and Development of Robotic Art." *Art Journal* 56, No. 3 (*Digital Reflections: The Dialogue of Art and Technology,* Special issue on Electronic Art), edited by Johanna Drucker (1997): 60–67. Available online at <http://www.ekac.org/articles.html>.

Kaprow, Allan. "The Happenings Are Dead: Long Live the Happenings." In *Essays on the Blurring of Art and Life,* 59–65. Berkeley and Los Angeles: University of California Press, 1996.

————. "The Education of the Un-Artist, Part III." In *Essays on the Blurring of Art and Life,* 130–147. Berkeley and Los Angeles: University of California Press, 1996.

————. "The Education of the Un-Artist, Part II." *Essays on the Blurring of Art and Life,* 110–126. Berkeley and Los Angeles: University of California Press, 1996.

————. "Self-Service: A Happening." In *Happenings and Other Acts,* edited by Mariellen R. Sandford, 230–234. London and New York: Routledge, [1968] 1995.

_____. "Excerpts from 'Assemblages, Environments & Happenings.'" In *Happenings and Other Acts*, edited by Mariellen R. Sandford, 235–245. London and New York: Routledge, [1966] 1995.

Kinder, Marsha. *Playing with Power in Movies, Television, and Video Games: From Muppet Babies to Teenage Mutant Ninja Turtles.* Berkeley: University of California Press, 1991.

King, Geoff, and Tanya Krzywinska, eds. *ScreenPlay: Cinema/videogames/interfaces.* London: Wallflower Press, 2002.

Kirby, Michael. "Acting and not-acting." In *A Formalist Theatre*, 3–20. Philadelphia: University of Pennsylvania Press, 1987.

Kittler, Friedrich. "On the History of the Theory of Information Warfare." In *Ars Electronica: Facing the Future. A Survey of Two Decades*, edited by Timothy Druckrey, 173–177. Cambridge, MA: MIT Press, 1999.

_____. "Happenings: An Introduction." In *Happenings and Other Acts*, edited by Mariellen R. Sandford, 1–28. London and New York: Routledge, [1965]1995.

Koschmann, Timothy, ed. *CSCL: Theory and Practice of an Emerging Paradigm.* Mahwah, NJ: Lawrence Erlbaum, 1996.

Kreisler, Harry. "Identity and Change in the Network Society: Conversation with Manuel Castells." *Conversation with History*, Institute of International Studies, University of California, Berkeley, May 9, 2001. Available online at <http://globetrotter.berkeley.edu/people/Castells/castells-con5.html>.

Kristof, Ray and Amy Satran. *Interactivity by Design.* Mountain View, CA.: Adobe Press, 1995.

Kubey, Craig. *The Winners' Book of Video Games.* New York: Warner Books; 1982.

Lacan, Jacques. "The Mirror Stage as Formative of the Function of the I as Revealed in Psychoanalytic Experience." *Écrits.* Translated by Alan Sheridan, 1–7. New York: W.W. Norton, 1977.

Laird, John E. "Research in Human-Level AI Using Computer Games." *Communications of the ACM* 45, No. 1 (January 2002).

Lakoff, George. *Women, Fire, and Dangerous Things. What Categories Reveal about the Mind.* Chicago: Chicago University Press, 1997.

Lara Croft: Lethal and Loaded. 50 min. West Long Branch, NJ: White Star Video, 2001. DVD.

Laurel, Brenda. *Utopian Entrepreneur.* Cambridge, MA: Press, 2001.

_____. *Computers as Theater.* London: Addison Wesley, 1993.

Le Diberder, Alain. "L'interactivité, une nouvelle frontière du cinema." (Dossier: Numérique, Virtuel, Interactif. Demain le Cinéma) *Cahiers du Cinéma* 503 (June 1996), 122–126.

Le Diberder, Alain, and Frédéric Le Diberder. *L'Univers des jeux vidéo.* Paris: Éditions La Découverte, 1998.

_____. *Qui a peur des jeux vidéo?* Paris: Éditions La Découverte/Essais, 1993.

Levy, Steven. *Hackers: Heroes of the Computer Revolution.* New York: Anchor, 1984.

Lewis, Michael, and Jeffrey Jacobson. "Game Engines in Scientific Research." (Special Issue: Game Engines in Scientific Research) *Communications of the ACM* 45, No. 1 (January 2002).

Lischka, Konrad. *Spielplatz Computer.* Heidelberg: Verlag Heinz Heise, 2002.

Loftus, Geoffrey R. *Mind at Play: The Psychology of Video Games.* New York: Basic Books, 1983.

Lombard, Matthew, et al. "Measuring presence: a literature-based approach to the development of a standardized paper-and-pencil instrument." Project Abstract Submitted for Presentation at *Presence 2000: The Third International Workshop on Presence.* Available online at <http://nimbus.temple.edu/~mlombard/P2000.htm>.

Lombard, Matthew, and Theresa Ditton. "At the Heart of it All: The Concept of Presence." *JCMC* 3, No. 2 (September, 1997).

MacLean, Paul D. "Ictal Symptoms Relating to the Nature of Affects and Their Cerebral Substrate." In *Emotion: Theory, Research and Experience*, Vol. 3, edited by R. Plutchik and H. Kellerman, 61–90. New York: Academic Press, 1986.

Macnab, Geoffrey. "*Pearl Harbor.*" *Sight and Sound* 11, No. 7 (July 2001), 49.

_____. "Bunk, But Unlikely to Bomb." *The Independent*, March 23, 2001, 12.

Malone, Tom. "Toward a theory of intrinsically motivating instruction." *Cognitive Science* 4 (1981), 333–369.

Mandler, Jean M. *Stories, Scripts and Scenes: Aspects of Schema Theory.* Hillsdale, New Jersey: Lawrence Erlbaum, 1984.

Manovich, Lev. *The Language of New Media.* Cambridge, MA: The MIT Press, 2001.

McBride, Sam. "Sing the Body Electronic: American Invention in Contemporary Performance." *Sycamore* 1, No. 3 (Fall 1997). Available at online at <http://www.unc.edu/sycamore/97.3/electron.html>.

McCloud, Scott. *Understanding Comics: The Invisible Art.* New York: Harper Collins, 1993.

McDonald, Neil. "Swashing and Buckling." *Quadrant* 45, No. 7 (July 2001), 85–89.

McLaughlin, Thomas. *Street Smarts and Critical Theory: Listening to the Vernacular.* Madison: University of Wisconsin Press, 1996.

McLuhan, Marshall. *Understanding Media: The Extensions of Man.* London: Sphere Books, 1964. Other edition: New York: McGraw-Hill Books Company, 1964.

McMahan, Alison. *Branching Characters, Branching Plots: A Critical Approach to Interactive Fiction.* Forthcoming.

———. "Sentient VR: The Memesis Project (Report of a Work in Progress)." In *Proceedings of the 6th World Multiconference on Systemics, Cybernetics and Informatics,* edited by Ngib Callaos, Marin Bica and Maria Sanchez, 467–472. International Institute of Informatics and Systematics, Vol. XII, 2002. Available online at <http://faculty.vassar.edu/almcmahan/memesis/home/index.html>.

———. "Spectator, Avatar, Golem, Bot: Interface and Subject Position in Interactive Fiction." Paper given at the Society for Cinema Studies Conference, Chicago, 2000.

———. "The Effect of Multiform Narrative on Subjectivity." *Screen* 40, No. 2 (Summer 1999), 146–157.

———. "Verbal-Visual-Virtual: A MUDdy History." In *Gramma: Journal of Theory and Criticism* 7 (1999), 73–90.

Metz, Christian. *The Imaginary Signifier: Psychoanalysis and the Cinema.* Translated by Celia Britton, Annwyl Williams, Ben Brewster, and Alfred Guzzetti. Bloomington: Indiana University Press, 1982.

———. "Notes Toward a Phenomenology of the Narrative." In *Film Language: A Semiotics of the Cinema.* New York: Oxford University Press, 1974: 16–28.

Microsoft Combat Flight Simulator 2: World War II Pacific Theater Pilot's Manual. Microsoft Corporation, 2000.

Miklaucic, Scott. "Virtual Real(i)ty: *SimCity* and the Production of Urban Cyberspace." Paper presented at the annual meeting of the Association of Internet Researchers, Minneapolis, MN, October 2001. Available online at <http://www.english.uiuc.edu/miklauci/simcity1.htm>.

Miller, Skyler. "The History of Square." *Gamespot.com* (2001). Available online at <http://www.gamespot.com/gamespot/features/video/hist_square/index.html>

Moreno, Julio L. "Subjective Cinema: And the Problem of Film in the First Person." *Quarterly of Film, Radio, and Television* 7 (1953), 341–358.

Moritz, William. "The Dream of Color Music, And Machines That Made It Possible." *Animation World Magazine* 2, No. 1 (April 1997). Available online at <http://www.awn.com/mag/issue2.1/articles/moritz2.1.html>.

Morse, Margaret. "What Do Cyborgs Eat? Oral logic in an Information Society." In *Culture on the Brink: Ideologies of Technology,* edited by Gretchen Bender and Timothy Duckrey, 157–189. Seattle: Bay Press, 1994.

Motte, Warren F., ed. *Oulipo: A Primer of Potential Literature.* Illinois: Dalkey Archive Press, [1986] 1998.

Moulthrop, Stuart, and Sean Cohen. "About the Color of Television." October 1996. Available online at <http://raven.ubalt.edu/features/media_ecology/lab/96/cotv/cotv_about.html>.

Mulvey, Laura. "Visual Pleasure and Narrative Cinema." In *Visual and Other Pleasures.* Bloomington: Indiana University Press, 1989. Originally published in *Screen* 16, No. 3 (1975), 6–18.

Münsterberg, Hugo. *The Film: A Psychological Study.* New York: Dover, [1916] 1970.

Murray, Janet H. *Hamlet on the Holodeck: The Future of Narrative in Cyberspace.* MIT Press, 1997. [Other editions: New York: Free Press, 1997; and Cambridge, MA: MIT Press, 1998.]

Nakamura, Lisa. *Cybertypes: Race, Ethnicity and Identity on the Internet.* New York: Routledge, 2002.

Ndalianis, Angela. "Special Effects, Morphing Magic, and the 1990s Cinema of Attractions." In *Meta Morphing: Visual Transformation and the Culture of Quick-Change,* edited by Vivian Sobchack, 251–271. Minneapolis: University of Minnesota Press, 2000.

_____. " 'Evil Will Walk Once More': *Phantasmagoria*—The Stalker Film as Interactive Movie?" In *On a Silver Platter; CD-ROMs and the Promises of a New Technology,* edited by Greg M. Smith, 87–112. New York: New York University Press, 1999.

Newman, James. "In Search of the Videogame Player: The Lives of Mario." *New Media & Society* 4, No. 3 (2002), 405–422.

Okorafor, Nnedimma, and Lucinda Davenport. "Virtual Women: Replacing the Real." Paper presented at the annual meeting of the Association for Education in Journalism and Mass Communication, Washington, DC, August 2001.

Ow, Jeffrey. "The Revenge of the Yellowfaced Cyborg: The Rape of Digital Geishas and the Colonization of Cyber-Coolies in 3D Realms' *Shadow Warrior*." In *Race in Cyberspace,* edited by Beth Kolko, Lisa Nakamura and Gilbert Rodman, 51–68. New York: Routledge, 2000.

Parlett, David. *The Oxford History of Board Games.* Oxford: Oxford University Press, 1999.

Pausch, Randy, Jon Snoddy, Robert Taylor, Scott Watson and Eric Haseltine. "Disney's *Aladdin:* First Steps toward Storytelling in Virtual Reality." In *Proceedings of the 23rd annual conference on Computer Graphics and interactive Techniques,* New Orleans, 1996.

Pearce, Celia. "Story as Play Space: Narrative in Games." In *Game On: The History and Culture of Videogames,* edited by Lucien King, 111–119. New York: Universe, 2002.

_____. "Sims, BattleBots, Cellular Automata God and *Go:* A Conversation with Will Wright by Celia Pearce." *Game Studies* 2, No. 1 (July 2002). Available online at <http://www.gamestudies.org/0102/pearce/>.

"Pearl Harbor: More or Less." *Air Power History* 48 (Fall 2001), 38–43.

"Perfect Dark," *Edge* 82 (March 2000), 26–27.

Perron, Bernard. "Jouabilité, bipolarité et cinéma interactif." In *Hypertextes. Espaces virtuels de lecture et d'écriture,* edited by Denis Bachand and Christian Vandendorpe. Québec: Nota Bene, 2002.

_____. *La Spectature prise au jeu. La narration, la cognition et le jeu dans le cinéma narratif.* Ph.D. thesis, Université de Montréal, 1997.

Picard, Michel. "La lecture comme jeu." *Poétique* 58 (March 1984), 253–263.

Pimental, Ken, and KevinTeixeira. *Virtual Reality: Through the New Looking Glass.* New York: Intel/Windcrest/McGraw-Hill Inc., 1993.

Poole, Steven. *Trigger Happy: Videogames and the Entertainment Revolution.* New York: Arcade, 2000. Other edition: *Trigger Happy: The Inner Life of Video Games.* London: Fourth Estate, 2000.

"Project Ego," *Edge* 101 (September 2001), 30.

Prothero, J. D., D. E. Parker, T. A. Furness III, and M. J. Wells. "Foreground/background manipulations affect presence." Paper presented at HFES '95, 1995. Available online at <http://www.hitl.washington.edu>.

Provenzo, Eugene. *Video Kids: Making Sense of Nintendo.* Cambridge, MA: Harvard University Press, 1991.

Rabinovitz, Lauren. "Temptations of Pleasure: Nickelodeons, Amusement Parks, and the Sights of Female Sexuality." *Camera Obscura* 23 (May 1990), 71–88.

Rampell, Ed. "Pearl Divers Toy with Reality." *Variety* 292, No. 11 (April 30, 2001), 1.

Ramsey, Steve. "*Tender Loving Care*." *Quandary Computer Game Reviews* (February 2001). Available online at <http://www.quandaryland.com/2001/tlc.htm>.

Reid, Elizabeth. "Text-based Virtual Realities: Identity and the Cyborg Body." In *Cultural Formations in Text-Based Virtual Realities.* Ph.D. Thesis, University of Melbourne, 1994, 75–95. Available online at <http://www.rochester.edu/College/FS/Publications/ReidIdentity.html>.

Resnick, Mitchell. *Turtles, Termites, and Traffic Jams.* Cambridge, MA: MIT Press, 2001.

"Rez," *Edge,* 105 (Christmas, 2001), 74–75.

Rheingold, Howard. *The Virtual Community* (1993). Electronic version available online at <http://www.rheingold.com/vc/book/intro.html>.

_____. *Virtual Reality.* London: Martin Secker and Warburg, 1991.

Rich, Adrienne. "Compulsory Heterosexuality and Lesbian Existence." in *Feminist Frontiers IV,* edited by Laurel Richardson, Verta Taylor and Nancy Whittier, 81–100. New York: The McGraw-Hill Companies, 1997.

Richard, Birgit. "Norn Attacks and Marine Doom." In *Ars Electronica: Facing the Future. A Survey of Two Decades,* edited by Timothy Druckrey, 336–343. Cambridge, MA: MIT Press, 1999.

Ricoeur, Paul. *Time and Narrative,* 2 vols. Chicago: University of Chicago Press, 1984–1985.

———. "Narrative Time." *Critical Inquiry* 7, No. 1 (Autumn, 1980): 169–190.

Ridgeon, Chris. "Planet Lara: Where the World Revolves Around Lara." Available online at <http://www.planetlara.com/index.asp>.

Robertson, George, Mary Czerwinski and Maarten van Dantzich. "Immersion in Desktop Virtual Reality." In *Proceedings of the 10th Annual ACM symposium on User Interface Software and Technology,* 11–19. Banff, Canada, 1997.

"Rollcage Stage II," *Edge* 82 (March 2000), 71.

Rossi, Leena-Maija. "Why Do I Love and Hate the Sugarfolks in Syruptown? Studying the Visual Production of Heteronormativity in Television Commercials." In *Conference Proceedings for Affective Encounters: Rethinking Embodiment in Feminist Media Studies,* edited by A. Koivunen and Susanna Paasonen. University of Turku, School of Art, Literature and Music, Media Studies, Series A, No. 49 (2001). Available online at <http://www.utu.fi/hum/mediatutkimus/affective/rossi.pdf>.

Rouse, Richard. *Game Design: Theory and Practice.* Plano, TX: Wordware, 2001.

Ryan, Marie-Laure. *Narrative as Virtual Reality. Immersion and Interactivity in Literature and Electronic Media.* Baltimore and London: The Johns Hopkins University Press, 2001.

———. "Beyond Myth and Metaphor—The Case of Narrative in Digital Media." *Game Studies* 1, No. 1 (July 2001). Available online at <http://www.gamestudies.org/0101/ryan/>.

———. "Cyberspace, Virtuality and the Text," In *Cyberspace Textuality, Computer Technology and Literary Theory,* edited by Marie-Laure Ryan, 78–107. Bloomington and Indianapolis: Indiana University Press, 1999.

Schank, R., A. Fano, B. Bell, and M. Jona. "The Design of Goal-Based Scenarios." *Journal of the Learning Sciences* 3, No. 4 (1993), 305–345.

Schechner, Richard. *Performance Theory.* London and New York: Routledge, 1988.

———. "Extensions in time and space: An interview with Allan Kaprow." In *Happenings and Other Acts,* edited by Mariellen R. Sandford, 221–229. London and New York: Routledge, [1968] 1995.

Schuemie, M. J., C. A. P. G. van der Mast, M. Krijn, and P. M. G. Emmelkamp. "Exploratory Design and Evaluation of a User Interface for Virtual Reality Exposure Therapy." In *Medicine Meets Virtual Reality,* edited by J. D. Westwood, H. M. Hoffman, R. A. Robb, D. Stredney, 468–474. IOS Press, 2002. Available online at <http://graphics.tudelft.nl/~vrphobia/mmvr2002.pdf>.

Sedgwick, Eve Kosofsky. "Gender Asymmetry and Erotic Triangles." In *Feminisms: An Anthology of Literary Theory and Criticism,* edited by Robyn Warhol and Diane Price Herndl, 463–486. New Brunswick, NJ: Rutgers University Press, 1993.

Sender, Katherine. "Selling Sexual Subjectivities: Audiences Respond to Gay Window Advertising." *Critical Studies in Mass Communication* 16 (1999), 172–196.

Sheridan, Thomas B. "Interaction, Imagination and Immersion: Some Research Needs." In *Proceedings of the ACM Symposium on Virtual Reality Software and Technology,* 1–7. Seoul, Korea, 2000.

"Shorter Men Earn Less Money in Careers." *Cosmiverse.com* (April 19, 2002). Available online at <http://www.cosmiverse.com/news/science/science04190206.html>.

Silverman, Kaja. *Male Subjectivity at the Margins.* New York: Routledge, 1992.

———. *The Subject of Semiotics.* New York: Oxford University Press, 1983.

Slovin, Rochelle. "Hot Circuits: Reflections on the 1989 Video Game Exhibition of the American Museum of the Moving Image." In *The Medium of the Video Game,* edited by Mark J. P. Wolf, 137–154. Austin: University of Texas Press, 2001.

Sluganski, Randy, and Tom Houston. "Interview with Rob Landeros et David Wheeler." *JustAventure.com* (1999). Available online at <http://www.justadventure.com/Interviews/Landeros_and_Wheeler/Landeros_and_Wheeler_Interview.shtm>.

Smith, Greg M. "Introduction: A Few Words about Interactivity." In *On a Silver Platter: CD-ROMS and the Promises of a New Technology,* edited by Greg Smith, 1–34. New York: New York University Press, 1999.

"Spanking good coin-op fun." *Edge* 102 (October 2001), 17.

Spector, Josh. "Hollywood puts on its game face." *Hollywood Reporter,* Daily Electronic Edition, June 1, 2001, 2.

Spencer, Donald D. *Game Playing with Computers.* New York: Spartan Books, 1968.

Squire, Kurt. "Interview with Steven Poole, Author Trigger Happy." *Joystick 101.org* (January 24, 2001). Available online at <http://www.joystick101.org/?op=displaystory&sid=2001/1/16/174911/133>.

Squire, Kurt, Henry Jenkins, and Games-to-Teach Team. *Games-to-Teach Project Six Month Report.* Cambridge, MA: MIT, 2001.

"St. Louis County's regulations on video games upheld." *The Nando Times,* April 25, 2002. Available online at <http://www.nando.com/technology/story/379154p-3030283c.html>.

Stallabrass, Julian. *Gargantua: Manufactured Mass Culture.* Verso: London and New York, 1996.

"StarCraft: Ghost." *Edge* 118 (Christmas, 2002), 37.

Stern, Gloria. "What Interactive Media Needs Is TLC: Gloria Stern Talks to Rob Landeros and David Wheeler."*Hollywood Interactive Network* (1997). Available online at <http://hollywoodnet.com/Stern/cyberflicks10.html>.

Sternberg, Meir. *Expositional Modes and Temporal Ordering in Fiction.* Baltimore: Johns Hopkins University Press, 1978.

Steuer, Jonathan. "Defining Virtual Reality: Dimensions Determining Telepresence." *Journal of Communication, 42,* No. 4 (Autumn, 1992), 73–93. Available online at <http://www.cyborganic.com/People/jonathan/Academia/Papers/Web/defining-vr.html>.

Stiteler, Bill. "*The Sims.*" *Applelinks.com,* 2000. Available online at <http://www.applelinks.com/reviews/sims.shtml>.

Stokstad, Marilyn. *Art History.* Revised Edition. New York: Harry N. Abrams, Inc., 1999.

Stone, Alluquère Roseanne. "Will the Real Body Stand Up? Boundary Stories about Virtual Cultures." In *Cyberspace: First Steps,* edited by Michael Benedikt, 81–118. Cambridge, MA, and London, UK: MIT Press, 1992.

_____. *The War of Desire and Technology at the Close of the Mechanical Age.* Cambridge, MA: MIT Press, 1996.

Suler, John. "The Psychology of Avatars and Graphical Space in Multimedia Chat Communities." In *Chat Communication,* edited by Michael Beiswenger. Stuttgart, Germany: Ibidem, 1999, 305–344.

Sullivan, George. *Screen Play: The Story of Video Games.* New York: F. Warne, 1983.

Taddei, François. "*Tender Loving Care.*" *Les Productions 640Kb inc* (May 1999). Available online at <http://micro.info/chronique/chronique.php?Id=123>.

Talbot, Ben. "Compete, Command and Conquer: Playing for Space at the International Games Cultures Conference." *Intensities: The Journal of Cult Media* (2001). Available online at <http://www.cult-media.com/issue2/CMRtalb.htm>.

"Tall men and slim women earn more." *BBC News,* 24 November, 2000. Available online at <http://news.bbc.co.uk/2/hi/uk_news/1038531.stm>.

Tattersall, Ian. *The Monkey in the Mirror.* New York: Harcourt Brace, 2001.

"*Tender Loving Care,* and *I'm Your Man* on DVD: Empowering Movies Put You in the Action." *Technofile.com.* Available online at <http://www.technofile.com/dvds/tlc_yourman.html>.

"The Croft Times." *Newsweek,* November 10 1997. Available online at <http://www.cubeit.com/ctimes/news0094a.htm>.

The Sims. San Francisco: Maxis, 2000.

Thomson, David. "Zap Happy: World War II Revisited." *Sight and Sound* 11, No. 7 (July 2001), 34–37.

Tomashevsky, Boris. "Thematics." Translated by Lee T. Lemon and Marion J. Reis. In *Russian Formalist Criticism,* edited by Lee T. Lemon and Marion J. Reis, 61–95. Lincoln and London: University of Nebraska Press, [1925] 1965.

Tronstad, Ragnhild. "Performing the MUD Adventure." In *Innovations: Media, Methods and Theories,* edited by Gunnar Liestøl, Andrew Morrison and Terje Rasmussen. Cambridge, MA: MIT Press, 2003.

Turkle, Sherry. *Life on the Screen: Identity in the Age of the Internet.* New York: Simon and Schuster, 1995.

_____. *The Second Self: Computers and the Human Spirit.* New York: Simon and Schuster, 1984.

Turner, Mark. *The Literary Mind.* Oxford: Oxford University Press, 1998.

Uston, Ken. *Ken Uston's Guide to Buying and Beating Home Video Games.* New York: Signet, 1982.

Vaihinger, Hans. *The Philosophy of "As If,"* 2nd edition. Translated by C. K. Ogden (1924). London: Routledge and Kegan Paul, 1965.

Virilio, Paul. *Desert Screen: War at the Speed of Light.* Translated by Michael Degener. London: The Athlone Press, 2002.

———. *Strategy of Deception.* Translated by Chris Turner. London: Verso, 2000.

———. *War and Cinema: the Logistics of Perception.* Translated by Patrick Camiller. London: Verso, 1989.

Virilio, Paul, and Sylvere Lotringer. *Pure War.* Translated by Mark Polizzotti and Brian O'Keefe. New York: Semiotext(e), 1997.

Waggoner, Ben, and Halstead York, "Video in Games: The State of the Industry." *Gamasutra.com* (January 3, 2000). Available online at <http://www.gamasutra.com/features/20000103/fmv_01.htm>.

Wagner, Peter. *A Sociology of Modernity. Liberty and discipline.* London: Routlege, 1996.

Walker, Trey. "*The Sims* Overtakes *Myst.*" *Gamespot.com* (2002). Available online at <http://www.gamespot.com>.

Walters, Suzanna Danuta. *All the Rage: The Story of Gay Visibility in America.* Chicago: University of Chicago Press, 2001.

Weber, Samuel. *Return to Freud: Jacques Lacan's Dislocation of Psychoanalysis.* Translated by Michael Levine. New York, NY: Cambridge University Press, 1991.

Weinbren, Grahame. "In The Ocean of Streams of Story." (Interactive Cinema) *Millennium Film Journal* 28 (1995), 15–30.

Wilson, Andrew. *The Bomb and the Computer: Wargaming from Ancient Chinese Mapboard to Atomic Computer.* New York: Delacorte Press, 1969.

Winnicott, Donald Woods. *Playing and Reality.* New York: Basic Books, Inc., 1971.

White, Hayden. *The Content of the Form: Narrative Discourse and Historical Representation.* Baltimore: The Johns Hopkins Press, 1989.

———. "The Value of Narrativity in the Representation of Reality." *Critical Inquiry* 7, No. 1 (Autumn, 1980), 5–23.

Wolf, Mark J. P. *The Medium of the Video Game.* Austin: University of Texas Press, 2001.

———. *Abstracting Reality: Art, Communication, and Cognition in the Digital Age.* Lanham, MA: University Press of America, 2000.

———. "Inventing Space: Toward a Taxonomy of On- and Off-Screen Space in Video Games." *Film Quarterly* 51, No. 1 (Fall 1997), 11–23.

Worringer, Wilhelm. *Abstraction and Empathy: A Contribution to the Psychology of Style.* Translated by Michael Bullock. Chicago: Elephant Paperbacks, Ivan R. Dee, Inc., [1908] 1997.

Wright, Steve. *Stella Programmer's Guide.* December 3, 1979. Reconstructed online in 1993 by Charles Sinnett. Available online at <http://www.classic-games.com/atari2600/stella.html>.

Young, Jeffrey Adam. "Ripper." *Gamespot.com* (January 5, 1996). Available online at <http://www.gamespot.com>.

Young, Kay and Jeffrey L. Saver. "The Neurology of Narrative." *SubStance* 30, Nos. 1–2 (2001), 72–84.

Zimmerman, Eric and Katie Salen. *Game + Design.* Cambridge, MA: MIT Press, forthcoming.

Žižek, Slavoj. "Virtualization of the Master." (Being On Line: Net Subjectivity, edited by Alan Sondheim) *Lusitania* 8 (1997): 178–188.

Zola, Émile. *Germinal.* Paris: Hatier, 2001.

About the Contributors

Mia Consalvo is an assistant professor in the School of Telecommunications at Ohio University. Her research explores the intersections of gender and sexuality, popular culture, and new media; including the Internet and computer and video games. She has published articles in *Television & New Media, Feminist Media Studies,* and *Journal of Communication Inquiry* and is most recently coeditor (with Susanna Paasonen) of the book *Women and Everyday Uses of the Internet: Agency and Identity* published in 2002 from Peter Lang Publishing. [Consalvo@ohio.edu]

Chris Crawford sold his first computer game in 1978; he joined Atari in 1979 and was later promoted to supervise the Games Research Group. After the collapse of Atari, he went freelance and created a number of games, including *Balance of Power,* his first big hit. He founded and led the Computer Game Developers Conference. He has also written a number of books about computer game design. He is currently working on technology for interactive storytelling. [chriscrawford@wave.net]

Patrick Crogan teaches media studies at the University of Adelaide, Australia. He has published work on film, animation, new media, and computer games in journals including *Angelaki, Theory, Culture and Society,* and *South Atlantic Quarterly.* He has a chapter in *Paul Virilio: From Modernism to Hypermodernism and Beyond.* [Patrick.Crogan@uts.edu.au]

Markku Eskelinen is an independent scholar and experimental writer of ergodic prose, interactive drama and critical essays. Excepts from his earliest fiction were published in *The Review of Contemporary Fiction* (Summer 1996) according to which he's "easily the most iconoclastic figure on the Finnish literary scene." He is also an editor of *Game Studies*—the international journal of computer game research (<www.gamestudies.org>) and a series of *Cybertext Yearbooks*. [markku.eskelinen@kolumbus.fi]

Miroslaw Filiciak is Ph.D. student at Audiovisual Arts Institute, Jagiellonian University, Cracow, Poland. He researches online games and their communicational aspects. [mirek@cyberforum.edu.pl]

Gonzalo Frasca currently works as a game designer at Cartoon Network. He also edits Ludology.org, a video game theory site that has been described by Edge Magazine as "*a heaven for those who want to engage with videogames on a more abstract plane*." He holds an M.S. from the Georgia Institute of Technology and is also a former editor of science and technology at CNN. [frasca@jacaranda.org]

Torben Grodal is Professor of Media Studies at the University of Copenhagen. He is the author of *Moving Pictures: A New Theory of Film Genres, Feelings, and Cognition* and numerous articles such as "Emotions, Cognition and Narrative Patterns in Film" in *Passionate Views: Film, Cognition and Emotion* and "Video Games and the Pleasures of Control" in *Media Entertainment: The Psychology of its Appeal.* [grodal@hum.ku.dk]

Walter Holland is a second-year master's degree student in the Comparative Media Studies program at MIT. His research encompasses a range of topics surrounding the intersection of media technologies, education, storytelling, and games (digital and otherwise). His M.S. thesis analyzes gameplay and pedagogy as engagements with imaginative narrative spaces. [wgh@alum.mit.edu]

Henry Jenkins, the Ann Fetter Friedlaender Professor of Humanities and Director of MIT Comparative Media Studies, has spent his career studying media and the way people incorporate it into their lives. He is the principle investigator for the MIT-Microsoft Games-to-Teach project which is examining the educational potential of computer and video games. He writes a regular column, "The Digital Renaissance," for *Technology Review* magazine and is currently writing a book designed to explain "why media change matters." He testified in 1999 before the U.S. Senate during the hearings on media violence that followed the Littleton, Colorado, shootings, testified before the Federal Communications Commission about media literacy, and spoke to the governor's board of the World Economic Forum about intellectual property law. His books include *From Barbie to Mortal Kombat: Gender and Computer Games* (coeditor with Justine Cassell, 1998), *The Children's Cultural Reader* (editor, 1998), *Science Fiction Audiences: Doctor Who, Star Trek and Their Followers* (with John Tullock, 1995), *Classical Hollywood Comedy* (coeditor with Kristine Brunovska Karnick, 1994), *Textual Poachers: Television Fans and Participatory Culture* (1992), *What Made Pistachio Nuts?: Early Sound Comedy and the Vaudeville Aesthetic* (1992), and *Hop on Pop: The Politics and Pleasures of Popular Culture* (2003). Jenkins earned his doctorate in communication arts from the University of Wisconsin, Madison and a master's degree in communication studies from the University of Iowa. [henry3@mit.edu]

Martti Lahti is chair at the department of Media at Laurea Polytechnic, Finland. He has edited several books and published numerous articles. His latest publications include an edited collection of essays on new technologies and following articles, "Powerful Innocents: Dis-sing White Men's Empowerment in *Regarding Henry* and *Forrest Gump*," in *Closely Watched Brains*, edited by Murray Pomerance and John Sakeris; "Almost Ashamed to Say I'm One of Those Girls: *Titanic*, Leonardo DiCaprio, and the Paradoxes of Girls' Fandom," in *Titanic: Anatomy of a Blockbuster*, edited by Gaylyn Studlar and Kevin Sandler (1999; with Melanie Nash); "Sylvester Stallone's Body: 'A Peculiar, Not To Say Pathological, Interest,'" in *Bending Bodies—Moulding Masculinities*, volume 2, edited by Søren Ervo and Thomas Johansson (2003). [Martti.Lahti@laurea.fi]

Alison McMahan is a Mellon Fellow in Visual Culture at Vassar College where she is building a sentient VR environment. In the 1980s and early 1990s, she worked in film and new media production, producing interactive training programs in New York. From 1997 to 2001, she taught early cinema and new media at the University of Amsterdam, where she helped develop the New Media Studies Major. Her analysis of the work of the first woman filmmaker and reconsideration of how we understand early cinema in general was recently published as *Alice Guy Blache, Lost Cinematic Visionary*. She also has published widely on software, interactive architecture, special effects, and new media issues in magazines and journals such as *Archis, Interiors, The Independent, Filmmaker, Millimeter,* and *Screen*. [alisonmcmahan@aol.com]

Bernard Perron is an Assistant Professor of Cinema at the Université de Montréal. His research and writings concentrate on cognition, narration, the ludic dimension of narrative cinema, and interactive cinema. He was the guest editor for the *Cinémas: Journal of Film Studies* issue on cinema and cognition (2002). [bernard.perron@umontreal.ca]

Bob Rehak is a doctoral student in the Department of Communication and Culture at Indiana University in Bloomington. His film and book reviews have appeared in the online journal *Scope*. While his passion for video games and computers—as objects of study as well as recreation—is as strong as ever, his dissertation research involves film and new media: the technologies, discourses, and aesthetics of CGI, with particular focus on "bullet time," the migration of special effects across media, and transformations of narrative space through the use of virtual cameras. [zencat@indiana.edu]

Warren Robinett is a designer of interactive computer graphics software. At the University of North Carolina , he coinvented the NanoManipulator, a virtual-reality interface to a scanning-probe microscope, which allows a scientist to be virtually present on the surface of a microscopic sample within the microscope. In the mid-1980s, at NASA Ames Research Center, Robinett designed the software for the Virtual Environment Workstation, NASA's pioneering virtual reality project. In 1980, he cofounded The Learning Company, now a major publisher of educational software. There he designed *Rocky's Boots,* a computer game, which taught digital logic design to upper-grade-school children, using an interactive, visual simulation. *Rocky's Boots* won Software of the Year awards from three magazines in 1983. In 1978, he designed the Atari video game *Adventure,* the first graphical adventure game. [warren@WarrenRobinett.com]

Kurt Squire is a Ph.D. candidate in Instructional Systems Technology at Indiana University, and is currently working as a research manager at MIT on the Microsoft-MIT funded Games-to-Teach Project. His research interests include the design of games and simulations, the use of games and simulations in formal learning environments, video game industry and culture, sociocultural learning theory, performance assessments, and qualitative research methods. Squire also cofounded *Joystick101.org,* which has been recognized by *Wired, Shift,* and several news outlets as a leading site for the discussion of game design, theory, criticism, and culture. [ksquire@mit.edu]

Ragnhild Tronstad wrote her Ph.D. dissertation on questing and character interaction in MUDs in the Department of Media and Communication, University of Oslo. She has published articles on theatricality and performance, on the performative aspects of questing, as well as on different modes of role-playing within textually defined online communities such as MUDs and Usenet. [ragnhild.tronstad@media.uio.no]

David Winter (Paris, France) is a long time collector and passionate for technology. He started collecting old computer parts at the age of 8, and started a serious computer and video game collection in 1994. He obtained his MSc in Software Design in 1998 and centered his collection on early video games. He now owns over 800 machines. He participated in several French TV broadcasts, press articles, and video game history books. He knows Ralph Baer very well and now has most of his original video game documents and hardware in custody.

Mark J. P. Wolf has a Ph.D. from the School of Cinema/Television at the University of Southern California, and is an Associate Professor in the Communication Department at Concordia University Wisconsin. His writings have appeared in *Film Quarterly, The Velvet Light Trap, The Spectator,* the online journal *Scope,* and his books include *Abstracting Reality: Art, Communication, and Cognition in the Digital Age* (2000), *The Medium of the Video Game* (2001), and *Virtual Morality: Morals, Ethics, and New Media* (2003). He lives in Wisconsin with his wife Diane and son Michael, and has just finished his first novel. [mark.wolf@cuw.edu]

Index